Outstanding Dissertations in Music from British Universities

Edited by
John Caldwell
Oxford University

A Garland Series

Medieval English Benedictine Liturgy

Studies in the Formation, Structure, and Content of the Monastic Votive Office, c. 950–1540

Sally Elizabeth Roper

Garland Publishing, Inc.
New York & London 1993

Library of Congress Cataloging-in-Publication Data

Roper, Sally Elizabeth.
  Medieval English Benedictine liturgy : studies in the formation, structure, and content of the monastic votive office, c. 950–1540 / by Sally Elizabeth Roper.
        p.   cm. — (Outstanding dissertations in music from British universities)
  Includes bibliographical references and index.
  ISBN 0–8153–0953–8 (alk. paper)
  1. Benedictines—England—Liturgy—History. 2. England—Religious life and customs. I. Title. II. Series.
BX2049.B4R66   1993
264'.0201—dc20   93–15812
                                                            CIP

Designed by Valerie Mergentime

Printed on acid-free, 250-year-life paper.
Manufactured in the United States of America

CONTENTS

TABLES

DESCRIPTIVE CATALOGUE

APPENDICES

BIBLIOGRAPHY

ACKNOWLEDGMENTS

My first and greatest debt can only be to Dr John Harper, who has nurtured the progress of this thesis from the beginning. To him I owe rather more than words can express here. Without his support, kindness and judicious criticism, this thesis would almost certainly never have reached the binder.

Special thanks are also due to Dr John Whenham of the University of Birmingham and Dr John Caldwell, both of whom helped the work on its way in the early stages. Many others have willingly given time and advice over the years: Dr David Hiley, Professor Nick Sandon, Père Pierre-Marie Gy O.P., Sister Benedicta Ward S.L.G., Dr Mary Clayton, Dame Gertrude Brown O.S.B. and Dame Catherine Wybourne O.S.B., Mr Christopher Hohler, Dr Antonia Gransden, Dr Valerie Edden, the late Mr Derek Turner and Professor Richard Pfaff. I would also like to thank Edward Kershaw, Jane Frogley, Sandra McColl and Catherine Harbor for sharing their liturgical expertise.

The financial burdens of devoting five years to writing a thesis have been greatly eased by the Principal and Fellows of Brasenose College, whose decision to award me the Senior Germaine Scholarship in 1985 and a further grant for a trip to Valenciennes in 1987 contributed much to my peace of mind. I offer them my very grateful thanks. I am similarly indebted to Magdalen College, which provided me with a home for two years, and the Music Faculty for awarding me the James Ingham Halstead Scholarship in 1985 and the John Lowell Osgood Prize in 1988.

Mention must also be made of several libraries and their staff. My thanks are due to the Bodleian Library, the Music Faculty Library and the College Libraries of Worcester and Exeter in Oxford, the British Library, Lambeth Palace Library, the Cathedral Libraries of Canterbury and Worcester, the Bibliothèque Municipale in Valenciennes, the University Library and the College Libraries of Emmanuel, Magdalene, Trinity, and St John's in Cambridge. Dom Daniel Rees O.S.B. and Dom Philip Jebb O.S.B. of Downside Abbey, Miss Sarah Cobbold of the Music Faculty Library, Oxford, Dr Frank Stubbings and Miss Angela Heap of Emmanuel College, Cambridge and Mrs Janet McMullin of Lambeth Palace Library were especially helpful.

Other people have contributed to this thesis in less direct ways. Tom Czepiel, Martin Souter and my house-mates Simon Heighes and Jonathan Wainwright have offered first-hand sympathy over the pains of writing; Sister Margaret of the Society of All Saints and Henry Rees have provided assistance in the technical area of word-processing, and my mother has provided constant encouragement. I thank them all sincerely.

Oxford, January 1989

INTRODUCTION

The catholic nature of the Western Church in the Middle Ages did not preclude important local divergences. In England, geographical factors contributed to independent practices. Such independence does not always imply a deliberately insular or conservative position, but the primary currents of change and their impact in England do not always correspond with contemporary continental movements. England was first to accept the Use of Rome as the liturgical norm in most regions during the seventh century, but it was less immediately influenced by the Carolingian reforms of the eighth and ninth centuries. There is no movement in Europe comparable to the Norman influx in eleventh-century England, nor to the resulting compromise in ecclesiastical organization. Between the Conquest and the Reformation, the autonomy of the English Benedictine monasteries, the adherence to the Use of Sarum (and its derivatives) in non-monastic churches, and the individual nature of the late medieval educational foundations all served to imbue the English church as a whole with unique characteristics and qualities.

Perhaps the most important innovation of the Anglo-Saxon church was the establishment of cathedrals staffed by monks: few examples of this phenomenon exist outside Britain. The cathedral adjacent to the royal Saxon palace at Winchester was monastic, and monks dominated most areas of cultural creativity: whether scholarly, artistic or musical. After the Norman Conquest, William I retained the English system of cathedral-monasteries despite its insularity, and its influence was enlarged in the eleventh century. The rebuilt metropolitan cathedral at Canterbury remained a Benedictine priory church with a Norman monk as archbishop, and until the second phase of the dissolution of the monasteries (1540), almost half of the English cathedrals were Benedictine monasteries, as were some of the richest and most influential churches of the land.

The liturgical use of medieval monasteries in England has received far less attention than the secular rites. The study of monastic liturgy is complicated by the individual characteristics of the autonomous Benedictine houses (although the Cluniacs and Cistercians were centrally organized and more consistent in their practice) and by the loss of monastic books. It has also been overshadowed by the study of the Use of Sarum. The post-Reformation rites of the Church of England are most closely related to the Salisbury use, and Sarum books naturally drew the attention of scholars in the wake of the Oxford Movement (1833-45). The work of such scholars as F.E. Brightman, J.W. Legg, Frederick Procter, H.A. Wilson, F.H. Dickinson, Christopher Wordsworth and especially W.H. Frere has been taken up by many musicologists concerned with liturgy. The Use of Sarum is dominant in the writing of the late Frank Ll. Harrison and in more recent work by Nick Sandon. It is also a frequent reference point in Andrew Hughes's more comprehensive study, *Medieval Manuscripts for Mass and Office*. Last but not least, Salisbury practice is more generously represented than any other use in facsimiles, editions and, more recently, reconstructions.

At a broader level, while liturgy has been recognized as an indispensible part of the study of the context and use of medieval chant and polyphony, most work has been directed to consideration of the principal forms of the office and mass. But throughout the Middle Ages these celebrations were constantly complemented or expanded by an abundance of supplementary observances.

This study attempts to redress the balance in two respects. First, it focuses on the liturgy of English Benedictine monasteries (including the cathedral priories); second, it is concerned specifically with the character and content of a range of accretions to the monastic office, and with the factors which contributed to their formation and proliferation.

Benedictine houses were effectively autonomous units. Although there were attempts at various times to produce agreed codes and regulations, their pattern of life was highly sophisticated and retained individual characteristics. Nowhere is this independence more apparent than in the complexity and individuality of their liturgies, and especially in the liturgical accretions. Integrated with the calendar of seasons and feasts, and interspersed within the daily pattern of mass and office, was a series of additional devotions of varying length and importance. Some of these were no more than small, self-contained groups of psalms forming an appendage to an office, but others were much more extensive structures, modelled on the regular office and occasionally replacing normal ferial observance.

Since none of these additional devotions were part of the main pattern of daily liturgy laid down in the calendar, they occupy an area commonly referred to today as 'votive observance'. This term was first introduced in this context by Harrison in the 1950s, and has subsequently been adopted generally in musicological literature.[1] Nevertheless, the varied contexts in which the term 'votive' is used by musicologists rarely reflects direct transference from the Latin, and is thus something of an anachronism. There is, for example, no Latin equivalent for the ubiquitous term 'votive antiphon': liturgical books, statutes and manuscripts containing such texts, with or without music, usually refer simply to an antiphon (*antiphona*); less frequently the more specific qualification *antiphona de beata Maria virgine* is used.

Some evidence for the use of the word *votiva* in contemporary sources does exist, but it makes only rare appearances. One of the earliest surviving instances of a complete votive office of the Virgin, copied into an eleventh-century source from Canterbury,[2] is headed *votiva laus in veneratione marie*, but no other office of this kind carries a similar rubric in any of the sources consulted. Theoretically, observances with the qualification *votiva* were offered for a particular *votum* (wish or desire), but some modern writers have used the term to embrace such occasions as ordination and nuptial masses (better termed ritual masses) as well as services for special intentions (including the dead, the saints etc.).[3] In every case the feature common to these observances seems to have been that their celebration was not dictated by the requirements of the liturgical calendar, and this general principle remains a useful guideline for the categorization of later votive practices. Most votive observances function either as non-specific replacements for the regular liturgy (such as the commemorative office), or else as simple appendages to it (like the daily Little Office of the Virgin and the votive antiphon); in both cases these devotions were not substantially affected by the cycle of the calendar.

The votive repertory is further characterized by its association with saints of local importance, and more particularly by the overriding dominance of texts addressed to the Virgin Mary. Marianism had reached cult proportions in England by the twelfth century, and in many respects votive practices served as a natural overspill both for the accommodation of such an emphasis in the general devotional climate, and for the particular interests of individual houses in local saints and relics.

This study recognizes two basic categories of votive observance. The first category implies a broad use of the term, covering all practices which are simply accretions to the liturgical pattern defined by St Benedict in his Rule (*c*.540). Several of the items within this group are not of major relevance to this study; there is no discussion of those items which in due course came to be regarded as an 'official' part of the liturgy, such as the daily chapter meeting (added during the eighth century), the creeds and the litany.[4] This category also includes a number of small-scale accretions to the office, most of which are constructed around groups of psalms and collects. Some of these items are non-specific devotions apparently intended for private use, and they have no association with any particular saint or intention. Nevertheless, they are important early examples of the general tendency for liturgical elaboration, and their formation and content in the pre-Conquest period are discussed briefly in Part One.

A second category of observances calls for more explicit definition. This group includes only those accretions which were offered for a particular purpose or to a specified saint: the Virgin was clearly emphasized above all other saints in this last respect, and Marian votive observances are especially familiar to musicologists. This category comprises relatively substantial liturgical structures, including complete masses and offices. Three areas are examined in Part Two: the parallel *cursus*, recited as a daily appendage to the regular office; the commemorative office, which was substituted for the regular office on specified weekdays; and the appended antiphon, which was recited with a versicle and collect after certain hours. The votive antiphon of Our Lady, which dominates the late fifteenth-century English polyphonic repertory, seems to have originated as a small-scale observance: there are references in the tenth-century English customary *Regularis Concordia* to the recitation of single antiphons after Lauds and Vespers.

This study is only concerned with votive accretions to the office: limitations of space preclude extensive discussion of the related phenomenon of the votive mass. But for this, examination of the series of votive masses ascribed to Alcuin (*c*.735-804) for prescribed weekdays would form a natural adjunct to the commemorative office discussed in Chapter Four. However, a brief history of such masses, which aims to place them in the wider context of votive observance, is given at the end of Chapter Two.

None of the votive observances discussed here were unique to the Benedictines. The question constantly arises as to how the monastic liturgy compares with its better-known secular counterpart, and while this question lies outside the scope of the thesis, it is clear that there is considerable potential for a further study of the interaction between monastic and secular practices. A small amount of comparison occurs here, but it is limited to the available Sarum books, and does not pretend to great detail. Because of the relatively late appearance of most of the secular liturgies, it is difficult to trace the formation and growth of their observances with the same degree of continuity as the Benedictines. In this respect the monastic tradition is more historically continuous and complete.

APPROACH TO STUDY

The nature and scope of this thesis have inevitably been conditioned to some extent by the range of sources available for study. Medieval liturgical books from English Benedictine monasteries do not survive in vast quantity, and the practices of some houses are better documented than others. The overall picture of observance presented here is drawn from some 150 manuscripts representing about thirty houses. The evidence is piecemeal and sporadic: it is difficult either to study a single period in detail or to trace the liturgical progress of a single Benedictine monastery from the time of its foundation to the Dissolution. Emphasis on a particular house within the context of the study rests almost entirely on the surviving manuscript evidence, and such emphasis therefore shifts from chapter to chapter. The observances of a few houses are so well documented that it is logical to take that centre as a case-study. Winchester, for instance, is an inevitable choice for the late Anglo-Saxon period, on account of its importance as a centre of reform, its associations with the customary *Regularis Concordia* and the status of its prolific scriptorium. After the eleventh century the quantity of extant Winchester manuscripts (and by implication the liturgical evidence) declines sharply: study of surviving material from other monasteries is forced to take precedence.

Location of appropriate materials for any liturgical study is never entirely straightforward. There is no centralized inventory of liturgical books, and the catalogues of individual libraries vary considerably in content and quality. The Bodleian Library is perhaps best provided for in this respect. Stephen Van Dijk's handlist of liturgical manuscripts in the Bodleian (available in typescript in Duke Humfrey's Library) remains one of the most comprehensive indices available, and its attempt to catalogue the category, date, provenance and content of a wide range of manuscripts is an invaluable tool in the initial task of tracing relevant books. Nevertheless, it contains a substantial number of inaccuracies and omissions, and would benefit greatly from revision.

Provision for liturgical manuscripts held by the British Library is less good. The only available catalogue (confined to the Students' Room) which attempts to list all liturgical sources, *Latin Service Books*, contains entries dating back to the nineteenth century of remarkably diverse content. Many of these are inaccurate and misleading, and some fail to provide any information on a manuscript beyond its classification number. The current project to produce a more complete index is long overdue.

The more general English catalogues are equally variable. Neil Ker's *Medieval Manuscripts in British Libraries* stands out to students in all medieval disciplines as a model of scholarly excellence for its insight and systematic accuracy, but it does not cover the two repositories which are most rich in liturgical books: the British Library and the Bodleian. W.H. Frere's *Bibliotheca Musico-Liturgica* is somewhat dated and also omits British Library holdings. Andrew Watson's *Dated and Datable Manuscripts . . . in the British Library* makes good the deficiency in some respects, although few of the sources examined for the present study can be dated with great precision. Initial location of relevant material for this thesis has been greatly aided by the inventory of English Benedictine manuscripts consulted by the late J.B.L. Tolhurst for the companion volume to his edition of The Hyde Abbey Breviary.[5]

Some fifty of the 150 or so manuscripts consulted have provided essential information for this study: these are referred to extensively in the text and are catalogued separately on pp.293-324, where each is provided with a brief description of its content and a bibliography. All manuscript citations in the text are given in the form of short references: a key to manuscript abbreviations is provided in the prefatory material (p.xxvii).

In a few cases, assimilation of source material is greatly simplified by the presence of an accessible modern edition. The extensive work of J.B.L. Tolhurst has provided readily available texts of a number of customaries and a complete breviary, all published by the Henry Bradshaw Society. The more recent series, *Corpus Consuetudinarum Monasticarum (CCM)*, also incorporates a substantial number of monastic documents, ranging from legislation produced during the reforms of Benedict of Aniane (*c.*750-821) to English and European customaries. Fourteenth-century sources from the monasteries of Eynsham and Chester are both included here, while two documents of major importance from an earlier period, the tenth-century customary *Regularis Concordia* and Lanfranc's *Consuetudines* (*c.*1080), have also been re-edited with revised commentaries for this series. The distinguished team of *CCM* editors (many of them members of Benedictine communities themselves) have in most cases produced invaluable critical material for the documents represented: textual indices, lists of manuscripts and commentaries accompany each volume. Further noteworthy introductory material also appears in several of the Henry Bradshaw Society editions, and in the facsimile reproduction of the Worcester Antiphoner (*Paléographie Musicale*, 1, xii). The commentary and index to the latter, although existing only in an (unsigned) French version, were both compiled by Dame Laurentia McLachlan, abbess of Stanbrook Abbey, Worcester between 1931 and 1953.

Any study of Benedictine liturgy needs to start with The Rule of St Benedict (hereafter *RB*), which formed the basis for the monastic liturgical pattern of the later Middle Ages. *RB* survives in three separate recensions, discussed in Chapter One. All references to *RB* in this study are taken from the most recent and reliable edition of the document, *RB 1980*, based on the manuscript thought to be closest to St Benedict's original.[6] This provides a parallel English text, copious footnotes and appended articles, and glossaries on sources and the characteristics of earlier monastic practice.

Chapter One also draws widely on some of the earliest documents which deal with liturgical legislation, many of them produced under the supervision of the Carolingian monk Benedict of Aniane. The majority of the Aninian documents have been collated and edited in the first volume of *CCM*, and this evidence is used in conjunction with a biography of Benedict of Aniane produced during the eighth century by his pupil, Ardo.[7] The impact of this early phase of liturgical reform is seen in an eleventh-century version of *RB* from Abingdon, which incorporates a number of modifications to St Benedict's original text.[8]

The main body of the study obviously draws on the central evidence of the liturgical manuscripts themselves. Most of the larger Benedictine houses are included, but adequate manuscript information on votive observance (usually from customaries or office books with particularly full rubrics) survives from only a small proportion. The formative stage of English liturgy is most fully represented by *Regularis Concordia*, the earliest extant monastic customary produced by the Council of Winchester in *c*.970. Votive accretions covered in this source are tabulated and discussed in Chapter Two. *Regularis Concordia* provides the bulk of our knowledge for this period, but information on tenth-century practice is enlarged by supplementary manuscripts. The first of these, the so-called *Worcester Portiforium* of *c*.1065, edited for the Henry Bradshaw Society by Dom Anselm Hughes, provides the earliest evidence of weekly commemorative offices in England; these are discussed in Chapter Four. The other manuscripts appear to illustrate private devotional practices: they provide a valuable record of the early Little Office of the Virgin, and its irregular construction (see Chapter Three).

All Benedictine houses in England continued to use *RB* until the Dissolution, but the increasing complexity of the monastic lifestyle necessitated the compilation of amplified codes of observance, setting out the finer details of liturgical practice and other matters. Such customaries inevitably supply a large part of the material examined here. The evidence of votive observance found in *Regularis Concordia* is discussed in some detail in Chapter Two. This and other liturgical documents from the Anglo-Saxon period indicate that many of the large-scale accretions, which came to fruition in the twelfth and thirteenth centuries, have their roots in the insular practices of the pre-Conquest era.

The immediate impact of imported Norman practices can be studied in a document drawn up by Lanfranc, the first Norman archbishop of Canterbury. Lanfranc's *Consuetudines* are in many respects similar to *Regularis Concordia* in content, but they are less systematic and less informative on votive questions. In most cases the later customaries are more rewarding. Customaries or relatively detailed ordinals survive from the Benedictine houses of Eynsham (after 1230), Bury St Edmunds (*c*.1234), Norwich (*c*.1260), Christ Church, Canterbury (later thirteenth century), Chester (*c*.1330-40), St Augustine's, Canterbury (*c*.1330-40), Peterborough (1371), St Mary's, York (*c*.1400) and Barking (1404).[9] All but one of these manuscripts (the Peterborough Ordinal at Lambeth Palace) exists in an accessible modern edition, and all have provided important evidence for at least one of the larger observances discussed in Part Two.

Breviaries and antiphoners have also been an essential part of this survey, partly for their evidence of text and music, but also in a few cases for their full rubrics. The Worcester Antiphoner (*c*.1230) has proved almost as useful as the customaries listed above for its unusually full provision of rital directions. The two earliest extant English breviaries, from Winchcombe and St Albans respectively (both copied in the middle of the

twelfth century), have few rubrics, but they both supply critical evidence for
the formation of a weekly commemorative office. The gradual development
of this form can be traced through later breviaries from Evesham
(*c.*1250-75), Muchelney and Ely (both late thirteenth century), Hyde Abbey
(*c.*1300), Christ Church, Canterbury (later fourteenth century),
Peterborough (after 1415), and Battle (early sixteenth century). The Hyde
Abbey manuscript was transcribed for the Henry Bradshaw Society by
J.B.L. Tolhurst. There are also two printed sixteenth-century breviaries:
rather surprising survivals, since the Reformation was so imminent. Henry
Herford produced a breviary for the community at Abingdon in 1528 (of
which two incomplete copies surive, one at Exeter College, Oxford, the
other at Emmanuel College, Cambridge), and John Scholar printed a
breviary for St Albans in *c.*1535. It is particularly fortunate that the latter
survives, for it complements the twelfth-century source from the same
foundation.

Medieval English Benedictine antiphoners or noted breviaries are less
prolific; indeed, only three complete antiphoners have proved useful here.
The Worcester Antiphoner has already been mentioned; its reproduction in
facsimile for *Paléographie Musicale*, complete with textual indices, is
particularly convenient, despite the reduced size and poor quality of many
of the manuscript rubrics. As a repertory of music it is extensive and
testifies to the individuality of the only house which retained an English
abbot in the years following the Norman Conquest. The music transcribed
in Appendix I (p.327) all comes from this source. The slightly later
antiphoner from Peterborough is a more condensed manuscript and contains
little evidence of votive observance, beyond the mention of commemorative
offices: it has not supplied much of the evidence discussed. That from
Gloucester comprises only the day hours, and like the Peterborough source,
it reveals little of the votive practices adopted at that house.

Post-Conquest psalters have been particularly significant witnesses for
certain categories of votive observance. Most of the lavishly illuminated
pre-Conquest psalters are primarily books of psalms with little additional
material, but the contents of later psalters are often less limited than their
title would suggest, and indeed, many of them were clearly seen as
appropriate books for the transmission of very miscellaneous contents.
Several of the extant manuscripts provide early evidence for additional
votive offices, usually recited on a daily basis, either as private or corporate
devotions. Eleventh-century psalters with appended offices survive from
Crowland and Winchester; twelfth-century examples from Wherwell and
Muchelney.

It must be stressed that this is a study based primarily on liturgical
manuscripts, and owing to limitations of space and time, it has not been
possible to tackle archival evidence in great depth. However, in a few cases
important liturgical survivals from certain houses (such as St Albans) have

prompted examination of related non-liturgical sources. Matthew Paris's *Gesta Abbatum Sancti Albani* provides information on the liturgical alterations introduced by some of the abbots who held office at this monastery. The development of the commemorative office described by Paris and other St Albans chroniclers is recorded in Chapter Four. Equally valuable is the later collection of documents from the national and regional chapter meetings of the English Benedictines: these record the centralized legislation imposed on Benedictine houses from the later thirteenth century.[10] Although they deal mostly with the abolition of long-established practices which were by now felt to be largely superfluous, there are occasional directions as to how certain offices were to be performed. Tolhurst has recorded some of the major changes effected by this legislation; this study only covers those areas of immediate relevance to the observances examined.

An important question which inevitably arises from a study of this kind concerns the impact of continental practices on English monastic observance during this period. In spite of its insularity, England was subject to the influence of continental monasticism at several stages of its history. First, the English monastic revival of the tenth century (discussed in Chapter Two) drew on the practices of reformed European monasticism; representatives were invited to the Council of Winchester from the central houses of Fleury and Ghent, and several of the practices laid out in *Regularis Concordia* follow the example of foreign models. Second, England was rapidly influenced by Norman monasticism in the wake of the Conquest. The effects of the reform at Christ Church, Canterbury are apparent from the practices described in Lanfranc's *Consuetudines*, but there is also substantial evidence that change on a wider scale was facilitated by the importation of monks from continental houses to head English abbeys. Third, later movements of reform originating on the Continent (chief among them Cluny and Cîteaux), did not delay in establishing daughter houses across the Channel. The success of the Cistercian Order in Britain is apparent simply from the scale of the buildings which survive: among them Fountains, Furness and Tintern. All of these varying strands of influence must have contributed to the general character of Benedictine life in medieval England, and it must be stressed that there is a need for review of existing scholarship in the light of surviving evidence.

Inevitably there are other angles which have not been pursued here. There is little investigation of the spiritual and theological aspect of votive observance, and only a brief discussion of the devotional issues. Nevertheless, some of these areas (and in particular the impact of Marianism) have been covered by scholars in other medieval disciplines. There is also no investigation of the practices of non-monastic orders in England, including the possible impact of the mendicant orders in the twelfth century. Similarly there is no extensive comparison with the phenomenon of votive observance in the Use of Sarum, or exploration of the evidence offered by choral establishments—Lady Chapel choirs, colleges and other musical foundations—although the surviving English polyphonic repertory testifies to the impact of votive (and particuarly Marian) observances. Research of other scholars which considers related issues is, of course, cited where possible.

SCOPE AND RANGE OF THE STUDY

The time-span of the survey is extensive, covering more than 500 years. But the problems of the surviving manuscript evidence preclude exhaustive study of a single period or house, and there are compensations in taking a wider overview. The primary focus of the work concentrates on the major votive observances which only came to fruition in the twelfth century or later. Nevertheless, these important practices clearly have some precedent in earlier monastic observances, and the emphasis on Anglo-Saxon liturgy in the earlier chapters is an attempt to provide a bridge between the practices of the English Benedictines before and after the Conquest. Each section of Part Two aims to trace the chronological progress of three individual observances, extending where possible into the sixteenth century.

A series of specific areas within this broad pattern is discussed in more detail. Part One examines the liturgical pattern set out in *RB*, and the possible precedent for periods of private prayer allowed to a monastic community in the sixth century. It is suggested that these 'free' periods may have formed the basis for more formed accretions of a votive nature in subsequent years. Early recensions of *RB* are set against a late copy from Abingdon, with particular reference to the liturgical modifications in the later document. Primarily these alterations are concerned with the manner in which each of the hours ended, an area which has been briefly examined by Tolhurst.[11] He felt that St Benedict himself expected short accretions to the office to occur, and his arguments related to these *capitella* are summarized and compared with the later evidence.

Chapter One also examines the first significant move towards liturgical expansion during the Carolingian period under Benedict of Aniane (*c.*750-821). The expansion of the Benedictine order brought with it a distortion of St Benedict's original conception of a lifestyle divided almost equally between *Opus Dei*, manual labour and study. It is from the Carolingian period that the earliest evidence for votive observance survives: mostly small-scale devotions modelled around psalms, but nevertheless formal observances intended for the corporate worship of the entire community. Evidence from the legislation produced at the Councils of Aachen and from Ardo's biography of Benedict of Aniane is examined and the earliest votive accretions are listed. Some of them are too unspecific to warrant extensive discussion, but other observances went on to form more substantial devotions of much greater import.

More detailed analysis of the practices of English Benedictine communities occurs in Chapter Two. There is a brief discussion of monastic life in England before the famous revival of the tenth century, but most of this chapter focuses on the monastic communities at Winchester, the compilation of an agreed national monastic customary in that city, and the external circumstances which influenced its content (and by implication the character of some of the later observances). The votive elements found in the customary *Regularis Concordia* are tabulated and analysed, and their overall significance is discussed. Chapter Two also examines the beginnings of the cult of the Virgin Mary in England, and the reflection of Marianism in slightly later pre-Conquest manuscripts.

Part One as a whole serves primarily as an introduction and context for the more detailed analysis of the monastic votive office presented in Part Two. Both the daily votive office and the weekly commemorative office first appeared at the end of the Anglo-Saxon period, so that there is both continuity and cross-reference. Chapter Three follows the adoption of complete parallel offices, from their early appearance as personal devotions in the private prayerbooks and psalters of tenth-century monks to the corporate recitation of complete duplicate hours at St Mary's York at the beginning of the fifteenth century. Parallels with other additional offices, particularly the ninth-century Office of the Dead, are discussed, and the non-monastic structure of the parallel office is investigated.

Chapter Four deals with a votive office of rather greater status: the commemorative office which served as a replacement for the prescribed calendar office on certain days. Evidence from a wide range of customaries and breviaries is collated, and the structure and content of the various types of office are discussed. This chapter addresses the question of how such 'complete' votive observances were compiled. Were they newly composed, or was the material simply borrowed? Is there evidence of new musical composition, and if so does this differ stylistically from earlier repertories? Which devotional areas appear to have been most prominent at this period? Were the practices of individual houses conditioned largely by their patron saint or by other saints of particular local interest?

The final chapter deals with the votive antiphon and those rather more contained observances which seem to be related to it. Each observance is modelled around an antiphon, said or sung with a versicle and a collect. In some respects such devotion can be traced right back to the *capitella* implied at the end of the hours in *RB*. *Regularis Concordia* also specifies the recitation of individual antiphons after Lauds and Vespers. But the most characteristic of these accretions is the so-called votive antiphon, usually appended to Compline and occasionally to other hours in addition. In spite of the four familiar seasonal texts associated with this form in the Roman

Use (*Alma redemptoris, Ave regina, Salve regina* and *Regina celi*), it appears that many Benedictine monasteries in England were content to use a single text: *Salve regina*. The obvious popularity of this antiphon in liturgical and devotional sources, and the large number of polyphonic settings from the fifteenth century, have prompted a discussion of its origins and early adoption by monastic communities. It is also considered in the light of the other Marian antiphons which appear in votive offices addressed to the Virgin.

NOTES

1. Harrison, *Music in Medieval Britain*, 77-88. Harrison's introduction to *PMFC* xvi and Hughes's introduction to *EECM* viii also discuss the term 'votive'.

2. *Lbl* A.III, ff.107v-15v

3. As, for example, Jungmann, *The Mass of the Roman Rite*, 97-99; 159-161.

4. Various additions of this kind are discussed by Tolhurst, *The Monastic Breviary of Hyde Abbey*, vi, 46-69. [Hereafter 'Tolhurst'.]

5. Tolhurst, 238-242.

6. Fry, *RB* 1980.

7. *PL*, ciii (cited as Aniane. Vita); English translation by Cabaniss, *The Emperor's Monk*.

8. *Ccc* 57; modern edition by Chamberlain, *The Rule of St Benedict*.

9. Manuscript sigla are not cited in the text at this point, but all sources referred to here are indexed by provenance on pp.289-91.

10. Pantin, *Chapters*.

11. Tolhurst, 14-46.

NOTE ON CITATION AND ABBREVIATIONS

All quotations from Latin sources in the main text are taken either from the original source or from a subsequent edition of the original. Citation from an edition reproduces exactly the orthography adopted by that editor, although this method inevitably results in occasional inconsistency. Citations from unedited sources also follow the orthography (and, where possible, the punctuation) of the original. There is no attempt to replace the familiar 'e' ending of words such as *glorie* and *sue* with the Classical form 'ae'. On the few occasions where 'ae' occurs in the original, it is retained in the transcription. All other contractions, where they exist, are expanded within square brackets.

For the sake of clarity, the modern terms 'Matins' and 'Lauds' are used for the first two hours of the regular office throughout, irrespective of the Latin original. References to the Office of the Dead form the only exception to this rule, where the study follows the majority of the sources in adopting the term 'Vigils' (rather than 'Matins') of the Dead.

References to Latin citations are given in the main text, using a system of short-references. A key to the editions used may be found in the first section of the bibliography (pp.353-63), together with full details of publication. References to editions in the text give both the page and line number of the edition where both are indicated; for example, Eynsham 113,64-114,2, indicates *The Customary of Eynsham*, page 113, line 64, to page 114, line 2. Where line numbers are not provided by the editor, a page reference alone is given. Any other method of citation is indicated in a footnote. Psalm numbering in the text follows that of the Latin Vulgate.

Manuscripts are also cited by short-reference sigla, following the system of *Répertoire International des Sources Musicales* (*RISM*). For convenience, all class-marks have been abbreviated to a recognizable form. This consists of the *RISM* siglum for place and library (and country other than Great Britain) followed by a condensed form of the shelfmark. A key to manuscript abbreviations appears on pp.xxvii-xxx. A select inventory of manuscripts which have particular significance within this study is given on pp.287-324, together with a brief description and a bibliography for each item. This is arranged alphabetically by library sigla.

Other abbreviations used in the text and liturgical abbreviations adopted in the tables are listed separately on pp.xxxi-xxxiv.

Notes to the text, indicated by superscript numbers, are printed collectively at the end of each chapter. Full details of publications referred to in the notes are given in the bibliography.

Pitch is indicated in accordance with the Helmholtz system: notes from C below the bass stave to low B in the bass stave are referred to as C-B; notes in the octave above c-b, then c'-b'. Editorial accidentals in the musical transcriptions are provided above the stave.

ABBREVIATIONS

1. Source Abbreviations

CA 3	Canterbury, Chapter Library, MS Additional 3
CA 6	Canterbury, Chapter Library, MS Additional 6
Ccc 57	Cambridge, Corpus Christi College, MS 57
Ccc 178	Cambridge, Corpus Christi College, MS 178
Ccc 201	Cambridge, Corpus Christi College, MS 201
Ccc 265	Cambridge, Corpus Christi College, MS 265
Ccc 368	Cambridge, Corpus Christi College, MS 368
Ccc 391	Cambridge, Corpus Christi College, MS 391
Ccc 422	Cambridge, Corpus Christi College, MS 422
Ccc 441	Cambridge, Corpus Christi College, MS 441
Ccc 465	Cambridge, Corpus Christi College, MS 465
Cec S1.4.6	Cambridge, Emmanuel College, S1.4.6 [Printed Book]
Cjc C.18	Cambridge, St John's College, MS 68 C.18
Cjc D.27	Cambridge, St John's College, MS D.27
Cjc F.31	Cambridge, St John's College, MS 168 F.31
Cmc F.4.10	Cambridge, Magdalene College, MS F.4.10
Ctc 0.2.30	Cambridge, Trinity College, MS 0.2.30
Ctc 0.7.31	Cambridge, Trinity College, MS 0.7.31
Cu Dd.1.20	Cambridge, University Library, MS Dd.1.20
Cu Ee.2.4	Cambridge, University Library, MS Ee.2.4
Cu Ii.4.20	Cambridge, University Library, MS Ii.4.20
Cu Kk.6.45	Cambridge, University Library, MS Kk.6.45
Cu Ll.1.14	Cambridge, University Library, MS Ll.1.14
Cu Mm.2.g	Cambridge, University Library, MS Mm.2.g
DO 26543	Downside, Abbey Library, MS 26543
DRc A.IV.19	Durham, Cathedral Library, MS A.IV.19
DRc B.IV.24	Durham, Cathedral Library, MS B.IV.24
DRu V.V.6	Durham, University Library, Cosin MS V.V.6
GL 35	Gloucester, Cathedral Library, MS 35
Lbl A.II	London, British Library, Cotton MS Nero A.II

Lbl A.III	London, British Library, Cotton MS Tiberius A.III
Lbl A.IV	London, British Library, Cotton MS Titus A.IV
Lbl A.VIII	London, British Library, Cotton MS Vespasian A.VIII
Lbl A.X	London, British Library, Cotton MS Faustina A.X
Lbl A.XIV	London, British Library, Cotton MS Galba A.XIV
Lbl B.III	London, British Library, Cotton MS Faustina B.III
Lbl B.VI	London, British Library, Cotton MS Claudius B.VI
Lbl C.110.a.27	London, British Library, C.110.a.27 [Printed Book]
Lbl C.XI	London, British Library, Cotton MS Otho C.XI
Lbl C.XII	London, British Library, Cotton MS Faustina C.XII
Lbl D.III	London, British Library, Cotton MS Claudius D.III
Lbl D.XXVI-II	London, British Library, Cotton MSS Titus D.XXVI-II
Lbl 2.A.X	London, British Library, Royal MS 2.A.X
Lbl 2.B.V	London, British Library, Royal MS 2.B.V
Lbl 155	London, British Library, Arundel MS 155
Lbl 157	London, British Library, Arundel MS 157
Lbl 460	London, British Library, Lansdowne MS 460
Lbl 944	London, British Library, Stowe MS 944
Lbl 1005	London, British Library, Harley MS 1005
Lbl 1804	London, British Library, Harley MS 1804
Lbl 2961	London, British Library, Harley MS 2961
Lbl 3950	London, British Library, Harley MS 3950
Lbl 4664	London, British Library, Harley MS 4664
Lbl 5431	London, British Library, Harley MS 5431
Lbl 17002	London, British Library, MS Additional 17002
Lbl 18302	London, British Library, MS Additional 18302
Lbl 21927	London, British Library, MS Additional 21927
Lbl 30850	London, British Library, MS Additional 30850
Lbl 37517	London, British Library, MS Additional 37517
Lbl 43405-6	London, British Library, MSS Additional 43405-6
Llp 198/198b	London, Lambeth Palace, MSS 198, 198b
Llp 368	London, Lambeth Palace, MS 368
Llp 558	London, Lambeth Palace, MS 558
Mch 6717	Manchester, Chetham's Library, MS 6717
Ob b.1	Oxford, Bodleian, MS Rawlinson liturg. b.1
Ob b.5	Oxford, Bodleian, MS Rawlinson liturg. b.5
Ob c.1	Oxford, Bodleian, MS Rawlinson liturg. c.1
Ob C.892	Oxford, Bodleian, MS Rawlinson liturg. C.892
Ob C.781	Oxford, Bodleian, MS Rawlinson liturg. C.781
Ob d.3	Oxford, Bodleian, MS Rawlinson liturg. d.3
Ob d.4	Oxford, Bodleian, MS Rawlinson liturg. d.4
Ob D.1.20	Oxford, Bodleian, MS Auct. D.1.20
Ob D.2.6	Oxford, Bodleian, MS Auct. D.2.60

Ob D.3.2	Oxford, Bodleian, MS Auct. D.3.2
Ob D.4.7	Oxford, Bodleian, MS Auct. D.4.7
Ob D.4.8	Oxford, Bodleian, MS Auct. D.4.8
Ob e.1*	Oxford, Bodleian, MS Rawlinson liturg. e.1*
Ob e.14	Oxford, Bodleian, MS Lat. Liturg. e.14
Ob f.1	Oxford, Bodleian, MS Rawlinson liturg. f.1
Ob g.1	Oxford, Bodleian, MS Lat. liturg. g.1
Ob g.10	Oxford, Bodleian, MS Rawlinson liturg. g.10
Ob g.12	Oxford, Bodleian, MS Rawlinson liturg. g.12
Ob 4	Oxford, Bodleian, MS Laud misc. 4
Ob 5	Oxford, Bodleian, MS Laud liturg. 5
Ob 6	Oxford, Bodleian, MS Liturg. 6
Ob 8	Oxford, Bodleian, MS Gough liturg. 8
Ob 9	Oxford, Bodleian, MS Lyell 9
Ob 10	Oxford, Bodleian, MS Jesus College 10
Ob 17	Oxford, Bodleian, MS Gough liturg. 17
Ob 22	Oxford, Bodleian, MS Barlow 22
Ob 41	Oxford, Bodleian, MS Barlow 41
Ob 48	Oxford, Bodleian, MS Hatton 48
Ob 101.E	Oxford, Bodleian, MS University College 101.E
Ob 104	Oxford, Bodleian, MS Liturg. 104
Ob 169*	Oxford, Bodleian, MS Tanner 169*
Ob 296	Oxford, Bodleian, MS Douce 296
Ob 358	Oxford, Bodleian, MS New College 358
Ob 435	Oxford, Bodleian, MS Bodley 435
Ob 579	Oxford, Bodleian, MS Bodley 579
Ob 1525	Oxford, Bodleian, MS Ashmole 1525
Occ 197	Oxford, Corpus Christi College, MS 197
Oec 9M	Oxford, Exeter College, 9M [Printed Book]
Ouc 169	Oxford, University College, MS 169
Owc 213	Oxford, Worcester College, MS 213
SB 152	Salisbury, Cathedral Library, MS 152
W n.s.	Wells, Cathedral Library, MS (not specified)
WO F.160	Worcester, Cathedral Library, MS F.160
WO F.173	Worcester, Cathedral Library, MS F.173
WRec 178	Windsor, Eton College Library, MS 178

Sources in Foreign Libraries

CH-E 235	Einsiedeln, Stiftsbibliothek, MS 235
CH-SGs 390	St Gall, Stiftsbibliothek, MS 390
CH-Zz Rh.28	Zürich, Zentral Bibliothek, MS Rh.28
D-Bds 194	Berlin, Deutsche Staatsbibliothek, cod. 194
F-LH 330	Le Havre, Bibliothèque Municipale, MS 330
F-O 129	Orléans, Bibliothèque Municipale, MS 129
F-Pn 987	Paris, Bibliothèque Nationale, MS lat. 987
F-Pn 3719	Paris, Bibliothèque Nationale, MS lat. 3719
F-Pn 12854	Paris, Bibliothèque Nationale, MS lat. 12854
F-Pn 17296	Paris, Bibliothèque Nationale, MS lat. 17296
F-R Y.6	Rouen, Bibliothèque Municipale, MS Y.6
F-R Y.7	Rouen, Bibliothèque Municipale, MS Y.7
F-TAM n.s.	Tamié, Abbey Library, MS (not specified)
F-VAL 116	Valenciennes, Bibliothèque Municipale, MS 116
I-BV V.21	Benevento, Biblioteca Capitolare, MS V.21
I-Lc 601	Lucca, Biblioteca Capitolare, MS 601
I-MZcap c.12.75	Monza, Biblioteca Capitolare, MS c.12.75
I-Rss XIV L.1	Rome, Biblioteca S. Sabina, MS XIV L.1
US-SM EL 34.B.7	San Marino (Calif.), Huntington Library, MS EL 34.B.7

2. Abbreviations for Journals and
Collected Editions

AH	Analecta Hymnica
ActaM	Acta Musicologica
ALw	Archiv für Liturgiewissenschaft
AnnMed	Annuale Médiévale
AnnMus	Annales Musicologiques
ASE	Anglo-Saxon England
BMQ	British Museum Quarterly
BQR	Bodleian Quarterly Record
CCM	Corpus Consuetudinarum Monasticarum
CMM	Corpus Mensurabilis Musicae
CS	Camden Society
CSS	Cistercian Studies Series
DACL	Dictionnaire d'Archéologie Chrétienne et de la Liturgie
DownR	Downside Review
DubR	Dublin Review
EECM	Early English Church Music
EETS (OS)	Early English Text Society (Old Series)
EG	Etudes Grégoriennes
EHR	English Historical Review
EL	Epheremides Liturgicae
EM	Early Music
HBS	Henry Bradshaw Society
JRMA	Journal of the Royal Musical Association
JTS	Journal of Theological Studies
LO	Lex Orandi
MAev	Medium Aevum
MB	Musica Britannica
MD	Musica Disciplina
MGH	Monumenta Germanicae Historica
ML	Music and Letters
MQ	Musical Quarterly
PL	Patrologica Latina
PM	Paléographie Musicale
PMFC	Polyphonic Music of the Fourteenth Century
PMMS	Plainsong and Medieval Music Society
PRMA	Proceedings of the Royal Musical Association
RB	Rule of St Benedict

RC	Regularis Concordia
RM	Rule of the Master
RS	Rolls Society
RevB	Revue Bénédictine
SM	Studia Monastica
SS	Surtees Society
STC	Short-Title Catalogue
VCH	Victoria County History

3. Liturgical Abbreviations

A	Antiphon
A3	Third Antiphon of a series
Adv	Advent
Adv III	Third Sunday in Advent
Anc	Annunciation
AS	All Saints
Asc	Ascension
Ash Wed	Ash Wednesday
Asm	Assumption
Ben	Benedictus antiphon
BVM	Blessed Virgin Mary
C	Compline
C.BVM	Compline of the Virgin
CC	Corpus Christi
Chr	Christmas
Chr Ev	Christmas Eve
Circ	Circumcision
CO	Commemorative Office
DO	Daily Office
Ep	Epiphany
Exalt HC	Exaltation of the Holy Cross
Fr	Friday
H	Hymn
HM	High Mass
Ho In	Holy Innocents
inc	Incipit
Inv HC	Invention of the Holy Cross
l	Lesson
l iii	Third lesson
L	Lauds
LX	Sexagesima
LXX	Septuagesima
mCon	Melodic concordance
M	Matins
MA	Memorial antiphon
Mag	Magnificat antiphon
Mag iv	Fourth Magnificat antiphon of a series
Mon	Monday

MS	Manuscript
N	None
Nat BVM	Nativity of the Virgin
Nunc	Nunc dimittis antiphon
Obl BVM	Oblation (Presentation) of the Virgin
Oct	Octave
Oct Ep	Octave of the Epiphany
pa	per annum
proc A	Processional antiphon
P	Prime
Pasch	Eastertide
Pent	Pentecost
Proc	Procession
Ps	Psalm
Pur	Purification
Quad	Quadragesima
R	Respond
R III	Third respond of a series
Rog	Rogation
S	Sext
Sat	Saturday
Sun	Sunday
tCon	Textual concordance
tmCon	Textual and melodic concordance
T	Terce
Tu Rog	Tuesday Rogation Day
Th	Thursday
Tr	Trinity
Tu	Tuesday
V1	First Vespers
V2	Second Vespers
VA	Votive Antiphon
Vig	Vigil
Vig Asm	Vigil of the Assumption
VS	Verse
v	Versicle
XL	Quadragesima
*	Indicates presence of complete text in source

Medieval English Benedictine Liturgy

Part I

THE FORMATION OF VOTIVE

OBSERVANCE IN ENGLISH MONASTERIES

BEFORE THE NORMAN CONQUEST

Chapter One

ST BENEDICT'S *OPUS DEI*:
THE BASIS FOR LATER VOTIVE OBSERVANCE

The liturgical scheme drawn up by St Benedict of Nursia (*c*.480-*c*.550) for the daily worship of the first Benedictine community at Monte Cassino is presented as Chapters 8-20 of The Rule of St Benedict. The pattern described in this document is simple and uncluttered, operating within a carefully planned routine, where the community was subject to strict discipline but 'nothing harsh or burdensome': *In qua institutione nihil asperum, nihil grave, nos constituturos speramus* (*RB* Prologue: 4).[1] The liturgical prayer of the community (*Opus Dei*), amounting to about four hours a day, was only one element of the prescribed lifestyle. Approximately six hours were devoted to manual labour, and a further four to *lectio* (reading or private prayer) and *meditatio* (memorization, repetition and reflection on biblical texts).[2] This particular balance, however, was not retained by all of the communities which adopted *RB* during the Middle Ages. The tendency for liturgical expansion which began during the eighth century (discussed at the end of this chapter) set a precedent for widespread proliferation of liturgical accretions, resulting in a serious distortion of St Benedict's original ideal. Nevertheless, the directions for *Opus Dei* presented in *RB* remained the basic foundation around which all subsequent liturgical change was made, and the purpose of this chapter is to consider the basic evidence of the document as a precursor for intercession of a votive nature.

Comparison with earlier monastic rules reveals that most of Benedict's directions for the structure of the office and the daily order of psalmody are more clearly regulated than those of his predecessors. But other areas within the liturgical scheme of *RB*—including the conclusion of the office hours and the regulation of periods of private prayer—are described with less precision. This may imply that certain practices were too familiar to merit explicit discussion, or it may be that genuine flexibility was thought to be desirable. The following discussion, some of which inevitably summarizes and conflates the extensive work of other scholars, aims to relate some of the ambiguities of *RB* to later sources which clarify the issue by providing more complete instructions or additional texts. It also evaluates the legacy of *RB* by examining its contemporary significance and derivation from other rules, the extent to which it was received during the Middle Ages and its early adoption in England. The second part of the chapter considers the aims of some of the earliest Benedictine reformers, most notably Benedict of Aniane, and the resulting proliferation of liturgical accretions.

THE RULE OF ST BENEDICT AND ITS PRECURSORS

Most of *RB* draws on existing monastic practice. It is but one of many Latin rules written between the fifth and sixth centuries, and was not conceived other than for use by the community at Monte Cassino. Its widespread circulation only began during the eighth century when it was promulgated throughout the empire of Charlemagne (768-814). *RB* demonstrates parallels with a group of more than twenty rules written at a slightly earlier date in Italy and Southern Gaul. Traces of Caesarius of Arles (*c*.470-542) and eastern rules are present, but much of the material is lifted directly from a code termed *Regula Magistri* (*RM*), a lengthy anonymous monastic rule of over 50,000 words written in Italy south-east of Rome in the first quarter of the sixth century.[3]

The close relationship between *RM* and *RB*, the obvious debt in the latter work to the Roman Office, the cathedral usage of Jerusalem and a variety of other monastic traditions, imply that St Benedict's code is a document of concensus rather than of originality. But in many respects fidelity to established practice was the key to its contemporary popularity: its traditionalism marked it out as a masterful distillation of earlier monastic experience. It also represents a considerable advance in quality on *RM*: it is more concise, structurally and stylistically superior, and more humane in its outlook.

Unlike *RM*, *RB* presents liturgical directions as a continuous sequence of chapters (*RB* 8-20; *RM* deals with the ordering of the liturgical day at a later stage, primarily in Chapters 33-37, but also 44-45 and 49). Table 1:1 (pp.181-86) presents in summary format the prescribed structure for each of the office hours in *RB*. In essence the structure of the office parallels the practice of the contemporary Roman basilicas served by monks, but Benedict's version of the Psalter (here presented alongside the later standard secular *cursus* of psalms as Table 1:2) is modified, eliminating some of the repetitions in the Roman monastic office, where the daily psalmody at all hours except Matins and Vespers was fixed. *RB* imposes firm regulation on the number of psalms at Matins (twelve) and Vespers (four)—*RB* Chapters

9, 11, 17—and introduces variable psalmody at Lauds, Prime, Terce, Sext and None. *RM* gives no indication of the ordering of the psalms.

The two documents also diverge significantly in that *RM* prescribes daily reception of the communion under both kinds. *RB* is notably silent on the matter of the communion. The term *communio* appears three times (*RB* 38:2, 38:10, 63:4) but not in the chapters specifically devoted to the liturgy. Opinion varies considerably as to the frequency of mass celebration amongst the early Benedictines. Adalbert De Vogüé is most cautious, considering that a conventual mass would 'at most' have been limited to Sundays and feastdays, or even without any sense of fixed regularity whatsoever.[4] C.H. Lawrence is less circumspect, arguing for a single celebration of conventual mass on Sundays, feastdays and other important occasions, including special needs. He sees this partly as the result of the small number of priests in the earliest Benedictine communities, and partly the result of an abbot's inability to legislate on the eucharistic liturgy: a task which had to be left to a bishop.[5] George Guiver, however, suggests that the communion was not celebrated at the monastery at all, and that the monks simply visited the local parish church.[6] The infrequency of eucharistic celebration implied in the liturgical scheme of *RB* was overturned in the later Middle Ages. Most communities were required to be present for at least two daily masses by the tenth century (the Mass of the Day and the Chapter or Morrow Mass), whilst a third celebration in honour of the Virgin was added in many foundations during the twelfth century.

MONASTIC PRAYER

As suggested above, *RB* allows for a surprising degree of flexibility in certain areas. This is most explicitly stated in the chapter dealing with the order of psalmody, which, after its enumeration of the psalms to be recited at each hour, gives the following modified directive:

> *Hoc praecipue commonentes ut, si cui forte haec distributio psalmorum displicuerit, ordinet si melius aliter iudicaverit, dum omnimodis id attendat ut omni hebdomada psalterium ex integro numero centum quinquaginta psalmorum psallantur, et dominico die semper a caput reprehendatur ad vigilas.*   RB 18:22-23

There is also very little formal direction for the manner in which periods of time for prayer should be structured. *RB* recommends private prayer but seems concerned to safeguard its spontaneity, and Chapter 20, which concludes the specifically liturgical section of *RB*, presents an ideal of brevity and purity:

> *Et ideo brevis debet esse et pura oratio, nisi forte ex affectu*
> *inspirationis divinae gratiae protendatur.*   RB 20:4

This recommendation is also applied to prayer in community, presumably
before or after an office:

> *In conventu tamen omnino brevietur oratio, et facto signo a priore*
> *omnes pariter surgant.*   RB 20:5

Chapter 52 (concerned with the oratory of the monastery) certainly implies
that private prayer might follow an office, an important factor when
considering the expansion of the hours in later years by the addition of
independent observances. (This will be further discussed in relation to the
imprecision of *RB*'s directions on the closing ceremonies of the hours,
below.) Indeed, private prayer was allowed in the oratory on all occasions:

> *Oratorium hoc sit quod dicitur, nec ibi quicquam aliud geratur aut*
> *condatur. Expleto opere Dei, omnes cum summo silentio exeant, et*
> *habeatur reverentia Deo, ut frater qui forte sibi peculiariter vult*
> *orare non impediatur alterius improbitate. Sed et si aliter vult sibi*
> *forte secretius orare, simpliciter intret et oret, non in clamosa*
> *voce, sed in lacrimis et intentione cordis. Ergo qui simile opus non*
> *facit, non permittatur explicito opere Dei remorari in oratorio,*
> *sicut dictum est, ne alius impedimentum patiatur.*   RB 52:1-5

Private prayer was also considered a suitable act of self-denial during Lent:

> *Ergo his diebus augeamus nobis aliquid solito pensu servitutis*
> *nostrae, orationes peculiares, ciborum et potus abstinentiam, ut*
> *unusquisque super mensuram sibi indictam aliquid propria*
> *voluntate . . . offerat Deo.*   RB 49:5-6

The term used here for private prayer, *orationes peculiares*, is one which
was used in a similar context three centuries later by Rabanus Maurus (776
or 784-856), Abbot of Fulda and Archbishop of Mainz, in a manual dealing
with the sacraments, communal prayer and other matters (*De clericorum*
institutione). Rabanus identifies three categories of prayer: private (*privatae*)
personal (*peculiares*) and secret (*furtivae*).[7] *RB* on most occasions refers
simply to private devotions as *oratio*, but in Chapter 17, part of the section
dealing formally with the Divine Office, *oratio* seems to be used to refer to
the entire office:

> *Tertia vero, sexta et nona, item eo ordine celebretur oratio, id est*
> *versu, hymnos earundem horarum, ternos psalmos, lectionem et*
> *versu, Kyrie eleison et missas.* **RB** 17:5

This may also imply a link with the reference to *oratio* in community at *RB* 20:5 (cited above). Timothy Fry's discussion of the liturgical code in *RB* suggests that the term *oratio* (when applied to communal prayer) may well indicate the use of psalter collects evident in cathedral worship at a similar period: a psalm 'Christianized' by a collect and followed by a brief period of silent prayer.[8] Both St Cassian and *RM* seem to have been familiar with the notion of private prayer after psalms, and de Vogüé argues strongly that this practice was very much a part of the monastic tradition.[9] It is, however, but one area where *RB* leaves room for speculation. Nevertheless, the psalm/collect structure serves as an obvious precedent for those devotions consisting of psalms and collects which became such a characteristic part of votive observance. A number of these structures are discussed in Chapter Two.

There are few other instances where particularized use of free time is specified in *RB*, with the exception of a passage dealing with the interval which falls after Matins during the winter:

> *Quod vero restat post vigilias a fratribus qui psalterii vel lectionum*
> *aliquid indigent meditationi inserviatur.* **RB** 8:3

Similarly after the midday meal during the winter, the community is exhorted to apply itself to sacred reading or to the study of psalmody:

> *Post refectionem autem vacent lectionibus suis aut psalmis*
> **RB** 48:13

PRAYER AT THE END OF AN OFFICE

If the notion of private prayer is still largely unformed in *RB*, most of the regulations for the Divine Office are remarkably clear. However, this is not the case at the conclusion and dismissal of the hours. Table 1:3 (p.192) presents the directions given in the liturgical section of *RB* for the termination of each hour. Although no mention is made of this observance in the relevant chapters, Chapter 67, dealing with brothers sent on a journey, indicates that the last prayer of the *Opus Dei* incorporated a commemoration of absent brethren:

> *et semper ad orationem ultimam operis Dei commemoratio*
> *absentum fiat.*   *RB* 67:2

It seems most likely that this refers to the prayer at the end of each hour rather than simply to the end of Compline. In addition to this commemoration, all hours appear to have closed with the litany *Kyrie eleison* (*supplicatio litaniae, id est Kyrie eleison: RB* 9:10) and the Lord's Prayer. Except at Lauds and Vespers, *RB* specifies that the latter was to be recited silently up to the customary concluding versicle (*Et ne nos inducas in tentationem*) and response (*Sed libera nos a malo*), both of which were spoken aloud:

> *Ceteris vero agendis, ultima pars eius orationis dicatur, ut ab*
> *omnibus respondeatur: sed libera nos a malo. RB* 13:14

At Lauds and Vespers however, *Pater Noster* was to be read aloud in its entirety:

> *Plane agenda matutina vel vespertina non transeat aliquando, nisi*
> *in ultimo per ordinem oratio dominica, omnibus audientibus,*
> *dicatur a priore.*   *RB* 13:12

The exact nature in which the hours terminated has been greatly disputed by scholars of all generations, owing to the ambiguity of the word *missa*.[10] This term occurs four times in Chapter 17 of *RB* in conjunction with concluding ceremonies: *et missas* (17:4,5), *fiant missae* (17:8), and *missae fiant* (17:10). Chapters 12 and 13, dealing with Lauds, do not use this phrase, stating simply *et completum est* (12:4, 13:11). Elsewhere in *RB* the term *missa* appears in a rather different context. Twice it unequivocally refers to the celebration of mass (*post missas et communionem*, 38:2; and *concedatur ei . . . benedicere aut missas tenere*, 60:4). In Chapter 35, however, which instructs the kitchen workers to wait until after 'the dismissal' (*usque ad missas*) on solemnities, before receiving a drink and a small portion of bread and then serving the community for its meal, the term seems to be used in the simple sense of conclusion:

> *In diebus tamen sollemnibus usque ad missas sustineant*
>   *RB* 35:14

DuCange also cites instances where the term is used merely to indicate dismissal: this usage appears twice in the second book of St Cassian's *De institutis coenobiorum: Quare post missam nocturnam dormire non oporteat*

(Chapter 13) and *Post orationum missam unusquisque ad suam cellam redeat* (Chapter 15).[11]

J.B.L. Tolhurst, however, by examination of the works of Caesarius of Arles argues for a more explicit use of the term.[12] He considers that *missa* was not simply a reference to 'some form of dismissal', but rather an indication of a prayer or series of prayers, to which a commemoration for absent brethren might be added. Caesarius of Arles in his *Regula ad monachos* (written soon after 502) used the term *missa* to imply a passage of scripture read from a book:

> *Vigilias . . . duos nocturnos faciant et tres missas. Ad una missa legat frater folia tria, et orate; legat alia tria, et levet se.*
>
> Caesarius, 1102

In his Rule Caesarius indicates that the hours were all to terminate with a series of short passages, primarily extracted from the psalms, which were used as intercessions in the manner of a litany. Here the term used is *capitella de psalmis*, a phrase which recurs in Canon 30 of the Council of Agde of 506 (over which Caesarius presided) in its prescription for the termination of Lauds and Vespers.[13]

Tolhurst considers that the term *missas* in *RB* refers to these same *capitella*. St Benedict was clearly familiar with Caesarius's Rule for Monks, since *RB* twice quotes from it in Chapter 58 (58:1-4, 24-25), and incorporates likely allusions to it on eight other occasions.[14] The commemoration for absent brethren mentioned in *RB* 67 may therefore simply have been appended to the end of a series of *capitella*, perhaps with a collect concluding the entire sequence (see below).

Capitella seem to have become regular features of several monastic liturgies by the seventh century. Two categories were in use by *c*.600: Gallican *capitella* (psalm verses only, without specifying any particular intention) and Celtic *capitella* (incorporating an introductory particularizing formula before each verse and sometimes a collect after it).[15] The latter species is prescribed in the Rule of St Columbanus, compiled *c*.590, where a variety of intentions is listed:

> *cum versiculorum augmento intervenientium pro peccatis primum nostris, deinde pro omni populo christiano, deinde pro sacerdotibus et reliquis deo consecratis sacrae plebis gradibus, postremo pro elemosinas facientibus, postea pro pace regum, novissime pro inimicis, ne illis deus statuat in peccatum quod persecuntur et detrahant nobis, quia nesciunt quod faciunt.*   Columbanus, 130.

Two series of Celtic *capitella* also appear in the Bangor Antiphoner,[16] a manuscript which in all probability was copied at Bobbio, one of several continental monasteries founded by St Columbanus who died there in 615. The Antiphoner appears to have been written between 680 and 691, during the abbacy of Cronanus. The *capitella* occur under the headings *Oratio communis fratrum* (p.22) and *Ad horas diei oratio communis* (p.31): both exhibit close correspondence with the series given in the Rule of Columbanus. Such intercessions appear in a similar form in several later manuscripts, amongst them the early tenth-century Durham Collectar (*DRc* A.IV.19), although with considerable rearrangement of the intentions specified. In later liturgical books they are often termed *preces*, a term which appears in some of the medieval recensions of *RB* (see below). In other respects the Celtic *capitella* suggest an obvious link with the series of memorials and suffrages which were commonly appended to Vespers and Lauds from at least the tenth century. This link is examined further in Chapter Five.

Despite the difficulty of precise interpretation of *missae sunt*, it seems clear that *RB* alludes to closing ceremonies which were familiar enough not to call for explicit definition. Tolhurst alone aims to provide a suitable interpretation for the termination of each hour in *RB*, although most scholars acknowledge that the term implies a group of prayers used to conclude an office. This notion is further supported by interpolations written into several surviving versions of *RB* copied during the eleventh and twelfth centuries, when monastic liturgy had expanded.

MEDIEVAL RECENSIONS OF *RB*:
FURTHER EVIDENCE FOR THE CONCLUSION OF THE OFFICE

Since the publication of Ludwig Traube's pioneer work in 1898, it has been widely accepted that by the eighth century there were at least three categories of the *RB* text in circulation.[17] Most modern critical editions of *RB* take the so-called *textus purus* (*A*) as their model, but it is unlikely that this particular version ever reached England during the Middle Ages. During the seventh and eighth centuries an amended version, *textus interpolatus* (*O*), circulated in England and on the Continent, but a mixed recension (*textus receptus*), amalgamating elements from both *A* and *O*, was dominant throughout Europe from the middle of the ninth century. All extant manuscripts of *RB* copied in England before *c.*1100 with one exception (*Ob* 48, the earliest extant copy of *textus interpolatus*, copied in the Midlands *c.*720[18]) belong to *textus receptus*. Such texts were probably derived from continental exemplars, although it is difficult to determine whether this occurred before the critical tenth-century Benedictine reform in England. Mechthild Gretsch lists sixteen extant sources of *RB* (*textus receptus*) and its Old English translation copied in England between the mid-tenth century and the beginning of the thirteenth century (Table 1:4, p.193).[19]

Many of the medieval additions to *RB* were of a liturgical nature. Table 1:5 (p.194) lists all interpolated passages in one of the surviving recensions: *Ccc* 57, copied at Abingdon in the tenth or eleventh century.[20] A number of these insertions are not directives but simply complete liturgical texts, presumably added to St Benedict's original prescriptions for the sake of convenience or clarity. The modified reference to each of the day hours in Chapter 17 of the Abingdon copy (Table 1:5 No.4) simply adds the words *cum precibus* to the original direction *et missa est* in the earlier version of *RB*: no particular texts are specified. But on four occasions (nos. 6-9 of Table 1:5) a complete series of versicles and responses followed by a collect is appended to St Benedict's original. Many of these additions are for very specific occasions: the blessing of the kitchen servers and the weekly reader, and the reception of a guest. Item 9a, however, provides texts for the commemoration of absent brethren prescribed in the earlier versions of *RB* at the end of each hour (see pp.9-19); these (as argued above) may well have concluded a series of unspecified *capitella*.

Like the other examples in Table 1:5 (nos. 6-9), the appended texts consist of a series of versicles and responses (taken from the psalms) followed by a collect:

Et sic oretur pro eis:

Salve fac servos tuos.
Responsorium: Deus meus, sperantes in te [Ps.85,v.2]

Mitte eis, Domine, auxilium de sancto
Responsorium: Et de Sion tuere eos. [Ps.19,v.2]

Nihil proficiat inimicus in eis
Responsorium: Et filius iniquitatis non noceat eis. [Ps.88,v.22]

Domine exaudi orationem meam
Responsorium: Et clamor meus ad te perveniat. [Ps.101,v.7]

Oratio: Deus qui diligentibus te misericordiam tuam . . .

Neither The Rule of St Columbanus nor the Bangor Antiphoner makes any mention of *capitella* for absent brethren, but Tolhurst's collation of six later sources containing *capitella* in the Celtic tradition shows an important parallel with the texts given in the Abingdon version of *RB*.[21] All six incorporate at least one verse marked *pro fratribus nostris absentibus*, and in four of the six sources *Salvos fac servos tuos* heads the series. Five of the six sources continue with *Mitte eis domine* and *Domine exaudi orationem*, while the Durham Collectar (*DRc* A.IV.19) inserts a further three texts between the last two items, one of which, as in the Abingdon copy, is *Nihil proficiat*. A number of sources with *capitella* of the Gallican rather than Celtic species (in that they tend to omit introductory intentions and collects) also contains similar series of verses.

The collect for absent brethren given in the Abingdon manuscript is found in a similar context in other liturgical sources. A slightly modified version of the text appears in the Gelasian Sacramentary as the first of a series of *orationes ad proficiscendum in itinere*;[22] it also occurs in Leofric A as the postcommunion of the *Missa pro iter agentibus*.[23] Textual duplication of this kind was common; the Abingdon collect prescribed when guests were received into the monastery, *Deus humilium visitator*, also appears in the Gelasian Sacramentary as the first of two prayers *super venientes in domo*.[24] Duplication of collects as part of appended devotions is discussed further in the following chapter.

The *capitella* for absent brethren given in *Ccc* 57 presumably occurred after each of the hours. It is likely that they were preceded by the unspecified *preces* prescibed after Prime, Terce, Sext, None and Vespers (Table 1:5, no. 5; p.194), which must have been modelled along similar lines, but directed towards other intentions. At this early stage in the elaboration of *RB*, the term *preces* seems to have been used synonymously with *capitella*. Sets of *preces* appear in different forms from at least the eleventh century, not only to conclude the monastic office, but also, as Tolhurst points out, in the appended daily office of All Saints and the earlier versions of the Little Office of the Virgin.[25] Their position at the end of the office is one of importance: from the earliest manuscripts of *RB* it seems that the termination of an hour was an area of considerable flexibility, allowing space for varied accretions. Many of the earliest instances of votive observance appear in the form of appendages to the end of the office, and the question of *missae*, *preces* and *capitella* will be re-examined in Chapter Five in relation to two slightly later but closely-related categories: memorials and suffrages.

ST BENEDICT OF ANIANE: LITURGICAL UNITY
IN THE CAROLINGIAN ERA

Although the Rule of Benedict of Nursia persisted in the later Middle Ages, it was overtaken by developments and reform in western monasticism. The first major phase of reform revolved around St Benedict of Aniane (*c*.750-

821). Most of the details of Benedict's life come from a contemporary account by the monk Ardo, a disciple of Benedict who served as monk, priest and teacher at Aniane.[26]

Prior to Benedict's reform *RB* seems to have fallen into disuse, and few monasteries practised the regular Benedictine life. During the seventh century fifty-three houses in Frankish territories followed the severe Rule of Columbanus, while old and new codes existed side by side during the eighth century: Chrodegang's Rule for Canons, the Egyptian tradition of St Cassian, the heremetical tradition of Lérins, and the Rule of Caesarius of Arles all had their adherents. Furthermore, secular control of certain houses meant that many monasteries became destitute and were forced to disband.

Benedict of Aniane's attempts to reform Frankish Benedictine houses were greatly aided by a close collaboration with the state. The project was supported by Charlemagne and his son Louis the Pious, both of whom cherished similar ideals: the imposition of a uniform liturgical and constitutional code amongst monasteries in Frankish territories. Charlemagne granted immunity to Benedict's own monastery at Aniane, and gave him the right of free election of the local abbot. Louis the Pious was equally supportive, making Benedict the superior general of all Benedictine houses in Aquitaine so that he might reform them in accordance with the model usage of his own monastery at Aniane. Later in his career (*c.*815-6) Benedict was elected abbot at Inde, a foundation built by Louis to serve as a model for all other houses in the Frankish empire, situated just six miles from the imperial palace. This physical and ideological co-operation between monk and emperor was crucial to the achievement of Benedict's plans for reform, and in one sense was a foreshadowing of the active patronage of the monks of Winchester by King Edgar in the later tenth century discussed below, pp.31-32). And like Edgar, Louis the Pious had sufficient power to influence and shape the direction of the monastic movement.

Much of Benedict's work as a reformer is chronicled in Ardo's biography. Evidence also survives in *Capitulare monasticum*, a series of eighty canons produced at the Council of Aachen in 817 (here cited as Aachen.817).[27] In the previous year, Louis the Pious sponsored a synod at Aachen to improve the life of the canons regular. Louis was equally important in his patronage of the monastic synod of 817, but it is clear that the document produced at this later council is almost exclusively the work of Benedict of Aniane. With the aim of achieving uniform observance, Benedict submitted the document to Louis the Pious who made it an official capitulary of the realm, and ordered that it be put to use in all Frankish monasteries within the space of one year. Adoption of the requirements expressed in the *Capitula* was supervised by monastic visitors (*missi dominici*).

The capitulary was produced with the intention of clarifying a confusingly wide range of monastic traditions. It took as its foundation *RB*,

which Benedict had studied for many years, seeing faithful observance of
the Rule as his true vocation:

> *Cujus ille obediens jussis, circumivit singulorum monasteria, non*
> *solum semel et bis, sed et multis vicibus, ostendens monita*
> *Regulae, eamque eis per singula capitula discutiens, nota*
> *confirmans, ignora elucidans.*   Aniane.*Vita*, 372

Yet it was widely acknowledged that *RB* had its limitations as a complete
code for the regular life in the ninth century. There were lacunae and
ambiguities in its directions for the execution of the *horarium*, customs and
discipline. Several matters were left to the discretion of the abbot. Ardo
records Benedict of Aniane's feelings on this area:

> . . . *permulta sunt quae usus explere quotidianus expetit, ipsa*
> *tamen reticet: ex quibus omnibus habitus monachi veluti gemmis*
> *ornatur, et sine quibus dissolutus ac fluxus incompositusque esse*
> *probatur.*   Aniane.*Vita*, 378

The 817 Aachen capitulary reflects Benedict's campaign for additional
legislation, although its dependence on *RB* is strikingly apparent in the first
forty canons, and especially in the opening items:

> *1. Capitulum, ut abbates mox ut ad monasteria sua remeauerint*
> *regulam per singula uerba discutientes pleniter legant et*
> *intellegentes domino oppitulante efficaciter cum monachis suis*
> *implere studeant.*
>
> *2. Ut monachi omnes qui possunt memoriter discant regulam.*
>
> *3. Ut officium iuxta quod in regula sancti Benedicti continetur*
> *celebrent.*   (Aachen.817, 457-8)

Liturgy is prominent in the *Capitula*, which suggest a growing passion
for elaborate or finely regulated ceremonies. At least sixteen of the canons
deal with the office, whilst a number discuss accrued practices nowhere
mentioned in *RB*: whether in the original text or in a medieval recension.
Ardo's *Vita* also gives details of some of these extraneous ceremonies.
Benedict of Aniane's codification of the liturgy prescribed the following
additions:

1. Recitation of fifteen psalms before Matins

Fifteen psalms were recited before Matins in choir: five for the faithful
living, five for the faithful departed, and five for those recently deceased.
Each monk was then to prostrate himself after each group, 'commending to
God those in general for whom he sang, and only then beginning to petition
for particular persons'.

> *Psalmos autem cantare jussit, quinque pro omnibus fidelibus in toto*
> *terrarum orbe vivis, quinque etiam pro omnibus fidelibus defunctis;*
> *pro eis quoque qui nuper defuncti sunt . . . quinque. Decursis vero*
> *psalmis quinque pronus orationi incumbat, eos pro quibus cecinit*
> *Deo commendans; et tunc demum pro aliis rogaturus initium sumat.*
>
> Aniane. *Vita*, 378

No reference is given to any particular group of psalms, but it is almost
certain that this devotion is equivalent to the so-called fifteen gradual psalms
(Psalms 119-133) which are prescribed in many later sources for recitation
before Matins. In the later sources these psalms become part of a more
fully-formed devotion called *Trina oratio* (see pp.37-38 and Table 2:4).

2. Daily visitation of all altars

a) before Matins
b) before Prime
c) after Compline

At the first visit the monks said the Lord's Prayer and the *Credo* at each
altar. At the second and third visits they were free to say either the Lord's
Prayer or the *Confiteor*.

> *In his tribus per diem vicibus circumire cuncta praecepit altaria,*
> *et ad primum ex eis orationem Dominicam dicant et symbolum,*
> *caeteris orationem Dominicam, vel sua confiteantur delicta.*
>
> Aniane. *Vita*, 379

3. A daily meeting in the Chapter House, after Prime:

> *Expleta Prima in unum aggregati solvant capitulum.*
>
> Aniane. *Vita*, 379

Ardo gives no details of the chapter office although he mentions its
occurrence (*officium capituli*). It is described more fully in the Aachen
Capitula:

> *Ut ad capitulum primitus martyrilogium legatur et dicatur uersus,*
> *deinde regula aut omelia quaelibet legatur, deinde Tu autem*
> *domine dicatur.*   Aachen.817, 532

The chapter is also mentioned in an account of the practices of the
monastery at Inde written by two Reichenau monks, Tatto and Grimalt.
Later forms of the chapter typically consist of the following elements:

a) Reading from the Martyrology
b) Versicle *Pretiosa*
c) *Deus in adiutorium* (three times)
d) *Gloria Patri*
e) *Kyrie eleison*
f) Reading from *RB* or homily
g) Versicle *Tu autem Domine*
h) Chapter of faults
i) Daily work assignment

It is unclear whether Benedict of Aniane can be credited with the
introduction of the chapter meeting, which occurs in a small number of
contemporary sources, including *Memoriale Qualiter* (*c.*770). *RB* itself
makes no reference to a daily meeting of the community, but provides for
an assembly of all the monks for matters of particular business (*RB*, Chapter
3).

4. The Office of the Dead

It seems even less likely that Benedict of Aniane was responsible for the
introduction of the Office of the Dead, for there are references to it in two
of the late eighth-century *Ordines Romani* and in Angilbert's *Institutio* (see
Table 3:2). Nevertheless it appears to have been a familiar observance when
the Aachen legislation was compiled. Ardo makes no mention of the Office
of the Dead, but it is discussed in the Decrees of the first Synod of Aachen,
held in 816, and in the report drawn up by Tatto and Grimalt (Table 3:2,
G). It is unclear whether the Office of the Dead was regarded as a daily
accretion to the office, or whether it was simply recited on certain
occasions. Its origins and early structure are examined in more detail in
Chapter Three (Table 3:2 and pp.58-64).

5. Psalms for benefactors and the dead

Canon 12 of the *Capitula* of 817 refers to special psalms for benefactors and
the dead:

> *Ut praetermissis partitionibus psalterii psalmi speciales pro elemosinariis et defunctis cantentur.* Aachen.817, 475

No particular context is specified, but certain later sources, amongst them *Regularis Concordia*, indicate that Psalms 6-9 were recited daily for the dead, after chapter (see Table 2:2, p.197).

Benedict also provides rather more precise directions for the occupation of the monk during periods of manual labour, emphasizing the non-liturgical use of psalmody. During work outdoors or in the kitchen, the community is enjoined either to remain silent or to recite psalms, singly or in company:

> *Expleta Prima in unum aggregati solvant capitulum: quo expleto, cum silentio, aut psalmos decantando exeant ad opus sibi injunctum. In monasterio quoque remanentes non fabulis occupentur otiosis, sed bini et bini, aut certe singuli in coquina, in pistrino, in cellario psalmos canant.* Aniane.*Vita*, 379

Periods of private prayer were also much more closely regulated: no-one was allowed to stay in the oratory after Compline, and permission was needed if a monk wished to pray alone:

> *Diurnis autem orationum horis ad suum quisque accedat oraturus locum: si autem peculiariter sibi vult orare, quibuscunque vacat horis, licenter peragat.* Aniane.*Vita*, 379

The lifestyle established at Inde was more authoritarian than that prescribed in *RB*. But as in the latter, it was the execution of the Divine Office which took precedence over all other activities. 'Excessive or indiscreet vigils during the course of the night' were to be avoided on practical grounds, in case the community became too fatigued to concentrate on the psalms of the regular hours:

> *Sic enim accidere solet ut nimiis vigiliis atterantur unius noctis indiscretione: horis autem quibus divinis psalmodiis esse intentum oportet, praeoccupatus somno non valeat divinum exsolvere censum.* Aniane.*Vita*, 379

Benedict of Aniane has been criticized for over-emphasizing community prayer and extraneous devotion. But in other respects the tendencies of his reform were paradoxically akin to the more austere movements of later monasticism: Cîteaux among them. This is most clearly seen in his concern to establish a uniformity of liturgical and constitutional practice, founded on the principles of *RB*. After his death in 821, many of the flourishing houses established along the lines of the Inde model failed to survive; hence, the Carolingian aspirations to uniformity were never achieved. Nevertheless, during the next phase of building, both in England and on the Continent, the pattern of Benedict of Aniane's foundations is indelibly stamped on the liturgical observance of the new communities.

NOTES

1. All references (Chapter: Line) to Fry (ed.), *RB 1980*, unless otherwise stated.

2. Fry, 446-7; Knowles, *The Monastic Order*, 4-7.

3. De Vogüé, *La Règle du Maître*. This edition also provides a comparison of the structure of the office in *RB* and *RM*.

4. De Vogüé, 'Problems of the Monastic Conventual Mass', 328.

5. Lawrence, *Medieval Monasticism*, 29.

6. Guiver, 57

7. Rabanus, *De clericorum orationibus*. Chapter 11 discusses *orationes peculiares*; other sorts of prayer are discussed in Chapter 12.

8. Fry, 412-3.

9. De Vogüé, *La Règle de Saint Benoît*, v, 582-3.

10. Delatte, 156, 174; *RB* (ed. McCann), 178-9.

11. DuCange, *Glossarium mediae et infimae Latinatis*.

12. Tolhurst, 14-16.

13. Tolhurst, 16-17.

14. Fry, 595.

15. For a detailed examination of Gallican and Celtic *capitella*, see Tolhurst, 18-46.

16. Edited as HBS, iv, x; see x, 22, 31.

17. Traube, *Textgeschichte der Regula S. Benedicti*. For a summary account of the three traditions, see Gretsch, 'Aethelwold's Translation'.

18. Facsimile and critical commentary in Farmer (ed.), *The Rule of St Benedict (Oxford, Bodleian Library Hatton 48)*.

19. Gretsch, 'Aethelwold's Translation'.

20. *Ccc 57* is the only medieval recension of *RB* which appears in a modern edition (Chamberlain (ed.), *The Rule of St Benedict*).

21. Tolhurst, 20-27.

22. Gelas.Sac., 1314.

23. Leof.Miss., 16.

24. Gelas.Sac., 1554.

25. Tolhurst, 19.

26. All references to Aniane. *Vita*. English translation by Cabaniss, *The Emperor's Monk*.

27. Edited in *CCM*, i, 501-36 (listed under 'Aachen.817' in bibliog.).

Chapter Two

THE PLACE OF VOTIVE OBSERVANCE IN
THE FIRST ENGLISH BENEDICTINE COMMUNITIES

What was conceived as a monastic rule for a single house in northern Italy had by the ninth century become the norm for a large number of houses throughout Europe. But in spite of the spread of St Benedict's Rule and its development in the Carolingian era, it was neither exclusive nor comprehensive. Other rules and traditions were found, especially in the extremes of Europe (such as the Celtic lands). Furthermore, the autonomous status of each monastery allowed it to interpret and enlarge *RB* within its own customs and traditions. But the monastic revivals of the ninth and tenth centuries saw a new direction most obviously represented by Cluny. At Cluny Odo and his successors not only established a strong and large house with its own concept and interpretation of *RB*, but from there were founded daughter houses. These houses followed the same practices as the mother house and belonged to a single congregation presided over by the abbot of Cluny.

The trend away from the autonomous monastery towards an integrated, centrally-controlled group of houses is a new feature in the history of monasticism. And although its manifestation is most obvious in the eleventh century with the new orders of the Carthusians and Cistercians, it was an important part of the revival of monasticism in England during the tenth century.

The English interpretation of *RB* is embodied in *Regularis Concordia* (hereafter *RC*), a document formulated at the Council of English monks held at Winchester (*c.*970). In a general way it demonstrates how *RB* was received in England, how it was coloured by contemporary practice both in England and on the Continent, and how an attempt was made to establish an agreed practice for an English Congregation. In the context of this study it serves to give more specific evidence related to votive observance. *RC* goes much further than *RB* in describing customs liturgical and otherwise. In its comprehensiveness, *RC* not only gives a more precise account of votive observance than any other contemporary document but also describes practices and emphases that are uniquely English. Although Anglo-Saxon in conception, it provides a historical base from which to evaluate votive observance in the context of later medieval practice.

In studying *RC* it is useful to summarize the reception of *RB* into English monasteries, and to examine the historical circumstances of the tenth-century revival and the Council of Winchester.

THE ADOPTION OF THE RULE OF ST BENEDICT IN ENGLAND

RB was certainly known in England as early as the seventh century, but probably not as an exclusive code. The exact circumstances of its introduction are unclear. The once popular theory that it was imported into Kent by St Augustine and his Roman companions in *c*.597 is now thought to be unlikely,[1] for although Bede's *Ecclesiastical History* (731) reports that the Roman missionaries were monks, there is no indication of the code of practice which they followed.[2] Roman monasticism of the period was characterized by diversity, and the abbot of each autonomous community was able to devise his own rule.[3]

Bede emphasizes the polarity of two separate strands of monasticism in seventh-century England. The Roman mission lost no time in establishing communities in the south based on its own customs, but insular Celtic traditions remained prominent in the north. Celtic monasticism was brought from Ireland to Iona by St Columba in *c*.583, passing from there to Lindisfarne and Northumbria by the agency of St Aidan (d.651). Most of the Celtic houses are likely to have adopted the Irish Rule of St Columbanus, at least in part, although Columbanus's asceticism, severity and harsh insistence on corporal punishment led to collaborative attempts at moderation of his Rule. A number of houses may well have used it in conjunction with *RB* during the later seventh century, despite their Celtic origins. Such eclecticism was also a feature of continental monasticism at this date: Luxeuil, Chelles and Faremoutiers all amalgamated *RB* and the Rule of Columbanus, while in seventh-century Gaul, Donatus's Rule for Virgins was compiled from extracts from *RB*, Columbanus and Caesarius.[4]

The spread of the Roman tradition within England centred around several figures mentioned by Bede. Eddius Stephanus, Putta and James the Deacon are all cited for their promulgation of reformed musical practices, and in 680 the founder of the twin monasteries of Wearmouth and Jarrow, Benedict Biscop (628-89), persuaded John, the Roman Archcantor, to come to England to teach the chant as it was practised at St Peter's.[5] Benedict Biscop is a key figure in the history of English monasticism. Six visits to Italy fuelled his great passion for Roman customs and artefacts, and Bede emphasizes his propensity for amassing items from abroad. Biscop undoubtedly knew of *RB* and is likely to have promoted its use within England. Nevertheless, he still favoured a mixed code, for his own rule for Wearmouth and Jarrow drew on the best practices of the seventeen monasteries which he claimed to have visited during his travels.[6]

Biscop's Northumbrian contemporary St Wilfrid (*c*.633-709) attached greater importance to the authoritative status of *RB*. His life is documented in a partisan and sometimes inaccurate biography by the singing-master Eddius Stephanus, who describes Wilfrid's early dissatisfaction with his education at Lindisfarne, a stronghold of Celtic insularity.[7] Like Biscop, Wilfrid sought inspiration from continental practices, travelling to Rome and eventually taking monastic vows at Lyons. From 661 Wilfrid was responsible for the foundation or reform of a number of English houses, including Ripon, Hexham and several Mercian monasteries. All appear to have adopted *RB* as a basis for uniformity, and it is quite possible that *Ob* 48 [*O*], the eighth-century copy of *Textus interpolatus* (see p.12), was produced in one of Wilfrid's Mercian foundations. His promotion of *RB* is mentioned by Eddius. In 709 Wilfrid was forced to recite his accomplishments during his forty years as a bishop before a council at Austerfield, Yorkshire. The recorded speech cites Wilfrid's standardization of the date of Easter, the form of the tonsure, and—most significantly—his attempt to establish *RB* (hitherto unknown in the area) as the normal code:

> *Vel quomodo vitam monachorum secundum regulam sancti Benedicti patris, quam nullus prior ibi invexit, constitueram?*   Eddius, 98

Wilfrid and Biscop undoubtedly established a precedent for Benedictine communities in England, but their potential was all but obliterated along with other centres of religious life by 900. This decline was largely the result of a series of Viking invasions which began in the last decades of the eighth century. Most of the northern houses perished at the hands of the Norsemen (Lindisfarne was sacked in 793 and Jarrow in 794), while some of the larger houses in the south fell into lay hands, their standards falling drastically. This marked the onset of a period of disruption extending until 878, when Alfred the Great checked the Danish advance at the battle of Edington. Alfred was keen to revive the monastic life from its desolate state, although it is significant that his instinct was not to attempt rejuvenation of the old sites, but rather to create new ones and import continental monks to fill the new houses. Indeed this was a period which saw the onset of new links with the Continent as England developed a new prestige across the Channel. Alfred's first foundation at Athelney consisted of a community of foreigners, headed by John the Old Saxon from Corvey. A second foundation carried out by Alfred's son Edward, in the New Minster at Winchester, was ruled by another foreign scholar, Grimbald of

St Bertin. In the final event, however, both foundations were short-lived, for neither survived the turn of the century.

THE TENTH-CENTURY MONASTIC REVIVAL

The revival of English monastic life in the tenth century only began to make real headway after the appointment of the monk Dunstan (*c*.909-980) to the abbacy of Glastonbury in 940, where he expelled the secular clerks, cancelled the overlordship of the laymen who ruled over them (*saecularium prioratus*), and set about restoring the regular life. This established a precedent for similar ventures elsewhere. Dunstan was joined by two further monk-reformers, Ethelwold of Winchester and the Dane, Oswald, and under this triumvirate, the revival gained considerable ground during the 960s. Dunstan himself was responsible for the return of monks to Malmesbury, Bath, Cerne, Sherborne, St Peter's, Westminster and the two houses of Christ Church and St Augustine at Canterbury.[8] He became successively Bishop of Worcester (957), London (*c*.958) and Archbishop of Canterbury (*c*.960-88). Ethelwold and Oswald were appointed respectively to the sees of Winchester (963-84) and Worcester (961-92, together with York after 972). All were greatly aided by the active support of the English monarch, King Edgar, who was responsible for conferring many of the most influential ecclesiastical appointments during this critical period.

Dunstan, Ethelwold and Oswald were further linked by their knowledge of continental monasticism, and the whole question of European influence within the insular reform is an important one. Dunstan took refuge at the monastery of Blandinium, Ghent (reformed by Gerard of Brogne *c*.937), during his enforced exile under King Edred (946-55); Oswald was a member of the Cluniac community at Fleury (founded from Cluny *c*.930) between 950 and 958, and Ethelwold was only prevented from joining him there by his appointment as Abbot of Abingdon (*c*.954). Nevertheless, Ethelwold invited musicians over from Corbie to Abingdon to teach the chant, and Osgar, one of his monks, was sent to Fleury to study its customs. There is also the familiar claim made in a list of Ethelwold's benefactions to Abingdon that Ethelwold had a copy of *RB* sent over from Fleury: *Fecit enim venire regulam Sancti Benedicti a Floriaco monasterio* (Abingdon, ii, 278). The document in question may even have been *Ccc* 57, mentioned in Chapter One (p.13).

The status of *RB* during this phase of the tenth-century reform was much more clearly defined than in previous years. Possibly in this the revival owed something to similar movements on the Continent, for recent scholarship has tended to stress the European context of the English reform. D.H. Farmer suggests that the resemblance of English reformed monasticism to its continental counterpart is most evident 'in the main framework of the life': its essentially liturgical nature, strict enforcement of celibacy and cancellation of private ownership—all three features 'most significantly synthesized and symbolized by the Rule of St. Benedict, transcending any divergence of detail in their customaries'.[9]

THE WINCHESTER COUNCIL OF MONKS
AND *REGULARIS CONCORDIA*

In *c.*970 a council of English bishops, abbots and abbesses met at Winchester, the ancient capital of Wessex and the seat of the royal household. Their aim was to establish a uniform pattern of monastic lifestyle. Representatives from Fleury and Ghent, 'personifying the two great foreign schools of monasticism', were invited,[10] and King Edgar and his queen presided. The outcome of this famous council was the customary *RC*, the most significant document of the tenth-century monastic revival. The status of *RC* among the other customaries discussed within this study is considerable. As the earliest extant English monastic customary, it incorporates most of the evidence we possess for the formation and early adoption of votive practices within the context of the monastic liturgy in English foundations. Indeed, detailed analysis of the nature and origin of the observances which it presents is of paramount importance to an understanding of the later pattern of votive accretions established in the centuries which followed.

It is impossible to attribute *RC* to a single author. Earlier this century historians tended to hold the view that the real guiding mind behind the document was St Dunstan, the most senior of the three monastic reformers. But more recently, scholarly opinion has tended to favour the younger and more radical Ethelwold (d.984) as largely responsible for the arrangement and codification of the document. The abridged copy of *RC* made for the community at Eynsham (*Ccc* 265) states explicitly that the book was put together by Ethelwold 'with his fellow bishops and abbots', although neither of his two biographers, Aelfric and Wulfstan, makes reference to *RC* or to the Winchester Council. Indeed, the fullest and most authoritative account of the Council that survives is recorded in *RC* itself.

Whoever was primarily responsible for its compilation, *RC*, like *RB*, cannot be seen as an entirely original document. It draws on existing codes of practice from various parts of Europe, and the prologue indicates that it was a joint production sanctioned by those present at the Council. Symons describes the document as 'a code of monastic law drawn up in response to a specific need', seeing the compilers as men familiar with European texts, 'who made it their business to seek out and study examples of the best monastic practice at the time'.[11] The combination of indigenous and foreign customs in the document is discussed below.

In spite of the attention it pays to the network of later liturgical accretions, *RC* leaves little doubt that it takes *RB* as its starting point. Reference to the supreme authority of *RB* is made on over twenty occasions in *RC*, and most overtly in the prologue. But the document also acknowledges the place of King Edgar, as an active patron of the reform:

> . . . *monuit, ut concordes aequali consuetudinis usu . . . regularia praecepta tenaci mentis anchora seruantes nullo modo dissentiendo discordarent, ne impar ac uarius unius regulae ac unius patriae usus probrose uituperium sanctae conuersationi irrogaret.*
>
> *RC* 71,3-7.[12]

Nevertheless, the prologue of *RC* is quick to acknowledge that observance of *RB* in itself is not adequate as a means of securing uniformity of monastic usage. Communities which simply aimed to follow *RB* faithfully (*norma honestissime*) are criticized for the disparity of their customs: *una fide, non tamen uno consuetudinis usu* (*RC* 70,14-15). The synthesis of native and reformed customs which it recommends is laid out in detail, but the compilers were careful never to contradict the precepts of *RB*:

> . . . *et cetera, quaeque patroni nostri beati Benedicti traditione uoluntarie suscepimus. . de consuetis sanctae regulae moribus tam a praedicto patre Benedicto quam a sanctis sequacibus et imitatoribus suis partim cum magna examinis discussione iugi custoditis usu . . .*   *RC* 77,13-17

On numerous occasions in *RC*, as if to enforce this issue, the phrase *uti regula praecipit* (129,8; 130,8; 131,1) or *secundum regulae praeceptum regulae* (85,5-6; 96,7) appears. Clearly, then, *RC* serves to uphold the authority of *RB*, whilst clarifying and supplementing the earlier document where its information is inadequate or absent.

CONTINENTAL INFLUENCES IN THE
COMPILATION OF *REGULARIS CONCORDIA*

In essence the customs of *RC* hark back to the era of Benedict of Aniane, although some draw on practices described in sources of an earlier date. Symons notes *RC*'s debt to the late eighth-century document *Memoriale* (or *Ordo*) *Qualiter* (hereafter *MQ*), written either in Italy or France.[13] There are several copies of this document in later English manuscripts, including one which contains *RC* itself, *Lbl* A.III, copied *c.*1040-70 at Christ Church, Canterbury.[14] Chapter One of *RC* contains a number of citations from *MQ*, although few of them are directly concerned with votive practices. Indeed the earliest copies of *MQ* scarcely mention extraneous devotions, referring rather to periods of silent prayer for which no particular structure is suggested. One later version however, written for a house of nuns in the tenth century, is amended to incorporate more specific accretions, including the *Trina oratio* and the Morrow Mass.

The emphasis placed on general accretions to the liturgy in *RC* links the document more closely with the spirit of the Anianian reforms, and some of the most overt parallels between the two movements are literary. Symons notes that the title of *RC* may well be in imitation of Benedict of Aniane's collection of monastic rules, *Concordia Regularum*, while part of the prologue to *RC* is clearly modelled on the preface to The Rule for Canons, compliled at Aachen in 816. Equally important is the reflection of Benedict of Aniane's phrase *una consuetudo, iubente imperatore* (Aniane *Ord.diurn*, 312) echoed *in uno consuetudinis usu* of the prologue to *RC*.

The influence of contemporary continental monasticism is equally pronounced, and the prologue to *RC* draws attention to the role of reformed continental monasticism in the compilation of the customary. Most historians agree that there are two primary streams of influence implied in the document: the first Cluniac, via the connection with Fleury, the second Lotharingian, via the connection with Ghent. The abbeys of Fleury-sur-Loire and St Peter's (Blandinium), Ghent were, of course, both represented personally at the Winchester Council (*RC* 72,2-4). Since there is no extant contemporary source from either foundation, the respective influences of these two strains is difficult to analyse. Symons's extensive collation of later sources has confirmed that some of the customs of *RC* are concordant with Cluny and Fleury; others with Trier, Einsiedeln and Verdun.[15] Although all of these groups followed a broadly similar pattern, Symons himself marginally favoured the Lotharingian influence on *RC*. On the other hand, Eric John, writing in 1960, argued that the compilers' principal sources were Cluniac, particularly because of the preponderance of monks in tenth-century England with Fleury connections.[16] Indeed, many 'common' practices must have been observed throughout Europe and it remains virtually impossible to trace precise lines of influence in these general areas. Those practices in *RC* which may well have been unique to English monasticism are discussed below.

THE ENGLISH FEATURES OF THE DOCUMENT

Despite its debt to European reformed monasticism, there are references to the authority of 'the customs of our fathers' throughout *RC* (*RC* 74,2; 77,17-18; 100,9-10; 104,10), and an emphasis on the status of the document as one of national import. Quite how ancient these English customs may have been is a matter for debate, taking into account the decline of the monastic tradition in England during the eighth and ninth centuries and the comparatively recent date of the reform. It may well be that Glastonbury, the most ancient of the English centres of Christianity (revived by Dunstan who became abbot there in 940) contributed most in this respect. Nevertheless, comparison with European sources strongly suggests that some of the customs of *RC* (summarized in Table 2:1, pp.195-6) are unique to English monasticism.

Dom Thomas Symons's work has again contributed most to our knowledge in this respect. Some of the customs which he draws attention to are concerned with the day-to-day running of the monastery rather than its liturgy. No European customary parallels *RC* in prescribing a room with a fire to be set apart for the brethren during the winter, and there is no reference elsewhere to the ancient English custom of pealing all the bells at Matins, Vespers and Mass between Holy Innocents and the Octave of Christmas. The wearing of the chasuble by the deacon and subdeacon during Lent is also cited as a venerable English practice: *usu praecedentium patrum* (*RC* 104,10). There are further idiosyncracies resulting from the position of the royal household. The king was expected to participate in the election of abbots and abbesses, and no monastery was to acknowledge lay dominion under any circumstances. The uniquely English system of monk-bishops prompts the direction that a bishop was to be elected in exactly the same manner as an abbot, provided that there was a suitable candidate in the monastery.

Other features of the document are more directly concerned with liturgical observance. *RC* is the only customary of this period which prescribes daily rather than occasional reception of the communion, and no other contemporary source requires recitation of the entire psalter after Prime on each day of the *Triduum*. But most significant in *RC* are three uniquely English practices which have an important bearing on votive observance. The document indicates that special groups of psalms and collects for the royal family were to be recited after each of the regular hours, and it provides special directions for the two daily masses. The Morrow Mass was to be said for the king, while High Mass on Friday was to be in honour of the Holy Cross, and on Saturday in honour of the Virgin. Each practice is examined in more detail below.

These unique insular features have led some scholars to view the customary as a retrospective document. David Parsons sees *RC* as witness to a 'clinging to traditional English forms with a gradual, perhaps in some cases grudging, acceptance of continental ideas and practices, of which the English were clearly aware'.[17] This opinion also seems to be given credence by Christopher Hohler's work on a variety of early liturgical manuscripts, where he concludes that most of the older English books based on Italian models were 'updated' to conform with northern European practice.[18] None the less, much of the re-writing seems to have been slow and no one continental model was adopted wholesale.

English insularity is also evident in artistic areas. Illumination and line drawings of the so-called Winchester School are found in some of the finest manuscripts of the period, while the ninth-century insular tradition in metalwork continued to flourish.[19] Parsons, however, stresses the strength of the leadership of the English monarchy: 'Nobody . . . in late tenth-century Europe could touch the English royal line for nobility and length of tradition, and it is almost a wonder that England bothered with the Continent at all.'[20] And it is the active patronage of the English monarchy in the revitalization of the monastic life which in many ways sets it apart from the post-Carolingian European reforms.

THE STATUS OF THE KING IN
THE ENGLISH MONASTIC REFORM

Almost all historians of the tenth-century English reform have emphasized the parallels between the role of King Edgar and that of Louis the Pious in the Frankish monastic reforms of the ninth century. C.H. Lawrence draws particular attention to this correlation, seeing the Winchester reform as 'a product of the Carolingian reform of the ninth century and a society that assigned a sacral role to kingship'.[21] Indeed, the notion is prefigured in an entry in the Peterborough Chronicle for 975, the year of Edgar's death, which stresses his importance as reformer:

> *Rex Edgarus obiit, non minus memorabilis Anglis quam Karolus Francis, Cyrus Persis, vel Romulus Romanis: quadraginta et quatuor monasteria fertur fundasse, vel saltem restaurasse.*   Peterborough, 31.

The prologue to *RC* itself draws attention to the importance of the king and queen in the restoration of the monastic life. The document opens with a glorification of King Edgar, emphasizing his active expulsion of secular clerks and his generosity in endowing the new monastic communities with wealth and security. Edgar is credited with summoning the Council at Winchester, but only after 'deep and careful study of the matter' (*archana quaeque diligenti cura examinans*: *RC* 70,16 to 71,1). He is 'the Good Shepherd' (*pastorum pastor*: *RC* 70,6), 'this excellent king' (*huius praecellentissimi regis*: *RC* 71,7) who dispenses wise advice, exulted by his subjects as 'so good and great a teacher' (*talem ac tantum. . . doctorem*: *RC* 71,9). All obey his commands 'with the utmost gladness', 'relying on the advice of our king'.

In practical terms the king has sovereign power over all monasteries, rendering earlier secular overlordship void. On the advice of the assembly, the king and queen and no other authority might be 'besought with confident petition, both for the safeguarding of holy places and for the increase of the goods of the Church' (*regis tantumodo ac reginae dominium ad sacri loci munimen et ad aecclesiasticae possesionis augmentum uoto semper efflagitare optabili prudentissime iusserunt: RC* 76,1-3). Further, all abbots and abbesses were to have 'humble access to the king and queen in the fear of God and the observance of the Rule', as often as necessary. The king also had considerable say over the election of an abbot: the Council decided that 'the election of abbots and abbesses should be carried out with the consent and advice of the king and according to the teaching of the Holy Rule' (*ut abbatum ac abbatissarum electio cum regis sensu et consilio sancte regulae ageretur documento: RC* 74,18-75,1). This practice appears to have had little precedent, and is certainly not envisaged in *RB*.

Although Edgar's role in the Winchester reform is easily exaggerated, the closeness of his relationship with his archbishop, Dunstan, clearly contributed to their mutual recognition of the possibilities of dissent amongst the growing number of new foundations in their land, and the desirability of establishing a common code of observance upon which all monasteries might build. The king's permission and support was an essential prerequisite for the monks. Aelfric's *Life of St Ethelwold* has several references which confirm this: Ethelwold was tonsured *jubente rege* (Abingdon, ii,256-7), and took charge of Abingdon *permittente Dunstano, secundum regis voluntatem* (ii,257); he expelled the clerks of the New Minster at Winchester *annuente rege Eadgaro* (ii,261), and the reform itself was only achieved *consentiente rege* (ii,262). Dunstan, Ethelwold and Oswald all received episcopal advancement from Edgar, thus establishing a precedent for the distinctively English phenomenon of monastic bishops and cathedral-monasteries. In return for the benevolent patronage of the monarch, the monasteries offered special prayers, psalms and masses for the royal family which formed an integral part of their liturgies. Liturgical obligation to the monarch and his welfare is stressed on numerous occasions in *RC*.

THE IMPORTANCE OF WINCHESTER

Royal patronage was by no means an English phenomenon, but the emphasis of the Winchester document on monastic obligation to the monarch is more overtly stated than in the decrees of Aachen. Partly this must have been due to the very particular interrelationship of monastic and secular life in Winchester. Extensive excavations made at Winchester (1961-71) have shown the extraordinary physical proximity of the royal palace to no fewer than three monastic foundations which existed during the ninth century.

Winchester was the residence of both king and bishop from the second half of the seventh century, after the transference of the see of Dorchester-on-Thames to Winchester during the 660s. The Old Minster, built by Cenwahl of Wessex in 648, consequently became a cathedral (dedicated to St Swithun) and the site for the coronation of several English kings. Martin Biddle has suggested that the Old Minster may indeed have been founded to serve as a palace church, forming part of a small royal 'estate' enclosed within a walled area in the south-east quarter of the city.[22] The royal palace lay immediately to the west of the church.

Under Edward the Elder (899-924) two further monasteries were founded at Winchester: the New Minster and the Nunnaminster, the latter a house of nuns probably founded simply as an act of royal piety. The New Minster was constructed just four metres from the north side of the Old Minster, with the earlier building probably continuing in use exactly as before. The reason for the foundation of New Minster has never been conclusively established by historians. Biddle suggests that it may have been intended as the burgh church of the replanned city, which now boasted renewed defences, new streets, a market and a mint.[23] Certainly it maintained a closer contact with the people, and all Winchester citizens were allowed burial there.

During Ethelwold's years as bishop (963-84), he lived apart from his monastery in the bishop's palace, probably built during his own episcopate. In 964 Ethelwold refounded all three minsters. The New Minster was placed under Ethelgar, formerly abbot of Abingdon, while monks were also brought from Abingdon to replace the secular canons then in residence at the Old Minster. All three buildings were rebuilt, doubtless to cater for the requirements of the new monastic communities. Edgar issued the famous 'Golden Charter' (*Lbl* A.VIII) to the New Minster in 966, commemorating the introduction of Benedictine monks into that house and supporting Ethelwold's general desire that all three foundations needed seclusion from the life of the town. It was witnessed by Edgar and the royal family, St Dunstan and various bishops including Ethelwold.

The intervention of the regional English royal houses had frequently been important to the spread of Christianity in different parts of the country. Under the Anglo-Saxon kings the region of Wessex was dominant, and it was there that the church found a natural centre. The influence of the king on the church and on monasticism has already been noted. What is more particular here is the response to the royal family in the monastic liturgy, and most especially in votive accretions.

VOTIVE OBSERVANCE IN *REGULARIS CONCORDIA*

RC provides details of a wide range of accretions, summarized comprehensively in Table 2:2 (p.197). Some of these concord with contemporary continental practice, but others—including the custom of praying for the royal household—are uniquely English, and call for special examination.

Additional devotions recited specifically for the king and the royal family are perhaps the most significant examples of votive observance in *RC*. Comparison with European monastic customaries, whether contemporary with *RC* or from the Carolingian era, suggests that liturgical obligation to king or emperor was never quite so pronounced as in England during the late tenth century. Contemporary continental monasticism certainly adopted observances related both in form and content to those discussed here, but the intention of such devotions is rarely stated in quite such direct terms as in *RC*, and the content of the observance is nowhere outlined with comparable precision. In England itself no customary compiled after the Conquest retains the same degree of emphasis on the royal household; the format and position of the Winchester royal devotions survive in a number of cases, but the intention specified in these later sources is usually modified to the exclusion of any mention of the monarch. Clearly the unique focus on the royal household in *RC* must have been influenced, if not inspired, by the prominent role of King Edgar in the revival of the English monastic life, and also by the exceptional circumstances of the monastic communities at Winchester, with their proximity to the royal palace. Nevertheless, it is not likely that all of the observances in honour of the king were actually conceived by the Winchester Council, since the prologue stresses their venerability:

> *ne ea, quae usu patrum pro rege ac benefactoribus, quorum beneficiis Christo larigente pascimur, intercessionis oramine consuete canimus, nimia uelocitate psallendo deum potius ad iracundiam inconsiderate, quod absit, prouocent quam prouide ad peccaminum ueniam inuitent.*   RC 74,2-7

But neither can such observances be regarded simply as 'local' practices, resulting from the peculiarities of the Winchester environment. *RC* not only emphasizes its own importance as a national document for the promotion of uniformity throughout England, but there is also proof that Winchester practices were transferred unaltered to other houses. Both of the extant manuscripts of *RC* (*Lbl* A.III and *Lbl* B.III) were probably copied for and used at Christ Church, Canterbury,[24] while the abridged version of the customary compiled for the community at Eynsham in *c*.1005 (*Ccc* 265), is substantially identical to *RC* in its description of liturgical practice. By and large this similarity applies to all instances of votive observance in the three manuscripts.

There are three areas in *RC* where the monks are instructed to pray for the royal family. First in specially appointed pairs of psalms, each pair said with three collects, which followed straight after High Mass and all of the regular offices except Prime (Table 2:3, p.202); second in the middle section of a tripartite devotion termed the *Trina oratio*, recited on this occasion before Matins (Table 2:4, p.203); and third in the second communal eucharistic celebration of the day, the Morrow Mass (*RC* 86,13-14). *RC* refers to the first (and most significant) of these observances as *psalmi pro rege et regina ac familiaribus*: psalms for the king, queen and *familiares*. On three occasions (after Terce (*RC* 86,7-9), after Compline (*RC* 93,7-9), and in the passage from the prologue cited above (*RC* 74,3-4)) *benefactores* is substituted for *familiares*; these terms seem to be more or less interchangeable in *RC*, although it is questionable whether they carry exactly the same meaning. *Benefactores* would seem to imply patronage, possibly with direct financial maintainance; *familiares* may well have included a rather wider group of associates, tied to the monastery simply by prayer and confraternity, or sometimes by kinship. In later English sources identically-placed psalms were almost invariably recited solely for *familiares* rather than for the king, and are consequently referred to simply as *psalmi familiares*: a modified term which does not occur in *RC*. This modified terminology is clearly indicative of the declining emphasis on liturgical obligation to the monarch in England after the Conquest. It is but one example of the manner in which a number of the earliest English votive practices were altered to accommodate the needs of the changing devotional climate.

Similar groups of psalms appended to the regular office survive in several other monastic sources. The Customary of Einsiedeln, copied *c*.970, specifies two psalms for recitation after Matins (6 and 19) which are identical to those in the corresponding position in *RC*. The accompanying collect, however, *Pretende . . . da famulis*, is different, and unlike the alternative given in *RC*, *Quaesumus . . . ut famulus tuus*, makes no mention of the king (Einsiedeln, 250). Although there is no indication that the Einsiedeln devotion was offered for any specific intention, the prescribed collect also appears in the Fulda Sacramentary as the collect for a *Missa Familiarium Communi* (Fulda 2273), and it seems probable that the Einsiedeln devotion was also offered for *familiares*.

Recitation of additional psalms after the regular office hours seems first to have been formalized during the reforms of Benedict of Aniane, and documents from this period frequently refer to them as *psalmi speciales*. This general term is often used in later sources to indicate very particular psalmodic groups, such as the seven penitential psalms or the fifteen gradual

psalms. But even in the Carolingian environment, where ties between monk
and monarch were equally pronounced, there are very few passages which
specify particular psalms or prayers for the king. Only one copy of the
Anianian legislation, from St Martial, Limoges, (dated before 850), includes
an explicit direction:

> *Ut psalmi quinque aestate ante horam Primam, tempore uero*
> *himali post interuallum pro rege et omnibus catholicis et*
> *familiaribus et elemosinariis omni die canantur, id est Miserere mei*
> *deus secundum. Deus in nomine tuo. Miserere mei deus miserere.*
> *Deus misereatur mostri. Deus in adiutorium meum et pro rege*
> *specialiter Exaudiat te dominus.*   Aachen.St Martial, 561,18-22

The first five psalms specifed here—50, 53, 56, 66 and 69—inserted before
Prime in summer, have no direct correspondence in *RC*, although three of
them occur in piecemeal fashion as psalms for the royal household (56 after
Terce, 66 after Sext and 69 after Compline). *RC* indicates that Psalm 50 was
recited after Prime, but this is the sole instance at Winchester where the two
psalms after the regular hours were not recited for the king and *familiares*.
The first psalm, 37, was said against temptations of the flesh, the second,
50, for deceased brethren. The sixth of the Einsiedeln psalms, 19,
specifically designated for the king, is the only one of the Winchester
psalms which was recited twice in the overall scheme. It occurs in *RC* as the
second of the two psalms after Matins, and as the first of the pair of psalms
after Mass.

The psalms selected for the royal household in *RC* were recited without
antiphons and were followed by collects. They were omitted from the
Octave of Easter to the Octave of Pentecost:

> *ab octauis Pascae . . . usque octauas Pentecosten . . . psalmi, qui*
> *pro benefactoribus solent cani necne laeetaniae ante missam,*
> *quoniam a genuflectione ordo aeclesiasticus declinari ammonet,*
> *omni modo intermittantur.*   *RC* 132,2-5

Each pair of psalms was selected individually with no obvious numerical
arrangement. Few of the psalms seem to have been chosen for a particular
reference to kingship, although the instructions after Matins indicate that the
first psalm of the pair was specifically for the king (*pro rege specialiter*),
and the second for king, queen and *familiares* together (*pro rege et regina*
ac familiaribus). This distinction was also maintained after the other hours.
After Mass, unspecified *preces* were inserted between the psalms and the
collects. There is no reference to *preces* after any of the hours with the
exception of Prime, where the intentions were different (see below).

Three collects followed each pair of psalms: the first for the king, the second for the queen, and the third for king, queen and *familiares* together. These texts remained standard for each occurrence, and were particularized items which mentioned both the king and the queen by name. However, none of them was written specifically for the observance in *RC*, for each occurs in another context in at least one earlier source, as the concordances listed in Table 2:5 demonstrate (p.206). The Gelasian Sacramentary, dating from the mid-eighth century incorporates the respective collects for king and queen; the third collect, also used for the *Trina oratio*, occurs in the supplement to the Gregorian Sacramentary, compiled during the latter part of the eighth century. All three collects also occur in the eleventh-century Leofric Missal (*Ob* 579). Each occurrence of the texts in concordant sources relates closely to the function prescribed in *RC*, and it seems likely that each collect was originally conceived for use in a votive mass. The compiler of the royal devotions in *RC* borrowed postcommunion prayers as well as collects; clearly there was little discrimination between these texts. Comparable interchange of material between observances remained a common practice in the compilation of much of the later votive repertory; it is discussed in more detail in relation to later observances in Part Two.

RC allotted specific attention to the royal household in another devotion with psalms and collects: the tripartite *Trina oratio* (Table 2:4, p.203), which was recited three times a day (before Matins, after Lauds or before Terce, and after Compline). Every recitation of the *Trina oratio* comprised three separate 'prayers' (*orationes*), each prayer consisting of one, two or three psalms, *Pater noster* and a collect. When the *Trina oratio* was recited after Compline, *Kyrie eleison* preceded *Pater noster*, and *preces* consisting of four verses from Psalm 50 were inserted between *Pater noster* and the collect in each section. No texts whatsoever are specified for the devotion after Lauds; they may simply have duplicated one of the other two forms, where all the texts are carefully prescribed. The Matins form of the observance is the only one which provides any indication that each of the three 'prayers' should be directed towards a particular intention. Here, the first *oratio* was for personal intentions (*pro seipso*), the second for king, queen and *familiares* (*pro rege et regina atque familiaribus*) and the third for the faithful departed (*pro fidelibus defunctis*). Before Matins, the psalms chosen for the *Trina oratio* were simply the seven penitential psalms, divided between the three sections as a group of three and two pairs (6, 31, 37; 50, 101; 129, 143). After Compline five different psalms, apparently specifically chosen for the devotion, were used. They were divided thus: 12, 42; 66, 126; 129.

Most of the collects used for the *Trina oratio*, like those recited with the psalms for the royal household, were borrowed from votive masses. Two of the prayers however, *Gratias tibi . . . in hac nocte* (the first of the

Matins group, *RC* 18,11-14) and *Gratias tibi . . . in hac die* (the first of the
Compline group, *RC*, 93,15-18) are exceptions. Both occur in only one
earlier source, the late eighth-century customary *MQ*, and in each case the
collect occurs in a directly comparable position to that prescribed in *RC*.
Before Matins, *MQ* specifies exactly the same waking routine as *RC* up to
the point where the community reaches the oratory: indeed, it clearly served
as a model for the later document. After this, however, *MQ* describes a
briefer and more personal preparatory ceremony. In the church each
member of the community went to his appropriate place and prayed silently,
prostrate; *Gratias tibi . . . in hac nocte* is the sole text specified, and it
immediately precedes the beginning of the office. The ceremonies preceding
the office in *RC* are more formed, but the retention of this same collect
demonstrates how the use of *Trina oratio* developed out of earlier practice.
The post-Compline use of the collect is again directly comparable. *MQ*
prescribes a largely personal penitential ceremony, observed by the whole
community, but specifies only one of the texts to be used; *RC* takes this
same text as a basis for a more fully formed devotion.

The other two collects of the *Trina oratio* before Matins, one for the
king and one for the dead, both occur in the supplement to the Gregorian
Sacramentary. *Inueniant quaesumus*, for the dead, also appears in the earlier
Gelasian Sacramentary, which provided some of the material for the
Gregorian supplement. These are the only two collects described in this
section which are duplicated elsewhere in *RC*: *Deus qui caritatis* was recited
for king, queen and *familiares* after each of the hours, as described above,
while *Inueniant quaesumus* was recited for departed brethren after Prime.
In the Gelasian and Gregorian sources it appears as the postcommunion in
a mass for the dead.

Collects for the post-Compline *Trina oratio* do not specify particular
intentions and they appear to be of a general personal nature, stressing
penitence. With the exception of the first collect (taken from *MQ*), the other
items are all borrowed from a weekly cycle of votive masses compiled by
Alcuin (735-804), a critical figure in the liturgical reforms of the
Carolingian period. Alcuin's cycle was subsequently copied into a large
number of sacramentaries throughout Europe, although sometimes with
minor modifications. Distribution of Alcuin's masses in a number of
sacramentaries is presented in Table 2:6 (p.208). All three of the masses
which supply the collects for the post-Compline *Trina oratio* are
particularized formularies: for the grace of the Holy Spirit, for the petition
of tears, and against temptation respectively.

The final instance of liturgical obligation to the monarch in *RC* occurs
as the Morrow Mass. Unlike the other devotions, a Morrow Mass for the
king was not an invariable daily observance, and *RC* does not supply texts.
The Morrow Mass was certainly celebrated as an integral part of the daily

liturgy by the end of the tenth century, but its intention was not fixed. Special needs took precedence over the king when necessary: *Eadem uero matutinalis missa pro rege uel quacumque inminente necessitate celebretur* (*RC* 86,13-14). Equally the selection process was different on Sundays, when the Morrow Mass was celebrated for the Trinity, unless displaced by a feast. Nevertheless, none of the extant European customaries of a comparable date indicates that this mass was ever said for the king. Einsiedeln and Fleury both specify that it was to be for the Trinity, and in the uses of Fulda and Trier it alternated between *pro defunctis* and *pro pace* on ferial days. It is also one of the few areas where the Eynsham version of *RC* deviates from its model. Although the appended psalms and the *Trina oratio* appear to have paralleled the practices described above, there is no indication that the Morrow Mass was ever said specifically for the king; at Eynsham any appropriate formula was to be used: . . . *ferialibus diebus de quacumque necessitate euenerit facienda est* (Aelfric, 158,8).

OTHER VOTIVE INTENTIONS IN *REGULARIS CONCORDIA*

Other instances of votive observance in *RC* are by and large more typical of mainstream European practice. They fall into six basic categories: devotions in honour of the dead, All Saints, the Trinity, the Holy Cross, the Virgin Mary and more personal observances dealing with self-discipline and general spiritual welfare. The devotions in honour of the dead and of All Saints are the most substantial. Both of these consisted of complete office hours (Vigils, Lauds and Vespers of the Dead, and Lauds and Vespers of All Saints), which followed the corresponding hour of the regular liturgy. Each of these partial appended *cursus* appears in contemporary continental monastic customaries, and is modelled on the secular rather than the monastic form of the office. They are discussed in more detail in Chapter Three, with particular reference to their role as precursors of the complete votive offices which appear in later sources.

The dead were also honoured in a number of more concise devotions. The third section of the *Trina oratio* before Matins, marked *pro fidelibus defunctis*, has already been discussed. The second of the two psalms appended to Prime is marked *pro defunctis fratribus*: the text chosen was *Miserere* (Psalm 50), the first psalm of Lauds of the Dead. It was accompanied by the collect *Inueniant quaesumus*, already used as the collect in the relevant section of *Trina oratio*. The collect was followed by the *preces Animae fratrum nostrum*. After the daily chapter meeting, there was a further independent group of five psalms for the dead. This consisted of 5, 6 (both from Vigils of the Dead), 114 (from Vespers of the Dead), 115 and 129 (the latter also from Vespers of the Dead). Private masses for the dead are also mentioned in *RC*, although these seem to be obligatory observances of a specific nature, recited when a member of the community died. But the possibility of celebrating masses for the dead in a votive context is also likely.

No other area of devotion was greatly emphasized. The Trinity was honoured in a general way in the *Trina oratio*, over and above the individual intentions of its three sections. This is overtly expressed in the rubrics in *RC*: *ut trinitatis reuerentia ab omnibus legitime teneatur, trina utantur oratione* (*RC* 82,10-11), and *ut . . . sanctae trinitatis ac indiuiduae unitatis reuerentia legitime a seruulis exibeatur catholicis, agant . . . tres orationes* (*RC* 93,9-12). This Trinitarian emphasis was represented tangibly only in terms of the tripartite structure of the devotion, and in its thrice-daily recitation. The only other devotion honouring the Trinity was the Sunday Morrow Mass, and even this was displaced if any other feast or intention took precedence.

The first of the group of three *antiphonae* following Lauds and Vespers was addressed to the Holy Cross, although no text is specified. Borrowing from the regular liturgy may well have been likely. The *Missa principalis* on Friday was also offered in honour of the Holy Cross unless displaced by a feast; the choice of this particular day was sanctioned by a long tradition which again seems to have its roots in Alcuin's cycle of masses (see below). Later sources sometimes provide an accompanying Friday Office of the Cross (see Chapter Three). The Virgin was honoured in two exactly parallel observances: the second of the antiphons after Lauds and Vespers, and the Saturday *Missa principalis*. Both of these customs were to have important implications for the expansion of votive observance in honour of the Virgin in later sources. The final antiphon in the series of three was addressed either to the saint whose relics were kept in the church, or failing this, the saint to whom the church was dedicated. This is the sole example of a more local emphasis within the votive items prescribed in *RC*. The implications of these independent antiphons within the context of the later tradition of votive observance is examined in Chapter Five.

A further group of observances has a more personal emphasis. The first section of the *Trina oratio* after Matins, marked *pro seipso*, has already been discussed, and all three of the post-Compline *orationes* suggest personal devotion of a penitential nature. The first of the two appended psalms after Prime, *Domine ne in furore* (Psalm 37), was specifically recited against fleshly temptation; it is accompanied by *preces* and the collect *Ure igne*, from Alcuin's *Missa contra tentationem carnis*. Psalm 50, the *Miserere*, was also recited independently three times a day: after Lauds, Vespers and Compline. In each case it preceded the psalms for the royal household, and its observance may well represent a unique English practice. Further devotions were offered at more specific times as a particular mark of devotion. Two prostrate psalms, consisting of one gradual and one penitential psalm were recited after each hour during Lent; they were followed by *Kyrie eleison*, *Pater noster*, the *preces Pro peccatis* and a collect. On the *Triduum*, after Prime, the community were to recite the entire psalter. These latter items, owing to their seasonal nature, can less readily be labelled as votive observances, but it is significant that several of the observances discussed above might also be recited in a more specific context when additional devotion was appropriate. This was particularly likely when a member of the community died and the Office of the Dead was used.

Two important issues emerge from the discussion above: first, many of the votive observances use material culled from other parts of the liturgy or at least correspond with them; second, the majority are based on psalms. All accretions in *RC* are listed in Table 2:2, together with concordances and correspondences in other parts of the liturgy. Examination of the table makes it plain that the additional observances in *RC* fall into three basic structural groups.

Most observances are formed around a nucleus of complete psalms: in some cases these are recited independently, as self-contained units (the fifteen gradual psalms, the seven penitential psalms and the five psalms for the dead), and in others they are accompanied by collects, *preces* and other items (the psalms for the royal household and the *Trina oratio*). The two votive offices of All Saints and the Dead also have a nucleus of psalmody but are obviously much more expansive devotions modelled on the regular office.

The psalmodic devotions are by and large constructed on a small scale. They appear to have been common to the majority of western monastic houses throughout the Middle Ages, and are symptomatic of the general epidemic of office accretions which originated during the liturgical expansion instituted by Benedict of Aniane.

Only a small number of the observances have no psalmodic nucleus. The masses are obvious examples, but clearly these were not created specifically as votive observances, but simply provided the framework for an appropriate formula. Masses fall into two basic categories: weekly formularies addressed to a particular saint or intention (the Holy Cross and the Virgin are the most common examples) and formularies compiled only for use in special circumstances. Masses for the dead or for particular petitions relating to temporal events fall into this category.

Only one of the office accretions has no psalmodic content: the independent antiphon. This was presumably borrowed from the central liturgical repertory rather than compiled especially for this observance, but it is one of the few instances in the liturgy where an antiphon was recited independently of a psalm. On the basis of evidence from other contemporary sources it is likely that such antiphons were accompanied by a versicle and collect. Observances with this structure are discussed in Chapter Five.

THE PROLIFERATION OF VOTIVE MASSES

Although this thesis is concerned with the office, it is already apparent that there is a comparable tradition of votive observance in the celebration of mass. Examination of *RC* has established that prayers from the mass were borrowed in votive accretions to the office, and it also cites votive intentions for the Morrow Mass which are identical to those in the office. In order to place the office in a wider context, it is valuable to outline the formative development of the votive mass and its place in the monastic liturgy.

RB makes no reference to a daily celebration of mass, and peripheral references to mass and communion on Sundays and feastdays occur only in chapters devoted to the duties of mealtime readers and servers at table (see Chapter One, p.10). The earliest communities would have been composed very largely of lay-monks who may have attended mass at a local church; the advent of the priest-monk was a later development.[25]

Ordination of monks only became widespread after the Roman Synod of 610, when Pope Boniface IV expressed positive approval of the practice. Increase in the number of priests in monastic communities led to the multiplication of private masses, where the celebrant recited all parts of the mass, including those which were usually sung. Some of the earliest surviving masses are simply headed *pro seipso*, with prayers in the first person singular, although large numbers of masses for use in times of trouble or for the sick were added to the liturgy during the course of the eighth century. Several masses for private celebration on special occasions survive in the third book of the Gelasian Sacramentary.

During the ninth century, when daily celebration of mass by each priest seems to have been the norm, a cycle of votive masses for much more regular celebration was copied into several continental sources. Examples of weekly cycles are listed in Table 2:6 (p.208), and it is widely accepted that Alcuin of York (735-804) introduced the practice. Alcuin's function as compiler is important in other respects, for he is known to have formulated an extensive collection of masses to supplement the rather slender resources of the Gregorian Sacramentary used under Pope Hadrian I. The increased demand for mass formularies was an obvious outcome of the tendency for more frequent celebration, particularly pronounced in monastic foundations.

Alcuin's series of votive masses seem to have been intended for both conventual and private use, although the covering letter sent with the masses to the community at Fulda under Abbot Baugulf (c.802) implies only the latter:

> *Misi chartulam vobis. . . ut habeatis singulis diebus, quibus preces*
> *deo digere cuilibet placeat.*   *MGH*, Ep.iv, 404

Other sources containing Alcuin's masses suggest corporate celebration: the cycle is usually placed at the head of the section of the sacramentary devoted to masses for general use, and may even be separated from occasional masses for special needs by formulae for the Common of Saints. Reputedly, it was the reformer Boniface (680-755), also an Englishman, who requested the compilation of a cycle of weekly votives for general use; Alcuin met the appeal with a collection which reflects a careful eclecticism, combining existing material culled from a variety of sources with a number of newly-composed prayers. Each weekday is supplied with two formularies, of which the first became the more widely adopted in each case. The significance of the collection was soon to become apparent. It achieved almost instant popularity and was copied into sacramentaries and missals in a virtually identical form for several centuries.

Within the wider context of votive observance, Alcuin's Saturday Mass of the Virgin takes pride of place over the others in the series. No source compiled before Alcuin contains such a mass, and it is likely that both of Alcuin's formularies were newly-compiled. The earliest appearance of the Mass of the Virgin in an English source occurs in the earliest part of the tenth-century Leofric Missal, Leofric A. Recent scholarship has rejected the traditional view that this manuscript was written in the diocese of Arras or of Cambrai: it is likely that the scribe was continental, but some of the texts point towards origin in England.[26] The masses in Leofric A are represented in Table 2:6, together with those from the eleventh-century monastic gradual sent from Christ Church, Canterbury to Durham, *DRu* V.V.6. In all cases the *Missa de beata Virgine* is prescribed for Saturday: a precedent for the practice described in *RC* of celebrating High Mass of the Virgin on this day.

RC recommends daily reception of the Eucharist by each member of the community, but the practice may not have been universal. Aelfric's modified version of the customary produced for Eynsham implies that the practice was limited to Sundays and feastdays:

> *Omni dominica die, siue sollempni eant fratres ad pacem et eucharistiam accipiant exceptis his qui antea missam fecerunt.* Aelfric, 157,20-22

The Conquest seems to have brought about no radical change for mass celebration in England. The *Consuetudines* drawn up for use at Christ Church, Canterbury, by the Norman archbishop, Lanfranc, contains more references to private masses, including a daily mass for the sick. Private masses were allotted to individual monks during chapter, and on the Feast of the Dedication a mass was to be celebrated at each altar if the number of priests allowed. Lanfranc makes one further reference to a mass which has no place in *RC*: the *Missa familiaris*, which might be celebrated either privately or conventually.

*. . . nec ad missas dicatur Gloria usque ad Pasca, nisi missa
familiaris sit in conuentu, uel extra conuentum . . .*

Lanfranc, 22,3-4

The ambiguity of the term *familiares* has already been discussed in
relation to the psalms recited after the offices at Winchester. Satisfactory
interpretation of *familia* and *familiaris* is equally problematic. All three
terms occur in a variety of liturgical sources in differing contexts. The
psalmi pro familiaribus are paralleled by masses celebrated *pro familiaribus*,
which appear in most of the early sacramentaries. In some cases the *missa
pro familiaribus* bears a close textual correspondence to the votive mass *pro
fratribus et sororibus*. Both of these masses tend to share the introit *Salus
populi* and the collect *Deus qui caritatis dona*.

The *Missa familiaris* mentioned by Lanfranc seems to have been
textually distinct from these earlier forms. *Familia* usually incorporates the
idea of subservience to a superior; in this case the monastic community
under the abbot. In secular foundations, the term was used for the entire
clerical community centred around the bishop's *domus*, consisting of
praepositi, clerics in priests' orders, married lectors and exorcists.[27] In this
sense the *familia* is composed of no more than the autonomous religious
community, whether secular or monastic, rather than its benefactors and
associates. During the reforms of Benedict of Aniane the entire Benedictine
order was styled 'the *familia* of Benedict'.

THE LATER MIDDLE AGES:
ST MARY'S YORK AS A CASE STUDY

Surviving sacramentaries, missals and graduals testify to the enormous
popularity of votive masses during the later Middle Ages. The range and
variety of such masses precludes any serious discussion in this section, but
one particularly informative source—the Ordinal of St Mary's York (*Cjc*
D.27), copied between 1398 and 1405—may serve as a representative model
for the practice of English monastic foundations at this period.

During the course of the fourteenth century, the *Missa familiaris*
mentioned by Lanfranc was often celebrated in honour of the Virgin Mary.
The York Ordinal prescribes daily celebration of the *Missa familiaris* at the
Lady altar, although there is no evidence that it was a conventual mass. Like
the daily *Missa pro defunctis*, offered for the souls of founders, benefactors
and all the faithful departed, the *Missa familiaris* was to be celebrated by
each ordained member of the community in turn, according to the *Tabula*.
Moreover:

> *Missa familiaris sive de Domina, quod idem est, ad altare beate Virginis cotidie celebretur . . . Nullus excusatur ab hac missa et pro defunctis, exceptis Domino Abbate et ejus capellanis, infirmario qui cotidie celebrat missam infirmis in capella officii sui, et plumbario in capella beate Virginis celebrante.* York.SM.Ord, i,56

A number of private masses were offered after Prime at the same time as the masses specifed above, but the *Missa familiaris* was distinct from all other non-conventual celebrations. Rather than following the early practice of private celebration where only the monk-priest and his lector were present, the *Missa familiaris* at York was sung by its own choir, comprising two monks and a team of boys from the almonry (a separate building within the precinct wall):[28]

> *Duo monachi deputantur ad custodiendum et regendum pueros elemosinarie cantates ibidem, et ad incipiendum et regulandum omnia, excepto officio sacerdotis, que legi et cantari debeant in hac missa.* York.SM.Ord, i,57-58

The formula for the mass was identical to that of the Saturday High Mass of the Virgin on Saturday, which was sung by the complete community in choir:

> *Ad hanc missam officium, collecta, epistola, graduale, Alleluia, tractus, evangelium et cetera omnia erunt omni tempore anni sicut cantatur pro eodem tempore sabbatis in choro.* York.SM.Ord, i,56

For this purpose the year was divided into several seasonal periods, each with its own liturgical formula. A series of five collects was to be said during every season. The first, addressed to the Virgin, was variable, but the others had fixed texts. The fourth collect gave the mass the title of *Missa familiaris*:

> *quarta pro familiaribus nostris, a quibus illa missa accipit nomen suum: Deus qui caritatis.* York.SM.Ord, i,57

Here the emphasis lies not with members of the monastic community, but with its benefactors, relatives and friends; the collect is identical to that of the *Missa pro fratribus et sororibus*. This provides an obvious link with the other devotions offered *pro familiaribus* discussed earlier, but the association of the *Missa familiaris* with intercession to the Virgin marks an important distinction from earlier practice, entirely typical of the devotional climate during the later Middle Ages.

Alcuin's Saturday mass and the observances derived from it did not completely overwhelm the other masses in the series. At York, the *missa principalis* sometimes took a votive formula in seasons when there was no proper calendar observance. In the week after the Octave of the Epiphany, the Ordinal indicates the following series based on Alcuin's cycle: Monday, *De Angelis*, Tuesday, *De Sancto Spiritu*, Thursday, *Corpus Christi*, Friday, *De Sancta Cruce*, Saturday, *De Reliquiis*. On all Sundays between Trinity Sunday and Advent, the *Missa Matutinalis* was in honour of the Trinity, unless a saint's day took precedence. There was also a weekly Morrow Mass of St Laurence, celebrated at the chapter altar:

> *Omni septimana per annum fiat missa de Sancto Laurentio pro incendio in conventu ad altare capitulare* York.SM.Ord, i,73

On some days the Morrow Mass followed an occasional formula, reminiscent of the masses for particular needs in *RC*:

> *alii diebus pro pace et serenitate, et cetera.* York.SM.Ord, i,73

The Marian emphasis at York is entirely typical of most English monasteries at this date. The Saturday *Missa Principalis* of the Virgin was ubiquituous by the twelfth century, when it was often recited in conjunction with a commemorative office of the Virgin which replaced the prescribed calendar observance (discussed in Chapter Four). Several sources testify to the practice of celebrating a daily Lady Mass from the twelfth century, although in a private rather than a conventual context. The earliest recorded example survives in *The Chronicle of John of Worcester* (1118-1140), which mentions a private daily celebration of Lady Mass and recitation of a Marian office by Abbot Benedict of Tewkesbury (*ob.*1137), *Sanctae Mariae capellanus*:

> *Magnae religionis et castitatis vir Benedictus Theodekesberiensis aecclesiae abbas obiit. Hic Dei servus in beatissimae ac gloriosissimae Virginis Dei genitricis servitio totus erat devotus. Diatim nanque horis decantatis aut missam ipse festive celebrare aut audire solebat in illius honore.* Worc.John, 41

There is also a reference in a Bury St Edmunds manuscript to the promotion of the re-instated Feast of the Conception and the institution of a daily Lady Mass and Little Office by Anselm of Bury (*c.*1080-1148), the nephew of St Anselm of Canterbury:

> . . . *et cotidie unam missam de ea et post canonicas horas alias in honore eius celebrandas decrevit.*[29]

Giraldus Cambrensis, the Welsh historian, states in *Speculum Ecclesiae* that the first Benedictine house to adopt the daily *Missa de Domina* was Rochester, at the request of William of Ypres during the reign of King Stephen (1135-54):

> *Haec autem prima missa fuit, ut fertur, in Anglia cotidie de Domina solemniter celebrata, sed postmodum ad loca plurima per Dei gratiam exemplo laudabiliter est derivata.* Giraldus, iv, 202.

Evidence thus points to the 1130s as the period when the Lady Mass became a daily observance, and it seems to have existed quite independently of the two conventual masses.

THE RISE OF MARIANISM IN THE PRE-CONQUEST PERIOD

Instances of Marian votive observance in *RC* have already been cited. By contrast with the psalms and prayers for the royal family, these additional devotions to the Virgin do not receive particular emphasis, but they prefigure some of the most important devotional trends in medieval monastic liturgy. For the tenth century marked the beginnings of English interest in Marianism; an interest which had almost reached cult proportions by the time of the Norman invasion. It has frequently been stated that Marian devotion in England far exceeded that of the rest of western Europe during these years,[30] although there are few studies which have examined the facts behind this assumption. The most recent and valuable evaluation of Anglo-Saxon Marian piety, which assimilates evidence from both Latin liturgical and vernacular manuscripts, forms the basis of an Oxford thesis by Mary Clayton: *An Examination of the Cult of the Virgin Mary in Anglo-Saxon England* (1983).[31]

Mary Clayton considers that English liturgical sources show few signs of a pronounced interest in Mary before *c*.900. All four of the major feasts of the Virgin—the Purification, Annunciation, Assumption and Nativity—are present in English manuscripts by the end of the eighth century, but there is little which distinguishes these festal observances from contemporary continental practice.[32] Indeed, interest in the Virgin as a figure in her own right was slow to become established in the western church as a whole, resulting largely from dissemination of eastern doctrine and the practices of the oriental church.

It is likely that the narrative and doctrinal aspects of English Mariology in the early tenth century were dependent on continental models. Latin and vernacular texts written in England during these formative years begin to emphasize Mary both as a historical figure and an object of devotion in her own right. Most of them were produced in learned, probably monastic, circles. The Old English Martyrology, compiled at the end of the ninth century, seems to have been a reference book for the use of a learned man, while the famous homily *Advent*, which stresses Mary's role as *Dei genitrix*, uses a number of texts peculiar to the monastic liturgy. The Old English Martyrology is one of the first sources to draw on apocryphal narratives dealing with Mary's birth, childhood and death: much material of this kind was to serve as a major source for Marian liturgical texts throughout the Middle Ages.[33]

Mary Clayton stresses the role of the English monasteries, and particularly Winchester, in the early propagation of a cult to the Virgin. She attributes the sudden wave of interest in Marianism to the Benedictine revival, seeing Winchester as a natural centre for liturgical, devotional and artistic innovation. The tangible effects of these innovations were felt in several areas. More new monastic churches were dedicated to Mary than to any other saint, and existing ones were rededicated in her favour.[34] Artistically, the work of the Winchester School reveals some of the first instances where Mary is shown as a figure in her own right rather than simply as an appendage to Nativity scenes. Clayton cites two prominent examples: the Ramsey Psalter (974-986), which contains the earliest example of the Virgin weeping into her mantle at the crucifix, and the Benedictional of St Ethelwold (971-84), with the earliest depiction of the Coronation of the Virgin.[35] J.J.G. Alexander even suggests that Winchester artists adapted other scenes to produce depictions of the death of the Virgin.[36]

Winchester's importance as a centre of liturgical innovation, embodied in the document *RC*, has already been discussed. It was suggested above that the two Marian observances occurring in this customary—the Saturday Lady Mass and the daily Marian antiphon after Lauds and Vespers—may well have been native innovations. There is no evidence for continental precedent, and the dissemination of both observances in later insular sources clearly demonstrates their intrinsic significance for the English. Winchester also seems to have served as a melting-pot for devotional observances of a more personal nature. The reformer Ethelwold reputedly recited a daily Marian *cursus* (see Chapter Three, pp.66-67), and the single hour to the Virgin modelled on Vespers in *Lbl* D.XXVI-II (*c.* 1023-35), the Prayerbook of Aelfwine (abbot of the New Minster), may well represent a parallel observance. Clayton also draws attention to one of the early prayers of St Dunstan which singles out Mary above all other saints: 'the first of a considerable number of prayers which were written in the reformed centres up to . . . and after the Conquest'. She sees Winchester as 'already at the centre of [the Marian] cult in England in Ethelwold's time', and that this new 'intensity of devotion' was a product of the Benedictine revival which had not been felt in England or elsewhere in Europe before the tenth century.[37]

Although not mentioned in *RC*, Winchester also appears to have been the first English centre which incorporated two new Marian feasts into its calendar in *c*.1030: the Conception of the Virgin (8 December) and the Presentation or *Oblatio Sanctae Mariae* (21 November). Both feasts were known in the East well before this date, although there is no evidence that they were celebrated in any other part of Europe; Winchester certainly did not take them from Fleury or Ghent, in spite of the obvious influence of these monasteries in other liturgical areas. Both the Conception and the Presentation are copied into two eleventh-century calendars from Winchester: *Lbl* D.XXVII, the Prayerbook of Aelfwine (*c*.1023-35), and *Lbl* E.XXVIII (*c*.1030), which once formed part of *Lbl* D.XXVII. The Conception (although not the Presentation) also occurs in the calendar of *Ccc* 391, the Worcester Portiforium (*c*.1065-6). Clayton considers that this feast may have been transmitted from the East by Greek monks residing in southern Italy.[38] There were apparently Anglo-Saxons in Constantinople and a Greek monk, Constantine, at Malmesbury in *c*.1030. Winchester circulated these feasts to at least three other establishments. Its entire calendar was transferred to Christ Church, Canterbury between 1010 and 1020, and although this obviously predates the establishment of the two new feasts, eleventh-century Canterbury manuscripts show that they were added into the existing liturgical repertory. The close connections between these two houses were reinforced between 1052 and 1070, when they shared the same bishop, Stigand. Winchester also influenced the secular community at Exeter. Bishop Leofric had copies made of several Winchester manuscripts, and the Feast of the Conception appears in both the Exeter layer of the Leofric Missal (*Ob* 579) and the Exeter Benedictional of *c*.1075-1100 (*Lbl* 28188), taken from a Winchester exemplar.

In spite of their limitation to selected centres in England, the insular importance of these two feasts is emphasized by their complete absence in all contemporary continental sources. Indeed, both were abolished from the English calendar by the Normans shortly after the Conquest. But the substance of these feasts, clearly modelled on material taken from the apocryphal infancy gospels, illustrates the salient characteristic of Marianism in the Anglo-Saxon church. Although developed primarily in monastic centres, its focus was devotional rather than doctrinal; Edmund Bishop referred to it as 'pure piety without doctrinal afterthought'.[39]

The status of Mary within the liturgy of the Anglo-Saxon church clearly became firmly established in the tenth and early eleventh centuries. All establishments celebrated at least four feasts of the Virgin, and some as many as six, although the Conception and Presentation have no place in contemporary sources from other parts of western Europe. Private devotions to the Virgin also proliferated, often taking the form of single hours or complete liturgical offices. Such devotions did not necessarily originate in England, although some of the earliest surviving texts are English. There are numerous early European references to the recitation of private *cursus*, but no texts survive until the Prayerbook of Aelfwine. The communal Saturday office of the Virgin first appears in the late Anglo-Saxon source from Worcester, the Portiforium *Ccc* 391. This weekly commemorative office gained enormously in importance after the Conquest, although it may well have been temporarily suppressed by the Normans. Nevertheless, all of the observances discussed in Part Two of this study were evidently known and practised in at least certain parts of England by the first half of the eleventh century, and many of them seem to have developed independently of continental influence.

THE ANGLO-SAXON HERITAGE AND
THE IMPACT OF THE NORMAN INTERVENTION

RC has been taken as the basis for this chapter because of its status as a national document, its importance within the history of Benedictine reform, and its sheer comprehensiveness where liturgical matters are concerned. As an English customary fashioned in the manner of continental documents, it lends particular perspective to devotions which were common elsewhere in Europe at the end of the tenth century. But although it is related in form and content to its continental counterpart, the individual emphasis of English votive observance sets it apart from European practice.

    RC is not the only Anglo-Saxon source which provides evidence for votive observance. One of the two extant manuscripts of *RC*, *Lbl* A.III, contains additional material: complete votive offices of All Saints and of the Virgin. Only the first of these offices is mentioned in *RC* itself, and no texts are provided there. A precursor of the complete Marian office of *Lbl* A.III also survives in a slightly earlier manuscript, the Prayerbook of Aelfwine (*Lbl* D.XXVI-II). Here a series of three independent hours modelled on Vespers is given, addressed respectively to the Trinity, the Holy Cross and the Virgin. It is likely that they were used as private devotions, but they show a clear correlation with the later complete votive offices.

    Two further Anglo-Saxon sources—the Leofric Collectar (*Lbl* 2961), copied between 1046 and 1072, and the tenth-century Durham Collectar (*DRc* A.IV.19)—clarify the probable structure of the *antiphonae* mentioned in *RC*, which were recited daily after Lauds and Vespers. Both of these manuscripts were initially copied for secular foundations, but it is likely that the series of memorials to the Virgin, the Cross and All Saints corresponds with contemporary monastic practice. Each memorial consists of an antiphon, versicle and collect. A third source, *Ccc* 391, the Portiforium of St Wulfstan (1065-6), is also important. It is later than the other sources listed here, but seems to have been modelled on an exemplar from Winchester and it reflects Anglo-Saxon customs. The Portiforium bears witness to the pre-Norman adoption of weekly commemorative offices to the Virgin and the Holy Cross.

Not all instances of votive observance contained in *RC* survived into the later Middle Ages. Some of the appended psalms were eliminated entirely during the reforms of the central Benedictine Chapters of the thirteenth and fourteenth centuries. The *psalmi familiares* which superseded the psalms for the royal household were abolished by the Southern Chapter in 1277, and reduced to recitation after Prime by the Northern Chapter in 1310; Tolhurst remarks that they were probably not recited after 1336 in either province, and there is no evidence in the manuscripts after the later thirteenth century.[40] Other devotions had a rather longer history. The Lenten prostrate psalms certainly survived the later reforms, for Acts of 1277, 1343 and 1444 require them to be said.[41] The penitential psalms and the *Trina oratio* also seem to have survived reforming legislation, while an effort to abolish the gradual psalms in 1278 was withdrawn.[42]

The liturgical aftermath of the Norman Conquest is seen most clearly in a document which shares several structural features with *RC*, Lanfranc's *Consuetudines*, compiled for Christ Church, Canterbury in *c.* 1080. Although not intended as a national code, the *Consuetudines* testify to the impact of Norman monasticism in England and provide a useful basis for comparison with pre-Conquest observance. Many of the practices outlined in *RC* survive in the later document, including the Offices of the Dead and All Saints and the *Trina oratio*, but the more idiosyncratic devotions of *RC* have vanished. Psalms recited after the hours are referred to simply as *psalmi familiares*, and there is no indication that the royal household was ever commemorated specifically in the Canterbury liturgy. One of Lanfranc's innovations was a much greater emphasis on the memorial. Some memorials simply marked displaced feasts, but others were more specifically devotional, directed towards a particular intention. There are references to a memorial of All Saints after Lauds, and the Holy Cross after Vespers (except between Advent and the Octave of the Epiphany), although both may have been recited more frequently than is explicitly stated.

The compilation of Lanfranc's *Consuetudines* at Canterbury is in itself significant. In spite of the building of the new Norman cathedral church, the importance of Winchester as a centre of learning, writing and government declined sharply during the eleventh century. The royal capital moved to London, along with William the Conqueror, while the liturgical focus moved to Canterbury with Lanfranc. Manuscripts and monks were imported wholesale from Normandy. Anglo-Saxon abbots were expelled from the major English houses to make way for eminent Normans from *c.* 1070. Winchester, Glastonbury, Peterborough and St Albans witnessed a succession of continental abbots, while other English houses formed affiliations with Norman monasteries: Abingdon and Jumièges, Battle and Bec, Glastonbury and Caen.[43] In most of the English houses the succession of continental abbots was to hold good until the reign of Henry II (1154-89), when foreign appointments became less of a feature.

The Normans did not always approve of what they discovered across the Channel: liturgical practices which they considered quaint, superstitious and not always founded on fact. Lanfranc's hints at English superstition in Eadmer's *Life of St Anselm* have often been cited:

> *Angli isti inter quos degimus, instituerunt sibi quosdam quos colerent sanctos. De quibus cum aliquando qui fuerint secundum quod ipsimet referunt mente revolvo.*   Eadmer, 51

The Norman abbot of Evesham, Walter (1077-1104), reputedly tested the relics of certain Anglo-Saxon saints by fire, while the Feast of the Conception, newly established in Anglo-Saxon England, disappears from liturgical manuscripts for several years.

Only one small pocket of land seems to have retained its earlier Anglo-Saxon tendencies through this period, centring on Worcester (under its English bishop Wulfstan), Malmesbury, and a few monasteries in the Severn Valley. Wulfstan, the only remaining English-born bishop (1062-95), placed great emphasis on past tradition. Colin Platt sums up the state of English monasticism in the years immediately after the Conquest: 'The attacks on Anglo-Saxon institutions, on property and on the reputation of the saints . . . stirred a concern for the past which found expression in numerous written histories.'[44] There were attempts to reconstruct pre-Conquest histories by several monks, including William of Malmesbury and Matthew Paris at St Albans. So far as liturgy is concerned, two liturgical sources from Worcester hold a place of great importance in the observances examined in Part Two of this thesis. The first, the Worcester Portiforium (*Ccc* 391), mentioned above, may even have been made for the use of Wulfstan himself. The second, the Worcester Antiphoner (*WO* F.160), was copied as late as the thirteenth century, but it appears to represent a much earlier musical tradition, distinct from the repertory in use in other parts of Europe. Both documents testify to continuing insularity in English monastic worship.

NOTES

1. Schmitz, *Histoire de l'Ordre de Saint-Benoît*, i, 38 and Deansley, *The Pre-Conquest Church in England*, 54 both suggest that St Augustine imported *RB*.

2. All references to Colgrave and Mynors (ed.), Bede, *Ecclesiastical History* (listed in the bibliography and cited as Bede.HE).

3. Ferrari, *Early Roman Monasteries*, 386.

4. Lawrence, *Medieval Monasticism*, 44-5.

5. Bede.HE, iv.2. Reference to Eddius, 334; Putta, 336; James, 206; John, 388.

6. Bede.*Lives*, 196.

7. Eddius, 518.

8. Butler, *Medieval Monasteries*, 26.

9. Farmer, 'The progress of the monastic revival', 10.

10. Knowles, *The Monastic Order*, 42.

11. Symons, '*Regularis Concordia*: History and Derivation', 43-4.

12. All references to Symons's edition of *RC, CCM*, vii-3, 69-147 (cited throughout as *RC*).

13. Symons, '*Regularis Concordia*: History and Derivation', 46.

14. Sources of *MQ* are listed in *CCM*, i, 179-194.

15. Symons, '*Regularis Concordia*: History and Derivation', 49-59.

16. John, 'Sources of the English monastic revival', 198-9.

17. Parsons, *Winchester Studies*, 7.

18. Hohler 'Some service-books', 60-83.

19. Alexander, 'The Benedictional of St Aethelwold'; Cramp, 'Anglo-Saxon Sculpture'; Wilson 'Tenth-century Metalwork'.

20. Parsons, *Winchester Studies*, 9.

21. Lawrence, *Medieval Monasticism*, 94.

22. Biddle, '*Felix Urbs Winthonia*', 123.

23. Biddle, *ibid.*, 131.

24. Ker, *Catalogue of Manuscripts containing Anglo-Saxon*, 155; 240-8.

25. Hope, 'The medieval western rites', 239.

26. For an extensive discussion of this manuscript, see Drage, *Bishop Leofric*.

27. Deansley, 'The *Familia* at Christ Church, Canterbury'.

28. For a survey of early Lady Chapel choirs, see Bowers, *Choral Institutions*, section 4.6.2.

29. *Lbl* Harley 1005, f.218v. Cited in Osbert, 198.

30. Barlow, *The English Church 1000-1066*, 18; Woolf, *The English Religious Lyric*, 114.

31. For more general surveys of Marianism, see Graef, *Mary: A History of Doctrine and Devotion*; Barré, *Prières Anciennes*; Warner, *Alone of all her Sex*.

32. For the most recent survey of the early adoption of these feasts in the West, see Clayton, 'Feasts of the Virgin'.

33. Some of the material is collected in James (ed.), *The Apocryphal Gospels* (listed as 'Apoc.' in bibliog.).

34. See Clayton, *An Examination*, Ch.5, 'Anglo-Saxon church dedications and Marian relics'.

35. Clayton, *ibid.*, 441.

36. Alexander, 'The Benedictional of St Aethelwold', 178.

37. Clayton, *An Examination*, 442.

38. Clayton, *ibid.*, 54.

39. Bishop, *The Bosworth Psalter*, 64, n.3.

40. Tolhurst, 90.

41. Tolhurst, 93.

42. Tolhurst, 68.

43. Knowles *et al.*, *The Heads of Religious Houses*.

44. Platt, *The Abbeys and Priories of Medieval England*, 15.

Part II

THREE CASE-STUDIES TAKEN FROM

LATER MEDIEVAL PRACTICE

Chapter Three

THE DAILY VOTIVE OFFICE

Most of the devotions discussed in Part One did not disturb the basic rhythm of communal prayer in the daily office required by *RB*. But the area discussed in this chapter—the proliferation of the parallel votive office—represents a disruption of the Rule and a climax in the adoption of liturgical accretions. By the twelfth century duplicate sets of hours were recited daily by many monastic communities in addition to the regular office, sometimes on a private basis, but increasingly as a corporate observance in choir. In most uses each appended hour of the votive cycle followed its regular counterpart, but there are instances where the position is reversed and the appended hour comes first. By the thirteenth century the most familiar appended office was that addressed to the Virgin Mary (hereafter referred to as the Little Office of the Virgin). Communal daily recitation of all or part of this office seems to have been commonplace in English Benedictine houses by *c.*1250. Surviving references to the Little Office of the Virgin are recorded chronologically in Table 3:1 (p.209), together with a small number of extant votive offices for other intentions.

The principle of observing independent duplicate hours in honour of particular saints or intentions as an appendage to the regular daily *cursus* is an old one. The occurrence of the Offices of the Dead and All Saints in both *RC* and Lanfranc has already been cited; each was recited as a corporate observance, sometimes in choir and sometimes in a separate chapel. Both of these offices are distinguished from most later votive cycles, however, in that neither forms a complete *cursus*. The Office of All Saints was limited simply to Lauds and Vespers, while the Office of the Dead incorporated a third hour, Vigils. Both observances were known to European (and probably to English) monastic communities before the conception of *RC*.

The Office of the Dead is first mentioned at the very beginning of the ninth century (see Table 3:2, p.210). Recited daily, it was both a commemoration of the departed and a reminder of human mortality. Such daily recitation was probably first observed in monastic circles, although its structural features suggest close parallels with secular uses. The Office of

All Saints was adopted at a later date than the Office of the Dead and follows the more conventional structure of the monastic office described in *RB*. It has not been possible to substantiate satisfactorily J.B.L. Tolhurst's unqualified statement that the Office of All Saints was 'in common use from the ninth century'.[1] In the sources consulted (both English and European), the earliest reference to the office is no earlier than the second half of the tenth century (Einsiedeln, 248-9: see Table 3:5) and there are far fewer surviving texts of the office from any period.

The first complete votive offices (comprising a full cycle of hours) begin to appear in English sources during the eleventh century. They may well have been influenced by the existing devotions to the Dead and to All Saints. But unlike the older partial offices, which were both recited as communal observances, it is clear that the first complete cycles were not originally conceived with a corporate or 'parallel' function in mind, but rather have their roots in more personal, devotional practices. The emergence and early circulation of single hours or complete offices intended for private recitation is examined in the second section of this chapter, although space precludes consideration of the later adoption of private offices in the most widely used of all medieval manuscripts, the Book of Hours.[2] The real thrust of the chapter is to consider the functions of the votive office within the context of the monastic liturgy where corporate recitation was the norm. Even here, however, there were occasions when votive offices were to be observed *privatim* (on an individual basis, whether in or out of choir), particularly on feast-days when the regular liturgy was more elaborate than usual.

THE ORIGINS OF THE DAILY VOTIVE OFFICE
I: EARLY CORPORATE FORMS

The partial Offices of the Dead and All Saints were adopted in monasteries throughout Europe from the latter part of the tenth century onwards. The Office of the Dead was one of the earliest of all the votive accretions considered in this study; it was certainly in existence in some areas before the introduction of Benedict of Aniane's revised liturgical scheme for the monastery at Inde, which itself makes no explicit provision for the office (see Chapter One, p.18). Table 3:2 lists the earliest major references to the Office of the Dead in European monastic sources: it draws mostly on material edited for the first volume of *CCM*, but also on the research of Edmund Bishop[3] and Thomas Symons.[4] Because of the great frequency of this observance within monastic manuscripts copied from the eleventh century onwards, and the relatively high level of textual and structural concordance it exhibits from one source to the next, this chapter does not attempt to record the occurrence of the Office of the Dead in individual manuscripts, as it does for the Lady Office and the small number of remaining votive offices addressed to other saints or intentions. Table 3:3 (p.212) presents the texts for the Office of the Dead as they appear in *WO* F.160 (the Worcester Antiphoner) of *c*.1230; common variants found in other manuscripts (some taken from Tolhurst's more extensive textual analysis of the office) are given in brackets.[5]

The Office of the Dead occurred in two different contexts, both of them involving corporate recitation. First and foremost it constituted part of the ceremonies following the death of a member of a community or of some other individual. In this case it was usual to recite the office at the burial, and on certain prescribed days (which varied from house to house) during the following month. This was undoubtedly a very ancient practice which has its roots in the Early Church, where psalms, hymns and prayers were recited not only at burial, but also on the third, ninth and fortieth days following.[6] It is unclear quite when the Office of the Dead was used in a second, less specific context, as a general memorial of the departed. Constant intercession for the dead was certainly an early feature in both eastern and western liturgies: the later recitation of the Office of the Dead on a regular basis presumably represents a ritualization of this custom.

References to the two different functions of the office in eighth- and ninth-century sources are not entirely without ambiguity. The extracts from the *Ordines Romani* (Table 3:2, A,C), stressing the omission of the *Alleluia*, could apply equally to either a votive or a proper office, although there can be little doubt that Angilbert (3:2, D) was prescribing votive use of the observance in his *Institutio*, indicating daily recitation of Vespers (*Vespertinos*), Vigils (*Nocturnos*) and Lauds (*Matutinos*). A few years later, in 817, the monks of Fulda (3:2, E) were also exhorted to practise a daily observance, but the *commemoratio* specified for them was not the full Office of the Dead. The ceremony described here is less extensive than the usual office, consisting of the 'antiphon' *Requiem eternam* and the first part of Psalm 64, *Te decet hymnus* (perhaps a reference to the introit of the Mass of the Dead, *Requiem eternam V. Te decet*) followed by a versicle and collect. On the first day of each month, however, it appears that the observance was more expansive, incorporating a 'vigil' and fifty psalms, said for the abbot Sturmi and the founders of the monastery. On the anniversary of the deceased, the community was to recite the entire psalter in addition to the vigil. The exact content of this latter observance is not specified, although recitation of specified groups of psalms for the dead (see p.39) persisted in many monasteries in addition to a daily office at least until the thirteenth century. The Aachen documents of 816-21 (3:2, F,G) also offer no precise testimony that daily recitation of the Office of the Dead was the rule, although it is clear from the frequency of reference that votive use of the observance was relatively familiar by the period of Frankish reform.

The earliest account of votive use of the Office of the Dead in an

English monastery appears in *RC* (see Table 2:2). No indication of the structure and content of the office is given in this source, but there are several references to the external factors which dictated the time at which it was to be celebrated or omitted. *RC* records the general principle that the individual hours of its two appended daily offices (the Dead and All Saints) should follow the corresponding regular hour. Sometimes this resulted in three consecutive sets (one regular and two votive) of Vespers or Lauds, but transference of one or both of the votive hours might occur during certain seasons, dependent on the varying hours of darkness and the position (or omission) of the second meal of the day, *cena*. During the summer period (from the Octave of Easter to 1 November), *RC* indicates that Vespers of the day was followed by Vespers of All Saints, Vespers of the Dead and Vigils of the Dead:

> *Uesperi: Sicut diximus superius agendum de antiphonis post Matutinas, ita agatur post Uesperam et Uespere de Omnibus Sanctis et Mortuorum et Uigilia usque kalendas novembris.*
>
> *RC*, 92, 2-4

Similarly, during the summer period Lauds of All Saints and Lauds of the Dead followed in succession after Lauds of the Day, but out of choir in another chapel (*porticus*):

> *Post quas eundum est ad Matutinales Laudes de Omnibus Sanctis decantando antiphonam ad uenerationem sancti, cui porticus ad quam itur dedicata est. Post quas Laudes pro Defunctis.*
>
> *RC* 84, 9-11

During the winter season, however, the position of the two appended offices was reversed, and the regular office was followed by Lauds of the Dead and then Lauds of All Saints (*RC* 96,8-12). Both of these offices were omitted entirely from Maundy Thursday; that of All Saints until the Octave of Easter, and that of the Dead until the Octave of Pentecost (*RC* 132,1-2). The mobility of each office is summarized in Table 3:4 (p.215).

The Office of the Dead remained a fairly standard element found in English monastic customaries until the later Middle Ages. It appears in numerous English and European manuscripts from the eleventh century onwards, and it is almost invariably restricted to the three component elements of Vespers (or *Placebo* after the opening antiphon), Vigils (*Dirige*), and Lauds (*Exultabunt*, but since it was almost invariably said as a single unit with Vigils, it is rarely referred to independently). Statutes produced by the presidents of a General Chapter of the York province, held at Selby in 1287, indicated that Vespers and Lauds of the Dead were never to be said without Vigils: *Item quod vespere et laudes mortuorum omnino omittantur nisi Dirige precedat aut sequatur* (Pantin, i,255). Tolhurst's observation that 'there is no indication that this office ever had other than these three hours'[7] holds good for all of the Benedictine manuscripts examined for the thesis. Among the other uses, however, there is at least one exception to this rule. *Ob 5*, an Augustinian psalter from Guisborough copied in the late thirteenth century, provides texts for the Office of the Dead from Prime to None (although not Compline). These appear on f.164 in a contemporary hand, after the Mass of the Dead. They follow the conventional monastic structure of a single antiphon, the appropriate sections of Psalm 118 (see Table 1:2), a versicle and a collect. There are no chapters and no responds, but this is in line with the unusual structure of the other hours of the Office of the Dead.

THE STRUCTURE OF THE OFFICE OF THE DEAD

The structural peculiarities of the Office of the Dead represent some of its most interesting features. Hitherto this area has largely been ignored in liturgical scholarship, but the issue of structural individuality raises a number of important questions, some of direct relevance to the formation of later votive offices. *RC* itself makes no explicit reference to the structure of the Office of the Dead, but the standard pattern which survives in the later English sources (including *WO* F.160, given in Table 3:3) is likely to have been adopted. This reveals significant departures from conventional monastic structure. First, there are major omissions in all of the hours: there are no opening versicles, and neither Lauds nor Vespers contains a chapter or a respond.

In other respects, Vespers and Lauds are almost identical in terms of their overall arrangement. Both comprise five psalms with five antiphons, a versicle, and a canticle with antiphon. (Vespers of the regular monastic office contained only four psalms.) The Lauds psalms (50, 64, 62 with 66, and 148-50) duplicate those prescribed in the secular ferial *cursus* for Wednesday, although the canticle given here, *Ego dixi*, was normally sung on Tuesday. The Vespers series (114, 119, 120, 129 and 137) suggests a proper festal series of psalms, but no other corresponding pattern has been found, and it is likely that the series was compiled especially for the Office of the Dead. All of the sources examined, including those of continental provenance, exhibit singular regularity in the choice of psalms for all three hours.

Vigils of the Dead demonstrates most clearly the deviation from the usual monastic structural pattern. It has three nocturns, each constructed identically with three psalms and antiphons, a versicle, and three lessons with responds. The majority of the extant Offices of the Dead adopt a fixed set of psalms for Vigils: 5, 6, 7; 22, 24, 26; 39, 40, 41, although an early occurrence of the office in a secular Antiphoner from Monza, dating from the beginning of the eleventh century follows a variant (although related) pattern: 5, 6, 7; 21, 24, 30; 34, 39, 41.[8] As with the Vespers group, neither of these two arrangements recurs elsewhere among the repertory of proper psalms allocated to various feasts, and again it seems likely that the group was chosen specifically for the Office of the Dead.

The secular features of Vigils of the Dead are most readily identifiable from the identical structure of the nocturns, the incorporation of nine rather than twelve psalms, and nine rather than twelve lessons. This directly parallels the festal form of Matins used by secular communities. Monastic Matins on feastdays also comprised three nocturns, but the third was dissimilar in structure (incorporating three canticles rather than six psalms), and there were twelve rather than nine lessons. All sources consulted to this point give Vigils of the Dead in the complete secular three-nocturn form described above, but in practice this complete form seems to have been recited only when the office was used in its proper context (related to the death of a specific individual). Many sources, however, fail to specify this. *RC* is first to suggest the structural distinction between the two functions of the office when it describes the ceremonies following the death of a member of the community. For a week after his death and on the thirtieth day after the burial, the office was to be said in full (*plenarie*: *RC* 142,13; 143,2), but between these times, daily recitation was observed *more solito cum tribus lectionibus* (*RC* 143,1) or *sub breuitate* (*RC* 145,13). This implies that only one of the three nocturns was recited, apparently indicating the usual manner (*more solito*) in which the office was performed in its less specific daily votive context.

Lanfranc's *Consuetudines* draw a similar distinction between the two forms of the office. As in *RC*, seven *plena officia* (Lanfranc 104, 32-3) were recited after the death of a member of the community, while a passage prescribing the offices when a brother died while away from the monastery is more explicit still: *uesperas mortuorum et officium cum nouem lectionibus et Laudibus dicant* (Lanfranc 106,1-2). The Statutes produced by the General Chapter of Black Monks in 1277 also discuss the distinction between the two functions, although the Latin in the relevant passage is obscure. Recitation of Vigils with no more than three psalms and three lessons (implying a single nocturn) is the norm, but on anniversaries nine lessons and psalms were the rule, whether with or without music:

> *Placebo et Dirige et novem psalmis et totidem leccionibus, nisi in anniversariis solempnibus, nunquam fiat ultimo responsorio cum tribus tantummodo versubus decantato, nec tunc in cappis vel in albis, ministris dumtaxat exceptis, et cum cantoribus tribus tantum, sequens officium celebretur, vel si fuerit corpus presens, in*

> *anniversariis aliis cum novem fiat leccionibus sine nota, aliis*
> *semper cum tribus psalmis et totidem leccionibus.* Pantin, i,69.

The use of secular forms in the Office of the Dead is closely paralleled in one other area of the monastic liturgy: the special form of the office recited during Holy Week. On the *Triduum*, it was common to substitute the Roman Office for the usual monastic office, resulting in a greatly curtailed format. There is no reference to this particular practice in *RB* iself, but a commentary on the Rule by Paul Warnefrid (*c.*780) refers to a decision made by an unspecified council that the office on the *Triduum* should follow the Roman rite.[9] *RC* also prescribes this form for the *Triduum*, Easter Day and the week following:

> *In quarum noctium sequentibus diebus ad nullam dicitur horam*
> *Deus in adiutorium meum, sed in directum capitula canonicus*
> *cursus dicantur: dehinc uersus et sequentia.*   *RC* 110,6

During this period, Matins consisted of three identical nocturns. It began at the first antiphon, omitting versicles, invitatory and hymn, and ended with the ninth respond, followed immediately by Lauds. Lauds and Vespers also omitted preliminary versicles, beginning with the first antiphon. Both of these offices had five psalms with antiphons, but there was no chapter, respond or hymn, and these were also standard omissions at the Little Hours.

The correspondence between the curtailed format of the *Triduum* offices and the Office of the Dead is striking. Burial in the Eastern church apparently followed the form of Matins on Holy Saturday,[10] and the liturgist Amalarius of Metz (*c.*775-80) specifically acknowledged a relationship between the Holy Week office and that of the Dead in *De Ecclesiasticis Officiis* (821 and subsequent revisions): *Notandum est etiam quod officium pro mortuis ad imitationem agitur officiorum quae aguntur in morte Domini* (Amalarius, *Eccl. Off.* 1161). Rather surprisingly (since much of his work deals with liturgical interpretation) Amalarius refrains from suggesting an allegorical significance of the model for the Office of the Dead. A later section of his work refers to the practice observed in certain places of singing the full office on the first day of the month: *Sunt etiam et alia in quibus in initio mensis novem psalmi, novem lectiones totidemque responsorii pro eis cantantur (Eccl. Off.* 1239).

The infiltration of secular liturgical practice into the monastic *cursus* occurred in a minor way in other areas. Passing reference has already been made to the secular office in the regulation of those periods of time allotted to private prayer (pp.7-9). *RC* contains a number of references to the recitation of the secular Roman *cursus* (*canonicus cursus* or *horas*

canonicas) on specified occasions of this type. Some of these simply refer
to Holy Week, but elsewhere the notion occurs that the community should
use the secular *cursus* as a form of private devotion during periods of
manual labour (*cum decantatione canonici cursus et psalterii operentur*: RC
91,2), and as the bell rings for Terce (*horas canonicas . . . psallendo*: RC
86,1). Lanfranc also mentions silent recitation of the secular *cursus* as a
suitable devotion while the hosts are being made and baked (. . . *dum ipsius
hostiae fiunt et coquuntur, dicant idem fratres . . . horas canonicas*:
Lanfranc 70,11), and when the brethren are shaved (*dicant omnes canonicas
horas*: Lanfranc 76,14).

Any observance cited in an early customary for use as a devotion to fill
a period of time allotted to private prayer may well be a precursor of a
later, more formalized observance of a votive nature, and the individual
recitation of the Roman *cursus* prescribed in *RC* is certainly a potential
candidate for later appended votive offices, most of which reveal a
predominantly secular structure. It is equally likely that the longer
established Office of the Dead influenced later observances, even though it
did not originate as a votive office, and there is no evidence that it was
recited privately. But whatever the exact interrelationship of these early
appended offices, it is clear that most of them, whether for corporate or
personal use, were at an early date given an individual structural framework
modelled on secular practice.

THE OFFICE OF ALL SAINTS

The second of the two early votive offices, that of All Saints, is almost the
only exception to the convention of secular structure. Both of its hours
(Lauds and Vespers) simply follow the conventional monastic format,
incorporating all of the usual elements (see Table 3:5, p.216). Tolhurst
prints texts for this office from two English manuscripts, *Lbl* A.III, from
Christ Church Canterbury, and *WO* F.160, the Worcester Antiphoner.[11] The
latter source provides a small number of alternative texts for the office
during the Easter period, but a missing leaf at the beginning of the book
precludes full analysis of the office in the form it took during the rest of the
year. None of the sources listed in Table 3:2 mention an Office of All
Saints. It first occurs in the St Emmeram version of the Einsiedeln customs
(Einsiedeln 248-9); Tolhurst had apparently not consulted this source, but
by and large the office represented there is not significantly different from
those in the two English sources. Unlike the Office of the Dead, which
survived well into the sixteenth century for use as a monastic, secular and
lay office, the Office of All Saints had a rather less auspicious history. In
England it was abolished by the Southern Chapter of Evesham in 1255[12] and

a simple memorial was substituted (at least in those foundations which troubled to follow the legislation).

Although the structure of the All Saints Office is predictably monastic, the psalmody is a hybrid. In all three sources the five Lauds psalms are borrowed from the Roman *cursus* for Sunday, a series used very frequently in votive offices of the commemorative and daily appended type: 92, 99, 62 (with 66), the canticle *Benedicite* and 148 (-150). The English sources, however, make a characteristic alteration to the series by moving Psalm 66 from its usual secular position after 62 to the head of the series, where it was said without an antiphon: a standard convention at monastic Lauds in use from *RB* onwards. The Einsiedeln source makes no reference whatsoever to this psalm, but it may well be that it followed the pattern of the other sources, the compiler simply assuming that it was such a standard element among the opening ceremonies of Lauds that its recitation could be assumed.

Vespers of All Saints comprises four psalms, 110, 115, 125 and 139, each with its own antiphon. Occasionally it appears that the series of antiphons was reduced to a single item both at Lauds and at Vespers. *RC* prescribes this curtailment from the Octave of Easter until the Octave of Pentecost: *Uesperae uero et Matutinae de Omnibus Sanctis ab octauis Pascae una canantur antiphona usque octauas Pentecosten* (*RC* 132,1-2). The psalms themselves are borrowed from Vespers of the Feast of All Saints (November 1). The two English sources incorporate a short respond after the chapter at this office, but St Emmeram diverges in prescribing no more than a versicle. The *Magnificat* in all three manuscripts is followed by a short series of *preces*, which precedes the collect.

THE ORIGIN OF THE DAILY VOTIVE OFFICE
II: PRIVATE DEVOTION

RC makes no reference to any other formal appended office besides those of the Dead and All Saints, but there is a clear indication that emphasis on particular saints outside the context of the regular office was already important by the end of the tenth century. Twice daily, after Lauds and Vespers and the *psalmi familiares* which followed both of these hours, the community was to remain in choir to recite a series of antiphons, addressed to the Holy Cross, the Virgin, and the saint whose relics were kept in the church.

> . . . *cantent antifonam de cruce, inde antiphonam de sancta Maria et de sancto cuius ueneratio in praesenti colitur aecclesia aut, si minus fuerit, de ipsius loci consecratione.*   *RC* 84,7-9

The significance of the Winchester antiphons is discussed in more detail elsewhere (Chapter Five, pp. 139-40); here it is sufficient to remark that the individual elements of the appended ceremony described above may have been modelled along the lines of a memorial, consisting of antiphon, versicle and collect, rather than a simple antiphon alone. But the tripartite structure of the observance has a wider importance. Related devotions focusing on three saints or intentions in the manner outlined in *RC* are mentioned on two further occasions in English pre-Norman sources, but in both cases they suggest complete hours rather than the short memorial implied here. Indeed, it may have been a natural step to expand the *antiphona* ceremony into a complete hour, possibly with the intention that it might function equally well as a form of private devotion.

Other than directions for recitation of the *horae canonicas*, there are few explicit references at this period as to how monks should conduct their devotions during periods allotted to private prayer: it may well be that much of the time they simply borrowed material from the regular liturgy and recited it out of context. Certain groups of psalms were used in this manner, and it is often a complex procedure assigning particular types of votive observance to a corporate or personal category, especially during this early formative period. Single office hours or indeed complete *cursus* for particular intentions were initially compiled specifically for use as private devotions, and often this is reflected by the nature of the sources in which they appear (psalters and private prayerbooks rather than larger books for use in choir).

The earliest reference to the use of what appear to be single complete hours for private devotion in England credits their introduction to Ethelwold (bishop of Winchester between 963 and 984). The source in which this claim appears is of slightly doubtful authority: an anonymous note appended to a *Vita* of Ethelwold, reputedly written in the twelfth century by Ordericus Vitalis. On the other hand three hymns which follow the *Vita* are not the work of Ordericus and the appended note may also be earlier than the main body of the text, drawing on an authentic tradition.[13] The account states that Ethelwold, bishop of Winchester, instituted a tripartite devotion for his own personal use, consisting of three hours addressed to the Virgin, the apostles Peter and Paul and all living members of the family of Christ, and All Saints respectively. The precise content of the hours is not stated, but the implication is that they were modelled around psalms (*in . . . cursibus ordinavit . . . psalmodiae cantilena*). It also seems likely that they were quite widely disseminated by the time of writing (*plerisque in locis habentur ascriptae*):

> *Praeterea beatus Pater Adelwoldus horas regulares et peculiares sibi ad singulare servitium instituit, quas in tribus cursibus ordinavit . . . Est enim primae psalmodiae cantilena ad laudem*

*beatae Dei genitricis semperque virginis Mariae procurata; secunda
autem ad honorem beatorum apostolorum Petri et Pauli omniumque
nostri Salvatoris humanitati praesentialiter famulantium; tertia vero
ad suffragia omnium sanctorum postulanda, ut eorum pia
intercessione protecti . . . Quae videlicet horae plerisque in locis
habentur ascriptae, et ideo in hoc codicello sunt praetermissae.*

Ethelwold, 107-108

The account does not make it clear whether Ethelwold's three *cursus*
consisted of a complete set of hours in each case, or whether all three
devotions comprised only a single hour. The exact sequence of saints
specified here apparently recurs in no other surviving source, but a similar
tripartite *cursus* with Winchester associations may well shed light on
Ethelwold's hours. This slightly later observance occurs in the Prayerbook
of Aelfwine (*Lbl* D.XXVI-II), copied *c*.1023-35. It consists of three single
hours with different intentions but of identical construction: texts are given
in Table 3:6 (p.217). The Winchester provenance of the book in which they
occur is most apparent from the calendar and the presence of two full-page
drawings in the style of the Winchester School. The ownership of Aelfwine,
who was a member of the New Minster community, is recorded in *Lbl*
D.XXVII on f.13v: *Aelwino monacho aeque decano . . . me possidit.* He
was later appointed abbot of New Minster some time between 1032 and
1035.[14]

Aelfwine's Prayerbook was clearly compiled for devotional purposes.
It contains miscellaneous material, mostly of a non-liturgical nature,
including computistical tables and a few Anglo-Saxon texts. The sequence
of hours, addressed respectively to the Holy Trinity, the Holy Cross and the
Virgin occurs on ff.76-85. In essence all three of these independent hours
correspond with the structure of monastic Vespers, comprising the usual
elements of introductory sentences, four psalms under a single antiphon,
chapter with respond, versicle and response, hymn, *Magnificat* with
antiphon, *Kyrie eleison, Pater noster, Credo,* versicles, and collect with
preces. Each office is followed by a series of additional prayers. The
accompanying rubric gives no indication of their exact context, but it seems
almost certain that the three hours were intended for private recitation
outside the context of the formal liturgy.

In some respects the likely extra-liturgical context of the three hours
seems to have conditioned their content, for again there are signs of secular
influence. The choice of psalmody (identical in each case) is borrowed from
the secular rather than the monastic *cursus* of psalms (Table 2:1): the three
psalms (53, 117, 118, v.1[-32]) and the Athanasian Creed, *Quicumque vult,*
are all prescribed for Sunday Prime in the Roman *cursus.* Nevertheless, the
secular influence is not wholesale, since the choice of three psalms (with
Quicumque) rather than five, means that the overall structure of the offices

is in line with monastic rather than secular Vespers. The vast majority of the later votive offices follow the secular model far more systematically, both in their overall construction and in their choice of psalms.

The three tripartite devotions discussed here are clearly related, although their content and position is not identical. Neither do the sequences of saints correlate exactly, although the Virgin is a common element in each case.

RC Antiphonae	Ethelwold's Hours	Aelfwine's Prayerbook
Holy Cross	BVM	Holy Trinity
BVM	Peter and Paul	Holy Cross
Relics or Patron	All Saints	BVM

All three sets suggest that the local significance of certain saints was an important factor in appended devotions. *RC*, intended as a model for the nation, is most explicit in this respect by providing a flexible option as the final item. At New Minster in the tenth century the principal relics were those of St Judoc and St Grimbald, while St Swithun's grave was translated to the Old Minster in 971.[15] Ethelwold's emphasis on the saints Peter and Paul is more puzzling in spite of the important early diffusion of the cult of these saints and the large number of churches dedicated to them. Winchester seems to have had no particular connection with Peter and Paul, although it may indicate a link with Canterbury, where St Augustine's often went under the better known name of the monastery of St Peter and St Paul. The Holy Trinity, the Holy Cross and All Saints may simply have been regarded as of general devotional interest, and certainly the Virgin would fall into this category. Indeed, the group as a whole suggests a correspondence with saints listed in later sequences of suffrages. It is significant, however, that the Virgin is not emphasized to the exclusion of all other saints at this period. A number of scholars have commented on the changing nature of early devotional trends, among them Dom A. Wilmart, who states that during the eleventh century, devotion to the Cross held a more prominent position than similar devotions to the Virgin, the Eucharist, the Holy Spirit and the Holy Angels, which only came to the forefront in later centuries (the Virgin in the twelfth century, the others as late as the fourteenth and fifteenth centuries).[16]

ELEVENTH-CENTURY DEVELOPMENTS:
THE FORMATION OF A COMPLETE VOTIVE *CURSUS*

Before the first half of the eleventh century there is no substantial evidence that votive offices, whether for corporate or private use, ever comprised a complete *cursus*. From the outset, the Offices of the Dead and of All Saints were both characterized by a partial format, while the tripartite personal devotions in Aelfwine's Prayerbook consist of no more than single hours modelled on Vespers. The first moves towards expansion of individual hours into a complete *cursus* are represented by votive offices occurring in three English manuscripts of the eleventh century. *Lbl* A.III and *Lbl* 2.B.V both contain similarly constructed Offices of the Virgin, while the psalter *Ob* 296 incorporates a rare instance of the Office of the Holy Trinity. From this point onwards the majority of the offices represented in Table 3:1 exhibit two common features: first they occur as complete *cursus*, usually beginning with Matins and extending through to Compline, and second, with only three exceptions, they are addressed to the Virgin Mary.

The seeds for the corporate recitation of a daily votive office of the Virgin appear to have been sown in the second half of the eleventh century, primarily on English soil. Indeed, the manuscript evidence suggests that the Normans excised the Little Office from the insular liturgical pattern soon after their arrival; its absence is conspicuous in Lanfranc's *Consuetudines* (*c.*1080), although both *Lbl* A.III and *Lbl* 2.B.V were in use at Canterbury shortly before the Conquest, and suggest that the Little Office was flourishing there shortly before the Norman invasion. It is not entirely clear, however, which houses pioneered the adoption of the office as a communal observance, or even whether its circulation was particularly wide in the earlier eleventh century. Personal use of the Little Office almost certainly preceded its adoption as a corporate observance, but the boundaries between the two functions are not always easily identifiable in the earliest sources. Nevertheless, it is clear that the daily form of the Marian office, irrespective of the manner in which it was observed, was conceived at an earlier date than the weekly commemorative form (see Chapter Four).

The initial ambiguities associated with the categorization of private and corporate daily votive offices and their commemorative counterparts are further complicated by the nature of the sources into which they are copied. The commemorative office tends to be least ambiguous in this respect, for since it was a liturgical replacement it usually appears in books which contain the collective parts of the liturgy: portiforiums, breviaries or antiphonals (see Table 4:1, p.239). Daily votive offices feature far more rarely in these books, particularly before the fourteenth century. Complete texts for such observances are more often found in manuscripts whose function lies somewhere between the liturgical and the purely devotional. The Prayerbook of Aelfwine, discussed above, is a clear candidate for the latter category, but over half of the sources listed in Table 3:1 are psalters and miscellanies which amalgamate both liturgical and devotional material. There are a few additional references to both commemorative and appended votive offices in monastic customaries, although these sources do not always provide texts.

Psalters were copied either as functional manuscripts for genuine liturgical purposes (for monks in choir singing the office) or for personal use, sometimes by wealthy individuals with sufficient resource to pay for their illumination. Books falling within the latter category effectively functioned as private prayer-books. James McKinnon distinguishes between these two types by applying the terminology 'choir-psalter' and 'gift-psalter'.[17] Gift-psalters tend to be preserved in greater numbers than choir-psalters on account of their uniqueness and their decoration, but, on the whole, these more lavish books tend not to incorporate votive offices at this period.

The content of a psalter, whether for private or choir use, was not rigidly defined. The nucleus of psalms usually came near the beginning of the book, preceded by a calendar. Thereafter representative monastic choir-psalters often include the monastic canticles, Athanasian Creed, litany and accompanying prayers, and sometimes a hymnal. Votive material varies from source to source. The Office of the Dead, (sometimes with the *Commendatio Animae*) is a likely element, but complete *cursus* addressed to the Virgin or for other intentions are less common, and in at least two cases noted in Table 3:1, a votive office is appended by a later hand on a flyleaf. The earliest liturgical psalters rarely incorporate a votive office of the Virgin; if the observance does occur, it is much more likely (as in *Lbl* 2.B.V) to be a later addition to the main body of the manuscript. Only three psalters listed in Table 3:1 are exceptions to this rule: *Cjc* 68, *Lbl* 21927 and *Mch* 6717, where the votive office is contemporary with the earliest part of the source. Later specimens with miscellaneous contents are perhaps better described as psalter-hours, a transitional genre most common during the thirteenth century. McKinnon comments that 'the psalter was the principal devotional book in England throughout the fourteenth and fifteenth centuries when the Book of Hours occupied that role on the Continent'[18]: it remains unclear quite why the earlier genre survived so much longer in England. So-called Books of Hours expanded the accrued devotional material of the psalter, eventually dispensing with the psalm element altogether. The irregularity of the contents of psalters or psalter-hours, and the uncertainty of their original use, often blurs the intended function or date of any votive office included.

One of the earliest extant examples of a complete votive office occurs as an appendage to a choir-psalter, *Ob* 296, from St Guthlac's, Crowland, copied around the middle of the eleventh century. This manuscript contains two full-page illuminations, a calendar, daily and weekly canticles, *Gloria in excelsis* and creeds, a litany and private prayers. The Office of the Trinity on f.127v, headed *Cursus de Sancta Trinitate*, ends the book. Although None is missing from the office, it is clear that the original plan was for a complete cycle from Vespers through to None. The absence of the final hour is presumably due to a missing leaf: Sext ends at the foot of f.130v, the last leaf of the source. There is no musical notation. Structurally the Trinity office follows the common secular pattern which lies at the heart of all the offices represented in Table 3:1, drawing its psalms from both the festal and ferial arrangements of the Roman use. Its content will be discussed in due course. All of the proper texts for the office are Trinitarian and were presumably borrowed from elsewhere in the liturgy. This is one of only three surviving examples of a votive office of the Trinity, excepting the single hour given as part of the tripartite *cursus* in Aelfwine's Prayerbook. There is no indication that it was used publicly or with music, although its appearance in a choir-psalter rather than a private book may be significant. Doubtless such an office intended for votive use would have been transformed for a rather different function when the Feast of Trinity Sunday became a standard feature of the liturgy in the thirteenth century.

THE MARIAN OFFICES IN *LBL* A.III AND *LBL* 2.B.V

The two Marian offices in the related eleventh-century sources, *Lbl* A.III and *Lbl* 2.B.V, are the earliest extant examples of complete votive cycles addressed to the Virgin: each has a full set of hours from Matins to Compline. Texts are presented in Table 3:7 (p.220). *Lbl* A.III is of additional importance in that it contains certain appended elements which demonstrate the gradual adaptation of a votive office initially conceived with a personal function, to a corporate observance forming an appendage to the regular hours. Both offices occur in non-liturgical sources with miscellaneous contents, typical of those categories described above.

The offices have been considered as a related pair since the publication of both sets of texts as a single volume by E.S. Dewick in 1902.[19] The relationship between them is also noted by Neil Ker, who comments on the correspondence in provenance of the two manuscripts.[20] Palaeographical details suggest that both books were copied for and used at Christ Church, Canterbury: *Lbl* A.III almost certainly corresponds with one of the books described in the medieval library catalogue. It is known first and foremost as the more complete of only two surviving sources of *RC*, but the volume as a whole is a particularly comprehensive miscellany, containing *RB* with an Anglo-Saxon gloss, the Aachen *Capitula*, *Memoriale Qualiter* and a final section comprising prognostics and prayers. The Little Office of the Virgin is copied into this final section on ff.107v-115v, headed *uotiua laus in ueneratione sancte marie uirginis*. Tolhurst emphasizes the importance of this section, for he sees it as a supplement to the practices prescribed in *RC*.[21] In spite of the Canterbury provenance of *Lbl* A.III, some of the liturgical details in other parts of the manuscript, particularly the invocation of certain Winchester saints (such as Swithun and Birinus), possibly indicate a Winchester exemplar.

The related manuscript *Lbl* 2.B.V is a tenth-century psalter, but the Marian office appears on prefatory leaves which were appended at a later date than the main body of the manuscript. Ker suggested a date of *c.*1066-87 for the office, surmising that the book itself was copied for the Nunnaminster, Winchester, but that certain features of the script of the appended passages pointed to its presence at Christ Church, Canterbury in the eleventh century and later. The later Marian office is thus likely to have been compiled at Canterbury.

At face value the Marian offices in these two books are markedly similar. Neither source gives any precise indication of the function of the observance; indeed, the term *uotiua laus* in the earlier manuscript, *Lbl* A.III, suggests considerable licence as to when the office was used. However, this office (although not that in *Lbl* 2.B.V) incorporates a sequence of memorials after both Lauds and Vespers, presenting a strong possibility that it was used as part of public worship in choir, rather than as a private office intended for personal use. Tolhurst stresses that the office in *Lbl* 2.B.V was different in this respect: 'there is nothing to show that it was ever in use in choir, or that it was other than a devotion of a purely private nature'.[22] Conversely, he suggests that the office in *Lbl* A.III has a crucial relationship with the series of three antiphons prescribed to follow Lauds and Vespers in *RC*, dedicated to the Holy Cross, the Virgin and the saint enshrined in the church. Vespers of the Marian office in *Lbl* A.III is followed by two (untitled) memorials, addressed to the Cross and to All Saints respectively. Lauds of the same office is followed by a series of six memorials, beginning with the Cross and ending with All Saints. In neither case does a memorial of the Virgin appear, and Tolhurst plausibly suggests that Vespers and Lauds of the Virgin followed the respective regular hours, thus replacing the earlier *antiphona* or memorial. Vespers and Lauds of the Marian office may well have been recited in choir, but this does not seem to be the case for all of the other hours. Indeed, examination of the texts of the absolution following the *Confiteor* at Prime suggests a personal function, for it uses the first person singular: *mihi* and *peccata mea*.

Tolhurst's reasoning led him to conclude that at least part of the Little Office of the Virgin was adopted for recitation in choir at Canterbury during the first half of the eleventh century. Lanfranc's omission of the office is interpreted as no more than a 'temporary eclipse', since the office reappears with complex rubrics and a variety of alternative texts in *Llp* 558, also from Christ Church, Canterbury, but copied as late as the fifteenth century. Edmund Bishop also favoured the English origins of the office, commenting that if it was in use before the Conquest, 'it was abolished by the newcomers, the men of model observance, as mere Englishry'.[23]

Whatever their intended function, the structure of both of these early Marian offices is curious, since they combine elements from both secular and monastic uses. Secular influence is apparent in both offices in the single nocturn of Matins with its three psalms, and the incorporation of psalmody borrowed from the secular *cursus* (discussed below) in the other hours. *Lbl* 2.B.V shows other secular features: a respond after the chapter at the Little Hours, and the canticle *Nunc dimittis* at Compline. In many respects both of these offices correspond structurally to later votive cycles, but there are certain features—much more pronounced in *Lbl* A.III—which suggest the retention of standard monastic practice. This avoidance of a wholesale adoption of the secular framework in *Lbl* A.III emphasizes the transitional character of the observances. Its 'monastic' features are summarized below:

Matins

Tripartite repetition of the preliminary *Domine, labia mea*
Presence of introductory Psalm 3, *Domine quid multiplicati*
Recitation of the Gospel *In principio* (John I,1) and the hymn *Te decet laus* after the *Te deum* (these features are common to both sources)

Lauds

Presence of introductory Psalm 66, *Deus misereatur*
Six memorials after collect

Prime to None

Omission of short respond after chapter

Vespers

Two memorials and Little Office of Dead after collect

Compline

Three psalms without antiphon
Omission of *Nunc dimittis* and its antiphon

Lbl 2.B.V avoids all of these monastic features with the exception of the gospel reading and hymn at the end of Matins, but in other respects the two offices are very similar. The adoption of the one-nocturn form of Matins and the correspondence of psalmody has already been noted; both also follow the general rule of providing one antiphon for every psalm. And although the chosen texts do not often concord, they draw on a similar repertory. A number are borrowed from *The Song of Songs*, a relatively new source for Marian texts which was to become increasingly popular in

Marian liturgy from the eleventh century onwards. Indeed, many of the texts
used in these two offices recur in later sources for similar observances, and
as the earliest examples of their kind, it is clear that both offices are of great
importance within the context of this chapter.

SECULAR FEATURES IN THE OFFICES LISTED IN TABLE 3:1

Without exception, all of the offices listed in Table 3:1 reveal certain
similarities which draw directly on structural features found only in the
secular *cursus*. This is more marked in the later sources, but present in
essence even in the eleventh-century offices considered above. This
phenomenon has already been mentioned in relation to the earliest
occurrence of a votive office, that of the Dead, which was first adopted into
the daily monastic liturgy at the beginning of the ninth century. The choice
of a secular model for a votive *cursus* may have resulted from a deliberate
attempt to differentiate between the respective character of regular and
votive hours; in many cases, appended hours followed immediately after the
regular counterpart. In practical terms, it must also have been desirable to
restrict the length of the parallel office; this was particularly true in the case
of Matins, where the secular ferial form was considerably shorter than the
monastic equivalent. Dissimilarity in the relative length of the other hours
in the monastic and secular uses is less of a feature, although some votive
offices are curtailed by the exclusion of introductory versicles or appended
items, such as *preces*. To what extent the adoption of secular liturgical
forms in monasteries represents direct influence from secular communities
is difficult to determine, for there is little evidence to suggest that the
earliest votive offices based on secular models are anything but monastic in
origin. Comparable observances in non-monastic books tend to be later in
date, but they are more or less identical in format. This is certainly the case
with those appended offices which feature in the Use of Sarum.

The individual structural features which distinguish the monastic and
secular forms of the office have already been discussed in relation to the
Office of the Dead and the Little Offices of *Lbl* A.III and *Lbl* 2.B.V, and
the following analysis of the later votive office is based on similar
observations. The apparent continuity in the structure of the votive office
from the ninth century onwards is very striking. Its distinction from the
regular monastic office which usually preceded it is seen most clearly in the
late-fourteenth century customary of St Mary's, York, where texts for
adjacent regular and votive hours are set out in succession. It is possible to
develop this analysis further by examining the selection of psalms for the
votive office. In the Office of the Dead it was clear that the psalmodic
pattern for all three component hours, irrespective of the date of the source,
was remarkably constant. This regularity is less pronounced in the later

Little Offices of the Virgin, but most sources in essence follow one of three alternative psalm patterns, all of which are borrowed from the secular cycle of psalmody.

THE PROCESS OF SELECTING PSALMS FOR VOTIVE OFFICES

Psalm patterns (where they are given) for all votive offices included in Table 3:1 are listed in Table 3:8 (p.227). The number of psalms selected for recitation at each office is important, but more so the choice of the individual psalms themselves. Here there were two basic options: psalms might be extracted from the weekly ferial pattern (which varied in monastic and secular uses, although the basic principle that all 150 psalms should be recited within one week was common to both), or from a proper *cursus* specially chosen for its appropriateness to a particular saint or season. In the main the weekday ferial *cursus* is sequential, while proper psalm patterns tend to be non-sequential, chosen rather for their textual relevance. Despite the varying number of psalms required for Matins and Vespers in the monastic and secular arrangement, the choice of psalms for the same feast in both uses is usually closely related, drawing on a common repertory. This principle is discussed further in the following chapter which deals with the weekly commemorative office: here it is clear that the manuscripts are more or less equally divided between adoption of proper or ferial psalms.

(a) Matins

Nineteen monastic sources are represented in the Matins section of Table 3:8. Of the nineteen, fifteen are Marian offices, with a further three addressed to the Holy Spirit (*Llp* 368, *Lbl* 155 and *Mch* 6717) and one to the Trinity (*Ob* 296). The Holy Spirit offices are the only examples which fail to provide the usual quota of three psalms, while the Marian office in *Lbl* A.III gives an extra psalm (3) in its characteristic monastic position. One thirteenth-century source, *WO* F.160, provides four alternative cycles, consisting of three psalms each. The apparent norm of reciting three psalms at Matins in the majority of the offices in Table 3:8 is paralleled nowhere else in the monastic office, with the exception of the one-nocturn form of the Office of the Dead. The secular implications of this structure and its relationship with the Holy Week Office have already been discussed.

All of the Matins psalms in Table 3:8 are drawn from a proper rather than a ferial *cursus*. The following analysis summarizes the three different patterns which occur in the fifteen Marian offices listed in Table 3:1, and the relative frequency with which each occurs:

Psalms	Sources
8, 18, 23	8 of 15
8, 23, 86	5 of 15
8, 14, 86	2 of 15

Just over half of the fifteen sources considered above opt for the sequence 8, 18, 23. For the most part the frequency of this pattern is concentrated in the later sources (thirteenth century and later), but it also features in a mid-eleventh century office which is not represented in the above analysis, *Ob* 296, since it is addressed to the Trinity (see below). But all three patterns listed above show an obvious relationship in that they draw on only five psalms: 8, 14, 18, 23, 86. All three groups begin with 8, and both 23 and 86 occur in two of the three groups. Further, every psalm listed here (with the exception of 14) occurs in the Matins cycle allotted to Marian feasts; the secular *cursus* consisting of

First Nocturn: 8, 18, 23,
Second Nocturn: 44, 45, 86,
Third Nocturn: 95, 96, 97,

to which the monastic *cursus* (see Table 4:8, p.253) adds 47, 84 and 98, in the following arrangement:

First Nocturn: 8, 18, 23, 44, 45, 47
Second Nocturn: 84, 86, 95, 96, 97, 98.

In the majority of sources (both secular and monastic) which specify particular psalms for feasts, this proper sequence is used for all of the Marian feasts, and usually for the Common of Virgins and the Saturday commemorative office of the Virgin in addition. The latter is discussed at length in the following chapter. The first three psalms of the Marian proper cycle were also identical to those prescribed for Matins of Trinity Sunday, (in those sources late enough to incorporate this feast) but thereafter the Trinity cycle fails to concord: in *Ob* e.1*, the Hyde Abbey Breviary, it is 8, 18, 23, 28, 46, 47, 61, 65, 71, 76, 95, 97. It may therefore be concluded that one manner of selecting the psalms for Matins of a votive office was simply to extract the first three psalms from the 'proper' psalmodic *cursus* used on a related feast. On this basis, it is very clear that the quadruple cycle of psalms prescribed in the thirteenth-century Worcester manuscript simply drew on all twelve festal Marian psalms and used them within a rota system. Votive offices to the Virgin in the Sarum and Exeter books also adopt this rota, although the secular rite had resource to only nine Matins psalms rather than the monastic quota of twelve.

Table 3:8 shows the use of two further psalm patterns for Matins of the votive office of the Virgin. Five sources opt for 8, 23, 86: this presumably represents a random selection from the Marian festal psalms listed above. In the two remaining sources, however (the related early pair *Lbl* A.III and *Lbl* 2.B.V) a 'foreign' psalm, 14, is incorporated. 14 appears in none of the psalm cycles for the Marian feasts in the twelve secular and monastic antiphoners collated by Hesbert; and in the Hyde manuscript the three psalms 8, 14, 86 occur together in a single cycle only once, on the Feast of Mary Magdalene.

The three Offices of the Holy Spirit all prescribe a single psalm, 1, at Matins. This suggests no obvious pattern: the closest proper cycle (Pentecost) begins with Psalm 8. Psalm 1 is mostly confined to Martyrs or Bishops (whether in the common or the sanctorale), although it also occurs as the first psalm of Sunday Matins in the secular *cursus*. All three of these offices incorporate only a single psalm for each hour, rather than following the more conventional secular model adopted in the other offices listed in Table 3:8.

(b) Vespers

The psalms of the other hours of the votive office do not always lend themselves quite so readily to this kind of straightforward analysis. Aside from Matins, Vespers is the only other element of the regular office where a proper cycle of psalms operates regularly on major feasts, although over half of the sources in the Vespers section of Table 3:8 suggest borrowing from the ferial rather than the festal *cursus*. Here only fourteen offices (twelve addressed to the Virgin, one to the Trinity and one to the Holy Spirit) are represented. The Holy Spirit Office is omitted from the following analysis since its psalmodic structure differs so radically from the other offices. Three manuscripts, two of which are in other respects central to this chapter (*WO* F:160 from Worcester, and *Cjc* D.27 from St Mary's, York) lack the Vespers section altogether.

Five of the twelve Marian offices represented in the Vespers section of Table 3:8, all of them in sources copied before 1300, again indicate recourse to a festal rather than to a daily Vespers *cursus*. All extant offices copied after this date are unequivocally ferial in their choice of psalmody. One striking feature of the Vespers *cursus* of the votive office is that not all of the sources opt for the same number of psalms: the choice is between four (in accordance with monastic tradition) or five (as in the secular uses). The following analysis covers thirteen offices, including the Trinity office in *Ob* 296, which subdivide as follows:

Four psalms (monastic)   6 of 13
Five psalms (secular)   7 of 13

Offices with four psalms:

109, 121, 126, 131	3 of 6
109, 112, 121, 126	1 of 6
109, 112, 121, 147	1 of 6
121-124	1 of 6

Offices with five psalms:

121-125	6 of 7
143-147	1 of 7 (*Ob* 296, the Trinity office)

Use of a ferial *cursus* for the votive office is easily distinguishable, since the numbers run in sequence. Whether four or five psalms are specified, two basic ferial patterns emerge: 121-124 [or 121-125] and 143-147. The first pattern occurs seven times, the second only once, and this is in the context of the Trinity office rather than in an Office of the Virgin.

The implications of this are important, for it provides further evidence of borrowing from a secular pattern. Reference to Table 1:2 shows that the psalms 121-125 formed the prescribed series for Vespers on Tuesday in the secular rite. In the monastic books these psalms form no logical group, but are scattered between Terce, Sext and None in the latter part of the week, and it is clear that the group conceived for votive use must have been taken from secular Vespers. A glance at the Sarum books indicates that the same psalms were used there for the daily Office of the Virgin except on Tuesday, when the psalmodic pattern of the ferial office would simply have been duplicated by the appended Marian Vespers. Consequently a festal series was substituted for the Marian office: 109, 110, 111, 129, 131 (see below). The ferial *cursus* (143-7) used for the Trinity office in *Ob* 296 is that prescribed for Saturday Vespers in the secular rite, and again it seems clear that the psalms for the votive office were simply lifted directly from this source. Less obvious is the method whereby the compiler of an office fixed on a particular group of psalms: perhaps selection of a ferial repertory allocated to a specific weekday was not of great significance.

The logic which lay behind the choice of psalms from a proper *cursus* is usually easier to follow. Table 3:8 again shows two basic 'proper' sequences for Vespers: 109, 121, 126, 131, and 109, 112, 121, [126], 147. The first set simply represents the Vespers psalms prescribed in the Benedictine manuscripts for the Marian feasts (although not the Common of Virgins, where the last psalm is different). The second set listed above, whether it consisted of four or five psalms, has not yet been traced as belonging to any particular feast. But the issue is complex since individual houses did not necessarily standardize a set of psalms for use on a particular day.

(c) Lauds

The psalms chosen for Lauds of the votive offices are much less variable than those for Matins and Vespers, and are very closely related to Lauds of the secular ferial *cursus*. Table 1:2 serves as a reminder that the secular form of Lauds on Sundays exchanged the usual opening psalm 50, *Miserere*, for 92, *Dominus regnavit* (which did not occur in monastic Lauds at any point), thereafter continuing with 99 and the psalms which were recited at ferial Lauds on all days: 62 with 66 and the *Laudate* psalms 148-50. The canticle *Benedicite* was inserted into the series before Psalms 148-150. In essence, all of the psalms listed in Table 3:8 conform with this Sunday arrangement. The Hyde Abbey source gives only the first psalm, 92, presumably taking the others as read, but the other thirteen sources specify all psalms. Only three sources reveal a minor mutation from the Sunday Lauds pattern, and in every case the inconsistency concerns Psalm 66. The position of 66, *Deus misereatur*, was the primary distinguishing factor between the respective psalm patterns of secular and monastic Lauds, and the manuscripts *Lbl* A.III and *Lbl* 157 both attempt to restore the psalm to its conventional monastic position at the head of the group. But in neither case does this affect the fundamental choice of Lauds psalms which still represents the direct influence of the secular Sunday pattern. The third source which deviates from the norm, *Lbl* 2.B.V, omits Psalm 66 altogether, but it is possible that its absence in the manuscript does not indicate its omission in the office: its presence among the prefatory items may have still been sufficiently commonplace at this date to warrant scribal omission. It seems likely that the weekly commemorative office also used the same pattern of secular Sunday psalms at Lauds, for most of the sources are content simply to prescribe the opening psalm, 92.

(d) Prime

Prime is one of the more complex votive hours in terms of the psalmodic options offered. Several sources seem to have provided a Sunday arrangement and a weekday arrangement, the former involving extra psalms. This was the case at St Mary's York, Durham and Pilton (all copied later than 1380). In all three manuscripts this optional Sunday form was based on the secular *cursus*; Prime in the monastic liturgy remained consistent for all days of the week, including Sunday. The Sarum Use offers 53, 117, four sections of the long psalm 118, and 120 for Sunday Prime of the regular office. None of the votive offices in Table 3:8 conforms exactly to this pattern, although Pilton (*Ob* g.12) comes near (53, 117, 118 x 4 and 116). York and Durham are quite different from this system, but are clearly related to each other: 53, 1, 2, 6 and 116 at York, and 53, 1, 2, 5 and 116 at Durham. Psalms 1, 2 and 6 were prescribed for regular Prime on

Monday in the monastic *cursus*. The standard votive pattern at Christ
Church, Canterbury also approaches this arrangement (2, 6, 116), although
here there are only three psalms and no alternatives are offered for Sunday.
One feature which clearly remains constant in all sources is the invariable
opening psalm, 53: indubitably borrowed from the ferial secular *cursus* for
Prime. Thereafter most sources continue with the first thirty-two verses of
Psalm 118 (as in the Sunday ferial office in both monastic and secular
liturgies), although these are not always divided in exactly the same manner.
Prime of the votive offices normally concludes with either the Athanasian
Creed, *Quicumque vult*, (mostly in the earlier sources) or Psalm 116, which
appears to have replaced this item in the later manuscripts.

(e) Terce to None

Two basic options operated for the other Little Hours of the votive office.
Most of the sources prescribe three sections of Psalm 118, each of sixteen
verses. Terce incorporates verses 33-80 in most cases, Sext verses 81-128,
and None verses 129-176. This corresponds exactly with the division of
verses for these hours in the ferial secular *cursus*. A few sources deviate
from this plan, or provide alternatives for Sunday (as in the manuscripts
from Christ Church, Canterbury and Pilton). Other sources have more
radical schemes and do not draw on Psalm 118 at all. In this case the psalms
from the ferial monastic *cursus* are substituted: 119-121 at Terce, 122-24 at
Sext, and 125-27 at None. In addition to the office in *Lbl* 157, of uncertain
provenance, the appended offices at Worcester, St Mary's York, Godstow,
the Sunday office at Pilton, and the offices of Sarum and Exeter all follow
this pattern.

(f) Compline

The Compline psalms are more regular. Four sources simply follow the
fixed Compline psalms of the secular regular *cursus*: 4, 30, 90 and 133 (*Ob*
296 from Crowland, *Lbl* 2.B.V from Canterbury, *Lbl* 21927 from
Muchelney and *Lbl* 157, of unknown provenance). Only one manuscript, the
early Canterbury source *Lbl* A.III, follows the monastic arrangement of 4,
90, 133. Two sources, however, prescribe psalms which suggest a
compromise between the two: 4, 30, 133 is found in a second, later
Canterbury manuscript (*Llp* 558) and at Gloucester (*Ob* f.1). Three other
sources use 30, 86, 116 (Hyde Abbey, St Mary's York and Pilton), while
the remaining three sources and the appended offices used at Sarum and
Exeter give the psalms 12, 42, 128 and 130. All but one of the sources (the
earlier Canterbury manuscript) follows the essential secular pattern by
including the canticle *Nunc dimittis*.

*

Analysis of the broad sweep of psalm patterns represented in Table 3:8 might be expected to produce evidence of links between individual monasteries, or at least some correspondence where their observance of the votive office is concerned. But no two monasteries followed exactly the same sequence of psalms for all hours. A particular group of houses linked by their choice of Matins psalms may well disintegrate and regroup within the context of Vespers. But one feature which does emerge is the greater regularity of psalmodic patterns in the sources copied after *c.*1300. There is an apparent shift towards two clearly defined groups in the later sources: 8, 18, 23 at Matins, and 121-125 at Vespers. It is not impossible that this increased regularity reflects the influence of the Use of Sarum. Secular patterns certainly influenced the formation of the votive office as a whole, but the particular sequence of psalms chosen for the Sarum Little Office was extremely influential in many later sources. Most of the later English Books of Hours follow the Sarum pattern, and it is also reproduced in one of the sources listed in Table 3:8, the psalter copied for the nuns of Godstow, *Mch* 6717. The wider implications of the choice of psalms for the votive office are discussed below.

ADOPTION OF THE DAILY VOTIVE OFFICE AFTER 1200

Table 3:1 suggests that the Little Office of the Virgin was a widespread—although not universal—observance in English monastic communities by the latter part of the thirteenth century. Like the commemorative office discussed in the following chapter, the content and position of the accrued hours were not regularized from house to house; indeed those customaries which refer to a daily office of the Virgin provide very diverse rules for its observance. Some monasteries, like Worcester and St Mary's York, sang a full set of appended hours, each one following the corresponding regular office, but other houses seem to have adopted only one or two additional hours which did not always have a fixed position in the liturgy, but shifted with the season. There is no evidence that the community at Norwich observed a daily Lady Office at all, while at Chester during the 1330s, the appended office was replaced by a simple memorial during those seasons when the liturgy dictated that its public recitation should be abandoned, as in the secular uses. Chester also makes reference to private recitation of the appended office during specified periods, as does Worcester, St Mary's York, and Barking.

All customaries considered here which refer to the daily Little Office also make provision for its weekly counterpart, the Saturday commemorative office. Three sources, Worcester, Hyde Abbey and Barking, provide texts for both forms of the office, and in all cases a number of the texts are common to each observance. On account of its more substantial structure (which corresponds to the liturgy of either a three-lesson or twelve-lesson feast) the weekly commemorative form incorporated more material than its reduced daily counterpart. Both of these offices may reveal evidence of new textual and musical composition, which is not duplicated elsewhere in the liturgy. The quality of new material for the Little Office is seen most clearly in *WO* F.160, the Worcester Antiphoner, which contains a unique cycle of nine *Magnificat* antiphons for use between Pentecost and the Nativity of the Virgin. Textual borrowing in other areas of the votive office, where several groups of texts are lifted direct from an existing related feast, is also commonplace, and this phenomenon is examined at the end of Chapter Four.

Two roughly contemporary customaries of the first half of the thirteenth century from Eynsham and Bury St Edmunds, both available in recent editions by Antonia Gransden, are the earliest sources of their kind which refer to the daily Marian office. *Ob* 435, the Eynsham manuscript (copied after 1230) contains details of the constitutional affairs of the house rather than the liturgy; it frequently refers to a complementary book (now missing) which dealt with liturgical observance in more detail. Nevertheless, *Ob* 435 contains two references to a daily Marian observance. Compline of the Virgin, said with a specially worded blessing, was to follow Compline of the day; *Pater noster* and the *Trina oratio* followed after, and then the community retired to bed.

> *Deinde dicatur Confiteor et Completorium. Si ad leccionem collacionis omnes extiterint, tunc sic incipiatur Adiutorium nostrum et deinde oracio et cetera. Post Completorium dei genitricis talis detur benediccio Per intercessionem suae matris benedicat nos filius dei patris. Deinde fiat oracio id est Pater noster aut tres simul et sub uno intervallo et terminetur cum prior ante et retro fecerit.*
> Eynsham, 112,35-13,6.

Ob 435 also mentions an observance termed *collacio dei genitricis*, presumably a short reading after Compline. Many monasteries observed the *collacio*, but no other reference has been traced to the use of a specifically Marian text:

> *Post capitulum horae ultimae si psalmi familiares non secuntur et post collacionem dei genitricis cum secuntur, exeat rector ad percuciendum cymbam.*   Eynsham, 146,1-3.

The Bury St Edmunds Customary, copied c.1234, is rather more generous in its liturgical information. Here a complete Little Office of the

Virgin was appended to the daily liturgy. On ferial days the office was sung as a communal observance (*in conventu*), but on feasts celebrated in copes modifications were necessary. When only two of the rulers were required to vest in copes for a feast (*duae capae*), Matins of the Virgin was not to be said communally (*publice*) as on ordinary days, although all the other hours of the Virgin remained unaffected. Where four copes (*quatuor capae*) are prescribed, however, public recitation of all of the Marian hours and additionally the *psalmi familiares* was to cease:

> *Hicque notandum est quod duae capae prohibent Matutinas de sancta Maria cantari publice in conventu. Sed omnes alias horas de ipsa permittunt cantari a conventu palam cum horis diei more solito exceptis suffragiis ad Vesperas et ad Matutinas . . . Quatuor vero capae numquam sumunt Matutinas vel aliquam horam de sancta Maria simul teneri a conventu in choro cum servicio iliius festi, cuius sunt ipsae capae, nisi ipsum festum fuerit de ipsa, nec psalmos familiares, nisi solummodo Voce mea vel Beatus qui intelliget, ut dictum est.* Bury, 47,10-22.

As part of the set of Statutes published by the General Chapter at Reading in 1277, the presidents enjoined either communal observance of all of the hours of the Lady office (*in conventu*), or private recitation out of choir (*penitus extra chorum*). In the latter case a memorial was appended to Lauds and Vespers of the Little Office:

> *Matutine et cetere hore de domina aut dicantur protractius et distinctius in conventu, et qui non interfuerint, proclamentur: aut dicantur penitus extra chorum. Et qui illas ex consuetudine non dicunt in choro, ad laudes et vesperas de domina faciant memoriam specialem.* Pantin, i,68.

The Northern Chapter, meeting at Selby in 1287, produced a similarly worded statute, specifying that a monk failing to recite the Lady hours was to confess his fault in chapter (*et qui non dixerint nec interfuerint, in capitulo proclamentur*: Pantin, i,256). A letter of the presidents of the Abingdon Chapter held in 1279 reiterated the desirability of reciting the hours privately on feasts of twelve lessons:

> *Hoc insuper eciam [est?] declaratum, quod cum xij leccionibus in spacio quo psalmi quindecim dici solent, matutinas de domina vel aliquid aliud utile dicant singuli singillatim.* Pantin, i,103.

But as with many of the Chapter Acts, the practices of independent monasteries, formed autonomously, often failed to tally with the general requirements. A set of instructions formulated for the novices at Christ Church, Canterbury towards 1300 refers to a single hour of the Virgin, which was to follow the second meal of the day, preceding the regular office:

> *Audito sonitu statim surgendum eundum ad ecclesiam et orandum super formas et dicendum Miserere quousque incipiatur Deus in adiutorium de beata uirgine, et quo audito statim surgendum et post uesperas de sancta Maria et post uesperas diei in suffragiis genuflectendum ut superius dictum est.*
>
> Cant.Ch.Nov.,148, 24-30.

The customary compiled for the community at Chester in the 1330s gives a rather fuller account of the daily Marian office. Here all hours of the Virgin, from Vespers to None, were recited, except during certain parts of the year. Vespers and Lauds had a single psalm antiphon and Matins consisted of the usual single nocturn, said with *lectiones consuete*. In all of the Little Hours there was a respond after the chapter, while Compline of the Virgin incorporated the votive antiphon *Salve regina*, which preceded the collect (see Chapter Five). The series of texts for the office is headed *De domina in Adventu*, although there are no further seasonal items in the manuscript. One of the problems of the Chester source is the difficulty of distinguishing between the two forms of the Marian office which it frequently refers to without clarification. It appears that both the Saturday office and the daily votive ofice were omitted from *O sapientia* (16 December) until after the Octave of the Epiphany. J.D. Brady's commentary on his edition of the Chester source suggests that the daily office was replaced by a simple memorial (*commemoratio*) during these periods, although the source does not state this explicitly. It is, however, apparent that private recitation replaced public recitation of the office at certain times of the year:

> *Ad privatas Vesperas et ad Matutinas de sancta Maria super Magnificat et super Benedictus antiphona Virgo verbo.*
>
> Chester, 281,1-2.

Vespers of the Little Office was clearly transferable, and during Lent, when the *missa principalis* followed None, it preceded Vespers of the day:

> *Diebus ferialibus per Quadragesimam dicantur omnes quatuor hore diurne ante maiorem missam. Post missam dicantur statim Vespere de domina, deinde Vespere de feria, deinde quatuor psalmi prostrales . . .*   Chester, 289,13-15.

On the Feast of the Exaltation of the Holy Cross, however, each votive hour followed the regular hour:

> *Decantatis Matutinis et horis de cruce dicantur hore de domina more solito cum orationibus de sancto spiritu.* Chester, 306,10-11.

A contemporary customary from St Augustine's Canterbury (*Lbl* C.XII) specifies that the hours of the Virgin were all to be said standing as a special gesture of reverence, *cum devocione et intenta mente* (Cant.SA.Cust. 313,20). Compline of the day, however, was said seated (313,11-12). The Marian office was presumably a daily occurrence here, omitted on appropriate occasions (although this is not stated explicitly). On feasts of the Virgin, however, (*quocienscumque de beata Dei genitrice fit in conventu obseqium*) the community was required to recite Prime and Compline of the Virgin, although it appears that the other hours might be omitted: *Quod unusquisque fratrum cotidie primam et completorium de Dei genitrice dicere debet.* On feasts of the Virgin these two offices were to be recited *secrecius ac devote* (Cant.SA.Cust., 313).

At Barking in 1404 the Little Office of the Virgin was to be omitted throughout Christmas week until after the Circumcision: *Nota quod matutine et hore beate marie sunt omittende per totam ebdomadam usque post diem circumcisionis* (Barking, i,31). From Wednesday of Holy Week, Matins of the Virgin followed Compline of the day, (Barking, i,89) while on Maundy Thursday Vespers of the Virgin followed the *Mandatum* ceremony, and was itself followed by Vespers of All Saints (i,94). Compline and Matins of the Virgin followed Compline of the day on this occasion: *Post completorium beate marie . dicat priorissa in audencia . Benediccio dei patris. Deinde dicantur matutine beate marie, et cetera sicut predictum est.* (i,96). This office, like that given in *WO* F.160 and *Ob* e.1* is equipped with a series of appropriate seasonal texts which changed at specified points during the year.

THE LITTLE OFFICE OF THE VIRGIN AT ST MARY'S, YORK

The Ordinal of St Mary's, York (copied 1398-1405) offers the fullest account of the appended office of the Virgin in an English Benedictine house. At York there was a complete *cursus* of hours, each hour of the Virgin following the corresponding regular hour. Directions for the observance of the Marian office are incorporated into the general account of the regular office on Advent Sunday. Eight missing leaves in this section of the York manuscript must have included Vespers; no information survives on either the office of the day or on Vespers of the Virgin which followed.

The account of the Little Office of the Virgin at St Mary's York reveals two interesting features. One is its adoption of a secular model, which has already been discussed; the second is the instruction that a considerable part of the office was to be spoken rather than sung. Psalms for each hour are marked *sine nota directe dicantur*, the hymn *sine nota*, and the *Nunc dimittis* at Compline appears with the verb *dicatur* rather than *cantatur*. The collect for this hour is marked *directe cantat*. The customary indicates specifically that antiphons at all hours (with the exception of the last antiphon at Compline, *Ecce completa sunt*) were to be spoken:

> *Notandum vero quod omnium antiphonarum ad vesperas, completorium, matutinas et ad omnes [horas] diei de Domina a versiculario nunciantur et in tempore suo omnes dicuntur excepta ultima antiphona ad completorium Ecce completa sunt et cetera que plenarie cantari debet.*   York.SM.Ord., i,48,34-36

A letter of the presidents accompanying the statutes of the provincial chapter passed at Northampton in 1343 suggests that spoken psalmody was not uncommon at the Marian hours and for the fifteen psalms:

> *Nec alia psalmodia voce submissa dicatur in conventu de cetero, exceptis quindecim psalmis, matutinis et horis beate Marie, ubi est consuetudo eas in choro dicendi . . . que omnia suis temporibus voce mediocri et pausacione facta in medio, prout decet, tractim et devote dicantur.*   Pantin, ii,34-35.

Compline of the Virgin followed that of the day at York. During the blessing at the regular office, the monks stood up in their stalls, uncovered their heads and reverently signed themselves with the cross. Then the community turned to the altar, and the priest (*sacerdos*) began Compline of the Virgin *mediocri voce*. The usual introductory versicles followed, and thereafter the office proceeded in accordance with the secular pattern. The two very different forms of Compline at York are presented in Table 3:9 (p.238). Three psalms only (monastic) were prescribed at the Little Office, although there was an accompanying antiphon (secular). The antiphon incipit before the psalms was begun by the *versicularius*, slowly (*lenta voce*). As at Chester, the votive office concluded with a short independent ceremony where the community remained in choir to sing the antiphon *Salve regina*, with tropes. This observance is discussed in detail in Chapter Five.

Matins and Lauds of the Marian office were said as one unit following Lauds of the day and the appropriate memorials and suffrages. The priest (*sacerdos*) officiated, and all present turned to the altar until the *Gloria Patri* of *Venite* (Psalm 94). After the usual introductory dialogue, the *versicularius* (who was exempt from singing Matins of the Virgin on ferial days, since no one was to sing *Venite* twice on ferial days) began the invitatory. As for most of the office, one melody sufficed for the entire year; the qualification *nisi quando plenarie celebratur de ea* refers to the weekly commemorative form of the office. All three psalms were sung under a single antiphon, and the *versicularius* read the three lessons and sang the solo passages in the responds which followed. The lessons remained constant throughout the year, but there were two further sets of responds which were used in alternation with the first set. If the office was said out of choir, then the first two responds of the first group and the final respond of the third group were always used. Matins concluded with *Te deum*, and then a versicle and response led into Lauds.

Lauds began with the usual *Deus in adiutorium*. Each of the five psalms had its own antiphon, and a *contraversicularius* on the opposite side of the choir began alternate antiphons. Psalms 62 and 66 were said under a single *Gloria Patri* (a convention of the secular uses). After Lauds of the Virgin, the community returned to the dormitory.

Prime of the York office followed the usual pattern, beginning with *Deus in adiutorium* after the concluding *Benedicamus Domino* of Prime of the day. Whether the office was sung in or out of choir, an extra two verses (*Memento salutis auctor* and *Maria plena gracie*) were added to the hymn, *O Christe proles*. The mutation of the Prime psalms, involving the substitution of four psalms on Sunday has already been discussed. Terce, Sext and None followed an exactly parallel pattern.

The Marian office was clearly not invariably said in choir, but on those occasions when choral observance was not suitable it seems (as at Chester and St Augustine's, Canterbury) to have been replaced by private recitation:

> *Notandum quod in nullis festis precipuis per annum dicitur servicium de Domina in choro, nec quindecim psalmi ante Matutinas, nec suffragia post Matutinas aut Vesperas, set quilibet hoc seorsum dicere tenetur per se.* York.SM.Ord, ii,183.

The evidence of the six customaries discussed above is supplemented by two sources which provide complete texts for a Little Office of the Virgin in four seasonal forms. *Ob e.1**, the Hyde Abbey Breviary of c.1300, provides no more than the texts and a few sparse rubrics, but the thirteenth-century Worcester Antiphoner, *WO* F.160, is invaluable as the sole surviving English source which provides chants for the two forms of the Marian votive office, both the Saturday observance and the daily Little Office. The characteristics of both of these offices and their relationship with one another are discussed in detail at the end of the following chapter.

*

Although the votive offices discussed here all share superficial similarities, more profound analysis reveals pronounced individual characteristics. Surviving customaries show that offices were not adopted consistently by all houses, and that the manner of their observance differed widely. Further, there are significant structural discrepancies. Only the Office of the Dead exhibits a really clear-cut structural framework, modelled on an early secular form which was presumably transferred from the rites of the Early Church. These deep roots undoubtedly account for its textual and structural stability, recalling Frere's notion of 'fixity means antiquity'.[24] Unlike any other votive office, both the structure and the psalmody of the Office of the Dead remained constant and universal, not only within English monastic books, but also across a much wider span of secular and monastic sources from both England and Europe. No serious attempt was ever made to modify its intial structure.

No other office discussed in this chapter adopts such a clearly defined secular model. Surviving votive offices certainly reveal secular influence, but their partial rather than wholesale incorporation of non-monastic features results in hybrid forms which fall somewhere between the two uses. This ambivalence is apparent even in the Office of All Saints, the only votive office besides that of the dead which was in wide circulation by the tenth century. Lauds and Vespers of All Saints use a predominantly monastic framework, but the psalms recited at Lauds follow the characteristic pattern of the ferial Lauds psalms in the secular *cursus*: 92, 99, 62 [66], 148-50. Most of the later offices, including the Little Office of the Virgin, follow this same scheme for Lauds, and indeed, it is one of the few consistent features of psalmody which remains fixed for virtually all daily votive offices. The only real diversion from the secular Lauds pattern is an occasional attempt to move Psalm 66 to its more usual monastic position at the beginning of the office, but by and large the level of concordance is high.

The discrepancy between the psalm patterns of the other votive offices seems to be an outcome of the two distinct strands which are combined in this form. Most of the later examples in Table 3:1 conform closely to the secular structure of the hours: the one-nocturn form of Matins with three psalms, the five psalms at Vespers, and the inclusion of an extra psalm and a canticle at Compline. But the choice of psalmody is much less overtly secular, and some of the offices even combine psalms from both the secular and the monastic *cursi* within a single hour. This is perhaps seen most clearly in Prime of the Office of the Virgin, where all sources adopt the invariable first psalm of secular Prime, 53, but thereafter follow divergent patterns. Most sources opt for the sequence of verses from Psalm 118 prescribed for Sunday Prime in the ferial secular *cursus* (vv. 1-32), but St Mary's, York, Durham and Canterbury all choose psalms from the monastic ferial *cursus* for Monday (1, 2, 6). The patterns of Terce, Sext and None of the votive offices are very similar. Most sources continue with the secular sequence of verses from 118, but Worcester, St Mary's, York, Pilton and a source from an unidentified monastery borrow psalms sung at the corresponding hours in the ferial monastic *cursus* from Wednesday to Saturday. Matins of the Worcester Little Office also combines secular and monastic features. It takes all twelve psalms prescribed for Matins on feasts of the Virgin in the monastic use, but arranges them as four alternate groups of three in line with the secular form of this office.

This intermingling of features from two separate uses may well result from the initial conception of the daily votive office as a private devotion, and its relatively late emergence in the tenth and eleventh centuries. It also seems that no fixed structure was ever established for the office in English Benedictine monasteries, even after its general adoption as a corporate observance. Compilation of votive offices from a diverse stock of material seems to have been accepted practice, and presumably duplication of texts, psalms and even the structure of the regular monastic office was to be avoided where practical. Indeed, borrowing of psalms from another liturgical use was not unique to the monastic votive office, for the corresponding form of the Little Office in the Uses of Sarum and Exeter transfers psalms from the monastic regular *cursus* at Terce, Sext and None. It is significant that the least variable psalms within the votive office are those at Lauds, for the *cursus* of psalms prescribed for regular Lauds in the monastic and secular uses shared several common features.

The daily votive office was also an important forum for newly-composed texts and melodies in the Middle Ages. Not only was it a comparatively recent observance, but its growing popularity as a corporate devotion within the wider framework of the liturgy led to the adoption of different seasonal formularies, necessitating a wider stock of texts and melodies. The process of compiling new offices is explored in more detail at the end of Chapter Four, with particular reference to *unica* and to the practice of borrowing texts from existing offices.

NOTES

1. Tolhurst, 113.

2. See Wieck, 39-44; De Hamel, 159.

3. Bishop, *Liturgica Historica*, 211-37.

4. Symons, 'Monastic observance', 137.

5. Tolhurst, 107-113.

6. Cross, art. 'Prayers for the Dead'; Davies, art. 'Burial'.

7. Tolhurst, 108.

8. *I-MZcap* c.12.75 (Hesbert.1, 413-5).

9. Tolhurst, 206.

10. Davies, art. 'Burial'.

11. Tolhurst, 114-119.

12. Tolhurst, 119.

13. Discussed in Winterbottom 'Three Lives', 198-99; Clayton, 84.

14. Ker, *Catalogue of Manuscripts containing Anglo-Saxon*, No.202.

15. Biddle, 134-6.

16. Wilmart, 'Prières Médiévales pour l'adoration de la croix', 23.

17. McKinnon, 'The Late Medieval Psalter', 133.

18. McKinnon, *ibid.*, 138.

19. Dewick, *Facsimiles of Horae de Beata Maria Virgine* (cited as 'Dewick' in bibliog.).

20. Ker, *Catalogue of Manuscripts containing Anglo Saxon*, Nos. 186, 249.

21. Tolhurst, 121.

22. Tolhurst, 121.

23. Bishop, *Liturgica Historica*, 227.

24. Frere, introduction to *Sar. Grad.*, x.

Chapter Four

THE COMMEMORATIVE OFFICE

From the twelfth century a new and substantial votive form begins to feature prominently in English Benedictine books; an observance which will be referred to here as the commemorative office, following the majority of liturgical manuscripts which term the form *commemoratio*. As such it is not to be confused with a much smaller-scale observance, here distinguished by the term memorial, which may also appear in sources of comparable date under the title *commemoratio* or *memoria*. These brief memorials (discussed in Chapter Five) consist of no more than antiphon, versicle and collect, and normally function as appendages to Lauds and Vespers.

The history of the commemorative office, whether in secular or monastic foundations, is less well documented than many of the other votive forms. Rather surprisingly, Tolhurst's companion volume to his edition of the Hyde Abbey Breviary contains little information on the commemorative office: Tolhurst simply remarks on its structural similarity to the regular office and provides a summary list of the commemorative offices observed in ten different monasteries with the weekdays to which they were assigned.[1] This list is valuable, but by no means complete; it also creates problems by referring only to the individual houses where the commemorative offices were observed, rather than to the mansucripts in which they occur. A more complete list of surviving offices is presented as Table 4:1 (p.239). An earlier brief examination of commemorative offices was made by Christopher Wordsworth in 1894, but his published survey deals almost exclusively with the secular liturgies, and its usefulness is limited by a failure to provide complete liturgical texts. Harrison also provides a very cursory reference to the saints represented in weekly commemorative offices at Salisbury, Exeter, Wells, Hereford and Lichfield, but there is no reference to their structure and content.[2]

Despite the apparent lack of scholarly interest in the commemorative office, the observance nevertheless held a position of considerable prominence among the other votive forms, for it had an independent liturgical status of its own. Some customaries indicate that irrespective of its structure, it was of equivalent rank to a twelve-lesson feast, although in most instances after *c*.1200, Matins of the commemorative office was not constructed on this 'festal' scale, and normally contained only three lessons (two nocturns). For most of the liturgical year commemorative offices took precedence over the prescribed office of the day (except on certain feasts and vigils) and virtually all surviving sources indicate that the commemorative office was to be celebrated on a weekly basis, usually on a specified day of the week. Whereas earlier surviving votive offices of the pre-Conquest period (with the notable exception of the two offices in *Ccc* 391, the Worcester Portiforium) seem to be private devotions, the later commemorative office was neither private nor a simple appendage to the prescribed ferial liturgy, but rather a replacement observance celebrated in the same manner as other feasts.

Most commemorative offices, and particularly the earliest extant examples, were addressed to the Virgin Mary and intended for celebration on Saturday, thus complementing the custom instituted by Alcuin (*c*.735-804) of celebrating a Lady Mass on this day (see pp.42-43). The Saturday office of the Virgin which emerged in the twelfth century had been adopted more or less universally by the Benedictines in England by the mid-thirteenth century. There is one early instance of a Friday office of the Holy Cross (given with a Saturday office of the Virgin in the Worcester Portiforium), but the form does not seem to have been generally revived after the liturgical revisions of the Norman Conquest. From the thirteenth century onwards a commemorative office of St Benedict was more widely established in several monasteries, but it seems never to have attained the universal popularity of the Marian office. This is also true of commemorative offices celebrated in honour of the relics of a house or of its patron, which feature in a number of books of comparable date. No office was allocated a specific day with the same consistency as that of the Marian office, where the invariable choice of Saturday was sanctioned by a long tradition of devotion to the Virgin on that day.[3] Nevertheless, all commemorative offices, whatever their intention, were likely to be transferred to another vacant weekday if displaced by a feast. The rules for transference vary from source to source and are sometimes complex; on occasion the offices of Matins and Vespers were even divided between a commemorative and a festal observance, so that the first part of the hour had a quite different emphasis from the second.

The majority of commemorative offices followed the structure of the regular monastic hours as set out in St Benedict's Rule: nevertheless, there were certain variations within this scheme which are reflected in the commemorative observance, so that there was no fixed model. Commemorative offices compiled after *c*.1200 for the most part demonstrate a substantial reduction in textual content, seen most prominently in Matins. The variability in the form and content of the Matins offices is important, for the structural permutations of this hour are the most immediately useful yardstick for categorization of any complete office, whatever its context. The three variant forms of Matins given in *RB* are set out in Table 1:1, with an indication of their respective function. Each of these three forms was conditioned not only by the status of a particular feast (major celebrations inevitably implied greater elaboration at all of the hours) but also by practical matters. The shortest form of Matins given in *RB* was constructed on the basis that the nights were of considerable brevity during the summer months: dawn broke very early, and Lauds was required to begin at this point. For the longer nights in winter a more extensive form of Matins, modelled on the Sunday office, was used, and it is to this form that the majority of the thirteenth-century commemorative offices approximate. It has already been observed that Matins of the daily appended office followed none of the three conventional Benedictine models and used a unique short one-nocturn form of Matins with only three psalms and three lessons. This category may also have formed the basis for Matins of the commemorative offices in the Worcester Portiforium: these are discussed in more detail below.

In structural terms then, the majority of commemorative offices fall into two broad categories readily identifiable from the organization of Matins. The earlier forms of the office (compiled during the twelfth century) tend to use the festal form of Matins with the full three nocturns and twelve lessons. During the thirteenth century in most English monasteries, this expansive structure was largely superseded by the more condensed two-nocturn format, which had only three lessons but a full complement of twelve psalms arranged in the following pattern:

First Nocturn	6 psalms (usually with a single antiphon)
	3 lessons
	3 responds
Second Nocturn	6 psalms (usually with a single antiphon)
	chapter
	versicle

Both categories seem to have retained their formal (although not necessarily textual) stability throughout the year, rather than being subject to the usual seasonal alteration of Matins which affected the main cycle of the office. The other hours of the commemorative office have fewer readily distinguishing features. Here, comparison can most nearly be made between the number of antiphons attached to the groups of psalms recited at Lauds and Vespers. Where a commemorative office has three-nocturn Matins, it is usual to find that all of the psalms at Lauds and Vespers have individual antiphons, while two-nocturn Matins normally implies that the whole group of psalms at Lauds and Vespers is sung under a single antiphon. Specific offices discussed below explore this distinction in more detail.

THE COMMEMORATIVE OFFICES IN
THE WORCESTER PORTIFORIUM (*CCC* 391)

The earliest surviving commemorative offices of English compilation occur in *Ccc* 391, the Worcester Portiforium of *c*.1065. Two votive offices are given: *De sancta cruce*, for celebration on Fridays, and *Sancta Maria*, celebrated on Saturdays (Worc.Port., ii,700). The content and construction of these observances is summarized in Table 4:2 (p.242), also showing concordances with the later Worcester Antiphoner, *WO* F.160. It has already been established that the Office of the Virgin went on to gain widespread popularity after the Conquest, but only one recurrence of the Office of the Cross has been located in an English source, and this is of surprisingly late date: *Ob* g.12, a Book of Hours copied in 1521 for Pilton, a cell of Malmesbury Abbey.

Both of the Worcester offices are singularly unelaborate in terms of content, and both are constructed identically, comprising first Vespers, Matins, Lauds, Prime, Terce, Sext and None. But in many respects the formal conception of both offices is something of an enigma. Categorization from a structural analysis of Matins is problematic, since not all of the required texts are supplied for either office. It is unclear whether Matins had only one nocturn, or whether the antiphon, chapter and respond of a second nocturn have simply been omitted: this is not impossible, since texts for all of the other hours of these two offices are limited to antiphons alone. The absence of the Matins antiphons, however, also prevents analysis of the psalmodic content of the office; indeed it seems probable that there was just one antiphon to cover the complete psalmodic group at Matins, whether this consisted of three psalms (as in some of the earliest personal Marian offices, *Lbl* A.III among them) or six psalms, as in all of the later examples of the commemorative office. This ambiguous relationship of antiphons and psalms is, however, less of an issue in Lauds and Vespers of the commemorative offices in *Ccc* 391, where the psalms were almost certainly sung under a single antiphon. The apparent simplicity of both of the pioneering offices in the Portiforium is thus matched neither by the private (or appended) English observances of comparable date and intention, nor indeed by the earliest of the post-Conquest forms of the commemorative office which are, without exception, far more extensive forms.

Comparatively few of the texts given for both of the commemorative offices in the Portiforium are borrowed from elsewhere in the manuscript, as the column of concordances in Table 4:2 shows. The Friday Office of the Holy Cross comprises eight antiphons, of which only three appear in the sanctorale of *Ccc* 391 (two for the Exaltation and one for the Invention of the Holy Cross). Of the three responds, none are borrowed, and this total absence of concordance also applies to the three lessons. In the Saturday Office of the Virgin, four of the seven antiphons are borrowed, while one is doubled (Lauds and None share the psalm antiphon). The lessons and responds of Matins are all without concordance. On the basis of this observation, it therefore appears that only about a quarter of either office is borrowed from elsewhere. Comparison with the slightly earlier private offices of the Cross and the Virgin in similarly dated non-liturgical manuscripts (such as *Lbl* D.XXVI-II, *Lbl* 2.B.V and *Lbl* A.III) also reveals remarkably few concordant texts.

At first glance, this paucity of textual concordance appears significant, but the likelihood that the non-concordant items were newly composed especially for the votive offices is less certain than it might appear. The complexity arises from the fact that *Ccc* 391 is a portiforium or collectar rather than a complete breviary, and thus (for the most part) does not contain material for the night office of Matins. Commemorative offices—and particularly Marian commemorative offices—of a later date (examined in a subsequent section of this chapter) demonstrate that a large proportion of votive material was often drawn from Matins of related feasts, and there is no reason why this principle should not have been in operation when the tenth-century Worcester offices were compiled. The apparent possibilty of new composition is therefore weakened by the limited content of the manuscript.

It is worth noting that almost a century and a half later, a number of the texts of *Ccc* 391 found their way into the Worcester source, *WO* F.160, but mostly in a festal rather than a votive context. *WO* F.160 makes no reference to a commemorative office of the Cross, although both forms of the Marian office (the Saturday commemoration and the appended Little Office) are represented in the source (see below).

OTHER EARLY COMMEMORATIVE OFFICES

In spite of their prominent position in the pre-Norman votive repertory in England, the two commemorative offices copied into the Worcester Portiforium cannot be viewed with certainty as an English innovation. A passage in the Customary of the Benedictine monastery of Einsiedeln, copied *c.*970, testifies to a comparable practice on the Continent:

> *Per totam Quinquagesimam paschalem infra ebdomadam fiant tres lectiones similiter. Sexta quoque feria et septima, si sanctorum natalitia non affuerint, de sancta cruce et sancta Maria tres eodem modo compleantur, excepto quod antiphonae in Matutinis et ymni*

> *non mutabuntur. Hoc quoque de sancta cruce et sancta Maria non*
> *dimittatur vsque in Aduentum Domini.*   Einsiedeln, 239, 5-9.

The intentions and weekdays specified for the two offices referred to here were thus identical to those established at Worcester almost a century later. The Einsiedeln Customary however, is more precise as to context: both offices were apparently to be omitted during Advent, and also when a saint's day took precedence. Here, as at Worcester, it is indicated that Matins had no more than three lessons, although the Einsiedeln source states explicitly that both the antiphons and hymns at Matins (if not for all of the hours) remained constant throughout the year. No other extant customary of comparable date of European or English provenance makes any reference to a commemorative office. This group, of course, includes the national English customary *RC* (also copied *c*.970), although there is a requirement for the celebration of a Mass of the Holy Cross on Friday and of the Virgin on Saturday in that source.

The presence of the weekly commemorative offices in the Worcester *Portiforium* establishes clearly that the phenomenon of liturgical replacement was accepted and practised before the Norman Conquest in England, and indeed a century earlier in certain parts of Europe. While there is no further conclusive evidence in any other extant English source pre-dating the Conquest which confirms the adoption of such offices, it is possible that the rather vague manner in which the content of the Portiforium commemorations is expressed enabled some of the existing 'private' Little Offices to be drafted into service at a more formal liturgical level in some of the other Benedictine houses.

THE POST-CONQUEST COMMEMORATIVE OFFICE
AT ST ALBANS AND WINCHCOMBE

After the Conquest, it seems likely that the commemorative office, like the Little Office, was submerged in the general liturgical reorganization effected by the Normans. Consequently, after its fleeting appearance in *Ccc* 391, the Saturday Office of the Virgin vanishes from the manuscripts until the early twelfth century, when it reappears in connection with two sources associated with St Albans. One of these is the *Gesta Abbatum*, a retrospective account of the deeds of the abbots of the house initially compiled by the historiographer Matthew Paris in the first half of the thirteenth century, but more familiar today in a later and more extensive revision of Paris's original by Thomas Walsingham.[4] This account is of considerable value since it contains several references to the Saturday commemorative office (not previously noted by scholars), the first of which specifically attributes its introduction to the abbot Geoffrey Gorron, a Norman who held office at St Albans between 1119 and 1146:

> . . . *et in refectorio inveniret caritatem vini, vel medi, omni Sabbato, vel una feriarum pro Sabbato, quando fit Commemoratio de Sancta Maria, quam idem Abbas Gaufridus statuit fieri in albis.*
>
> St Albans, i,76.

This passage suggests that the commemorative office carried considerable status in the St Albans liturgical hierarchy: there is particular reference to an accompanying allowance of wine or mead, and the office was to be celebrated in albs. Designation of a feast as *in albis* denoted a degree of ceremonial splendour, with the convent vesting in albs at least for High Mass; such feasts were second in rank only to the ten or so 'principal' feasts of a house (such as Christmas and Easter), and those celebrated with the convent vested in copes, *in capis*.[5] The calendar of the twelfth-century St Albans breviary *Lbl* 2.A.X (see below) indicates that fourteen feasts at St Albans fell into the category *in albis* at about this date, among them the Feast of Relics, the Invention and Exaltation of the Holy Cross, and the Octave of the Assumption.

Saturday was again the desired day for Gorron's new observance, with the usual possibility of transference if Saturday was already occupied. The commemorative office was by no means Gorron's sole innovation if Paris's account is correct, for he seems to have been at the forefront of more general liturgical remodelling at St Albans. The *Gesta* reports that he instituted the feast of the Conception of the Virgin, which was to be celebrated in copes (although this possibly took some while to filter through into liturgical manuscripts) and raised the status of several existing feasts: the Ascension became a major feast, while St Matthew, St John before the Latin Gate, St Giles and St Catherine were all celebrated *in capis*.[6]

Further references to the Saturday office appear in the accounts of three later abbots of St Albans in *Gesta Abbatum*: Radulf, seventeenth successor to the title (1146-51), John, twenty-first abbot (1195-1214) and William, his successor (1214-35). During the time of Radulf, the Saturday office was celebrated in albs as before, but with an accompanying procession to the Lady altar:

> *Hic etiam processionem in Commemoratione Beatae Mariae, quae singulis hebdomadibus in albis celebratur, ad altare ejusdem Virginis fieri statuit.*
>
> St Albans, i,107.

A passage from the abbacy of John tells of a miraculous occurrence during the singing of Matins, when John heard the twelve lessons and responds of the Virgin sung by unknown voices:

Legebantur autem Duodecim eadem nocte de Beata Virgine
lectiones, quas corde tenus, sine candela, bajuli transcurre
consueverunt, cum suis, quae sequuntur, responsoriis, tenui tamen
lumine cruciboli per vitrum diapharum translucente.

St Albans, i,231.

Not only does this testify to the presence of a three-nocturn commemorative
office at St Albans around 1200, but it also indicates that the office was
sung by heart, without candles.

Nevertheless, the later account (from William's abbacy) suggests that
the observance was still relatively uncommon in England even in the
thirteenth century:

. . . licet in nostra ecclesia, quod non fit in aliis, qualibet
septimana, die Sabbati, nisi obstet causa rationabilis, fiat
Commemoratio de Beata Virgine, totaliter per diem et noctem in
albis solemniter . . .   St Albans, i,284-5.

There are also references from William's abbacy to the procession
which accompanied the Saturday office. William is said to have presented
an image of the Virgin to the church at St Albans, carved by Walter of
Colchester and referred to as the Mariola. A candle burned before it on all
principal feasts, *et in processione quae fit in commemoratione ejusdem* (St
Albans, i,286). The procession is also mentioned in a passage stating that
a daily service of All Saints was to be said in choir without interruption
from processions, excepting that attached to the Saturday office (St Albans,
i,293).

These documented accounts of the adoption of the Saturday observance
are satisfactorily supported by the physical presence of a Marian
commemorative office in an extant St Albans breviary of the
twelfth-century, *Lbl* 2.A.X. Extensive analysis of the post-Conquest library
of St Albans by Rodney Thomson has established that a number of liturgical
books of considerable importance survive from St Albans from this period;
he dates *Lbl* 2.A.X at *c.*1140-50, thus placing its compilation during the
reign of Geoffrey Gorron's successor Ralph Gubuin.[7] (Gubuin was the first
English abbot of St Albans after the Conquest and had earlier been in charge
of the scriptorium.)

Lbl 2.A.X is a small breviary which was presumably compiled for use
in choir. Copied into its small sanctorale section on f.135 is an office
headed *In commemoratione sancte Marie*, consisting of first Vespers,
Matins, Lauds and second Vespers, the latter with an alternative series of
psalms which in turn is followed by an alternative set of readings for the
third nocturn of Matins (see Table 4:3, p.244).[8] In spite of the likely
function of this office as a replacement for use on Saturday, its position in

the manuscript is curious. It is immediately preceded by the Exaltation of the Holy Cross and the Feast of Cornelius and Cyprian (both on 14 September) and followed by Michaelmas (29 September). The arrangement of the manuscript is further complicated by the fact that in addition to the small sanctorale section (ff.126-145), four Marian feasts (the Purification, Annunciation, Assumption and Nativity of the Virgin, although not the Conception) occupy a separate part of the manuscript between ff.111v and 121v. All four feasts begin at the third nocturn of Matins, and provide all of the hours up to second Vespers; the appropriate texts for the four sets of first Vespers are given as a group at the end of the section on f.121v. Investigation of the source by K.D. Hartzell prompted him to suggest that the commemorative office might be connected with the Octave of the Nativity of the Virgin which fell on 15 September; this octave is included in the calendar of the manuscript where it is marked as a twelve-lesson feast *in albis*. But one would expect proper texts for this occasion to be grouped with the other Marian items on ff.111v-121v, and the possibility that the office on f.135 was intended exclusively—indeed, if at all—for this day is very slight.[9] The independence of the Marian commemorative office from the series of feasts listed above is likely on two counts. First the use of the conventional term *commemoratio* as a title, and second, the rubric attached to the series of replacement psalms supplied for second Vespers:

> *Si n[on] ev[en]erit Sabb[ato] dicantur hi Ps[almi] Dixit d[ominus].*
> *P. Letat[us] sum. P. Nisi d[ominus] edif[f]icaverit]. P. Memento*
> *d[omi]ne. et cet[er]a de s[an]c[t]a Maria.*

If not entirely direct in its wording, this rubric unequivocally refers to the transference of the commemorative office to another weekday if Saturday is impracticable. In this case the usual selection of Vespers psalms (the monastic set used on all Saturdays: see Table 1:2) had to be altered, and the standard series of 'Marian' psalms common to second Vespers of the Assumption, Nativity and Annunciation (although not the Purification) was substituted.

The texts of the commemorative office in *Lbl* 2.A.X are given in Table 4:3. The presence of two sets of Vespers together with Matins and Lauds has already been remarked, but all of the Little Hours are absent, a feature which is also common to most of the offices given in the sanctorale of the manuscript. Provision of two sets of Vespers for commemorative offices seems to have been an early practice; comparable offices compiled after *c*.1200 are almost invariably supplied with texts for first Vespers alone. It is equally significant that second Vespers of the commemorative office in *Lbl* 2.A.X is incomplete; four psalms with four antiphons are given (thus in fact receiving more weight than the single antiphon allotted to the four psalms at first Vespers of this office), but from the chapter onwards, proper texts from first Vespers of the following day presumably took precedence. This phenomenon of sharing an office between two contingent observances was by no means uncommon, and is discussed in more detail in relation to the later Chester source on p.106.

Matins of the commemorative office in *Lbl* 2.A.X follows the three-nocturn festal structure described in *RB*. All twelve psalms have individual antiphons, and most items are given in their complete form rather than as incipits. In the majority of cases the texts given in the first and second nocturns of Matins have no concordance elsewhere in the manuscript, although this is less true for the final nocturn where all four responds (IX-XII) are duplicated, three from the Assumption, the other from the Annunciation. But in spite of the paucity of concordant texts, it seems unlikely that large portions of this office were newly composed. The issue is complicated, however (rather as in the tenth-century Worcester MS *Ccc* 391, discussed above) by the provision of incomplete offices elsewhere in the breviary. The most likely candidates which could provide appropriate material for the commemorative office are quite clearly the four Marian feasts on ff.111v-121v, but all four begin only at the third nocturn of Matins, and consequently give no indication of the antiphons and responds intended for the first part of the office. Quite why this omission occurred is not clear. Comparison with the same four feasts in a wide range of books indicates that it is highly unlikely that the first two nocturns of the four offices in *Lbl* 2.A.X were simply common, for in all cases quite separate groups of texts are provided for each feast, often with a particular textual significance for that day.

The isolated presence of nocturns one and two in the St Albans commemorative office could therefore not have doubled for all four of the deprived feasts in the same manuscript. But examination of the antiphons provided for the Saturday office reveals an exact parallel with the Assumption series used in many other Benedictine manuscripts, most immediately recognizable from the emphasis on texts drawn from *The Song of Songs*. Certainly the evidence of many of the later Marian offices, whether for use as Saturday commemorations or as daily appendages, demonstrates that the Assumption was a major source for textual borrowing. The practicality of compiling a new office quickly by lifting material directly from another source is plain. Borrowing appears to outweigh new composition in most of the manuscripts discussed below, and it seems very likely that much of the commemorative office in *Lbl* 2.A.X was borrowed. The very fact that the St Albans office is the earliest surviving instance of the twelve-lesson Saturday observance, and the references in *Gesta Abbatum* to its newness and unfamiliarity elsewhere in England, perhaps suggest that Geoffrey Gorron was indeed the first of a long line of compilers of the votive office. And even if his finished product was not adopted in its entirety as a fixed model by other houses, the general principle of constructing material for new observances—and particularly votive observances—was clearly adopted elsewhere.

Bearing in mind the limitations of *Lbl* 2.A.X, Table 4:3 aims to show the proportion of borrowed material in the St Albans commemorative office. One may assume that items appearing as incipits will be borrowed from elsewhere, although the 'parent-text' may not always be located in the same source (as is the case with the respond at first Vespers, *Speciosa facta*). A few texts are simply common: this almost invariably occurs with psalms, hymns and versicles. The collect *Concede nos*, however, apparently intended for use at all hours of the commemorative office, may well have been unique to this observance since no other function is suggested for it in the collectar section of the manuscript. Borrowing of other items is dominated by the Marian feasts. Only one item, the respond *Felix nanque*, is taken from a less closely related source: the Feast of All Saints. Nothing is borrowed from the Common of Virgins, although textual duplication between votive offices and the Common is relatively frequent in some of the later sources. The prominence of Assumption borrowing has already been established, and several texts are taken from the Annunciation (as in other instances of the commemorative office). A survey of the entire repertory of commemorative and appended Marian offices in extant English Benedictine sources suggests that these two feasts were most frequently used as source-material by compilers. In *Lbl* 2.A.X, most of the Annunciation elements are transferred in piecemeal fashion, and with the likely exception of the twelve psalm antiphons at Matins, the same is true of the borrowed Assumption texts.

Relatively large-scale borrowing (outside the first two nocturns of Matins) is seen most clearly in the third nocturn of the office in *Lbl* 2.A.X: responds IX-XI are directly transferred from identically placed Assumption responds. The final Assumption respond, *Gaude Maria virgo V. Gabrielem archangelum* is not transferred; instead respond XI from the Annunciation, *Styrps iesse V. Virgo dei genitrix* (also found elsewhere, as Table 4:3 shows) is taken over in the commemorative office. The series of Lauds antiphons also reveals a straightforward method of compilation: four of the five are lifted from Lauds of the Annunciation (although the ordering is shuffled), but no concordance has been found in this manuscript for the second antiphon, *Beata mater et innupta*. The short respond and the versicle from this office are, less conventionally, extracted from the Nativity of the Virgin, for with the exception of the Matins Respond VII (which the Nativity probably borrowed from Matins of one of the other Marian feasts), there are no other examples of this office serving as a single source for texts in the commemoration.

The main areas of original composition in this office appear to focus on the antiphons. The second psalm antiphon for Lauds is a *unicum*, as are those for the *Benedictus* and *Magnificat* of first Vespers. The latter is particularly interesting. The commemorative office simply supplies the incipit *Ave regina celorum*, but the full text appears in isolation, in the principal hand of the manuscript, on f.62, headed *In veneratione sancte Marie ad vesperas*. Although this text was commonly used independently as a votive antiphon after Vespers or Compline from the second half of the thirteenth century, there is no evidence that this particular paraliturgical devotion had achieved recognition in any of the Benedictine houses as early as the mid-twelfth century, and it is most likely that the *Ave regina* in *Lbl* 2.A.X was intended for use either as an alternative *Magnificat* antiphon at one of the Marian feasts or as a processional antiphon used after Vespers. There is some evidence for the processional usage of *Ave regina* in a number of Benedictine manuscripts, and there may well be a link between this text and the procession accompanying the Saturday office mentioned in *Gesta Abbatum*, which was allegedly introduced during the time of Abbot Radulf (1214-35). But whatever alternative function the antiphon was intended for, its presence in the commemorative office is apparently clear evidence that this new observance not only utilized familiar material from well-established feasts, but also much more recent compositions.

Certainly there was a new vogue for creating Marian texts and music once the cult of the Virgin had achieved secure status in England in the twelfth century. The sudden influx of these pieces into the liturgy must have been regulated by the requirements of the new Marian observances which were gradually being accepted as standard elements of monastic ritual. The commemorative office is an obvious candidate for new texts, as is the slightly later votive antiphon, for while some monasteries were clearly content to borrow large numbers of texts from elsewhere to meet demands, others produced quantities of new texts, which have no parallel elsewhere. This penchant for original composition is perhaps most clearly seen in the Marian observances in the Worcester Antiphoner (*WO* F.160), discussed below.

THE COMMEMORATIVE OFFICE
IN THE WINCHCOMBE BREVIARY (*F-VAL* 116)

Only one manuscript with a comparable office of similar date to that in *Lbl* 2.A.X survives: a mid-twelfth century breviary from the abbey of Winchcombe. The Winchcombe breviary, *F-VAL* 116, is with *Lbl* 2.A.X one of the two earliest extant English breviaries. J.B.L. Tolhurst used it as a major source of comparison with the thirteenth-century Hyde Abbey Breviary, and evidently regarded it as of considerably more importance than the St Albans book.[10]

F-VAL 116 also contains a commemorative office of the Virgin of comparable structure to that in *Lbl* 2.A.X, but sadly the observance is incomplete, consisting only of Matins and part of Lauds (Table 4:4, p.247). The three-nocturn form of Matins is identical to that of the St Albans office, although there is no indication of the psalms used in the first nocturn, or of the lessons ix-xii in the final nocturn. Several of the texts are borrowed, and in some cases lifted directly in pairs or groups from the sanctorale. All six of the antiphons in the first nocturn of Matins and the first two (A7-8) of the second nocturn duplicate both the identically placed texts for the Feast of the Assumption in this manuscript, and the equivalent antiphons in the commemorative office in *Lbl* 2.A.X. The five Lauds antiphons of the Winchcombe office are of directly parallel extraction from Lauds of the Assumption. Elsewhere the borrowing is less schematic, but again the Assumption is clearly the major source of textual derivation. Seven of the twelve Matins responds in the commemorative office (III, IV, V-VIII and XI) are taken from this feast, although in a re-ordered form (responds VII, VIII, VI, IV, II, III, X are the Assumption correspondences). One further respond (II) comes from the Purification, while the Lauds respond is also derived from this feast, although it is doubled by the Annunciation in addition. The Matins hymn is again common. There are no textual correspondences for the lessons.

The newly composed 'sung' items of the Winchcombe commemorative office, as in *Lbl* 2.A.X, are thus primarily concentrated in the antiphon repertory. Antiphons 9-12 in the second nocturn are all given in complete form rather than as incipits, and they are not duplicated by the Marian feasts. The one possible exception, *Ortus conclusus amica mea*, appears as an incipit for the Nativity of the Virgin, where it is referred to simply by the words *Ortus conclusus*, but there is no certainty that the Nativity incipit actually refers to the commemoration antiphon rather than that used during the Octave of the Assumption, *Ortus conclusus es dei genetrix*. In either case its incompleteness implies that it was borrowed from one or other office. Two of the responds (IX and XII) and the canticle antiphon of the final nocturn are also unique to the commemorative office. About a quarter of Matins therefore consists of newly composed texts, while all of Lauds is borrowed from the sanctorale. As in *Lbl* 2.A.X the insertion of these new items seems to be random, and there is no attempt in the manuscript to signify the source of borrowed material.

The component items of Matins and Lauds of the commemorative offices in *F-VAL* 116 and *Lbl* 2.A.X are thus comparable but not identical. The clearest instance of direct concordance is the parallel in both offices between all six antiphons of the first nocturn and the first two antiphons of the second nocturn: furthermore, in *F-VAL* 116 these eight texts are identical to the first eight antiphons of Assumption Matins. Four of the twelve responds in the two commemorative offices also correspond, but not in directly comparable positions.

SURVIVAL OF THE THREE-NOCTURN COMMEMORATIVE
OFFICE AFTER 1200

The related three-nocturn commemorative offices of *Lbl* 2.A.X and *F-VAL* 116, both apparently compiled in the twelfth century, have few direct structural parallels among the later sources. But in many respects our understanding of the dissemination of the commemorative office for at least a century after the Conquest is hampered by a lack of material, and it is not entirely clear to what extent the limited quantity of surviving evidence is representative of mainstream tendencies. This issue is less critical after *c.*1250, for thirteenth- and fourteenth-century manuscripts survive in greater abundance, and comparison of particular observances at several of the larger monasteries is made possible by the range of material.

Examination of the commemorative office in later sources suggests that in most cases the observance underwent an important structural mutation. The majority of available sources testifies to the substitution of a two-nocturn form of Matins for the three-nocturn form discussed above, and both Lauds and Vespers also tend to adopt a reduced format, opting for single rather than multiple antiphons for their respective groups of psalms. This more conventional scaled-down office will be examined in due course, but it is equally interesting to consider the survival of the earlier and structurally more substantial three-nocturn commemorative office.

Evidence for the survival of this retrospective form has been traced to eight sources compiled later than the St Albans and Winchcombe breviaries: a miscellaneous manuscript from Reading Abbey written between 1250 and 1300 (*Owc* 213), the Chester Customary of *c.*1330-40 (*D-Bs* 194), the Barking Ordinal of 1404 (*Ouc* 169), a breviary copied for Battle shortly after 1500 (*Ctc* 0.7.31) and a collection of miscellaneous hours from Pilton, cell to Malmesbury Abbey, with a colophon dated 1521 (*Ob* g.12). Two extant printed breviaries, produced in the first half of the sixteenth century for the monasteries of St Albans (*Lbl* C.110.a.27) and Abingdon (*Cec* S1.4.60) also contain the observance. Most of these sources are of relatively late date, but there is an additional earlier reference to a three-nocturn office in *Ob* 435, a customary compiled for the community at Eynsham some time after *c.*1230. This account provides little information beyond the fact that the observance incorporated twelve lessons:

> *Si tercia die festivitas duodecim leccionum communis historiae,*
> *quae in albis vel cappis non celebretur, evenerit vel dei genitricis*
> *commemoratio duodecim leccionum celebretur, non ideo dimittetur*
> *quin regulariter licencia minuendi petatur.*
>
> Eynsham, 106,17-20

THE COMMEMORATIVE OFFICE AT ST WERBURGH, CHESTER

The Chester Customary has already been cited for its reference to the Little Office of the Virgin; it also contains evidence of a Saturday commemorative office, daily recitation of the votive antiphon *Salve regina* during Compline of the Virgin, a Saturday procession to the Lady altar, and memorials of the Virgin after Lauds and Vespers.

Two cursory passages deal with the Saturday commemorative office of the Virgin. The first lists incipits of some of the texts used for this office in Advent (given below), while the second gives general directions for the regulation of the observance at all times of the year (Chester, 274,8-16; 287,9-16). The Chester office clearly incorporated twelve lessons: *fiat sinaxis de sancta Maria in duodecim lectionibus et responsoriis* (274,11). The second passage indicates that the office was celebrated on all Saturdays throughout the year, except from *O sapientia* (16 December) to the Circumcision, from Ash Wednesday to the Octave of Easter, and during the Octave of Pentecost:

> *Singulis septimanis anni fiat sinaxis de sancta Maria exceptis istis temporibus, scilicet a die quo incipitur O sapientia usque post Circumcisionem et a Capite Ieiunii usque post octabas Pasche et octabas Pentecostes.*   Chester, 287,9-12

This passage goes on to specify three occasions when the office was transferred from Saturday to some other vacant day. Displacement of the observance resulted from the occurrence on Saturday of a twelve-lesson feast, Ember Day or Vigil:

> *Si autem sabbatum occupetur per festum duodecim lectionum aut Quatuor Temporum aut per vigiliam quo minus possit de domina celebrari, celebretur de ea alio die magis vacante.*
> Chester, 287,12-15

The rules of precedence expressed here are typical of many sources which contain commemorative offices, but Chester makes exceptions to these general guidelines in a few cases. If the Vigil of the Nativity of the Virgin (7 September) fell on Saturday, the customary indicates that although the feast was not to be transferred, the usual Saturday commemorative office was to be used, with psalm antiphons provided from the Vigil of the Assumption (Chester, 305,25-306,3). The same procedure was followed at Matins and Vespers of the Vigil of the Assumption itself (14 August), when the texts for the Saturday office were used, but with a different *Magnificat* antiphon and antiphons for the Little Hours borrowed from the octave of the Assumption (Chester, marginal note in a later hand following 304,7).

The customary is also particularly specific in indicating that certain individual hours were shared between two feasts or observances when concurrence of two observances was a factor. The rubric for the feast of St Hippolytus (13 August) specifies that if that feast fell on a Saturday, the first eight lessons of Matins were to be of the Virgin (*de domina*), and the last four of Hippolytus.

> *Si festum Ipoliti sabbato evenerit, sint octo lectiones de domina,*
> *quatuor de Ipolito . . .*   Chester, 303,15-16.

Matins was also split in the same fashion on the Saturday following the feast of the Ascension, with the Virgin taking the first two nocturns (Chester, 297,14-17); the same procedure may also have applied on the Octave of St Stephen (283,14-15) and the Feast of St Agnes *secundo* on 28 January (286,20-21). This division of an office between two observances also occurred from time to time at first Vespers; it is by no means uncommon to find that the proper texts provided for first Vespers begin only at the chapter, omitting the psalm antiphon which was either taken from the common according to the day of the week, or else from second Vespers of a feast which fell on the previous day.[11] Traces of this practice may often be seen in commemorative offices which incorporate texts only for the second half of first Vespers, and will be discussed in more detail below. The Chester source implies that second Vespers of the commemorative office was optional: *si debeat habere secundas Vesperas* (274,13-14); presumably its omission or inclusion was dependent on the status of the Sunday or feast occupying the following day.

The previous examples demonstrate the precedence of the Saturday commemoration over contingent feasts, but more often the reverse actually applied in most houses, and the commemorative office was moved to some other free day in the week, while the feast was celebrated in the normal manner on the Saturday. Sometimes a memorial of the Virgin was made on this day, and if the feast of St Nicholas fell on a Saturday, the standard set of psalms almost invariably used for Marian feasts (109, 121, 126, 131) was said at first Vespers (Chester, 275,1-4).

The Chester source distinguishes the Saturday office from the daily Little Office of the Virgin by varied terminology. The daily appended office is described as *hore de domina* (298,6 and 306,11) *de domina* (275,24) or *de sancta maria* (275,16). The Saturday commemorative office is also referred to in several ways: sometimes the conventional *commemoratio* (306,2), once as *servitium de domina* (306,1) and three times as *sinaxis de sancta Maria* (274,11; 287,10, and a marginal note following 304,7). This seems to be the only surviving instance of the term *sinaxis* for a commemorative office.[12] Quite possibly the varied terminology is employed to distinguish the observance both from the daily votive office and from the small-scale memorial, which appears in this manuscript with the qualification *commemoratio* (274,1 and 4; 281,7-8; 292,6-12; 302,8).

One of the problems of the Chester source is that it gives very few details of the proper items making up the Saturday office, and this makes comparative analysis difficult. No texts whatsoever are supplied for Matins, although it is clear that it had the full quota of twelve lessons and responds. Somewhat ambiguous notes referring to the celebration of the Vigils of the Assumption and the Nativity on a Saturday, hint rather vaguely that the Saturday office may well have taken some of its texts from the Assumption propers, but this is by no means certain (305,25 to 306,3; a later addition follows 304,7). First Vespers during the Advent season is the only one of the hours provided with its full complement of texts, and even here the Marian propers began only at the chapter, presumably because the first half of the office was shared with whatever observance fell on the preceding day. Second Vespers however, when it was appropriate to celebrate it, had a full set of four psalm antiphons as at St Albans:

> *In qua ad primas Vesperas capitulum Ecce virgo, responsorium Rorate celi, versus Post partum < antiphona Ne timeas. Ad utrasque Vesperas oratio Deus qui > et si debeat habere secundas Vesperas, sit ad illas antiphona super psalmos Missus est cum tribus sequentibus.* Chester, 274,12-15.13

The first two items listed here duplicate those said at the daily Marian office during Advent at Chester; this appended office provides a considerably more complete selection of texts for use at all of the hours during this season. No other texts for the commemorative office are given, but the particularized seasonal character of the items given for the office in Advent most certainly suggests that they would have been replaced during the other seasons of the year. Such seasonal variation became a particularly prominent feature of the commemorative office from the thirteenth century onwards: it is first seen in the the Worcester manuscript *WO* F.160 of *c*.1230.

The Chester Customary also indicates that there was a procession to the Lady altar on Saturdays, incorporating the antiphon *Ave regina celorum*: quite possibly the appearance of this same antiphon in the St Albans breviary *Lbl* 2.A.X was also intended to function in a processional context (see above, p.102). Although the time of day of the Saturday procession at Chester is not specified, it may well have been regarded as an extension of the commemorative office itself:

> *In sabbatis Adventus ad processionem versus altare beate Marie antiphona Ave regina, versus Egredietur, oratio Quesumus omnipotens < deus > tua nos. Extra Adventum versus Post Partum,*

oratio Concede quesumus omnipotens deus. In tempore paschali versus Benedicta tu, oratio Gratiam tuam. Chester, 275,10-14.

THE BARKING COMMEMORATIVE OFFICE

A later instance of the Saturday commemorative office with a twelve-lesson form of Matins appears in the Ordinal of the Nuns of Barking, compiled in 1404. A section headed *Hore Beate Marie,* placed between the Octave of St Andrew (7 December) and the Conception (8 December) gives instructions for both the daily appended form of the Marian office and the Saturday observance (Barking, ii,168-9). Elswhere the commemorative office is referred to as *eius obsequium* (ii,176) and *seruicium beate marie in sabbatis* (i,20).

At Barking, the commemorative office follows the usual ruling of Saturday celebration with the option of transference where necessary. In the event of displacement, however, the Saturday Chapter Mass continued to be of the Virgin; during Advent the introit of this Mass was *Rorate Celi,* preceded by a prefatory trope, possibly rhythmical, *Ave sponsa* with music (*cum nota*) (ii,169). Barking provides texts for the commemorative office for Advent (ii,168-9), Christmas to the Purification (ii,175-6) and Eastertide to Trinity (ii,212-3). The section dealing with the celebration of the office before the Purification is imperfect: it follows the Feast of St Thomas of Canterbury on 21 December, but a missing leaf at the end of his office means that only a remmnant of the Saturday office survives, and nothing of the daily Little Office for this period.

Matins of the Barking Office follows the three-nocturn pattern with twelve lessons and responds, but it is not entirely certain whether its overall structure corresponds with that of the three-nocturn offices in *Lbl* 2.A.X and *F-VAL* 116. The Barking manuscript suggests a condensed form of the conventional twelve-lesson structure: a single antiphon for the psalms of both first and second nocturns at Matins is given, apparently curtailing the more conventional one-to-one relationship of psalm and antiphon seen in the earlier sources. At a cursory glance through the texts supplied for most of the major feasts of the source it would seem that this reduction in the antiphon content was common practice in the Barking liturgy, and the rubric attached to Matins of Christmas Day: *Antiphone et responsoria sicut stant in antiphonario* (i,24) suggests that the appropriate items were supplied from other more comprehensive books. Quite possibly the single antiphon in the commemorative office of the ordinal simply functions as an index to the complete set, although a similar office in the Battle manuscript discussed below unequivocally opts for single antiphons in the first and second nocturns of commemorative Matins.

The final nocturn of the commemorative office at Barking incorporated a passage from the Gospels marked *cum exposicione Exordium*. The practice of modelling the third nocturn on the gospel of the day with the homily upon it serving as material for the four lessons was common to Matins of many Sundays and feasts as early as the twelfth century;[14] indeed, the commemorative office in the St Albans manuscript *Lbl* 2.A.X demonstrates this practice exactly.

The Barking office departs further from the conventions of three-nocturn construction witnessed so far, in that it is provided only with first Vespers, and as at Matins no more than a single antiphon is given for the entire psalmodic group. All of the other three-nocturn commemorative offices comprise both first and second Vespers, and common practice is to supply the latter with individual antiphons for each of the four Vespers psalms. Lauds matches Vespers in providing a single psalm antiphon. Compline is omitted; undoubtedly this office was borrowed from the liturgy of the daily Marian office given in the same source, as were the Little Hours: *[Ad horas] antiphone, capitula, uersiculi, et oraciones ad omnes horas sicut prenotatum est* (ii,169). The Barking commemorative office also incorporates a mass, with specific directions for the choice of sequence. As with the hours, proper texts of the mass changed with the season.

THE THREE-NOCTURN OFFICE
IN FOUR SIXTEENTH-CENTURY SOURCES

It is something of a surprise to find the commemorative office of the Virgin reverting to what appears to be its earlier structural form as late as the sixteenth century. All four of the sources discussed below contain groups of commemorative offices, and in all cases the group is headed by the Saturday Marian office with three-nocturn Matins. The other commemorative offices in the series, without exception, adopt the reduced format which became more common from the thirteenth century.

Ctc 0.7.31 is an early sixteenth-century breviary written in a small, rather indifferent hand. There are very few rubrics. James, Frere, Tolhurst and J.D. Brady[15] maintain that the book was used at Battle, but without providing supportive evidence. There is no calendar, although there is some emphasis on St Martin and St John the Evangelist in the suffrages and the commemorative offices. The Saturday Office of the Virgin heads the commemorative group on f.196v, but without explicit reference to a particular weekday. The office begins at the chapter of first Vespers, and provides a series of three alternative *Magnificat* antiphons: *Virgo dei genitrix*, *Rogamus te virgo* and *Ave regina celorum*. Matins, as mentioned above, gives only a single antiphon for each of its three nocturns. There is no indication that the chosen texts followed the St Albans and Winchcombe tendency of borrowing texts from the Assumption; indeed they bear no particular relationship to any of the feasts. *Benedicta tu* is given as the antiphon in the first nocturn, *Dignare me* in the second, and *Ortus conclusus es* for the canticles. The Matins psalms chosen are those used for all of the Marian feasts at the majority of monastic houses (see pp.122-24 and Table 4:7). Alternative texts are provided for use during Advent, although celebration of the commemorative office of the Virgin was not always permitted during this period.

Two other surviving sixteenth-century sources examined are unique examples of liturgical books which were specially printed for the use of individual monasteries. Although several Sarum books found their way into print from the latter part of the fifteenth century, the production of monastic books so very near to the date of the Dissolution is rather remarkable. J.B.L. Tolhurst knew of only one of these printed sources, a portiforium produced by John Scholar for the community at Abingdon in 1528.[16] Two copies of the book are known to survive, both incomplete. The Oxford copy, *Oec* 9M, comprises only the psalter section with calendar, litany and hymnal. A second copy at Emmanuel College, Cambridge (*Cec* S1.4.6) is much more extensive but consists only of the *Pars Aestivalis* (the summer period from Eastertide to the beginning of Advent). Fortunately this section also incorporates an abundance of miscellaneous material, which duplicates all of the material in *Oec* 9M, and also provides the Common of Saints, blessings, and a series of four commemorative offices. The first of these, addressed to the Virgin, preserves the extensive three-nocturn structure, while the following observances to the saints Vincent and Edward, Relics and St Benedict are constructed with only two nocturns.

A second similar printed book was printed for St Albans in *c.*1535.[17] No title-page or colophon survives, but Pollard and Redgrave's *Short Title Catalogue* (No. 15793.5) identifies the printer as J. Herford. One apparently complete (unpaginated) copy survives as *Lbl* C.110.a.27, comprising temporale, psalter and sanctorale with several miscellaneous additions. Three weekly commemorative offices are given, the first addressed to the Virgin with the usual three-nocturn format, the remaining two-nocturn offices to St Alban and St Benedict respectively.[18] Both of these printed sources are invaluable in that they represent the latest possible record of the standard liturgical practices of each house, for the most part fully equipped with copious rubrics.

The three-nocturn office in the St Albans book is remarkable for the degree of textual and structural correspondence which it exhibits with the parallel observance in *Lbl* 2.A.X, the twelfth-century St Albans breviary. This is a most useful comparison, for it testifies to the stability of the Marian observance at one house over a very long period. Changes to the office are in all respects minor: a small number of seasonal alternatives are provided, but these are single items rather than complete groups of texts.

The later source is also much more fully rubricated: all three commemorative offices at St Albans in the 1530s were to be omitted from Advent Sunday to the Octave of the Epiphany, from Ash Wednesday to the Octave of Easter, within the octaves of principal feasts and on Rogation Days. The Saturday Marian office was also impeded by twelve-lesson feasts, St Hippolitus, the Vigils of Pentecost and St Alban, All Souls, and the Feast of St Matthew if they fell on Saturday. On free Saturdays Matins of the office and an accompanying Mass of the Virgin were to be celebrated in albs, a practice which had clearly remained consistent from the time of Geoffrey Gorron.

Like the office in *Lbl* 2.A.X the St Albans office of the 1530s begins with first Vespers, but at the chapter rather than the psalm antiphon. All Vespers texts in the two sources concord (with the exception of the versicle), but the printed source supplies an extra canticle antiphon. The first, *Ave regina celorum* matches that given in *Lbl* 2.A.X, but in the sixteenth century this text was to be sung only from Trinity to Ash Wednesday. A second antiphon, *Speciosa facta es*, was substituted on the seven Saturdays which fell between the Octave of Easter and Trinity Sunday, and all of the seasonal alternatives provided in the later source were intended for this short period.

At Matins the invitatory *Ave Maria* replaced *In honore* (which operated throughout the year in the twelfth century) from the Easter Octave, but in most other respects the two Matins offices are identical. The only real deviation occurs with the arrangement of readings in the final nocturn. The later source provides a section of Luke's Gospel, *Loquente Ihesu*, with part of Bede's Homily on the same passage (here beginning at *Magne devotionis*). This was used from Trinity to Ash Wednesday. The responds remained constant throughout the year, but on Fridays from Trinity to Advent, from the Purification to Ash Wednesday and from the Octave of Easter to Trinity Sunday, a passage from St John's Gospel, *Stabant iuxta crucem* with a Homily from St Augustine replaced *Loquente Ihesu*. As shown in Table 4:3, *Lbl* 2.A.X also provides two alternative sets of readings but only one of them corresponds with those in the later source. *Loquente Ihesu* and the readings from Bede were substituted for the main set (the Gospel Luke, I,39 *Exurgens Maria*, with Homily *Quia per te meritatem*) during part of the year, but there is no explanatory rubric. The set of texts given for Friday in the sixteenth-century source seems not to have featured at all in the twelfth century, although it is clear that the process of seasonal substitution did operate in some of the earliest sources.

One further complication arises from the St Albans books, however. Comparison of *Lbl* 2.A.X with the slightly later Winchcombe breviary, *F-VAL* 116, led to the speculation that the antiphons of the first two nocturns of Matins of the St Albans commemorative office were really transferred direct from the Feast of the Assumption as at Winchcombe: a hypothesis which cannot, however, be verified, because of the incomplete character of all four Marian feasts in *Lbl* 2.A.X. All of the evidence in the printed breviary suggests that the St Albans tradition remained relatively constant over the years. But if this is so, the Feast of the Assumption was not the source for the twelfth-century commemorative office—or at least, not in the form that the Assumption took at St Albans. The printed source provides an entirely different series of twelve antiphons for Matins of this feast which has no parallel in any of the other sources consulted (Table 4:5, p.249). A number of the Matins responds correspond with those in the commemorative office, but they are not transferred into directly corresponding positions. The Lauds antiphons for the Assumption are those common to the majority of Benedictine sources, but these were never used for Lauds of the St Albans commemorative office as they were for the Winchcombe observance. This lack of correspondence between the two sources is puzzling, but the unfamiliar set of Assumption propers in the later book may simply be later texts compiled especially for the uses of that house. Sources from Ely (*Cu* 4.20) and Muchelney (*Lbl* 43405-6) also contain less conventional texts for Assumption Matins (Table 4:5), although there is no evidence that they represent a later tradition of compilation.

Like the Battle breviary, the St Albans office also opted for a scaled-down version of the office, but only during the summer period. From the Octave of Easter to the Feast of St Egidius (1 September, marked *in capis* in the calendar) only one antiphon of the six was to be sung at the first and second nocturns of Matins; in each case this was the first antiphon of the respective group. During the same period all but the first of the five Lauds antiphons was also omitted, the remaining four distributed at the Little Hours. One further change also occurred, although for no apparent reason: the texts for the versicles at Sext and None were exchanged.

The latest surviving manuscript example of the three-nocturn form of the commemorative office occurs in *Ob* g.12, a small Book of Hours from Pilton (a cell of Malmesbury Abbey). As in the other late sources discussed above, the Marian office alone follows the more substantial 'festal' structure; accompanying offices addressed to St Benedict, the Holy Cross and St Aldhelm, have reduced two-nocturn Matins. *Ob* g.12 is a curious combination of personal and corporate devotions. Several seasonal versions of the Little Office of the Virgin occur, along with blessings and a table for calculating the responds to be used at Matins. The colophon of the source mentions both the date (1521) and the name of the scribe: *Nomen scriptoris Thomas Olston plenus amoris* (f.295). Olston was chosen to be prior of Malmesbury in 1472, and the book may well have been compiled for his own personal use.

The real interest of the offices discussed in this section is the apparent attempt to distinguish the Marian commemorative office from other commemorative observances. Their more extensive structure equates their status with that of the main feasts of the calendar, effectively appending a weekly twelve-lesson feast of the Virgin to the calendar cycle. The primary concentration of the three-nocturn offices in sources of the twelfth century and the sixteenth century is of particular interest: the implication is almost that there was renewed emphasis on the Marian office shortly before the Reformation. No commemorative office addressed to any other saint has been found with a comparable structure, and few of the extant examples are provided with the seasonal alternatives of the Marian office. For the most part the compilers of the comemorative office during the thirteenth and fourteenth centuries seem to have been concerned to reduce the content of weekly observances, the Marian office included.

THE MAINSTREAM COMMEMORATIVE OFFICE AFTER 1200

The twenty-five English Benedictine sources compiled after 1200 listed in Table 4:1 confirm that the commemorative office went on to enjoy increased prominence within the framework of the regular liturgy during the thirteenth and fourteenth centuries. Indeed, during these two centuries virtually all Benedictine office books, ordinals and customaries of English provenance consulted make some reference to the observance: the thirteenth-century breviary from Coldingham (*Lbl* 4664) is a rare exception to this rule. Several of the manuscripts still term the Saturday observance *commemoratio* or in *commemoratione Sancte Marie* as before, but alternative titles appear with comparable frequency: *seruicium de Sancta Maria* (Evesham and Norwich, where the term *commemoratio* is reserved for the simple memorial), *officium de Sancta Maria* (Gloucester and Ely), and at Worcester, *tabula de sancta Maria*. Use of the term *sinaxis* for the Chester commemorative office has already been discussed.

The early years of the thirteenth century also marked the rise of more varied weekly offices in honour of other saints. From *c.*1200 onwards most houses kept at least one other office, often with particular local significance, in addition to the weekly office of the Virgin. The provision of alternative texts for various liturgical seasons also seems to have gained widespread currency during the thirteenth century, a phenomenon which was not limited to the observance discussed here, but also extended to the daily form of the Marian office and also to the post-Compline antiphon. For the most part textual substitution in the commemorative office is most overt in the longer established Marian office, but a few of the other observances listed in Table 4:1 supply seasonal texts in the same manner. Presumably this was partly to encourage conformity with the structure of the regular liturgy, and partly to provide variety in offices which were celebrated so frequently that their familiarity may well have begun to turn to tedium. It is also a predictable outcome of the late medieval tendency for particularization, codification and proliferation.

The proliferation of commemorative offices and the abundance of appropriate material compiled for them perhaps makes the widespread structural modification of the form seem anomalous. The substitution of the two-nocturn structure after *c*.1200 implied a substantial reduction in the scale of the commemorative office: this is most overtly apparent at Matins, where the common pattern of twelve lessons and responds seen in the earlier commemorative offices was reduced to three. Proper psalm antiphons at Matins, Lauds and Vespers were usually limited to a single text for each group of psalms in a comparable manner, although the total quota of psalms (twelve at Matins, five at Lauds and four at Vespers) remained unchanged. The choice of psalms used for commemorative offices will be considered below.

No source examined offers any reason for the reduction in the scale of the commemorative office, and, paradoxically, the observance appears to have retained the status of a twelve-lesson feast in spite of its structural modification. *Cjc* D.27, from St Mary's York, (*c*.1400) explicitly equates the Saturday Marian office with twelve-lesson feasts:

> *Et habeat illa commemoratio quamvis trium lectionum vim et effectum duodecim lectionum in omnibus . . .*
>
> York.SM.Ord, i,163.

Possibly the general augmentation of the calendar in most establishments after 1200 by the infiltration of local or newly-emphasized feasts had a dampening effect on large-scale votive observances such as the commemorative office, for certainly the number of days when ferial and occasional observances were necessary or even possible must have been greatly reduced. Indeed it is apparent that the Marian observance was now much more likely to be displaced from Saturday by a concurring feast. The aggrandization of the liturgy by these later accretions to the calendar, many with their own proper texts and some of them very elaborate, may well have made the notion of a weekly twelve-lesson 'feast' of the Virgin less practicable and even less attractive. Consequently, in spite of the apparently universal popularity of the Saturday office from the latter part of the thirteenth century, and the healthy implications of its seasonal expansion, the reduction of the textual and musical content of each individual office seems to have been a simultaneous and virtually invariable policy in English Benedictine monasteries. Seen in the light of other areas of votive observance, however, the curtailment of the scale of the commemorative office comes as no surprise, but rather unexpectedly, no formal legislation concerning the structure of the commemorative office ever appeared: there is only a single reference to the observance in the Chapter Acts of the

English Benedictines dated 1278, and this deals with nothing more significant than the method of selecting an appropriate weekday (see below).

The structural change in the commemorative office is partly matched by the manner in which the observance tends to be copied into the manuscripts after *c.*1200. Physical presentation is often considerably less prominent in the later sources than in the earlier manuscripts discussed above; as the Worcester Antiphoner of *c.*1230 illustrates, the office may well be masked by obscure rubrics where texts are given only in incipit and sometimes omitted entirely. At one level this would appear to confirm the expected familiarity of a well-established weekly observance where most of the texts were borrowed from other feasts; at another it suggests perhaps an accompanying decline in its status and interest. Obscure presentation of the commemorative observance is one of the particularly irksome features of *WO* F.160, the Worcester Antiphoner, where the texts and general directions for the two weekly offices observed there during the early thirteenth century (of the Virgin and the Worcester saints Oswald and Wulfstan) are given as highly abbreviated rubrics written in a small, cursive hand. Successive references to the Marian office, which changed with the season, are spread rather arbitrarily between sanctorale and temporale: there is no question of their being allotted a separate section of the manuscript with all offices grouped together.

A few scribes did adopt this more convenient mode of presentation. The Norwich Customary (*Ccc* 465) for example, provides an independent section dealing with the weekly Marian office (Norwich, 202-26), although even here the selection of textual incipits is limited, and there are also rubrics dealing with the rules of precedence of one observance over another. Equally, where manuscripts do provide for seasonal variations of the commemorative office, they often fail to indicate clearly the point at which a new cycle of texts was substituted for the previous cycle: sometimes seasonal texts for the Marian office can only be identified by the inexplicit rubric *De Sancta Maria*, without indication of the exact function. This imprecision is a feature of both the Gloucester and Evesham Breviaries, where the intended seasonal change can only be postulated by consideration of the adjacent regular liturgy forming part of the temporale.

In virtually all of the manuscripts examined, the piecing together of the complete commemorative office for any season involves a certain degree of speculation. Texts borrowed for commemorative use from a feast are usually indicated only by short incipits, and it is rare to find that the position of the parent-text is indicated clearly. (This issue is particularly complex in those cases where two different texts share the same incipit.) Indeed, where texts for a single commemorative office are borrowed from several sources, including the common, sanctorale and sometimes temporale in addition (as occasionally occurs, for example, in the commemorative Office of Relics), the process of identifying each individual element is slow and laborious. The fruits of such an investigation, which offer some insight into the methodology underlying the compilation of commemorative offices, will be examined in due course.

THE MARIAN OFFICE AFTER C.1200

Throughout the period under consideration, the weekly Office of the Virgin remained the most popular and widely occurring of the commemorative offices. Without exception, it appears in all twenty-nine sources listed in Table 4:1, mostly favouring the reduced Matins format after *c.*1200. As a rule those offices which do retain the older three-nocturn structure are given in isolation without reference to any other weekly observance, but the opposite is true for the two-nocturn offices. In the latter case, all but one source (the Norwich Customary) present the Marian office in conjunction with at least one other weekly office. Nevertheless, the presence of the other offices did not really detract from the priority of the Marian observance. In the Pilton, Battle, Abingdon and later St Albans books, this is emphasized (rather unconventionally) in physical terms by the structural distinction of the Saturday office from its three weekly counterparts: the Marian observance alone comprises the full twelve lessons and responds at Matins, the other offices following the more common three-lesson structure.

Several sources suggest similar precedence of the Saturday office over the other devotions by two further factors: first the provision of a far greater repertory of variant seasonal texts; second, the ruling that when the Marian office was transferred from Saturday, another commemorative office would be displaced. The Ordinal of St Mary's York of *c.*1400 gives instructions that the Office of St Benedict was to cede its usual day of Thursday to Mary if Saturday was occupied. In this case the office of St Benedict moved to Tuesday:

> *Sed si omnes ferie vacent preter sabbatum in quo contingit festum duodecim lectionum vel trium habentium proprias laudes tantum, feria quinta agitur de ea; et feria tertia de Sancto Benedicto quando de eo cantari debeat in conventu.*   York.SM.Ord, i,163.

But in spite of its supremacy in the commemorative hierarchy, even the Marian office was subject to the whims of the calendar. Without exception it seems to have been displaced by feasts of twelve-lessons, and there was usually a substantial number of three-lesson feasts with their own proper texts which had the same effect. Feasts which came into the latter category varied from one monastery to another. The St Mary's, York list names St John before the Latin Gate, the Translation of St Andrew, St John and St Paul, St Hippolytus and his companions, St Bricius and St Anne. Norwich has a similar list but omits the Translation of St Andrew and St Anne, and adds the Vigil of St John the Baptist, the Ordination of St Martin, the Octave of St Laurence, and St Agnes *secundo*. Both manuscripts also specify longer periods when the Saturday office was omitted entirely and not simply transferred: at York during the third week in Advent, from Christmas Eve to the Octave of the Epiphany, from Ash Wednesday to the Octave of Easter, during the Octaves of Pentecost and Corpus Christi; at Norwich within the Octaves of the Epiphany, Ascension and Trinity, during Advent and in Lent, although during Advent (as at Chester) the office was replaced by a simple memorial.

COMMEMORATIVE OFFICES IN HONOUR OF OTHER SAINTS

Expansion of the repertory of weekly votive offices during the thirteenth century is apparent from Table 4:1. The majority of sources after 1200 represented here contain at least one additional commemorative office in addition to that of the Virgin: St Benedict, Relics, and the patron of the house occupying the most prominent positions. Specific weekdays for these later offices are not always given and may sometimes be contradictory; Thursday was the most popular day for the Office of St Benedict, but most offices may simply have been allotted to any conveniently free day. Neither did all monasteries follow the same pattern. Tolhurst's statement that 'commemorative feasts . . . were almost invariably allotted to Tuesdays, Thursdays and Saturdays'[19] holds some truth but is not an infallible rule: this is apparent in the Pilton source, where the prescribed psalmodic pattern makes it clear that Friday and Monday were the favoured days for the offices of the Holy Cross and St Benedict respectively. However, the General Chapter decreed in 1278 that the choice of day was partly a matter for the cantor's discretion:

> *Et quando sic de domina, patronis, seu reliquiis officium*
> *celebratur, non eis certa dies ebdomade deputetur, set nunc hec,*
> *nunc illa, pro discrescione cantoris, quatinus regule veritas*
> *teneatur, et psalmi, responsoria feriarum et huiusmodi melius in*
> *usu habeantur.* Pantin, i,97.

The choice of commemorative offices in honour of patrons and local saints is illustrated in the Worcester Antiphoner, where in addition to the Marian office (given with four sets of seasonal texts) there is a weekly office referred to in the rubrics as *de confessoribus*, prescribed for Thursday. This commemorated the two major local saints at Worcester, Oswald and Wulstan, elected as bishops in 961 and 1062 respectively. Both receive considerable emphasis in the calendar of *WO* F.160, which contains a Deposition and a Translation for each saint (28 February and 8 October for Oswald; 19 January and 15 June for Wulstan). All four of these days ranked as principal feasts, of which there were thirteen at Worcester: the other nine were Christmas, Easter, Pentecost, the Assumption, the Nativity of the Virgin, Sts Peter and Paul, the Translation of St Benedict, All Saints, and the Dedication of the Cathedral Church. At a later stage the Worcester liturgy also incorporated a third commemorative office, that of St Thomas of Canterbury celebrated on Tuesday, although one of the rubrics appended to the source in a later hand is cancelled: *Feria iii si uacauerit < Tabula de s[an]c[t]o thom[i] cantuar[ensis]>* (*PM*, 1-xii, 164; erased material is enclosed in angle brackets.) Another reference to a weekly Office of Thomas of Canterbury is made in a separate section of the manuscript which gives the Feast of the Visitation, but no texts are supplied.

The late fourteenth-century Canterbury 'Burnt Breviary', *CA* 6, also makes reference to a weekly Office of Thomas of Canterbury, but the required texts are missing from the manuscript. Like the other Canterbury commemorations to the Virgin and to Relics, the Thomas office was to be omitted on twelve-lesson feasts and during octaves, but as at St Mary's, York, the commemorative office still retained the status of a twelve-lesson feast:

> *Et [nota] quod quando sit seruicium de sancta maria uel de sancto thomo uel de reliquiis . . . fiet totum seruicium solempniter sicut in xii leccionibus.*   CA 6, f.81

Six further sources in Table 4:1 make reference to a weekly Office of Relics. Evesham, Hyde Abbey, Abingdon and the Peterborough source *Ob* 17 all provide a complete set of texts for the office, mostly borrowed from the Common of Confessors. The later thirteenth-century *Instructio Noviciorum* (*Ccc* 441), written for the novices at Christ Church, Canterbury draws attention to the status of its two commemorative offices (of the Virgin and of Relics) both of which seem to have been treated in certain respects as twelve-lesson feasts. Two references dealing with the conduct of the novices in choir state that at the two weekly commemorative offices, on Sundays, and on twelve-lesson feasts, the community was not to bow or to incline over the desks while praying:

> *Diebus dominicis uel festo xii leccionum, uel quando agitur de beate uirgine uel reliquiis, nunquam in curta uenia uel super formas est orandum.*   Cant.Ch.Nov., 142-3.

Evesham specifies Thursday for the Office of Relics: the usual choice for a second weekday when only two commemorative offices were said at a monastery. The Peterborough Customary of 1371, *Llp* 198-198b which contains four commemorative offices, is less easy to interpret, but appears to favour Tuesday for this same office.

Other instances of local commemorative offices are found at Ely (the two offices for the patron saints Etheldreda and Peter), Westminster (Edward, after the founder, and Peter and Paul, the former being the dedicatee), Bury St Edmunds (St Edmund), Peterborough (St Peter), Pilton (St Aldhelm) and Muchelney (St Peter). The companion customary to Westminster, that of St Augustine, Canterbury (*Lbl* C.XII), contains an incidental reference to two commemorative offices in a passage which indicates that *Gloria in excelsis* was to be omitted from the Mass on three-lesson feasts. Exceptions to this rule occurred within octaves of principal feasts and on the two weekdays when commemorative offices, one in honour of the Virgin, the other patron saints, were recited:

> *Numquam Gloria in excelsis ad missam in tribus lectionibus, nisi intra principales octavas, et in quinta feria quando commemoracio sanctorum fit hujus loci, et in Sabbato de sancta Maria . . .*
>
> Cant.SA.Cust., 268.

The Customary of Bury St Edmunds, written *c.*1234, makes several brief references to two weekly commemorative offices of St Mary and St Edmund, both of which seem to have maintained twelve-lesson status in spite of their three-lesson structure, and consequently called for modification in certain practices which were normally restricted to feastdays. The following example is one of several:

> *Si autem de sancta Maria vel sancto Eadmundo vel duodecim lectionibus teneatur illa prima missa ad magnum altare, tunc tantum erit una oracio.*   Bury, 90-91.

Other areas where the Bury commemorative offices affected normal ferial practice focused around the appropriate number of candles, periods when talking was allowed, the ringing of bells at the hours, and the punishment of minor faults (Bury, 94-5, 37, 51, 52, 84-5, 88, 96).

Peterborough also adopted local observances of this kind, for a weekly Office of St Peter, celebrated on Thursday, had been added to the Saturday observance by the beginning of the fourteenth century. This foundation is virtually unique in this survey, in that it possesses no fewer than four surviving manuscripts, each testifying to the presence of the commemorative office. Viewed in chronological order, it appears that the community added individual commemorative offices in succession: the Virgin and St Peter are joined by St Benedict by the early fourteenth century (*Ob* 22), the Office of Relics by 1371 (*Llp* 198/198b), and a fifth weekly office of St Oswald at some stage after 1415 (*Ob* 17).

Another frequently appearing office, that of St Benedict, was chosen for its relevance to the entire order rather than for any particular local significance. Eight of the English houses which appear in Table 4:1 incorporate some reference to a weekly office of Benedict (Gloucester, Peterborough, Westminster, St Mary's York, Battle, Pilton, Abingdon and St Albans), and the thirteenth-century Fleury Customary also provides texts for a weekly *Servitium beati Benedicti* (Fleury, 309-11). Fleury and York observed this office on Thursday, but at York the Marian office sometimes took precedence (see above).

The *Gesta Abbatum* provides further information on the Office of St Benedict at St Albans. During the abbacy of Michael, twenty-ninth abbot (1335-49), a change was made to the antiphons at the commemorative offices of St Benedict and St Amphibalus (St Albans, 311), while one of the observances discussed in the new ordinal of Thomas de la Mare (1349-96) was a three-lesson office of St Benedict:

> *Ordinavit praetera, ut singulis septimanis fierent tres lectiones de Sancto Benedicto, quotiens extra Adventum et Quadragesimam, non impedientibus festivitatibus, ejus Commemoratio fieri potuisset.*
>
> St Albans, ii,396.

SEASONAL TEXTS

The Hyde Office of Relics, the Peterborough Office of St Peter in the antiphoner *Cmc* F.4.10, the three two-nocturn offices in the Pilton source and the Marian commemorative offices in all of the sources with the exception of Westminster, give alternative sets of texts for use during certain seasons of the year. In most cases relatively complete seasonal offices are substituted rather than simple individual texts or groups of texts: those monasteries where no more than the Matins readings changed are not included for consideration here. Most of the weekly offices were omitted entirely during the octaves of principal feasts and during Lent, and all but the Marian office was omitted during Advent in addition (see above, in relation to the customaries of Norwich and St Mary's, York).

Seasonal divisions in the commemorative office were not standardized from one monastery to another. The divisions adopted for the two-nocturn Marian offices in the manuscripts consulted are listed in Table 4:6. Advent was an uncomplicated season and the appropriate office was recited from the Saturday after Advent Sunday, and lasted at least until *O sapientia* (as specified by the Chester Customary). All other commemorative offices were omitted during this season, and occasionally this regulation also applied to the Marian office, as at Norwich. Six manuscripts prescribe a set of texts for Advent; Norwich and Chester replaced the office with a memorial.

Christmas and the various feasts which fell during the last days of December implied that the commemorative office was not resumed until January, and in most cases probably not until the Feast of the Epiphany on 6 January. Several of the Marian offices in Table 4:6 specify that a new cycle of texts was to start at Epiphany (Evesham and Norwich) or at the Octave of the Epiphany on 13 January (Worcester and Gloucester). Offices marked simply *In Natali Domini* (Ely, Hyde, Peterborough) presumably refer to the same period. In almost all cases the Christmas (or Epiphany) cycle terminated on the Feast of the Purification (2 February), when it was replaced by another set of texts. The period which followed Christmas thus lasted just under four weeks, or a week less if the cycle did not start until the Octave of the Epiphany. From the Purification to Lent, texts for the commemorative office often doubled those during the summer, and are simply labelled *per annum* in the manuscripts. Theoretically, as Tolhurst points out, the term governs the Octave of Epiphany to Septuagesima, and Trinity Sunday to Advent.[20] Most sources also provide texts for Eastertide, although sometimes the alterations are very minor, calling for no more than the addition of an *Alleluia*. This period was also short, usually commencing on the Saturday after Easter Sunday (or the Saturday after the Octave) and terminating with Trinity Sunday.

THE COMPILATION OF THE COMMEMORATIVE OFFICE

Analysis of the two twelfth-century Saturday offices discussed in the first part of this chapter led to the supposition that much of the material used to construct a commemorative office was borrowed from the repertory of proper texts used on related feasts. In both of these offices (*Lbl* 2.A.X and *F-VAL* 116), it emerges that the most popular source for borrowing was the Feast of the Assumption, with some emphasis on the Feasts of the Annunciation and the Nativity (Tables 4:3 and 4:4). The commemorative offices in both the St Albans and Winchcombe manuscripts borrow the first eight antiphons of Matins directly from Assumption Matins, and the Winchcombe compiler extended the same principle to the Lauds antiphons. The lifting of texts from areas of the sanctorale other than the Marian feasts does not seem to have been a prominent feature in these manuscripts. Both offices, however, probably incorporated a small number of newly-compiled items: non-musical texts such as collects, lessons and chapters commonly fall into this category in many votive offices, and it is likely that votive observances drew from the current repertory of devotional texts to supply material for lessons, rather than from the established readings used at the feasts.

The method of assembling a new observance by extraction and redistribution of material from related offices remained a persistent feature for the compilers of votive offices after 1200. Non-concordant items, for the most part, are increasingly less frequent. In some respects, the curtailment of the proper content of the weekly commemorative office by the transition from three-nocturn to two-nocturn format implied that fewer texts were needed for its construction. For the psalms at Matins the antiphons were reduced from thirteen to two and lessons and responds from twelve to three; at Vespers a single psalm-antiphon served, although not all monasteries replaced the original five antiphons of Lauds with a single text: the number of antiphons at Lauds often varied according to the time of year, as demonstrated in Table 4:6 (p.250).

But the process of compilation was now made more complex by the predominance of seasonal variants in the Marian office: rather than assembling a single set of hours, the compiler seems to have been expected to produce full offices for at least two separate seasons, and sometimes more (Table 4:7, p.252). There was also the question of assembling not only the well-established Marian office, but weekly offices for patron saints and relics in addition, and here the individual character of each monastery implied that the compiler was not always able to turn to an existing model.

CHOICE OF A PSALMODIC *CURSUS* FOR
THE COMMEMORATIVE OFFICE

In spite of the options available to the compiler of a commemorative office, certain features seem to have remained constant in virtually every manuscript, and the choice of psalmody is a case in point. Indeed, many sources fail to indicate the full range of psalms for any commemorative office, sometimes relying on a single incipit, or even omitting all mention of psalms. Indication of the psalmodic element is most commonly present for Matins, which included more psalmody than any of the other offices. Lauds, for example, seems to have been entirely unchanging in this respect, and presumably it was not thought necessary to include any reference to its psalms.

In the Marian office there seem to have been two basic options for the Matins psalms. Whether this office comprised two or three nocturns, twelve psalms were required: six for each of the first two nocturns, whether they were said under a single antiphon for the whole group or with an individual antiphon for each psalm. Almost unquestionably Matins of the two twelfth-century commemorative offices in *Lbl* 2.A.X and *F-VAL* 116 used the same psalmodic pattern at Matins, although the Winchcombe compiler failed to indicate the psalms for the first nocturn (Table 4:4). The St Albans manuscript, however, gives the whole set in incipit (Table 4:3). This particular set of psalms is listed separately in Table 4:8 (p.253), and will be referred to as Series A.

Examination of the Matins psalms used for the later Saturday offices of the Virgin suggests widespread use of Series A. Not all sources give incipits for the full set of twelve psalms (the manuscripts from Pilton (*Ob* g.12) and St Peter's, Westminster (*Ob* g.10) are exceptions), but most supply an indication of the first psalm of each nocturn: *Domine dominus noster* (8) and *Benedixisti* (84) respectively. Further investigation reveals that Series A was the set of psalms used by most monastic houses on each of the Marian feasts and also for the Common of a Virgin Martyr. Indeed, a small number of sources (the Norwich Customary, *Ccc* 465, amongst them) simply prescribe *psalmi unius virginis* for the commemorative office (Norwich, 205). At Winchcombe (*F-VAL* 116) Series A is given for the Purification, Annunciation, Assumption, Nativity of the Virgin, Common of the Nativity of One Virgin and the Feast of St Agatha. At Hyde Abbey, which also lists psalms for most of the sanctorale feasts, Series A was used for the Assumption, Purification, Nativity, Conception and the Common of a Virgin Martyr. The same set also appears for Marian feasts in the Antiphonals of St Maur-lès-Fosse (s.xii), Silos (s.xi) and Rheinau (s.xiii), and is clearly of considerable antiquity.[21] The surprising consistency of the series over a wide range of sources was noted by Henri Barré, who proposed that the set was derived from early psalmodic forms prescribed for Christmas Day Matins.[22] Barré points out that Psalm 18 had been given a Marian interpretation by the time of St Augustine, partly on the basis of its sixth verse, *In sole posuit*, later extracted to serve for a variety of independent Marian proper texts. The third verse of Psalm 44, *Speciosus forma . . . diffusa est gratia*, received similar treatment.

Use of Series A was not limited simply to the Marian feasts and weekly commemorative offices of the monastic rites. The uses of both Sarum and Exeter (where Matins followed the usual secular arrangement of nine lessons and psalms), took the psalmody required for Matins of the Marian feasts from the same set of twelve, omitting psalms 47, 84, and 98. Psalms for the weekly Saturday office in these uses followed an identical pattern. It has already been established that the daily Little Offices of the Virgin in both monastic and secular foundations also drew on the same repertory. In both uses only three psalms were sung at Matins of the daily votive office, and these, if not entirely consistent in all houses, were almost invariably drawn from the Marian set and always began with Psalm 8, *Domine dominus noster*.

The second psalmodic series for Matins of the Marian commemorative office in the Benedictine sources did not draw on a festal (or common) repertory, but on the monastic *cursus* of ferial psalms: the pattern prescribed in essence in *RB*, and modified in certain respects during the Middle Ages. Table 1:2 lists parallel ferial psalms for each day of the week for both secular and monastic uses. Commemorative offices opting for this alternative psalmodic series simply used the ordinary set of psalms prescribed for ferial

Saturdays: these are given in Table 4:8, where they are referred to as Series B. Few monasteries seem to have used the second series for the entire year. At Evesham, Norwich and Ely, A and B were used in alternation; all three houses taking 1 November (which marked the beginning of winter in the monastic calendar) as the point when substitution occurred. Either Lent or Easter marked the change to Series A, but since the commemorative office was omitted during Lent, in practice the new psalms came into use as the Easter cycle of texts began. Only the Pilton office (*Ob* g.12) seems to have used Series B for the entire year. This information is summarized in Table 4:6.

Psalms are listed less often for the other hours of the Marian commemorative office, but it may be assumed that the psalmodic pattern for all of the hours was consistent with the two options described above, using either ferial or festal (common) psalms. The twelfth-century St Albans Breviary, *Lbl* 2.A.X, is more explicit in this respect, indicating that the festal Marian series was to be used at second Vespers if the office fell on Saturday, but that the Saturday ferial series was to be substituted in the event of transference to any other day.

Commemorative offices in honour of other saints, where they prescribe psalms, follow similar principles to the psalmodic patterns of the Marian office. At Pilton the Offices of St Benedict and the Holy Cross used the ferial *cursus* for Monday and Friday respectively, but at Westminster, the Offices of St Edward and Peter and Paul both used festal series, identical to the proper psalms for the relevant feasts. The simplicity of these two basic options for all commemorative offices presumably accounts for the omission of appropriate psalms in several of the manuscripts.

THE COMPILATION OF MARIAN VOTIVE OFFICES

The apparent demand for seasonal variation in Marian votive offices meant that the compiler was faced with a more varied task than his earlier counterpart. Offices used throughout the entire year without textual change, in the manner of the two twelfth-century commemorative offices, could not hope to incorporate texts of equal relevance for all seasons of the year, and consequently the two examples cited seem to have drawn primarily on the Marian feast with least specific texts—the Assumption. In the later seasonal offices, Assumption borrowing becomes rather less pronounced except during those 'general' liturgical periods marked *per annum*: covering Epiphany to Quadragesima, and Trinity Sunday to Advent. This was appropriate even in terms of seasonal relevance, since the Assumption fell within the second period.

In an attempt to establish some of the problems which lay behind the compilation of a new votive office, the final section of this chapter considers borrowed and newly-composed elements in both the Saturday commemorative office and the Little Office of the Virgin. Although the function of these two observances was very different, their textual relationship is so pronounced that it makes it entirely logical to discuss the two forms together.

The parallel between the two observances is seen most clearly in the Hyde Abbey Breviary (*Ob* e.1*), where both forms of the votive office are copied into the source as a unit, the commemorative form (marked *sabbato*) following the daily form for each season (ff.442-449). The only other extant manuscript which provides a substantially complete set of texts for both offices is the Worcester Antiphoner (*WO* F.160), and this source is used as the basis for the greater part of the following analysis. The Worcester manuscript is less clear in its layout then the Hyde Abbey Breviary, since—as noted earlier—the texts for the votive offices are dispersed throughout the source in a slightly haphazard manner. Nevertheless, it is the only extant source which gives some indication of the musical characteristics of commemorative and appended votive offices in an English Benedictine foundation.

Items for the respective seasonal forms of the Worcester votive offices are given as Table 4:9 (p.254)—the weekly commemorative office, and Table 4:10 (p.260)—the daily Little Office. References to *WO* F.160 in this chapter relate to the accessible (although only partial) facsimile of the manuscript published as *PM* 1, xii: examination of the unpublished parts of the source has revealed no further references to Marian votive offices. For convenience, page references (in the extreme right-hand column of Tables 4:9 and 4:10) follow the numbering of the facsimile rather than the foliation of the manuscript itself. The majority of the texts for the commemorative office and the Little Office appear as abbreviated incipits. The small number of texts which do appear in their complete form in these offices are indicated by an asterisk (*). Columns of concordances in Tables 4:9 and 4:10 indicate all of the occasions where a votive text appears elsewhere, whether as an incipit or in full, and in the latter case, whether both text and melody concord (indicated by the abbreviation tmCon), or simply the text (tCon). Any complete text (including concordances), with or without melody, is marked with an asterisk.

Tables 4:9 and 4:10 both reveal the complexities of layout in *WO* F.160. The Advent form of the commemorative office (*PM* p.238) is copied into a quite separate part of the manuscript from its daily counterpart (*PM* pp.7-8), although texts for both the Saturday office and the Little Office during Eastertide (p.310) and the post-Octave Epiphany period (p.59) are juxtaposed. In the daily cycle, however, the post-Octave Epiphany office (operating from January 14) was observed only until the Feast of the Purification (February 2), when it was replaced by a further set of texts until Easter. The post-Purification texts are provided at *PM* pp.272-3. This explicit seasonal division is not paralleled in the commemorative office, although a group of texts marked *ab oct[avis] epiph[anie] usque xl et p[ost] t[ri]n[itatem] usque adv[entum]* (*PM* pp.360-61) presumably served the same purpose as the post-Purification texts of the Little Office. (The commemorative office was omitted entirely during Lent.) In other manuscripts 'general' texts for use from the weeks between early February and Lent (or Easter), and during the summer, are often not given with precise directions, but are simply marked *per annum*. The Little Office at Worcester, however, has a small number of texts (all of them *Magnificat* antiphons) expressly for use during the summer period (*PM* 162).

NEWLY-COMPILED TEXTS IN THE VOTIVE OFFICES IN *WO* F.160

Only a small proportion of the material in the Worcester votive offices is newly composed. This may be summarized as follows:

Newly-composed texts in the Weekly Commemorative Office

1. Advent

   Magnificat antiphon (later addition to the manuscript; also used as the Terce antiphon for this season)

2. Octave Epiphany to Purification

   Matins invitatory (partial concordance with invitatory for Little Office during the same season)

3. Eastertide

   First of two alternative responds at Vespers
   Matins invitatory (melodic concordance only with invitatory for the Saturday office from Epiphany to the Purification)

4. Octave of Epiphany to Lent and Trinity to Advent

   Four of five alternative *Magnificat* antiphons
   Prime antiphon
   Terce antiphon
   Three processional antiphons after None

Newly-composed texts in the Daily Little Office

1. Advent

    Matins invitatory (new melody, although text is borrowed)
    Three lessons at Matins
    Short responds for Lauds, Prime, Terce, Sext and None

2. Eastertide

    Short responds for Vespers, Compline, Prime, Terce, Sext and None
    (Texts for responds from Compline to None of Eastertide duplicate
    responds from Lauds to None of the Advent period)

3. Pentecost to 8 September

    Nine alternative *Magnificat* antiphons

Within the Little Office, the most prominent of these items are the short responds for use during Advent and Eastertide, and the *Magnificat* antiphons for the summer period. The majority of the newly-composed responds (see Table 4:10) occur only in the context of the daily votive office and nowhere in the regular liturgy: the Sext respond *Speciosa facta es* (for the Easter and Advent seasons) is the sole exception to this rule, since it appears as the Vespers respond on two occasions in the regular liturgy (on the Vigil of the Assumption and during its Octave), and once in the Saturday commemorative office. Textually, there is an exact correspondence between the groups of responds for the Little Hours of the daily votive office during the respective seasons of Easter and Advent. The sole distinction is that the Easter group incorporates appended Alleluias after the verse and respond sections. Only once is there evidence of non-direct transference of a text, when the Advent Lauds respond reappears at Eastertide Compline. The choice of respond for Eastertide Lauds is not indicated.

    Melodically, however, the two seasonal groups of responds for the Little Office are clearly distinguished. The six Easter responds (including those for Vespers and Compline) all follow the same formulaic melody:

Ex.4:1 *WO* F.160, Compline respond, *PM*, 310.

The Advent group, however, presents two further alternatives, with Lauds and Prime taking one option:

Ex.4:2 *WO* F.160, Lauds respond, 7.

and Terce, Sext and None another:

Ex.4:3 *WO* F.160, Sext respond, 7.

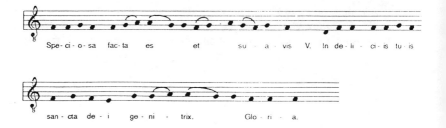

The three melodies represented here broadly correspond to the seasonal series of responds given in *LU* 229-30. Ex. 4:2 follows a mode 4 contour resembling the respond-melody for Advent in *LU* 230; Ex.4:3 follows a mode 6 pattern which has an obvious parallel with *LU* 229, prescribed for use throughout the year. The Worcester group for Easter (Ex.4:1) also adopts mode 6, and the melody is similar in outline to the Eastertide option in *LU* (230). Since no further alternatives are given in the Worcester manuscript, it is likely that the Advent series prevailed *per annum*, except during Eastertide.

The simplicity of the Worcester respond-melodies barely merits the suggestion that they are specimens of new musical composition. Nevertheless, they do represent items which were in some respects unfamiliar in the monastic rite, since short responds were not normally a feature of the regular Little Hours. It is possible that some of the texts represented here were borrowed from secular sources, although a parallel series has not been traced. The relationship with the Sarum series of responds for the corresponding hours of the Little Office of the Virgin is negligible; textual fragments from the Worcester responds do occur in the Sarum books, but not in direct correspondence, and there is a further major difference between the two rites in that the Sarum Little Office of the Virgin did not incorporate a respond after the chapter at Vespers and Lauds. *Gemma virginum lux*, the Vespers respond for the Little Office in Eastertide at Worcester (*PM* p.310) may well have been peculiar to this particular house. It is slightly more elaborate than the formulaic items given for the Little Hours, and this stylistic difference may have been observed as a general principle. Only once does a respond double both for Vespers and one of the shorter offices: *Speciosa facta es*, prescribed for None of the Little Office during Advent and Eastertide, corresponds with one of the responds used at Vespers of the regular office during the Assumption octave.

NEWLY-COMPILED TEXTS: ANTIPHONS

If the formulaic construction of the responds is not of major musical interest, the group of nine *Magnificat* antiphons provided for use at the Little Office from Pentecost to the Nativity of the Virgin (8 September), is far more significant. The antiphons are the only elements provided for the Little Office during this particular season, and it seems clear that the other items for the office were simply duplicated from one of the other cycles listed in Table 4:10 (most probably that prescribed from the Purification to Easter). The nine *Magnificat* antiphons have no textual or melodic concordance elsewhere in the source. Their relatively lengthy texts are all taken from *The Song of Songs*, (as are a number of the festal texts in the

Worcester Marian repertory, particularly those occurring around the Assumption period). Sometimes the antiphons are simply single verses from this section of the Bible, but more often they conflate sections of individual verses, or occasionally two whole verses. They do not necessarily follow the order of the biblical verses. A textual analysis of the nine Little Office antiphons is presented in Table 4:11 (p.267); the antiphons with music are transcribed complete as Appendix 1 (p.327).

The contemporary popularity of texts from *The Song of Songs* was unquestionably a result of its relatively recent Marian exegesis by several eminent figures of medieval scholasticism. The book had always been enormously popular; Leclercq comments that it was the text 'most frequently read and most frequently copied in the medieval cloister'.[23] Cluny possessed no fewer than fifteen commentaries on it in the time of Peter the Venerable, for it was the contemplative text *par excellence*.

In addition to their textual homogeneity, the antiphons also reveal a very striking method of melodic organization. The nine items run through the sequence of eight modes in series order, so that each pair of antiphons shares the same final, the first in authentic form, the second plagal. Mode seven occurs twice, so that the final three items all share one final (g). Such conscious modal planning is by no means uncommon in the Worcester Antiphoner, although its use is most frequently limited to cycles of Matins antiphons and responds on major feasts. Instances of serial modality in this source are listed in Table 4:12 (p.269). Recent work by Andrew Hughes has demonstrated that a good deal of later chant was organized in this careful manner, particularly in the case of metrical and rhymed offices.[24] Giulio Cattin sees the device partly as 'an indication of the systematic approach of the medieval mentality', but perhaps also 'a device for committing pieces to memory.'[25]

Aside from their modal organization, the nine *Magnificat* antiphons are also characterized by a clearly defined emphasis on a single tonal centre, heightened by the proximity of notes closely related to it. This is particularly apparent in the mode six antiphon *Sexaginta sunt regine*, where triadic cells built around f, a and c are prominent. Two of the nine melodies exploit an uncharacteristically wide range, incorporating both the plagal and authentic form of the mode: the mode one/two *Osculetur me* (B-f') and the mode five/six *Veni dilecte mi* (c-g') both fall into this category. (Table 4:11 and Appendix 1 follow Laurentia McLachlan's analysis in categorizing both antiphons as authentic.)

Cycles of alternative texts of the same genre, like those for the Little Office, do not occur frequently in the Worcester manuscript. Thirteen antiphons for use at the regular office during the middle of the week (Monday to Thursday) after the second Sunday in Lent (*PM* p.94) have no cyclic modal features; most of the items are in mode eight. Similarly a group of antiphons sung successively with the *Magnificat* and *Benedictus* from the Octave of Easter to the Ascension (*PM* p.138) are largely confined to this mode, with occasional instances of mode seven. There is, however, one further example of a cycle of *Magnificat* antiphons for votive use: this time at the Saturday commemorative office of the Virgin from the Octave of the Epiphany to Lent and after Trinity until Advent. Here, only three of the five items are without concordance (although a fourth simply reappears at the Saturday office during Eastertide). The items in question are all of considerable length; two of them frequently appear as post-Compline antiphons in later sources: *Salve regina* (here borrowed from the Vigil of the Assumption) and *Ave regina celorum*, characterized by its rhymed metrical text. Only two of the five texts are taken from *The Song of Songs*, *Tota pulchra es* (*Song of Songs* IV, 7) and *Introduxit me* (II, 4); the others are typical examples of newly-composed devotional texts, emphasizing the Virgin's role as Queen of Heaven. The cycle of five antiphons demonstrates no apparent modal organization (the modal sequence is 1, 6, 8, 4, 5) unless the antiphons are extracted from an earlier and more extensive cycle.

BORROWED TEXTS IN THE VOTIVE OFFICES

In spite of the opportunities for new composition, substantial *unica* of the kind described above do not often feature in great quantity in votive offices. New devotions, in spite of their variety, are usually relatively derivative structures, suggesting that compilers were content to draw material from a variety of related feasts and rearrange it as they chose. A Saturday office and a Little Office of the Virgin for the same season often follow broadly similar principles in this respect, in spite of their obvious structural disparity.

Analysis of the concordant texts listed in Tables 4:9 and 4:10 reveals that most of the material used for the votive offices occurs in at least two other contexts elsewhere. Theoretically, one of these occurrences, as the 'parent-text', should appear in complete form, and such items are easily identifiable in the tables by the presence of the asterisk. Occasionally it is impossible to trace a parent-source: a series of identical incipits may occur throughout the manuscript, but the complete version may simply not exist. In some cases this is due to missing leaves. In *WO* F.160, texts given as incipits for the Advent votive office, which also appear as Annunciation incipits, are almost certainly borrowed from the mother-source of Advent, from which part of Matins is now lost. Similarly, in other cases the presence of a two-word incipit may be insufficient for the identification of the complete text. One example of this ambiguity occurs with the incipit *Paradisi*, supplied as both *Magnificat* and *Benedictus* antiphon for the Little Office during Eastertide, and as the first *Magnificat* antiphon at the corresponding Saturday office of the Virgin during the same season. There are two possible parent-texts here, and both appear to be equally likely candidates: *Paradisi ianue*, the Sext antiphon for the Vigil of the Assumption, and *Paradisi porta*, used at the memorial of the Virgin after Lauds on the Thursday after Easter.

In the majority of manuscripts, wholesale lifting of a series of texts from one particular feast to form a Little Office or a Saturday office is uncommon (although the earliest Saturday offices were exceptions in this respect). Rather, compilers selected their material from a wide range of observances, and not exclusively from Marian feasts: Christmas Day, the Circumcision and Ember Days are just a few such examples. The three Matins responds of the Advent Little Office are a particularly diverse collection, representing Christmas Day, the Purification and the Sunday falling within the Octave of the Assumption. These have no correspondence with the items chosen for the Saturday Advent office. Textual correlation between the two forms of the votive office was thus not a rule, and neither was a votive office invariably compiled from a group of texts from a single feast.

However, certain trends for borrowing are apparent. Marian votive offices for use in Advent are normally characterized by the number of texts borrowed from the Feast of the Annunciation. The doctrinal correlation in operation here is very apparent, but close examination of the Annunciation propers in several manuscripts (among them the Worcester Antiphoner) reveals that many texts were simply lifted direct from the Advent period. This tendency is stressed by Henri Barré, who observed that many of the texts for both Advent and the Annunciation are drawn from St Luke's Gospel or from the prophetic texts of Isaiah, where medieval exegesis assumed a pronounced Marian character.[26] Indeed, texts for both feasts tend to be considerably more 'biblical' in terms of derivation than those of other periods in the liturgical year where the Virgin has a prominent role, including the Christmas season.

The Marian commemorative office following the Christmas period, which began at Epiphany or its octave, and usually extended to the Purification, was characterized by very different sets of texts. Both *WO* F.160 and the Hyde Abbey Breviary, *Ob* e.1*, draw on the Feast of the Circumcision, and the borrowing is particularly pronounced in the Lauds antiphons of the Hyde manuscript. Worcester supplements material from the Circumcision with items from the Octave of the Assumption and also from a set of texts which were not from the regular liturgy, but were themselves of a votive nature: the memorials which formed appendages to the office of second Vespers on the Feast of Holy Innocents, also part of the Christmas cycle of feasts.

Borrowing in the Marian offices used during Eastertide, predictably enough, was closely linked with Easter Day and its octave and often presents texts which cannot be readily identified, since they begin with the simple incipit *Alleluia*. Worcester used the Matins invitatory from the corresponding commemorative office prescribed for Epiphany to the Purification, but the concordance is not exact. The melody of *Laudemus omnes virginis* corresponds with the Epiphany equivalent, but the latter part of the text is altered.

THE MARIAN OFFICES IN THE HYDE ABBEY BREVIARY

The Hyde Abbey Breviary (*c.*1300), in spite of its absence of notation, provides an invaluable parallel insight into the compilation of the votive office. Like Worcester, the Hyde source supplies substantial seasonal alternatives for both the Saturday office and its daily counterpart: Advent, from Christmas to the Purification, Eastertide (Saturday only) and a general set of texts used *per annum*. Its textual content is more complete than the Worcester format: it gives not only musical items but also collects and chapters, and there are far fewer incipits.

In terms of structure the offices given in the two manuscripts correspond closely. Hyde Abbey, however, has proportionally fewer *unica* than Worcester in both forms of the office, and its borrowing is arranged slightly more schematically. Instances of schematic borrowing, where clearly defined groups of texts are lifted from their original context to form part of the votive office, are listed below. The phenomenon is particularly striking in the choice of the five Lauds antiphons required for the Saturday office (Worcester supplies only a single Lauds antiphon here). On three occasions Hyde Abbey lifts at least half of the Lauds antiphons from a single feast (the Annunciation, the Circumcision and the Assumption respectively), and once the entire series is directly transferred (from the Circumcision) with no alteration whatsoever. Some of the Matins responds are similarly unified. Seasonal borrowing in general seems to be more restricted than in the Worcester offices: the Hyde Advent offices limit themselves to texts from Advent Sunday and the Feast of the Annunciation, the Christmas Office to the Feast of the Circumcision, and the offices used *per annum* draw substantially on the Nativity of the Virgin. The number of texts common to both forms of the office, where schematic borrowing occurs, is prominent.

Schematic Borrowing in the Hyde Abbey Saturday Commemorative Office

1. Advent

Matins Responds I-III   Advent Sunday, Matins Responds III, IV, VI
Lauds Antiphons 1,2,3,5   Annunciation, Matins Antiphons 7,8,9,4

2. Christmas to the Purification

Matins Responds I-II	Circumcision, Matins Responds IV, XII
Lauds Antiphons 1-5	Circumcision, Lauds Antiphons 1-5

3. Eastertide

Matins Responds I-III	First Sunday after Octave of Easter, Matins Responds X-XII

4. *Per annum*

Alternative *Magnificat* Antiphons at First Vespers	During Octave of Assumption, Antiphons 6,1,2
Matins Responds III-V	Nativity BVM, Matins Responds IV, VIII, XII
Lauds Antiphons 3-5	Assumption, Lauds Antiphons 3-5

Schematic Borrowing in the Hyde Abbey Little Office

1. Advent

Matins Responds I-III	Advent Sunday, Matins Responds III, IV, VI
Lauds Antiphons	Annunciation, Matins Antiphons 7,9
Vespers Antiphons	Annunciation, Matins Antiphons 1,3
Compline Antiphons	Annunciation, Matins Antiphon 8, Lauds 4

2. Christmas to Purification

Matins Responds II-III	Advent Sunday, Matins Responds XII, VIII
Lauds, Terce, Sext and None Antiphons	Circumcision, Lauds Antiphons 1,3,4,5
Compline Antiphons	Christmas Eve, Sext and None Antiphons

CONCLUSIONS

The groups of texts for both forms of the votive office in the Worcester and Hyde sources emphasize two features: first, the desirability of providing a substantial quantity of alternative material for each season, whether newly composed or borrowed from elsewhere, and second, the intrinsic musical value of the office. There can be little doubt that the greater part of both votive offices at Worcester were sung (by contrast with the partly-spoken Little Office at St Mary's York), and that the music provided for both forms was often elaborate and sometimes completely original. The implication is that not only the 'festal' commemorative office had risen to a position of musical importance by the middle of the twelfth century, but that the Little Office had also been transformed from its early position as a private devotion, to an appended observance with an independent musical status of its own.

The sudden vogue for votive offices, and in particular those to the Virgin, must have provided the compilers of liturgical books with something of a challenge. As with many of the later medieval observances, including those offices and masses for newly-canonized saints like Thomas à Becket, the compiler had to choose between re-arranging existing material, or creating anew. Festal observances, including many of the 'local' feasts in the Worcester Antiphoner, seem to incorporate mostly original composition, much of it recognizable by its modal organization and melodic elaboration. Sometimes the principle of careful planning also extended to textual composition, centring around considered metrical and rhythmic schemes. Such originality, however, seems to have featured rather less prominently in the Marian votive repertory. In some respects the small number of extant texts makes this difficult to determine, but on the whole borrowing outweighs new composition by a substantial margin.

However, the proliferation of Marian feasts from as early as the sixth century onwards provided a compiler with a substantial repertory of material on which to draw. Creation of a votive office, none the less, must have required a degree of ingenuity. Seasonal relevance is seen to be a prominent factor in both of the manuscripts discussed, involving not only festal material of direct relevance, but also items culled from the temporale or even from smaller-scale votive observances such as memorials. The Worcester Antiphoner is a most fortunate survival in that it contains such a large proportion of Marian material, both for the Marian feasts and their vigils and octaves, and for the less specific memorials and votive offices. In this respect it far outweighs any other contemporary source, both English and European, and is particularly striking for its emphasis on *The Song of Songs*.

The extent of weekly commemorative offices of the Virgin and other intentions is a significant factor in the declining use of the ferial psalter in at least some monastic houses during the Middle Ages. Taken together with the expanded number of double feasts in the calendar, these observances largely ousted ferias, especially in the period referred to as *per annum*. Although principal feasts and their octaves and the Lenten season saw their omission, the use of commemorations and supplementary daily offices shows even the monasteries abandoning the continuous cycle of the recitation of the psalter in favour of devotional observance not far removed from popular piety, exemplified by lay Books of Hours.

NOTES

1. Tolhurst, 120; 149-50.
2. Wordsworth in Maydeston, 157-213, and Harrison, *Music in Medieval Britain*, 76 respectively.
3. See, for example, Barré, 'Un plaidoyer monastique', 375-99.
4. All references to H.T. Riley, *Chronica Monasterii S. Albani*, vol.i, (Rolls Series, xxviii, 1863-76), cited here as 'St Albans'.
5. See Tolhurst, 146-7.
6. St Albans, 93; See also Thomson, *Manuscripts from St Albans Abbey*, 38-44.
7. A brief description of the manuscript is given by Thomson, 94; there are further references to its importance on 28-30 and 37-8.
8. Christopher Wordsworth prints part of this commemorative office in Maydeston, 187-8, and K.D. Hartzell also gives it in rather more complete form in his thesis, *The Musical Repertoire at St Albans*.
9. Hartzell does mention the replacement Saturday observance as a possible function for the office discussed here, but in rather negligible terms: 'These forms [i.e. daily and Saturday offices of a votive nature] were in use in England sporadically before the Conquest. They either were repressed by the Normans or died out because the Normans had no place for them in the liturgy.'
10. Tolhurst's research was based on a rotograph of the source now at Downside Abbey, although his collation of this manuscript was never published.
11. Tolhurst, 153.
12. The nineteenth-century *Glossarium mediae et infimae Latinitatis* cf DuCange lists several instances of the term simply to suggest an office consisting primarily of psalmody, as for example in the Rule of St Donatus: *De synaxi, id est de cursu Psalmorum.*
13. Bracketed words in this citation are added in the margin of the source, and relegated to the apparatus in the modern edition.
14. Tolhurst, 187.

15. James, 1359, Frere, 953, Tolhurst, 238; Brady, *The Derivation of the English Monastic Office Books*, index of sources.

16. Tolhurst, 242.

17. Tolhurst makes no mention of the St Albans book in his handlist of sources in the Hyde Abbey companion, but a xerox of the entire breviary survives among his papers at Downside Abbey, presumably acquired after the publication of Hyde Abbey vi.

18. Offices to St Amphibalus and the Trinity follow within the same section, both under the general heading *commemorationes*, but neither seems to have been treated as a conventional commemorative office and there are no references to specific weekdays. There are occasional references to an office of St Amphibalus in *Gesta Abbatum*.

19. Tolhurst, 149.

20. Tolhurst, 144.

21. Hesbert, ed. *Corpus Antiphonalium Officii*, ii, Rome, 1965.

22. Barré, 'Antiennes et réponds de la Vierge', 153.

23. Leclerq, *The Love of Learning and the Desire for God*, 84.

24. Hughes, 'Modal Order and Disorder in the Rhymed Office', 29, and 'Chants in the Rhymed Office of St Thomas of Canterbury'.

25. Cattin, 117.

26. Barré, 'Antiennes et réponds de la Vierge'.

Chapter Five

THE VOTIVE ANTIPHON

By the thirteenth century two kinds of observance in honour of the Virgin were current in English monasteries: the Little Office and the Saturday commemorative office. A third observance became increasingly common in the succeeding centuries, employing what has become known as the votive antiphon. To avoid confusion this particular term is used consistently throughout this chapter, but it must be stressed that there is no medieval equivalent, and contemporary sources usually refer simply to an *antiphona*. The votive antiphon forms part of a group of related self-contained ceremonies, each consisting of three elements: an antiphon, versicle with response, and a collect.

The earliest reference to the singing of a Marian antiphon after an office occurs in *RC*. On all days throughout the year, except in Advent, a series of three antiphons addressed respectively to the Holy Cross, the Virgin and the patron saint, followed Vespers and Lauds:

> . . . *cantent antifonam de cruce, inde antiphonam de sancta Maria*
> *et de sancto cuius ueneratio in praesenti colitur aecclesia aut, si*
> *minus fuerit, de ipsius loci consecratione.*   *RC* 84,7-9

Comparison with three slightly later English sources suggests that *antiphona* implies rather more than an antiphon alone: indeed, it is likely that this passage refers to a sequence of three common commemorations, where the antiphon formed the first element of the tripartite ceremony described above. A series of observances with this structure appears among the additions to the tenth-century Durham Collectar (*DR*c A.IV.19), copied in southern England *c.*900-925. Miscellanous additions were made to the manuscript in *c.*970 in Northumbria by several scribes. The antiphon elements of the Durham observances are all short texts, and like the accompanying versicles and collects, they appear to have been borrowed from the regular liturgy rather than newly composed. As in *RC* they form part of a group of intercessions after Vespers, and are directed towards a variety of intentions, commencing with the Holy Cross, the Virgin and St Michael. Similar observances also occur in the mid-eleventh century Leofric Collectar (*Lbl* 2961), and, most significantly, after Lauds and Vespers of the Virgin in the Canterbury manuscript *Lbl* A.III, copied *c*.1032-50 (see p.71 and below).

The absence of psalmody within these structures is in some respects unusual, for most antiphons were conceived as refrains or framing texts for psalms: their function was often to clarify context by referring to the feast-day or season. Neverthless, there are other occasions in the liturgy where antiphons are prescribed without psalms: processions, the ceremonial *Mandatum* antiphons on Maundy Thursday, and the Aspersion antiphons, *Vidi aquam* and *Asperges me*. Some of these examples are not entirely divorced from psalmody since they incorporate integral psalm-verses; indeed, the *Mandatum* antiphons in the Use of Sarum retain an entire psalm as part of their structure. Processions in the Early Church were also accompanied by antiphons with integral psalms, which continued until the procession reached its station. Vestigial remmnants of the same practice may be seen in the antiphonal chants of the mass: the introit, offertory and communion, each of which originally accompanied a procession, although only the introit consistently retains its verse in medieval practice. However, these more complex forms do not feature within the repertory of votive antiphons, which correspond structurally to the more familiar office items. Indeed, most antiphons used independently in memorials were simply transferred from their original office context to function as part of a separate ceremony.

MEMORIALS AND SUFFRAGES

Memorials and suffrages account for the greater part of the independent antiphon repertory. These two observances usually share a common structure, although they vary slightly in function. The memorial also bears some relationship to processional forms, not only because a memorial for a particular intention (especially the Virgin and All Saints) often concluded the procession when it returned to choir, but also because the movement of the procession to its station was accompanied by an antiphon, while the station itself frequently consisted of a versicle followed by a collect, imitating the structure of a self-contained observance.

Nevertheless, memorials and suffrages most commonly occur as appendages to an office, where they function in several different ways. Fundamentally, they may be seen as part of a long line of tradition which stresses prayer for special intentions as a conclusion to the office (see pp.9-12). The roots of this practice appear to go back to two different sources: first, the commemoration of absent brethren prescribed by St Benedict at the end of the hours, and second, the series of Gallican and Celtic *capitella*.

Gallican *capitella* consist simply of psalm verses, but the Celtic type exhibit closer parallels with later memorials and suffrages. Although they do not incorporate antiphons, some of the psalm verses are followed by a short collect and they are often preceded by particularized intentions. A typical series might include appropriate verses for priests, the king, the abbot, peace, the sick and the faithful departed.

The exact manner in which the offices terminated is left ambiguous in Benedict's Rule, and none of the early sources provide explicit directions for the use of *capitella*. Even those sources which have provided much of the early material discussed in Part One—the Anianian documents, *RC* and Lanfranc—offer few clues as to how *capitella*, *preces*, memorials and suffrages inter-related. Intensive examination of a much wider range of sources from all parts of western Europe would be necessary to tackle this fascinating question properly: it constitutes a study in its own right.

Observance of memorials and suffrages is much more explicitly documented in medieval sources, although the exact circumstances of their evolution remain vague. Both were appended to Lauds and Vespers after the collect, where they were often interspersed with other additional ceremonies such as processions or votive offices.

In spite of their relationship with *capitella*, memorials are perhaps most easily understood as compressed offices, retaining some of the main features of the office—its psalm antiphon, versicle and collect—but omitting the psalmody. In their simplest manifestation, memorials arose when two holy days coincided, so that second Vespers of one feast clashed with first Vespers of another feast on the following day. There were two solutions to this problem. In some cases, Vespers would simply be divided equally between the two concurring observances, so that the first took precedence up to the chapter, and the second from the chapter to the conclusion. Examples of divided offices have already been noted on p.106. But more frequently a second solution was used. Here, one office was forced to give way completely to the other, and the displaced office was effectively recited in abbreviated form as a memorial following straight after the full office. The notion of a compressed office is clarified by the occasional appearance of memorials of more elaborate construction. Tolhurst identifies two examples with less regular structure. At Ely, the memorial of St John the Baptist after second Vespers of St Etheldreda consisted of the standard elements of antiphon, versicle and collect, but with *Magnificat* and its antiphon inserted before the versicle. Gloucester prescribed a yet more complex memorial if the Feast of St Andrew fell on the Vigil of Advent Sunday, consisting of a respond, versicle, *Magnificat* with antiphon before and after, and the collect, all taken from the displaced office.[1]

In each of the above examples the memorial provides a solution to the problem of two concurring feasts, and in particular the juxtaposition of two sets of Vespers, by compressing one of the hours. Memorials of this kind also arose if one feast fell on the same day as another, or on a Sunday, necessitating transference. In this case the transferred feast was commemorated on its original day in the usual manner after Lauds and Vespers.

Other memorials were common or simply devotional rather than proper. General memorials in honour of the Virgin, All Saints, the Trinity and the Holy Cross were observed by most houses during the Middle Ages. The last two were usually limited only to appropriate liturgical seasons, but those of the Virgin and All Saints occurred on a much more regular basis. Such memorials display more properly 'votive' characteristics in that they do not arise from the exigencies of the regular office.

Memorials in honour of the Virgin and All Saints are again excellent examples of the principle of compressing an office. Multiplication of appended ceremonies after the hours often resulted in a long and complex sequence of observances, sometimes calling for recitation of no fewer than three votive hours (of the dead, the Virgin and All Saints) after the regular office, in addition to any proper or daily memorials which might occur. Vespers and Lauds of All Saints seem to have disappeared from this scheme in most monasteries by the fourteenth century at the latest. Tolhurst indicates that the office was officially abolished by the Southern Chapter in 1255, and although its elimination was not effected immediately, most of the later manuscripts replace both of the hours with a simple memorial.[2] Like the Little Office of the Virgin, memorials of All Saints are often provided with variable seasonal texts.

Memorials of the Virgin have rather more complex associations. Tolhurst's argument that the Little Office of the Virgin in *Lbl* A.III simply represents an expansion of the *antiphona* in *RC* has already been discussed, but in some foundations both the Little Office and a memorial of the Virgin seem to have been recited as appendages to Vespers. At Chester, where the Little Office preceded Vespers of the day in Lent, the memorial followed the regular office, and this may also have been the case at St Mary's, York. Elsewhere, the memorial was used more conventionally as an abbreviated replacement for the Little Office on certain days, but several monasteries still recited the office privately, out of choir. The same is true of a third observance employing the antiphon; this often appeared as a successive appendage to Compline of the Virgin, rather than as a replacement for it. These rather unconventional methods of using memorials once again testify to the proliferation of Marian devotion in English monasteries; appendages in honour of the Virgin, unlike those for most other intentions, by and large seem to have escaped legislative pruning.

The Virgin also featured in series of suffrages as well as memorials. Suffrages imitate the standard structure of the memorial but occur as a fixed, ferial sequence, distinct from both proper (displaced) memorials and the daily or seasonal devotional memorials prescribed for non-ferial days.

In some respects, the devotional memorials to the Trinity, the Cross, the Virgin and All Saints discussed above, are perhaps best understood as a reduced series of suffrages. This point is clarified by Van Dijk's discussion of reformed Roman practice:

> The former [suffrages] were said on ferias after the final *Benedicamus* of Lauds and Vespers, a second *Benedicamus* being added to conlude the series. The latter [memorials, or, as Van Dijk terms them, 'common commemorations'], numbering only two, were restricted to Sundays and feasts. They preceded the one *Benedicamus* and followed the collect of the day or a *memoria* of an occurring feast.[3]

Choice of one group or the other thus seems to have been conditioned purely by the status of the day: a principle equally applicable to English Benedictine use. From this viewpoint, the fixed series of three devotions in *RC* is perhaps closer to an embryonic set of suffrages rather than a series of devotional memorials, for it seems to have been intended for regular use throughout most of the year.

In essence the suffrages are close to the early *capitella* (and their direct descendants, *preces*), reflecting the old tradition of praying for a sequence of special intentions at the end of an office. English Benedictine books reveal that the sequence of intentions had grown to vast proportions by the thirteenth century: a typical series included upwards of a dozen items, beginning with the general devotional intentions (the Trinity, the Cross, the Virgin), and ending with All Saints. Saints with a particular local significance, Apostles, Martyrs, Virgins and Relics were all likely to be interspersed. On occasion the Lady Office was also incorporated into the series in the accepted place for the suffrage of the Virgin. In this instance suffrage and votive office seem to have been alternative rather than successive devotions, although there was usually little reason to compress the full hour on a ferial day. Suffrages were a particular target for the reforming chapters, which aimed to reduce numbers to manageable proportions. Tolhurst notes the particularly drastic suggestion of the Southern Chapter in 1277, which proposed the substitution of a mere three suffrages—St Benedict, the Patron and the Virgin (when her office was not said in choir)—for the existing series.[4] Unfavourable response to this proposal led to its modification, and most of the later sources settle for a series of six or seven items.

Three classes of 'memorial' existed by the later Middle Ages: proper commemorations of displaced or concurring feasts, common or seasonal commemorations, and ferial suffrages. Suffrages and common devotional memorials are closely related, although suffrages are distinguished in some rites by two occurrences of *Benedicamus domino*, first as a conclusion to the office, second to mark the end of the suffrages themselves. The tripartite form common to all three categories was also imitated in a processional context, especially at stations and at the return to choir. Processional antiphons of the Virgin hold an important position in the repertory of independent antiphons, and in particular to the 'post-Compline' antiphon which forms the basis of this chapter. Their relationship is explored below.

Memorials and suffrages normally occurred after only two of the offices (or their votive counterpart)—Lauds and Vespers—and in this respect it is somewhat surprising to witness the emergence of an independent antiphon after Compline in English monasteries during the thirteenth century. It seems never to have been customary to recite a memorial after Compline, even when there was good reason: a memorial of the Virgin did not replace Compline of the Little Office on the occasions when it was omitted from choir. The post-Compline ceremony cannot, therefore, be classified as a conventional memorial, in spite of its identical structure. It is best understood as a quite independent observance, added to the liturgy as a special mark of adoration to the Virgin.

THE POST-COMPLINE CEREMONY

This observance, usually sung after Compline or Compline of the Virgin, began to assume prominence in English Benedictine houses during the later thirteenth century. It was distinct from the memorial in several ways. First, it was almost invariably addressed to the Virgin Mary; second, it tended to appear as a single item rather than as part of a group of similar observances addressed to other saints or intentions; and third, it was observed with greater ritual emphasis than the memorial, often preceding the *Trina oratio* which rounded off the day's devotions before the community processed to the dormitory. Some of the extant customaries, and particularly that of St Mary's, York, describe the details of its observance with considerable care.

Most of the texts for the earliest post-Compline ceremonies were apparently drawn from a relatively small repertory of items. Sometimes the choice of antiphon seems to have been a matter for the discretion of the cantor, but in other cases a particular text was expressly prescribed. In the latter instance, *Salve regina* is by far the most common of the antiphons given in the extant sources. Like the majority of memorial antiphons, *Salve regina* was borrowed from the existing repertory of the office rather than composed specifically for the ceremony. This also applies to three other familiar post-Compline antiphons: *Alma redemptoris, Ave regina celorum* and *Regina celi*.[5] All four of these items were adopted on a seasonal basis by the Franciscans in 1249 and were subsequently taken into the Roman Use, although the appearance of these particular texts, aside from *Salve regina*, is far more sporadic in English Benedictine and secular books.

Borrowing of liturgical material remained a common phenomenon until the Reformation, but a few of the later sources, particularly those associated with the collegiate foundations of the fourteenth and fifteenth centuries, contain a number of newly-written texts. Most of these utilize stereotyped imagery and are of no great literary merit. Some of the 'new' texts were simply troped versions of all or part of an existing liturgical text: there are several such versions of *Salve regina*.

Because of the prominence of the post-Compline antiphon within the English pre-Reformation polyphonic repertory, it has long been a form familiar to musicologists. During the 1950s, F.Ll. Harrison's research on the Eton Choirbook first drew attention to the richness and vast scale of many of these compositions, and the potential importance of the ceremony for which they were conceived became apparent.[6] It was Harrison who first introduced the term 'votive antiphon' as a convenient label for such pieces.

Votive antiphons were not observed exclusively after Compline. From at least the fifteenth century, English sources offer evidence that similar antiphons might be recited after the other hours, whether those of the regular office or those of the Little Office of the Virgin, and even after the daily chapter meeting in addition. In some cases a single antiphon might simply be repeated several times a day: this was often the case with *Salve regina*. Table 5.1 (p.273) lists fourteen extant English Benedictine sources which prescribe votive antiphons, remarking on their respective positions in the daily round. In most cases the ceremony seems to have been performed in choir after the office or mass in question, but secular practice in England (particularly at the new collegiate foundations) sometimes decreed that the singers were to assemble at some other more appropriate location, such as a side chapel, an image of the Virgin, or the founder's tomb.[7]

THE EMERGENCE OF THE VOTIVE ANTIPHON AS A PRACTICE

The major thrust for the adoption of the most widely occurring of all votive antiphons, *Salve regina*, seems initially to have come from the Cistercians. Nevertheless, the earliest references to the text in the statutes of the order do not specify a post-Compline position. (Relevant passages are recorded with references in Table 5:2, p.275.) In 1218, it was decreed that *Salve regina* (with an accompanying versicle and collect) was to be sung daily in Cistercian houses, after an (unspecified) respond following the chapter. In 1220, however, this requirement was modified to private daily recitation, and the 1228 statutes mention only that the antiphon was to be observed *mediocri voce* after chapter on Fridays. The daily singing of *Salve regina* as a communal observance after Compline seems not to have become a prescribed requirement for the Cistercians until 1251.

The earliest recorded occurrence of the singing of *Salve regina* after Compline suggests that the Dominican order may have taken the initiative for this particular position. In 1221, Jordan of Saxony, head of the Dominican order, decreed that the antiphon was to be sung in Bologna in procession after Compline, as an act of thanksgiving to the Virgin for the deliverance of a Bolognese friar, Bernard, from devilish torments. Reputedly this observance rapidly became the custom throughout Lombardy, and in 1334 a General Chapter in Limoges decreed that it was to be formally adopted throughout the Dominican order. The formal prescription of *Salve regina* and three other post-Compline antiphons by the Franciscan order in 1249 is discussed further below. Cluniac adoption of the antiphon was slightly later: a reference to *Salve regina* or some other antiphon of the Virgin after Compline, *alta voce et cum nota*, appears in the 1301 statutes of Bertrand I.

Formal prescription of the votive antiphon as an essential appendage to Compline in English Benedictine houses only occurred in 1343, when the presidents of the General Benedictine Chapter (meeting in this year at Northampton) issued a set of statutes for promulgation through the provinces of Canterbury and York. In the statutes relating to liturgy, there are items concerned with the abolition of votive practices which by this date were clearly felt to be extraneous or superfluous. Certain items of additional psalmody recited *submissa voce* met with disfavour, and the Chapter also aimed to reduce substantially the number of suffrages recited after Lauds and Vespers. Reference to this antiphon-ceremony occurs as part of Item 20 in the section dealing with the Divine Office (Table 5:2).

It is significant that a directive of the General Chapter primarily concerned with curtailment should also make provision for expansion of the repertory of appended observances. In this respect the post-Compline antiphon is a further instance of the Marian phenomenon which began to change the face of English devotion as early as the eleventh century. Indeed, reference to the antiphon in the Northampton statutes may simply have been a move to formalize a practice which had unofficially been adopted by some Benedictine houses at a much earlier date. Certainly at St Peter's, Westminster, in *c.*1266, the monks were to sing *Salve regina ex moderno et non ex veteri usu* (West.Cust., 201), implying that the antiphon had already been in use for some years before this date. Later statutes of the General Chapter indicate that the votive antiphon maintained its approved position as an appendage to Compline in Benedictine houses well into the fifteenth century. At the last recorded meeting of the General Chapter in 1444, again at Northampton, the 1343 reference to the item is reproduced almost verbatim (Pantin, ii,197).

The Benedictines were clearly not pioneers in their adoption of the post-Compline antiphon. Nevertheless, the Benedictine statute of 1343 ante-dates the Roman secular usage; it was in 1350 that Pope Clement VI sanctioned the use of the four seasonal Marian antiphons (listed above) in all churches following the Roman Use. The Roman church itself apparently borrowed this particular four-fold scheme from the Franciscan order, where it seems to have originated a century earlier. The transference of the custom is in itself symptomatic of the important links between Roman and Franciscan uses, which have been revealed by Stephen Van Dijk's extensive research into the origins of the late medieval Roman liturgy and its relation to Franciscan books.[8] Franciscan promulgation of the post-Compline antiphon is first mentioned in 1249, when the Minister General of the Franciscans, John of Parma, issued a letter to the superiors of the Tuscan province, largely concerned with the observance of certain liturgical books. A passage relating to the post-Compline antiphon (cited in Table 5:2) specifies the four familiar texts, and the regulation took on a wider importance when it was made obligatory for the entire Franciscan order by the Chapter of Metz in 1254. Nevertheless, the liturgical arrangement did not remain constant in Franciscan liturgical books of the fifteenth century, and a slightly different seasonal division was adopted by the Roman Church in 1350 (Table 5:3, p.277). Fifteenth-century Franciscan books are usually distinguished by the insertion of a fifth antiphon, *Quam pulchra es*, sung after Compline from the Nativity of the Virgin (8 September) until Advent.

EVIDENCE OF THE POST-COMPLINE CEREMONY IN SURVIVING ENGLISH BENEDICTINE MANUSCRIPTS

By comparison with the other votive forms considered so far, which are by and large richly represented in the extant sources, the votive antiphon appears more sporadically in English Benedictine manuscripts. Only three of the sources listed in Table 5:1 antedate the 1343 statute, and there is no reference to the custom in other early manuscripts of major importance from Worcester (*WO* F.160 of *c.*1230), Norwich (*Ccc* 465 of *c.*1260) and Hyde Abbey (*Ob* e.1* of *c.*1300). The matter is not entirely clear-cut, however, in that paraliturgical observances like this ceremony, although often mentioned in customaries, are not entirely appropriate for inclusion in the principal office books. Indeed, a greater proportion of the evidence for the adoption of this observance at the larger monasteries is found in rather miscellaneous sources with varied content.

Five miscellanies of this type, all with complete texts (although with little information on the manner of their observance), date from the fifteenth century. Four of the foundations represented were large houses of considerable importance: Christ Church, Canterbury (*Llp* 558), Durham (*Lbl* 1804), St Peter's, Gloucester (*Ob* f.1) and Winchester (*DO* 26543). The fifth was a small Benedictine nunnery on the outskirts of Oxford, Godstow (*Mch* 6717). The books are similar in content, and incorporate a variety of

material for occasional and votive use: the Office of the Dead and the Little
Office of the Virgin, weekly commemorative offices and prayers of a
private nature. The manuscripts from Canterbury and Godstow have a
psalter as their nucleus: *Llp* 558 has already been discussed in Chapter
Three for its incorporation of the Little Office. Few manuscripts of this type
are known before the fifteenth century, and they may be seen to represent
the contemporary importance of miscellaneous additional devotions. Tolhurst
saw them as 'supplementary volumes containing those parts of the daily
round of prayer which are not strictly speaking parts of the original *Opus
Dei* of St Benedict and which form a class of manuscripts by themselves'.[9]

Aside from these five manuscripts, only two other books listed in Table
5:1 present the three elements of the antiphon ceremony with complete texts.
One of these, *Ob* 358, is a psalter which includes the antiphon as an
unrubricated appendage, but the other, *Cjc* D.27—the Ordinal of St Mary's
York (*c.*1398-1405)—presents not only the text of the antiphon, but also
notation and rubrics describing the ceremony. This is the sole surviving
noted text of the antiphon *Salve regina* as used at a Benedictine house for
votive purposes, and it supplies the fullest account of how it was observed.
The three other customaries/ordinals in Table 5:1 provide only fleeting
references to the observance, and lack complete texts.

The earliest known reference to the post-Compline antiphon in an
English source occurs in *Lbl* C.XI, the Westminster Customary of
*c.*1266-74. It occurs in a section dealing with discipline and punishment.
Offenders were to take the lowest place in choir during certain specified
ceremonies, of which the antiphon was one:

> *Sed inter letaniam quae privatis diebus dicitur ante missam, et dum
> canuntur missae, atque dum canitur antiphona, Salve regina, quae
> ex moderno et non ex veteri usu cum oracione de Dei Genetrice
> post completorium cantatur, non ad scabellum sed ultimo loco erit
> in choro; atque post completorium versus dormitorium incedendo,
> sicuti et ad omnem processionem, ultimo loco incedet.*
>
> West.Cust., 201.

The choice of the antiphon *Salve regina* accords with most of the later
sources, while the accompanying prayer confirms the notion of the short
independent ceremony. The most intriguing feature of this passage is the
suggestion that although the custom was established at Westminster at the
time of writing, the antiphon itself had previously been used in some other
manner and subsequently modified. It is not entirely clear how the phrase
may be interpreted: possibly it qualifies the original liturgical function of the
antiphon, with *cum oratione . . . post completorium* as a gloss on *ex
moderno . . . usu*. In this case, the earlier function of the antiphon,

probably as a processional or office antiphon, may well have been discarded when the post-Compline use was adopted.

From this it may be inferred that the votive antiphon was established in at least one English Benedictine house by the middle of the thirteenth century. Nearest in date to *Lbl* C.XI is the St Albans psalter *Ob* 358, for which Neil Ker suggested a copying date of mid-thirteenth century.[10] The provenance of the book is identifiable from its calendar, which gives the Feast of the Dedication on 28 December and obits to the father, mother and uncle of Abbot John VI (Whethamstede) on 5 March. The antiphon *Salve regina* appears at the end of the book on f.145v, after the Office of the Dead. Ker considered this to be a slightly later addition made at the end of the thirteenth century. Again the presence of a versicle, *Ave Maria gratia plena*, and collect, *Omnipotens sempiterne deus*, suggests a self-contained form. There is no specific reference to context, but presumably the observance was viewed as an accretion in a similar category to the Office of the Dead (f.140) and the litany (f.134). The text of the antiphon is particularly significant since it is one of only four English Benedictine sources which present *Salve regina* with a trope. One of the other examples, the Ordinal of St Mary's York, dates from around a century later, although it exhibits an almost exact textual correspondence. The other instances of the trope—longer versions with five and seven verses respectively—occur in the Processional of the Nuns of Chester (*US-SM* 34.B.7) and the Godstow Psalter, both copied during the fifteenth century. The trope to *Salve regina* has particularly interesting implications, not least because it is an invariable occurrence in English secular sources of similar date. It is considered separately below.

After the St Albans Psalter, no other reference to the votive antiphon in an English Benedictine source occurs until the fourteenth-century Customary of St Werburgh's, Chester. The calendar of this manuscript (f.121) is dated 1330, although the editor, J.D. Brady, considers that the incorporation of *Salve regina* may imply a rather later date on the basis of the 1343 Chapter Act.[11] This factor is not, however, entirely reliable, first because the votive antiphon may well have been adopted prior to the statutes as at Westminster, and second because the Chester Customary disregards certain other Chapter directives which were supposedly in force by the mid-fourteenth century. It thus seems plausible to assume a copying date of *c.*1330.

At Chester the votive antiphon was appended not to Compline of the day but apparently incorporated into Compline of the Virgin, which normally followed straight after the regular office. The text sung—*Salve regina*—remained fixed throughout the year, although the accompanying collect changed during certain seasons. The versicle following the antiphon was always *Post partum* [*virgo inviolata permansisti*, with response *Dei genetrix intercede pro nobis*]. On most occasions the collect was *Deus qui*

de beate, but during Advent it was *Gratiam tuam* and on the Feast of the
Exaltation of the Holy Cross (14 September) *Imploramus*, which was
followed by a collect of the Holy Spirit, *Ure igne*. The votive antiphon
ceremony as a whole seems to have occurred between the hymn and the
Benedicamus of Compline of the Virgin. This is unique: in all other extant
sources it forms a straightforward appendage after the office.

No other reference to the post-Compline antiphon occurs until after the
1343 statute. But the *Gesta Abbatum Monasterii S. Albani* indicates—in a
passage written under the supervision of Thomas Walsingham, precentor and
chief copyist of the Abbey—that the priory of Redbourn, Hertfordshire,
acquired by St Albans under Abbot Leofstan before the Norman Conquest,
had certainly adopted the custom by the latter half of the fourteenth century.
Thomas de la Mare, abbot of St Albans between 1349 and 1396 often used
Redbourn as a place of retirement, and while staying there, the Chronicle
reports, he would sometimes ring the bell for services.

> *Ad Completorium quoque tres ictus fieri fecit in campana, more
> Monasterii; faciens tres orationes, et dicens salutationes Angelicas
> in Capella. Ad quas quidem orationes ipse, manibus suis, erigendi
> fecit signum. Antiphonam quoque de Sancta maria, post
> Completorium, cantari fecit ibidem.*   St Albans ii,401.

Redbourn presumably followed the mother-house in matters liturgical,
although none of the extant St Albans manuscripts aside from *Ob* 358,
suggests that a post-Compline antiphon was recited. Thomas de la Mare,
like several of his predecessors, was an important figure in the area of
liturgical reform: he is credited with publishing a new Ordinal for the
regulation of services, excising many of the old *historiae* and substituting
new ones, and attempting to improve the style of psalmody at St Albans.
His establishment of the weekly commemorative office of St Benedict is
discussed on p.120. His influence was not solely confined to his own
house, for in 1351 he was appointed president of the General Chapter of
black monks, and in that year published a set of Constitutions on the
discipline of the order.

The Ordinal of St Mary's, York has the fullest account of the
post-Compline antiphon, complete with notation (York.SM.Ord, 27-8). At
York the antiphon *Salve regina* was sung after Compline of the Virgin,
which followed Compline of the day as at Chester. Immediately after the
Benedicamus at Compline of the Virgin, the cantor turned to the altar and
intoned the word *Salve* loudly (*alta voce*). The choir took up the antiphon
with the words *regina misericordie*, bowing slightly over the benches
(*capiant curtas venias ob honorem Sancte Marie super formas*), the cantor
following suit after the intonation. Facing the altar, the monks raised their
heads and removed their cowls, continuing with the antiphon until the word

Ostende. At this point a trope of three verses was sung by soloists (see below). The first verse, *Virgo mater ecclesie*, was sung by the junior monk who read the first lesson at Matins during that particular week, and the second verse *Virgo clemens*, by the monk who read the second lesson. The third verse, *Funde preces*, was allotted to a senior. If the abbot was present, the cantor left his stall during the second verse to see if the abbot was willing to sing the following verse; if he declined, the cantor did it himself. The verses were separated by the phrases *O clemens, O pia, and O dulcis Maria,* sung by the whole choir. The antiphon with its verses was followed by the versicle *Post partum,* with response *Dei genetrix.* The priest (*sacerdos*) then intoned the collect *Omnipotens sempiterne deus* in a ferial tone, the choir responding with *Amen.*

After this all rose at once and filed into the middle of the choir in accordance with seniority, covering their faces with their cowls, the juniors preceding the seniors, with the novices at the choir step. All bowed and recited *Pater noster* three times, with *Ave Maria.* Then, at a signal from the prior, who stood at the rear, all rose, crossed themselves without removing their cowls and inclined again. Meanwhile, one of the great bells in the church was rung three times, and when the prior clapped his hands, the brothers followed him out of the church, the seniors leading. The prior led the way to the dormitory, where he stood at the door next to the priest who sprinkled the community with holy water as they passed through. This final procession to the dormitory can also be inferred at Westminster 150 years earlier.

At York the antiphon was sung each day except during the *Triduum,* when silence was observed: *Salve regina ad Completorium dicatur sub silencio super formas* (York.SM.Ord. ii,274). The precision with which the ceremony is described and the status associated with each verse of the trope implies that it was regarded as an important part of the daily liturgy; furthermore it suggests that the house may well have been influenced by secular practice, or vice versa, since the troped version invariably occurs in books of the Sarum rite, although in only one of the other later monastic manuscripts containing a full text of *Salve regina* (see below). On the other hand, the community at York may well have borrowed the custom from a secular foundation rather than relying on existing monastic tradition: possibly the secular Use of York was influential in this respect. This is clearly one of the areas where St Mary's proved its novelty in liturgical matters, and the scarcity of Benedictine houses in the northern province from which it might have borrowed established customs may well have been an important factor.

The Ordinal of the Nuns of Barking, compiled in *c.*1404, also reveals certain peculiarities in its liturgy. (It is one of the few extant English sources which contains the Easter *Visitatio sepulchri* drama.) At Barking *Salve* *regina* was not sung after Compline as in most of the monastic foundations represented in Table 5:1, but rather after High Mass on prescribed feast days: St Bridget (1 February, also the Vigil of the Purification), and Christmas Day. On the Feast of All Saints (1 November), an antiphon was sung after Compline, but this was *Mater ora filium* rather than *Salve regina*. No other reference to a votive antiphon is made in the Barking Ordinal, although it may be that the antiphon following High Mass was sung on a greater number of feasts than the source specifies. Such omissions suggest that not all houses were greatly influenced by the decrees of the General Chapter, although Barking may well have been exempt from certain items of jurisdiction since they were not represented at meetings of the Chapter.[12]

The fifteenth-century Processional of the Nuns of Chester, which belonged to Dame Margery Byrkenhed of Chester, is also unconventional in certain respects. Most of the items given are specifically processional texts with English rubrics, but in other instances general items are provided. Following the texts for Maundy Thursday ('Shere Thursday'), a number of Marian antiphons are given for general use after Compline. A lengthy versified 'payer' [sic], *Ave sponsa incorrupta*, was followed by *Pater noster* 'as the use is', *Adoramus te Christe*, *Ingressus angelus* and *Ave Maria*. Thereafter *Gaude dei genetrix*, *Ave regina celorum*, *Salve regina* 'with the fyve versus' and *Alma redemptoris mater* were said, with the respond *Aspice domine* and a series of *preces*. Clearly this is a further reference to the troped form of the *Salve* in rather fuller form than at St Mary's, York: the Chester version may have corresponded with the five-verse trope found in some Sarum sources (see Table 5:8).

The five miscellaneous fifteenth-century sources discussed above all testify to the expansion of the votive antiphon in later years: *Llp* 558, *Lbl* 1804, *Ob* f.1, *DO* 26543 and *Mch* 6717. The text selected in these manuscripts is almost invariably *Salve regina*, but it is no longer confined exclusively to its post-Compline function in all sources. The Durham book (*Lbl* 1804) is most conventional: Compline is followed by a memorial of the passion, consisting of a short antiphon related to the passion, versicle with response and collect. Such memorials were commonly said after each of the hours by the fifteenth century. The text of *Salve regina* follows in its full (untroped) form, with the versicle *Ave Maria gratia plena* and the collect *Omnipotens sempiterne deus*.

However, at St Peter's, Gloucester (*Ob* f.1), *Salve regina* was said after the *Benedicamus* at Lauds with the versicle *Post partum* and collect *Omnipotens sempiterne deus*. The memorial of the passion followed. *Salve regina* was also said with the same versicle and collect after None and Vespers. The daily chapter meeting and Compline, however, were both followed by a different antiphon, *Sancta Maria non est tibi similis*. After

Compline the antiphon was recited twice: once after the *Benedicamus*, and once after the *Trina oratio*.

The Godstow source (*Mch* 6717) also provides alternative antiphon texts, but in this case all for use after Compline: *Salve regina, Gaude virgo mater* and *Gaude flore virginali*, each with their own versicle. A seasonal scheme may well have been implied. The last two items are both newly-composed, non-liturgical votive antiphon texts, rare occurrences in Benedictine books, although texts of this type frequently feature in later secular devotional manuscripts and also within the English polyphonic repertory. There are surviving settings of *Gaude virgo mater* by Aston, Sturton, Horwood, Mundy and Wylkynson (the last three fragmentary), and of *Gaude flore virginali* by Horwood, Kellyk, Lambe, Turges, Cornysh and Davy (all in the Eton Choirbook) and Carver. The original index of the Eton manuscript also refers to a lost five-part setting of this antiphon by Dunstable.

Llp 558 from Christ Church, Canterbury prescribes only *Salve regina*. It appears with a slightly modified ending, accompanied by the versicle *Ave Maria* and collect *Omnipotens sempiterne deus*. These texts followed Lauds, None, Vespers and Compline of the Virgin, and were accompanied by the blessing *Per intercessionem sue sacratissime matris benedicat nos filius dei patris*.

The latest reference to the singing of a votive antiphon at a Benedictine house is also from Durham, and occurs in a retrospective account of the customs of the house as practised before the Reformation (popularly known as *The Rites of Durham*) probably written by an elderly monk after the dissolution of the foundation. The roll in which the following passage occurs is dated *c.*1600. After supper, which ended at five,

> they departed all to the chapterhouse to meet the prior, every night
> there to remain in prayer and devotion till six of the clock, at
> which time upon the ringing of a bell they went to the Salvi, all the
> doors both of the cellar, the frater, the dorter, and the cloisters
> were locked even at six of the clock . . .   Durham Rites, 86

In this case *Salve regina* seems to have preceded Compline, but the same roll also refers to the practices of the lay choir at Durham, which consisted of a team of boys from the neighbouring school, who assembled each Friday evening to sing a Jesus anthem before the Jesus altar in the nave after evensong. Following this 'the choristers did sing another anthem by themselves sitting on their knees all the time that their anthem was in singing' (*Durham Rites*, 34). This passage from the Durham Roll is important on two counts: first for its reference to a separate non-monastic body of singers, which in some Benedictine foundations was employed to sing polyphony in a separate Lady Chapel, and second for its emphasis on the Jesus antiphon. Hostility to Marian devotion at the eve of the Reformation led to the excision of many antiphons to Mary and the Saints, and in part this was responsible for the decline of the custom and the shift of emphasis seen in the polyphonic repertory of Latin sacred music from the 1530s.[13]

COMPARISON WITH SECULAR PRACTICE

The sporadic evidence of the Benedictine houses can valuably be compared with secular usage. While most manuscripts of the Sarum Use make no reference whatsoever to the singing of a post-Compline votive antiphon, the evidence from several statutes, particularly from the new collegiate foundations from the fourteenth century onwards, indicates that the custom was a daily requirement in such houses, most of which followed the secular Use of Sarum. Representative documents are cited by F.Ll. Harrison in *Music in Medieval Britain* with much valuable comment on context and performance. Harrison is, however, misleading when he states that the evening antiphon is not mentioned in the Sarum Ordinal.[14] This is true only of the New Ordinal, represented in the rubrics of later Sarum Breviaries including the printed edition of 1536 edited in three volumes by Procter and Wordsworth. The Old Ordinal, edited by W.H. Frere for *The Use of Sarum*, does contain a reference to such an antiphon, although without mentioning a specific text. It was to be sung straight after Compline of the Virgin, followed by the versicle *Post partum* and collect *Omnipotens sempiterne deus* (identical to the texts specified in a number of monastic manuscripts):

> *Post completorium canitur aliqua antiphona de sancta maria ante altare eiusdem: et dum canitur executor officii stet ad lectrinum quod ante altare est ubi scilicet cotidie de ea celebratur missa solempniter et ibi dicat V. Post partum . . . Or. Omnipotens sempiterne deus . . .*   Sar.Use, ii,6.

Frere dates the manuscript in question at *c.*1270—roughly contemporary with the earliest monastic source for the votive antiphon, the Westminster Customary of *c.*1266. This again raises important questions as to interchange of customs between monastic and secular practice: the prominence of secular features within the daily Little Office of the Virgin has already been discussed. Where the votive antiphon is concerned, however, monastic uses may well have set the precedent. Certainly the Cistercians seem to have been the first order to adopt *Salve regina* for votive use, and it was perhaps their influence which caused its subsequent propagation in the other orders.

One of the manuscripts used for Frere's facsimile edition of the Sarum Antiphoner, *SB* 152, a large noted breviary of *c.*1450-1500 also contains the complete text of *Salve regina* in the post-Compline position. As in several of the monastic sources discussed above, the votive antiphon follows Compline of the Virgin rather than ferial Compline which preceded it. The *Benedicamus* of Compline of the Virgin is followed by the memorial of the passion, with antiphon *Hora completorium datur sepulture*. Then *Salve regina* is given without notation, but with a trope of five verses: *Virgo mater, Virgo clemens, Funde preces, Gloriosa Dei* and *Dele culpas*. The versicle *Ave Maria* and collect *Omnipotens sempiterne deus* follow, and finally the psalm *De profundis*.

The absence of the votive antiphon in most of the earlier Sarum sources is somewhat puzzling, since both the extant polyphonic repertory from the fifteenth century and quantities of archival material testify to the widespread importance of this liturgical appendage. In some respects, however, as was suggested for the absence of the observance in English monastic books, it may well have been the peculiar paraliturgical status of the votive antiphon which excluded it from most breviaries and antiphoners. The most common place for a votive antiphon within the Sarum liturgical books is the processional. Richard Pynson's printed processional of 1502 contains several such antiphons, including *Salve regina*, followed by a versicle and collect, although without indication of context. It is unlikely that all of the antiphons listed were intended simply for processions, since Pynson's edition provides a collection of Marian antiphons specifically for use in procession at the end of the temporale (f.119v). The earlier and more complete Sarum processional *Ob* d.4 (1350-1400) reveals an almost identical layout in this respect, also providing two groups of Marian antiphons in separate parts of the source. Both books suggest a close correlation between votive and processional antiphons, both in terms of text and musical style, and this relationship will be examined below in the general context of independent antiphons.

The secular uses of York and Hereford offer no reference to votive antiphons in any of the accessible manuscripts. Bishop Grandisson's Exeter Ordinal of 1337, *Que eis fecimus et extraximus ex Exonie et Sarum usibus*, is rather more enlightening. At Exeter, Compline of the day was followed by the psalm *De profundis* with *Kyrie eleison* and other items. Then those who were assigned went to the Lady Chapel to sing Vespers and Compline of the Virgin, while the boys went to the altar of St Paul to sing a Marian antiphon:

> *Postea uadant qui assignantur ad officium beate Marie pro ebdomada sequente coram altari eiusdem, et cantent ibidem Uesperas et Completorium eiusdem, prout in Ordinali episcopi Johannis de Grandissono continentur. Pueri uero interim uadant ad*

> *altare sancti Pauli, et ibidem cantent antiphonam de beata Maria,*
> *cum alijs prout est consuetum.*   Exon, i,29.

The Marian Office and votive antiphon were thus sung by only a section of the Exeter community, the former operating according to a rota. The role of boys within the liturgy was rapidly assuming greater importance during the fourteenth century, both in secular and monastic foundations, and the singing of a votive antiphon by boys alone seems not to have been uncommon.

There can be no doubt that the votive antiphon became increasingly common in both monastic and secular foundations from the fourteenth century. In Benedictine foundations its adoption must have been spurred on by the 1343 Chapter Act, although it is unlikely that the results were felt in all houses immediately. The origins of the practice are shrouded in uncertainty, but in England a date in the first half of the thirteenth century seems plausible, possibly influenced by the early Cistercian custom of reciting *Salve regina* after the daily chapter. It is most apparent that this text dominated the repertory of votive antiphons, and that its popularity was extremely enduring. This issue is the subject of a separate section below.

Structurally the votive antiphon belongs to the family of independent antiphons, although the greater majority are borrowed from related feasts. Duplication of Marian antiphons in other areas of the liturgy, notably processions, memorials, commemorative offices of the Virgin and major feasts (where they often occur as antiphons for the *Magnificat* or *Benedictus*), raises the question of how particular texts were selected and how they relate to earlier customs where an antiphon was sung without an accompanying psalm.

COMPILATION OF VOTIVE ANTIPHON TEXTS

The great majority of surviving votive antiphon texts, particularly in manuscripts datable before the fifteenth century, were borrowed from the central liturgical repertory rather than newly composed. This principle of textual borrowing has already been established as an important means of creating a 'new' votive observance. It was seen to be particularly prominent in the compilation of two major Marian observances in English Benedictine houses: the Saturday commemorative office and the daily Little Office of the Virgin. Analysis of the texts used in these observances reveals that many of the items were taken from Marian feasts, notably the Assumption, or in the case of seasonal votive offices, from a feast which fell within the same season or which had some other relevance to it.

Three textual patterns predominate in the earlier votive antiphon repertory. Certain manuscripts simply specify that any antiphon of the

Virgin was appropriate for votive use, and indeed this was the policy recommended in England by the presidents of the 1343 Benedictine Chapter. A second group of sources is more explicit in prescribing a single text, which was almost invariably *Salve regina*. The third group, comprising Franciscan and Roman books, follows the centralized decree passed in these uses that four texts were to be used after Compline in accordance with the season: *Alma redemptoris*, *Ave regina celorum*, *Salve regina* and *Regina celi*.

None of these four seasonal antiphons was composed specifically for use in the post-Compline context. Rather they were borrowed from the liturgy in exactly the same manner as antiphons for memorials, the commemorative office, and the Little Office. Like most chants selected to serve as votive antiphons, the four seasonal chants come from the later phase of chant composition—the eleventh and twelfth centuries—and in this respect they form only a small proportion of a large corpus of antiphons to the Virgin composed during these years. Many Marian antiphons were composed for use at existing feasts: the large collection of *unica* for the Assumption period in *WO* F.160 is a good example. A rather smaller proportion was written exclusively for 'new' observances, as with the Worcester cycle of *Magnificat* antiphons compiled for the Little Office.

The following analysis examines the type of antiphon which was chosen for transference from its original liturgical context to the post-Compline position. The four seasonal antiphons discussed above are taken as convenient 'case-studies' for the analysis, largely because they are known examples of texts selected to function as votive antiphons in certain uses, but also because of their familiarity and accessibility in *Liber Usualis*. Nevertheless, it must be stressed that only *Salve regina* was regularly prescribed as a votive antiphon in English Benedictine books, and many other unspecified Marian chants might have been transferred in those monasteries where there was greater freedom of choice.

Tables 5:4, 5:5 and 5:6 (pp.278-280) show the liturgical position of the four antiphons in three groups of manuscripts: English Benedictine, European monastic and English secular. No instance has yet been traced where one antiphon appears simultaneously both as a liturgical antiphon and as a votive antiphon in a single source. The Westminster Customary of *c*.1266 is the only book which hints at this issue, with its references to 'old' and 'new' uses. Although the requirements are not entirely clear, it is apparent that there was a distinction between the two practices, and it is certainly a possibility that the later (votive) function actually superseded the earlier (presumably office) function.

Table 5:4 lists all liturgical occurrences of the four seasonal antiphons in seven English Benedictine manuscripts, presented chronologically. Only the three latest sources contain any mention of a votive antiphon, and in all cases it is *Salve regina*. (This text does not occur in these three manuscripts

with any other function.) *Salve regina* also occurs in a proper context in two
of the earlier sources in Table 5:4: *WO* F.160 (the Worcester Antiphoner
of *c.*1230), and *Ob* e.1* (the Hyde Abbey Breviary of *c.*1300). In both
manuscripts the antiphon appears twice, in similar circumstances. *WO* F.160
presents it with complete text and melody as the *Magnificat* antiphon for the
Vigil of the Assumption, and in incipit as the first of five alternative
Magnificat antiphons for the Saturday commemorative office of the Virgin
from the Octave of the Epiphany to Quadragesima, and from Pentecost to
Advent (see Table 4:9, p.254). *Ob* e.1* indicates that *Salve regina* was sung
as a *Magnificat* antiphon during the Octave of the Assumption, and as
Magnificat antiphon for the weekly commemorative office in Eastertide.
Neither manuscript makes reference to any other use of the antiphon.

Alma redemptoris and *Ave regina celorum* occur rather more widely in
the sources listed in Table 5:4. *Alma redemptoris* appears no fewer than six
times in the Hyde Abbey Breviary, four times as a *Magnificat* antiphon and
twice as a processional antiphon after Vespers. Three of the six occurrences
relate to the Assumption period, one to the Annunciation, one to the Nativity
of the Virgin, and one to the Saturday commemorative office. *WO* F.160
simply prescribes *Alma redemptoris* as the Terce antiphon for the
Annunciation, and indeed the substance of its text is more closely linked to
this feast than to any other. But in other respects Table 5:4 suggests that
Alma redemptoris had no pronounced link either with the Annunciation, or
with the related Advent period, in spite of its position as the antiphon for
Advent in the Franciscan and Roman post-Compline arrangement. At St
Mary's, York, *Alma redemptoris* was used for the final stage of a
procession in honour of the Virgin from the Purification until Advent, and
at Barking for a Pentecost procession. Barking also used the text as
Magnificat antiphon on the Feast of the Oblation (Presentation) of the
Virgin, which fell on 21 November. At Norwich in *c.*1260 there is no
mention of *Alma redemptoris* being sung in any festal context, although it
occurs with *Ave regina* as one of two *Magnificat* antiphons sung
sollempniter (i.e. with *Gloria Patri*) at the Saturday commemorative office
from Quadragesima to Pentecost.

Ave regina celorum is the only one of the four Marian texts which
occurs in the earliest of the seven sources: the twelfth-century St Albans
Breviary, *Lbl* 2.A.X. Here it is given in incipit for the Saturday
commemorative office, the complete version occurring in isolation on f.62,
headed *In veneratione sancte Marie ad vesperas* (see p.102). In Chapter
Four it was suggested that this antiphon might well have been intended for
a Saturday procession in honour of the Virgin, since this particular
observance took on a new significance at St Albans in the twelfth century.
Clearly *Ave regina* was used in exactly this manner at Chester in *c.*1330,

and for at least part of the year at St Mary's, York in c.1400. Barking also specified two separate processional contexts for *Ave regina* in 1404.

The fourth text, *Regina celi*, has more overt connections with the Easter period and occurs less frequently as an office item than the other three votive antiphons. It is absent from all sources except the Barking Ordinal (where it occurs as *Magnificat* antiphon on the Annunciation and at the Saturday commemorative office from Easter to Trinity), and the St Mary's, York Ordinal, where it appears as an office accretion: one of the memorial antiphons after Second Vespers during Easter week.

Taken in conjunction, the evidence of these seven manuscripts reveals several things. First, that all four of the antiphons under consideration retained their original liturgical function in certain uses well after they had been adopted as post-Compline antiphons in others; second, that each antiphon often had not one liturgical position but several; third, that the texts most commonly appear as *Magnificat* antiphons, but increasingly as processional antiphons in the later sources, and once as a memorial antiphon; fourth, that the antiphons were predominantly sung on the Marian feasts, but after the widespread adoption of the Saturday commemorative office in the thirteenth century, they were frequently lifted from their original festal context to serve as duplicate commemorative items. Finally, it is worth emphasizing that all four antiphons discussed here are random samples from a large Marian repertory, and that the exercise could be extended to cover many more Marian antiphons with similar characteristics. Those foundations where no particular text was specified for the post-Compline antiphon might well have drawn on any item of this kind.

Table 5:5 applies the same procedure to monastic manuscripts of European provenance. None of the sources here refers to a votive antiphon. By and large, the findings are similar, although the four chosen antiphons tend to occur rather more sporadically. Only the later Fleury Customary indicates an Assumption context for any of the texts, although the secondary emphasis on the commemorative *Magnificat* antiphon remains apparent. The twelfth-century St Denis Antiphoner (*F-Pn* 17296) is the only source which indicates a processional context for any of the texts, and here *Alma redemptoris* and *Ave regina* occur as part of a set of six antiphons.

The results of the same analysis in the secular manuscripts are slightly different. The Use of York is most conventional, adopting two of the four texts as *Magnificat* antiphons during the Octave of the Assumption, with the possibility of transference to the commemorative office or an Eastertide procession to the font. In the related Sarum and Exeter Uses however, there is no suggestion of any of the four items functioning as antiphons attached to psalms or canticles. Rather, they occur most predominantly as texts for the final stage of processions, termed variously *in redeundo, in introitu chori,* or *ad introitum chori*. In this respect they may be compared with the later English monastic books in Table 5:4. The relationship between texts specified for use as votive items in certain books and as processional antiphons in others is an important one, and necessitates some understanding of the characteristics of the procession itself. Investigation of the necessary evidence is frustrated, however, by the small number of extant English monastic processionals, and much of the following survey has had no option but to resort to the more plentiful and informative Sarum sources. Although the exact extent of the interchange between secular and Benedictine customs is still to be quantified, it is worth remembering that the observances discussed here are typical of late medieval practice, and may well have been adopted in comparable circumstances by monastic foundations.

THE RELATIONSHIP BETWEEN VOTIVE AND PROCESSIONAL ANTIPHONS

The following section deals with three areas which imply an important relationship between votive and processional antiphons. First, the duplication of several of the texts chosen to function as post-Compline antiphons within the processional repertory; second, the structural relationship between the votive antiphon ritual and the final stage of the procession (effectively a memorial); third, the custom of copying antiphons for votive use into processionals rather than other books. Given the structural similarity between post-Compline ceremonies, memorials and the third stage of the procession, the implications of this last issue are not entirely clear cut, particularly as likely texts appear in several surviving processionals without rubrics. This ambiguity is discussed more fully below.

Many of the texts required for a procession—antiphons, responds, collects and versicles—were simply borrowed from the office. As Terence Bailey points out, this is particularly true of the earlier sources, where office antiphons and responds form most of the processional items.[15] Nevertheless, a few chants were composed specifically for independent use in a processional context: those items sung at processions on Sundays in Advent, the Purification, Palm Sunday and the Rogation antiphons are examples.

Most processions consisted of three stages: *in eundo*, where the procession left the choir, a focal *statio*, or station, and finally *in redeundo*, the return to choir. The outward phase was normally accompanied by a borrowed respond, or sometimes a proper processional antiphon or hymn. At its destination (an altar or chapel, the rood or some other focal point), the procession stopped for a versicle and collect, sometimes said with an antiphon. The third stage of the procession, *in redeundo*, was effectively a self-contained memorial. An antiphon (or less often a respond) was sung as the procession moved off from the station, usually halting for the versicle and collect at the choir-step. Often the independence of this final stage was emphasized in that it honoured a quite different saint or intention from the preceding parts of the procession (quite commonly the patron).

The third stage of the Vespers procession in the Use of Sarum was usually in honour of the Virgin, first patron of the new cathedral at Salisbury.[16] This custom appears to have been observed on a universal basis by those churches which adopted the Sarum Use, even where they were not dedicated to Mary. There were a few standard exceptions to this rule—particularly on important feast days when the entire procession was *de festo*—but in most cases stage three took on the character of a Marian memorial. In this case, the antiphon sung *in redeundo* was often left for the cantor to choose. In most of the Sarum processionals (two of which are represented in Table 5:6), six alternative Marian antiphons are provided. These six antiphons were intended to double both for the closing section of the procession before Mass on Sundays, and for the procession appended to the Saturday commemorative office. Any of the six Marian antiphons given in the processional might be chosen *per ordinem*; *Ob* d.4, a Sarum processional of the latter part of the fourteenth century, gives the following rubric:

> *In introitu chori dicitur una de istis antiphonis de s[ancta] m[aria]*
> *per ordinem tam in proc[essione] in sabbatis quam ad*
> *proc[essionem] ante missam in dominicis.*   *Ob* d.4, f.119

The antiphons given in most Sarum books (including the mid-fifteenth century processional *Ob* 6 and Pynson's printed processional of 1502) are as follows:

> *Beata dei genitrix*
> *Ave regina celorum ave domina*
> *Alma redemptoris mater*
> *Speciosa facta es*
> *Ibo michi ad montem*
> *Quam pulchra es.*

This group served for most of the year, but between the Octave of the Assumption (22 August) and the Nativity of the Virgin (8 September), another group was substituted. All of the prescribed antiphons also occur as part of the regular office during the Assumption period:

> *Tota pulchra es amica mea*
> *Ascendit christus super celos*
> *Anima mea liquefacta est*
> *Descendi in ortum meum.*

The versicle and prayer for the third stage of the procession were often taken from an appropriate memorial; indeed, the revision of the Sarum books in the fourteenth century, which led to the 'New Use', specified that memorials of the Virgin sung at stage three of the procession were to be brought into correspondence with office memorials by standardization of the versicle and collect.[17] Consequently, the final stage of processions to the Virgin simply incorporated part of the standard Marian memorial which followed Vespers. Bailey also observes that Vespers processions in the Use of Sarum which are preceded by a Marian memorial exchange the usual Marian intention of the third stage for that of All Saints.[18] In this case the antiphon *in redeundo* borrows the *Magnificat* antiphon for the Feast of All Saints, while the collect is taken from the current Vespers memorial of All Saints.

The parallel between the third stage of the procession and the memorial is thus an important one, particularly when the versicle and collect of the procession were simply drawn from the memorial in current use. The antiphon element, however, seems to have been less derivative, for it was not necessarily drawn from a memorial. In the case of those processions where stage three was specifically directed to the Virgin, the antiphon used sometimes had no other apparent place in the liturgy. But in other cases these same antiphons seem to have doubled as post-Compline votive antiphons: a possible explanation as to why many votive antiphons are copied into processionals rather than other books.

Several of the Sarum processionals provide not only the 'standard' collection of Marian antiphons for the third stage of the procession, but also a further group, usually without explicit rubrics but of markedly similar style. An unrubricated collection of antiphons of this kind appears on ff.167-169v of Pynson's printed processional of 1502. This consists of the following antiphons:

> *Salve regina (with five-verse trope)*
> *Regina celi*
> *Nesciens mater*
> *Ave regina celorum mater regis.*

Thereafter the versicle *Ave Maria* with response *Benedicta tu* is given, together with the collect *Omnipotens sempiterne deus*. Three further items follow, similarly unrubricated:

> *Sancta Maria non est tibi (a respond)*
> *Mater ora filium*
> *Sancta Maria virgo intercede.*

The inclusion of a versicle and collect within this self-contained group on ff.167-169v suggests that it is possibly a collection of chants for use either as votive antiphons or in memorials. The occurrence of two of the prescribed seasonal texts discussed in this section perhaps offers a stronger case for the votive antiphon, particularly as *Salve regina* appears so frequently as a post-Compline devotion in other sources. Similar Marian antiphons without rubrics occur in the fourteenth-century Sarum processional *Ob* d.4. This manuscript includes a troped version of *Salve regina* on f.181, which follows straight on from the genealogy and hence is quite separate from the other groups of Marian antiphons used for the third stage of the procession. A further group of Marian antiphons without rubrics appears in the mid-fifteenth century Sarum processional *Ob* 6, f.99v: *Regina celi*, *Ave regina celorum*, and *Salve regina* with trope.

Of other secular uses, that of Exeter (which, of course, drew many of its customs from Salisbury), unequivocally emphasizes the processional funtion of the antiphons used as the basis for analysis in this chapter. Although it incorporates only three of the four chants, omitting *Salve regina* (see Table 5:6), there is no indication that any of these items were used in anything other than a processional context.

The secular Use of York is less regular in this sense. Here only two of the four texts appear, and only one of them, *Ave regina celorum*, is used processionally. Emphasis lies rather on their function as *Magnificat* antiphons, as in most of the Benedictine sources listed in Table 5:4.

At the Benedictine abbey of St Mary's, York, which (as already noted) reflects an eclectic agglomeration of liturgical customs, two of the four Marian antiphons under consideration are specified for processional use. *Alma redemptoris* and *Ave regina* have an almost identical function to the same texts in the Use of Sarum, operating on a seasonal basis for the Vespers procession which followed part of the Saturday commemorative office. But once again analysis is hampered by the absence of a sanctorale in the York manuscript, making it impossible to establish whether any of these texts were also used liturgically on the Marian feasts.

The small number of extant monastic processionals presents similar problems. It is difficult to ascertain whether the apparent Benedictine emphasis on the use of the four Marian antiphons as *Magnificat* antiphons (rather than processional antiphons) is mere chance. However, of all the extant self-contained monastic processionals consulted, none of them includes any of the four antiphons considered here, whether for festal or commemorative purposes. This may be pure chance; most of the extant Bendictine processionals are relatively early books, and the analysis of secular practices suggests that the antiphons prescribed in those books may well have been adopted late on.

In the secular uses the conclusions are less conjectural. Sarum demonstrates the processional function of all four of the antiphons discussed here, Exeter three of the four. And indeed, as Bailey points out, at Salisbury five of the six antiphons prescribed for the commemorative Marian procession have no other place in the liturgy.[19] Nevertheless, this absence of concordance among the repertory of processional items is comparatively rare, for few chants were composed exclusively for processional use, and those which were are usually for very specific occasions. Possibly Salisbury simply borrowed certain Marian antiphons from books of other uses purely for processional purposes, disregarding their original context in the chosen source. Certainly many of these items were used elsewhere at a considerably earlier date. The proliferation of Marian texts, some for festal offices and others for votive observances, has already been stressed. Salisbury itself, with its early dedication to the Virgin, must have had no little demand for Marian texts, particularly for processions.

Is it possible that votive antiphon texts and texts for the third 'Marian' stage of processions were simply interchangeable? This question of a particular function in the late antiphon repertory is a difficult one. Certainly many of the extant antiphons share similar characteristics which make it difficult to distinguish one group from another, whether for use in a festal, commemorative, processional or post-Compline context. And there can be no question that the compilers of Marian votive offices thought little of transferring existing material from one observance to another. Again it is difficult to be certain of the exact manner in which various types of text were used; what does emerge is that any attempt at straightforward categorization of Marian antiphons is unviable.

THE ORIGINS AND TEXT OF *SALVE REGINA*

As the antiphon most often specified for use in the ceremony after Compline, *Salve regina* has already been established as the most prominent of the texts selected to function as votive antiphons. And it is a text which also held a special place in the contemporary medieval repertory, for not only was it liturgically ubiquitous, but at the same time part of the European movement of popular Mariology. Its origins and its authorship aroused particular interest from as early as the twelth century, and have been the subject of debate ever since. During the Middle Ages the dispute over *Salve regina* was supplemented by myth, offering a glimpse of the significance which medieval divines attached to the antiphon. Few texts occasioned contemporary debate as to their origin, and even fewer were clothed with myths to substantiate their importance. Not surprisingly, a text so widely circulated was subject to emendation, and both its verbal and melodic formation, and its frequent inclusion of the extended concluding trope *Virgo mater ecclesie* warrant special examination.

There are several accounts of *Salve regina* which examine the possibilities of authentic authorship, and it is not necessary to present more than a very brief summary of these arguments here.[20] The fullest (although not entirely unbiased) examination of the evidence, which draws together the work of several earlier scholars, is J.M. Canal's *Salve Regina Misericordiae*, published in 1963. Canal, a Cistercian himself, argues strongly for the role of St Bernard of Clairvaux (1090-1153) and the Cistercians in the propagation of the text. Bernard was first advanced as a likely candidate by one of his biographers, John the Hermit, in 1180-82. John recounts a miraculous story where Bernard is awoken one night by angelic voices, and sees the Virgin standing in the church at Clairvaux. During the vision one of the angels intones *Salve regina* and sings it through. Bernard recalls the antiphon the following morning, writes it down, and sends a copy to the Cistercian pope Eugenius III, who orders it to be sung *per ecclesias ut adhuc plerique testantur*.[21]

Canal claims that the multiplicity of early references to the antiphon in Cistercian sermons and miracle collections adds weight to John's account, but other scholars consider that *Salve regina* was in existence well before Bernard's election as abbot of Cîteaux. Certainly the melody does not demonstrate all the usual features of Cistercian chant compiled during Bernard's abbacy, when much of the existing repertory was revised to conform to certain set rules. No chant was to exceed the compass of a tenth, the B flat was to be excluded, and general simplification was favoured.[22]

During the nineteenth century, popular belief favoured the authorship of Hermannus Contractus (1013-54), a monk at the Benedictine abbey of Reichenau who was also known as a chronicler, writer and composer.[23] One of the earliest of the *Salve regina* ascriptions occurs in an entry for the year 1049 in the Chronicle of Jacobus de Bergamo (1434-1520), which claims that Hermannus edited and composed many sacred hymns, among them *Salve regina*.[24] But recent scholarship is far more cautious. Lawrence Gushee states that only two works can safely be attributed to Hermannus, an Office of St Afra, and the sequence *Grates, honos, hierarchia*. De Valois also rejects Hermannus's authorship on the grounds of musical style.[25]

Two further candidates are acknowledged as possibilities: Adhémar of Monteil (d.1098) and Peter Mezonzo, bishop of Compostela (d.1103). Durandus of Mende commented in *c.*1286 that *Petrus Compostellanus fecit illam antiphonam Salve regina misericordie*, but there is little evidence to substantiate his claim.[26] Many historians now accept Adhémar as a more likely author. A later account of St Bernard's vision of the Virgin appears in a Chronicle of 1227 written by Alberic of Trois-Fontaines (d.1241). In an entry for the year 1130, Alberic recounts that Bernard first heard *Salve regina* sung not at Clairvaux, but at St Bénigne, Dijon, referring to it as 'the antiphon of Puy' (Alberic, 828). Adhémar was bishop of Puy from at least 1087 until his death in 1098, and the account certainly implies that the melody, at least, was in use at the church of Notre Dame, Le Puy, during his lifetime.

Although the debate on origins and authorship has never satisfactorily been resolved, modern liturgical scholars are by and large in agreement that the text and melody of *Salve regina* are contemporaneous (later eleventh or early twelfth century), if not necessarily the work of a single figure.

The text of the antiphon itself was not 'standardized' until the appearance of the 1569 Roman Breviary, although the version given there occurs in many sources of a much earlier date. Initially the text seems to have been shorter. Instances in the sermons of Pseudo-Bernard stop at the phrase *lacrymarum valle*,[27] but several accounts dealing with the history of the antiphon, irrespective of their views on its authorship, consider that the text was at least 'completed' by St Bernard. Wilhelm Eisengrein, a German chronicler of the sixteenth century, reports that at the time of the preaching of the Second Crusade (1147), St Bernard received one of its leaders, Emperor Conrad III, in the cathedral of Spire. In a moment of enthusiasm Bernard intoned *Salve regina* to the word *ostende*, adding on impulse the familiar concluding invocations: *O clemens, o pia, o dulcis Maria.*[28]

During subsequent years more words were inserted into the original text: *Salve regina (mater) misericordie*; *O dulcis (virgo Maria)*, and in some places *ostende (benignum)*. The most common variant in the later sources listed in Table 5:1 (*Llp* 558, *Lbl* 1804, *Ob* f.1, *DO* 26543 and *Mch* 6717) is the addition of the word *mater*. This is likely to be a further reflection of popular myth, based on the Cluniac legend *Mater misericordie*. John of Cluny, Odo of Cluny's biographer, recounts the story of the Virgin appearing to a monk of Cluny on his deathbed, where she identifies herself as *mater misericordie* and offers reassurance that she will lead the dying monk to the joys of her Son. This legend recurs in several medieval miracle collections, many of them English. Dominic of Evesham gives a variant version, while the miracles of William of Malmesbury (*c*.1090-*c*.1143) expand the legend in explaining that to that time, Cluniac monks hold the Virgin in special honour, praising her in communal celebrations of her hours.[29]

TROPED VERSIONS OF *SALVE REGINA*

Most of the textual sources in Table 5:1 are consistent where the main body of the text is concerned. With the exception of the word *mater* in the five sources listed above, the sole point of discrepancy is the presentation of the three petitions. *WO* F.160 rearranges the usual order to *O pia, o clemens, o dulcis Maria*; two of the fifteenth-century sources, *Lbl* 1804 and *Ob* f.1, add *salve* to the final petition, and *Ob* e.1* adds *alleluia*.

However, four of the sources listed in Table 5:1 incorporate more substantial variants, giving rise to a text quite distinct from that adopted by the majority of English and continental monasteries. The dissimilarity results from the presence of a trope: a variable number of hymn-like verses appended to the closing lines of the more familiar form of the antiphon (Table 5:7, p.281). Three of the four manuscripts in Table 5:1 (*Ob* 358 from St Albans, *Cjc* D.27 from St Mary's York and *Mch* 6717 from Godstow) give the complete text for both the antiphon and its accompanying trope. In *Ob* 358 and *Cjc* D.27, each of the three verses precedes one of the closing invocations of the antiphon: [Verse 1] *O clemens*; [Verse 2] *O pia*, [Verse 3] *O dulcis Maria*. The third source, the mid-fifteenth century psalter from Godstow (*Mch* 6717), provides no fewer than seven troped verses arranged in the following sequence: [Verse 1] *O clemens* [Verse 2] *O pia* [Verse 3] *O mitis* [Verse 4] *O felix* [Verse 5] *O benigna* [Verse 6] *O benedicta* [Verse 7] *O dulcis Maria*. The fourth source, the fifteenth-century processional of the nuns of Chester, (*US: SM* 34.B.7) is less informative in that it provides neither text nor music for the antiphon, but simply indicates that *Salve regina* was to be sung 'with the fyve versus'. The St Mary's, York source is the most valuable of the three listed above in that it also supplies full notation for the antiphon and its verses.

Although the troped *Salve regina* seems to have been the exception rather than the rule in monastic foundations, expanded versions of the antiphon, usually with five verses, are particularly prevalent in Sarum manuscripts. Table 5:8 (p.282), which lists both secular and monastic troped sources of *Salve regina*, includes four Sarum sources which present complete texts with the trope: three of the four are also provided with notation. Indeed, no Sarum source has been identified which presents the antiphon without its verses, and this also holds good for extant polyphonic settings of *Salve regina* written for foundations following the Sarum rite. Harrison cites Robert de Eglesfield's statutes for Queen's College, Oxford, where there is specific reference to the singing of the troped antiphon on Fridays: *Salve regina cum versibus*.[30] The Eton Choirbook contains fourteen such compositions, with tropes of three or four verses. Dunstable's setting (*MB* viii, 46) also incorporates the trope, as does that of Leonel Power (*CMM* 1, 10) and another similarly-dated setting which was probably written by Power (*MB* viii, 63; *CMM* 1, 22). Sandra McColl lists a further six large-scale troped settings of the antiphon, written during the latter part of the fifteenth or the early part of the sixteenth century,[31] and there are numerous smaller-scale troped compositions in a variety of English manuscripts copied in the years preceding the Reformation.

The origins of the expanded form of *Salve regina* are not entirely clear. The evident hymn-like construction of the trope suggests that it may also have been used as an independent text, and indeed two German sources of the fifteenth century (*AH* xxiii, no.82) contain an identical six-verse hymn, *Virgo mater ecclesie* (Table 5:7), which incorporates at least part of the material used in those versions of the trope listed in Table 5:8. In both of these sources the hymn is prefaced by the rubric *Salutatio BVM*, presumably a reference to the Annunciation (March 25) rather than to any other Marian feast. But the case for the independent existence of the hymn/trope before the fifteenth century is not entirely straightforward. Not only is there no evidence for a self-contained hymn in earlier manuscripts, but the collection of material in Morel's *Lateinische Hymnen des Mittelalters* suggests that hymn-like texts written specifically as tropes either to *Salve regina* or to other Marian antiphons were by no means uncommon. No fewer than three tropes for *Salve regina* are given in Engelberg sources: *O flos virginitatis* (fourteenth century), *O summa clementia* and *O virgo spes humilium* (both thirteenth century), all headed *Versus super Salve regina.*[32] There are also comparable tropes for the antiphons *Alma redemptoris, Ave regina, Pulchra es* and *Nigra sum*. All of these accretions are constructed in the manner of hymns, with a regular metrical structure, but there is no firm indication that they were intended for use in any independent context detached from the antiphon.

All of the troped sources listed in Table 5:8 (with the exception of the unique text used by the Bridgettines of Syon, *Salve celi digna*) draw on a common group of verses. The exact arrangement of the verses, which range in number from three to seven, varies from source to source, although the trope invariably begins with the verse *Virgo mater ecclesie*. For the sake of convenience, verses of the trope are referred to here in accordance with their numerical appearance in the fifteenth-century hymn, *Virgo mater ecclesie*, cited above, although this is not intended to imply direct transference.

The hymn *Virgo mater* comprises six verses. Two of these, *Stella maris* (No.3) and *Alma mater* (No.6) are not known to have been used as part of the trope in any source. Instances of *Salve regina* in the Sarum sources tend to duplicate four of the hymn stanzas (in the order 1, 4, 5, 2) usually with the addition of a fifth independent verse, *Dele culpas*, which has no place in the hymn. Versions of the trope in two mid-fifteenth century sources, the Godstow psalter *Mch* 6717 and the Sarum processional *Ob* 6, incorporate another verse which has no known concordance, *Et nos solvat*, while *Mch* 6717 has a further unique verse (totalling seven in all), *Supra celos exaltata*. The three verses used by the Bridgettines on certain specified feasts, including those of St Bridget, are also apparently *unica*. Table 5:8 compares Sarum, Bridgettine and monastic versions of the trope.

All stanzas (excepting those in the Bridgettine version), whether they occur in the hymn or the trope, are constructed in accordance with the same general principle. Each verse consists of four octosyllabic lines with occasional irregularites: the closing lines of the hymn stanzas 2 (*Qui tui memoriam agimus*) and 5 (*Spinis puncto felle potato*), and the independent trope stanza *Dele culpas* (*Vitam tuis precibus*) are obvious exceptions. Stress patterns vary from stanza to stanza: the underlying metre is predominantly trochaic with occasional instances of iambic lines (hymn stanza 1, line 2 and stanza 4, lines 3-4) or other irregularities where the stress pattern shifts in mid-line (*Virgo mater ecclesie; Esto nobis refugium*). The imagery is extremely conventional, and indeed, the literary quality of the trope scarcely matches that of the antiphon which it accompanies.

Selection of the stanzas which constitute the trope seems to have been a somewhat arbitrary process. The two Benedictine sources from St Albans and York, and the first option used by the Bridgettines of Syon (on the Feasts of Peter and Paul, John the Baptist, Augustine and Michael) all concur in their choice of the same three stanzas, but the later Benedictine Chester processional is closer to the Sarum sources in opting for five (here unspecified) stanzas. Three of the four Sarum sources have five stanzas (1, 4, 5, 2 with *Dele culpas*), while the fourth (*Ob* 6) simply appends an extra verse to this arrangement. Rather surprisingly none of the settings in the Eton Choirbook, *WRec* 178, concurs with the Sarum pattern. Eleven sources opt for only three verses rather than five, and the characteristic Sarum incorporation of verse 2 occurs in none of them. Dunstable and Power also opt for the three verses 1, 4, and 5.

The most striking deviation from any of the arrangements cited above occurs in the earliest troped version of *Salve regina*: that found in the famous 'Hartker Antiphoner' (*CH-SGs* 390), copied for the illustrious Benedictine monastery of St Gall in Switzerland. Although the troped antiphon is not contemporary with the material in the earliest parts of the source (copied between *c*.980 and *c*.1100), it is still earlier than any of the other extant manuscripts which contain the trope. The Solesmes editors of the manuscript suggest that the antiphon was added to the source at some stage during the thirteenth century, in spite of its archaic adiastematic notation.[33] Unlike the other instances of the trope, the St Gall manuscript indicates that the antiphon was not intended for use in a votive context after one of the hours, but rather as the *Magnificat* antiphon on the Feast of the Annunciation. This is the only known instance of the troped *Salve* being used in a specific liturgical context, and it suggests a possible correlation with the two fifteenth-century hymns prescribed for the *Salutatio*.

The three-verse Hartker trope, as shown in Table 5:7, does not correspond with the usual layout of the English Benedictine sources. The first two stanzas both have the expected first couplet but exchange the second, effectively resulting in two unique stanzas. The final Hartker stanza, *Gloriosa dei*, also has no place in the St Albans or St Mary's, York version of the trope, but is familiar as the penultimate verse in the Sarum sources.

The arrangement of invocations and verses is also unique in this early source. The antiphon itself ends complete, as in the untroped sources, with the triple invocation *O clemens, o pia, o dulcis Maria*. Thereafter the three verses of the trope follow on without interruption, complete with neumatic notation. The rearrangement of verses and interpolated phrases seen in the other sources listed in Table 5:8 seems to have come later in the history of the trope, for in the Hartker Antiphoner, a later hand has added the phrase *O dulcis Maria*, without notation, after the final verse of the trope. In all other sources, the verses of the trope invariably fall between the three exclamatory phrases.

The textual instability of the trope suggested by these sources provides no clear directive towards a possible prototype. It seems likely that verses were added to the trope at random, quite possibly at intervals of several years, and that the arrangement of verses was never standardized. Given that there is no evidence for a self-contained hymn before the fifteenth century, it may well be that the verses of the trope were simply extracted from the antiphon at some stage after its composition to serve as a hymn, possibly with newly composed verses.

A single strophic melody is used for all the stanzas of the trope. This is slightly more elaborate than most hymn melodies, with neumatic groups of three and four notes. Like the antiphon itself, it is in the first mode with rather haphazard addition of B flats. The descending four-note motif which characterizes the final cadence of the interpolated petitions (*O clemens, o pia*, which of course belong to the antiphon proper) suggests a certain motivic correspondence with the trope, where the final word of the first, second and fourth lines of each stanza uses a similar figure: perhaps a further suggestion that the trope was written specifically as an adjunct to the antiphon. On the whole those sources with notation reveal only minor discrepancies in all extant versions of the trope melody: apparently even in the case of the Hartker manuscript (in spite of the problems of its imprecise notation).

SALVE REGINA IN ENGLISH MONASTIC SOURCES

Although *Salve regina* is just one of the many antiphons sung in honour of the Virgin, it has particular significance in English sources in general, and can contribute more especially to the understanding of votive observance in English Benedictine monasteries. From Westminster Abbey in 1266 to the dissolution of the cathedral priory at Durham in 1540, there are fourteen extant Benedictine sources which refer to a votive antiphon (listed in Table 5:1), of which thirteen specifically identify *Salve regina*.

The references are spread thinly across the centuries and it is impossible to build a comprehensive picture of influence and dissemination. But in two

areas it is possible to extend the examination a little further: the evidence for
the use of the trope, and the characteristics of the surviving melodies. Eight
of the fourteen surviving sources include the text of *Salve regina*, and just
two of these include music: the thirteenth-century Worcester Antiphoner and
the Ordinal of St Mary's York (*c.*1400). In both areas of investigation there
are the questions not only of the interrelationship between monastic sources
but also of the interchange with secular practice. The second of these
questions is addressed in dealing with the appearance of the troped version
of *Salve regina*.

Three sources include the troped form of the antiphon: the
thirteenth-century psalter from St Albans, the Ordinal of St Mary's York,
and the mid-fifteenth century psalter from Godstow. There is also the
reference in the Chester Processional (*c.*1425) to the 'five verses' of the
antiphon. These examples appear to be rather exceptional. In most instances
the presence of the trope seems to be an important distinguishing feature
between monastic and secular uses. Without exception, all surviving
instances of *Salve regina* in English secular sources incorporate the trope,
and it is possible that two—if not three—of the four troped sources listed in
Table 5:1 were influenced by secular customs.

At some stage after the exodus of monks to found the Cistercian house
at Fountains in 1135, the re-established abbey at St Mary's York seems to
have come under the influence of the Use of Sarum. Other instances have
been identified earlier in this study, and here it is most apparent in the
musical correspondences that the York monks used a version of *Salve regina*
closely related to the Salisbury chant. (The musical details are discussed
further below.) The ordinal includes only three verses of the trope but these
are the first three of the five used most commonly in Sarum sources, and
the three regularly used in secular polyphonic settings of the fifteenth
century.

It is even more likely that *Mch* 6717, the Godstow Psalter, was
modelled on the Use of Sarum. Examination of the Little Office of the
Virgin in Chapter Three revealed that this was the sole suriving instance of
the Hours of the Virgin in a monastic manuscript which concorded exactly
with the text and psalms prescribed in the Sarum Hours, and since *Salve
regina* appears as an appendage to Compline of the Little Office, it is
equally likely to derive from a Sarum prototype. However, there is the
anomaly of the seven-verse trope found here. Although no other example of
a seven-verse trope has been identified, the lengthy appendage to the
antiphon in the Godstow source certainly suggests a closer parallel with the
Sarum sources discussed above than the majority of the Benedictine
manuscripts which contain *Salve regina*. The Godstow book, it may be
recalled, is also one of the few Benedictine sources to incorporate two
newly-composed votive antiphon texts, both of much greater length than
their established counterparts.

The occurrence of the troped *Salve* in the psalter from St Albans (*Ob* 358) is by far the earliest and the most puzzling. The Marian innovations at St Albans in the twelfth century seem entirely monastic in origin and form, and this troped version of the antiphon antedates every surviving secular example. The issue is further complicated since *Salve regina* makes no appearance (either as post-Compline antiphon or in a specific liturgical context) in the two other St Albans sources discussed in this thesis, the twelfth-century breviary *Lbl* 2.A.X, and the printed breviary *Lbl* C.110.a.27 of *c*.1535. The absence of any rubric in *Ob* 358 makes it impossible to locate a context for the antiphon with certainty, but it seems most likely that its presence in a psalter—along with versicle and collect—implies a paraliturgical, post-Compline function. Given the date of the manuscript and the apparent independence from secular influence, this instance of the troped *Salve* stands apart from those discussed above: its closest parallel is the version found in the almost contemporary Hartker Antiphoner from St Gall.

THE MELODY OF *SALVE REGINA*

In spite of the tiny sample of English monastic sources which include the chant for *Salve regina*, it is possible to make some observations which help to elucidate further the question of a relationship between monastic and secular practices. This can be achieved by comparing a sample of surviving versions of the chant from English and continental sources compiled over three centuries. Eight versions of the chant are presented in parallel in Appendix II (p.337). These exclude the tropes (indicated by an asterisk in the transcription) and the concluding *Alleluia* found in the Cistercian source. All but the two Sarum versions are from regular or monastic houses, two of them continental.

F-TAM	Monastic	Cistercian	Tamié	s.xii^2
I-Rss	Regular	Dominican	St Sabina, Rome	s.xiii
WO F.160	Monastic	Benedictine	Worcester	*c*.1230
Cjc D.27	Monastic	Benedictine	St Mary's, York	*c*.1400
Ob.d.4	Secular	Sarum	St John's, Dublin	*c*.1350
Ob 6	Secular	Sarum	St Mary, Belton?	s.xv med.
Cjc F.31	Monastic	Carthusian	Witham, Somerset	s.xiii
Ob e.14	Regular	Franciscan	Marches, Italy	1429

(Although it has not been possible to include a transcription of the melody found in the Hartker Antiphoner, an examination of the neumes suggests that it does not diverge significantly from the principal shape of the melody.)

Salve regina has a memorable, well-articulated melody which responds to the ordering of the verse. Even if it does not include exact conjunctions of musical and verbal rhyme, the musical cadences are made more pronounced by the repetition of the same basic melodic figure at the end of many of the lines. The opening phrase is repeated (in most uses almost exactly) both for the second line, and for the concluding petition *O dulcis Maria*. There are other musical correspondences and echoes throughout the melody.

Not surprisingly all eight versions follow the same basic melodic contour. Equally predictably, none of the eight correspond exactly, and at certain points those variants seem particularly significant.

1. *Salve* and *Vita*
Despite small variants (some of which are distorted by differences in underlay) the two opening phrases are concordant in all the sources, but one detail stands out. Only the text of the Worcester Antiphoner opens with the pitch sequence a-g-d; the others all return to the dominant before falling to the final (a-g-a-[g]-d).

2. *Ad te suspiramus gementes et flentes*
This is the most striking and inexplicable example of a variant reading. All but two of the melodies have the characteristic upward surge from d to c' at this point, descending in the second part of the phrase to end on c. But the versions found in the Worcester Antiphoner and in the Carthusian miscellany begin in a more confined way (reaching respectively only to g and a), while the second part of the phrase falls to A with the insistent repetition of the figure A-c-[d]-d for *gementes et flentes*.

3. *Eia ergo advocata nostra*
The variation is most striking in the early Cistercian source. Reaching up to d rather than c' it makes more use of the dominant in the phrase. But here again Worcester is alone in ending the phrase on g, and the scalar contour is most evident in the Worcester and Carthusian versions. (In the following phrase Worcester and Carthusian versions are alone in ending on d rather than c).

4. *Et Iesum benedictum*
Predictably the Cistercian source replaces the extended ambit to A with a setting of *Iesum* that reaches up to a. This accords with the basic principle of the reform of the chant by the order; melodies were contained within the ambit of a tenth. More surprising is the fact that the Sarum source *Ob* 6 follows the Cistercian version closely.

5. *Fructus ventris tui*

Here Worcester has an entirely individual melisma on *ventris*.

6. *O clemens, o pia*

Again the Worcester source is individual in providing a continuous melody. The Carthusian text follows suit, though with two more closely related phrases. All the others repeat the melody of *O clemens* for *O pia*.

What emerges from these very basic observations is the individuality of the reading in the Worcester Antiphoner. Whether or not this indicates the survival of an independent and ancient tradition of chant at Worcester as Knowles claims,[34] it is plain that the Worcester version is independent of the versions circulating among the friars, the Cistercians and secular churches following the Use of Sarum. Its closest relation is the Carthusian text. Both are sufficiently close and sufficiently different from one another to suggest a stemmatic relationship that dates back earlier than either.

Also standing alone is the Cistercian reading. Given the claims of Canal for the Cistercian origins of *Salve regina*, one might expect a greater degree of correspondence in other sources, although obviously the editing out of the tetrachord below the final was taken over in at least one surviving Sarum version of the melody. This abbreviation of the overall range suggests that the Cistercian version is a revision of an existing melody, rather than an original composition.

The largest group of sources, as might be expected, are those with Roman roots: the versions of the friars who promulgated the use of the Marian antiphons, the two Sarum texts (bar the Cistercian interpolation in *Ob* 6 noted above), and the version from the Benedictine abbey of St Mary's, York. The independence of St Mary's from the other Benedictine text (Worcester) is likely to have less to do with the autonomy of Benedictine monasteries than with the debt to secular practice that seems so characteristic of St Mary's.

In other words, there appear to be three melodic groupings for *Salve regina*: a mainstream of 'Roman' readings (including Sarum with its tropes); a 'reformed' version made by the Cistercians; and a third, independent version which surfaces in at least two unrelated English monasteries. The sample is too small to suggest an independent English monastic version of *Salve regina*, let alone that this third version is further indication of the spread of Marian observance in English monasteries. But it is clear that these two texts were borrowed neither from the 'Roman' group (whether from the friars or from secular use) nor from the Cistercians. Furthermore, the implications of the stemmatics suggest that the original melody had diffused into a number of related versions by the thirteenth century.

In the larger context of this chapter as a whole, the musical sources continue to underline the difficulties of assimilating interrelating fragmentary evidence. It does, however, confirm the complexity of the transmission of texts and customs from one foundation to another and from one use to another. Nevertheless, nothing here cuts across the basic pattern of the independence of votive observance in English monasteries in the thirteenth and fourteenth centuries from both the popular devotional cults inspired by the friars and from the practice of the secular church.

CONCLUSIONS

The consideration of the votive antiphon—and of *Salve regina* in particular—brings this study to the point where it meets the accepted view of musicologists: the current view continues to emphasize the votive antiphon as the dominant Marian observance in the office, and to concentrate on secular examples. But what has emerged here is the extent of votive observance in English monasteries stretching back to Anglo-Saxon times. Marian devotion is seen to become increasingly prevalent, and the votive antiphon provides a common apex at the end of the Middle Ages for older monastic and secular foundations as well as a ritual focus for the emerging new collegiate establishments. So far as the English Benedictine houses are concerned, their position can be summarized succinctly by reference to four key centres of English monasticism in the Middle Ages: Winchester, St Albans, Worcester, and St Mary's, York. Each assumes its greatest importance in various ways and at various times within the context of this study, but all four houses share a valuable and significantly distinct repertory of surviving manuscripts.

The three monasteries in tenth-century Winchester provide an outline of the gradual adoption of votive observance in the late Anglo-Saxon period. The Winchester houses are the best examples of the increasing momentum in the monastic movement brought about by the English revival, and the unique circumstances which contributed to its liturgy. *Regularis Concordia* embodies the customs of English monasteries during this period, illustrating how practices which were also observed in continental reformed monasteries took on new characteristics in the Winchester climate. The appended psalms, prayers, commemorations and appended offices have all been established as critical precursors of the observances of English monasteries during the later Middle Ages. Other Winchester manuscripts of the tenth and eleventh centuries, less central than *RC*, although no less significant, supplement our knowledge of monastic observance during this period. Private prayerbooks represent the gradual formalization of personal devotions modelled on offices, and more importantly, testify to the beginnings of an English cult of the Virgin.

Marian observance dominates most of the later votive repertory discussed in this thesis. It is first seen to take on significant proportions in twelfth-century sources from St Albans, a major centre of post-Conquest monasticism, closely-connected with Lanfranc and other eminent Norman clerics. It is here that the commemorative office of the Virgin seems to have materialized in a fully-developed weekly form: a far cry from the pre-Conquest versions of this office in the Worcester Portiforium. Not only does the earliest version of the three-nocturn commemorative office appear in a St Albans breviary, but the documentation of Matthew Paris and successive St Albans chroniclers bears witness to the process of its compilation, the myth attached to its observance, and the later adoption of an accompanying procession. If the St Albans account of the life of Geoffrey Gorron is accurate, St Albans may well have been the first English monastery to adopt the commemorative office. Certainly, taken chronologically, it heads the lengthy sequence of Saturday Marian offices found in surviving monastic sources. Of all the observances discussed here, it is perhaps the most prominent.

Worcester, in a sense, represents a different view of liturgical observance in post-Conquest England. Unlike St Albans, where the Normans lost little time in establishing themselves as the decision-makers, Worcester retained its Anglo-Saxon bishop, and possibly the remnants of earlier liturgical customs. The thirteenth-century Worcester Antiphoner, in many ways the most valuable of all surviving English Benedictine liturgical manuscripts, certainly shows evidence of customs and chants which have no parallel in comparable continental sources. Indeed, it possibly represents a unique survival of a much earlier insular tradition. Within this study it offers evidence of new composition of text and chant specifically for votive observance. The Worcester Antiphoner contains one of the earliest exmples of a daily Marian office sung in choir, and it is one of very few surviving sources testifying to the musical significance of the office. Its collection of unique *Magnificat* antiphons for the Little Office are fine examples of late-medieval chant compostition, unified not only by their texts, but also by a carefully planned modal sequence. Indeed, the extent of original Marian composition in the manuscript as a whole is witness to the increasing proliferation of English monastic interest in the Virgin.

The waves of change implicit in late fourteenth-century observance are perhaps most fully represented in the informative, although idiosyncratic, document from St Mary's York, bringing us full-circle to the adoption of a votive antiphon and the ritual significance attached to its observance. The York Ordinal also affords much evidence of other Marian observances which at this period must have been standard: a commemorative office, a daily Lady Office in choir, and a Lady Mass, here fully established as a daily observance with seasonal texts. York is equally significant for its implications of liturgical interchange with secular orders. Even as an isolated example, it represents what seems to be an increasing tendency towards less rigid distinctions between uses. It is part of an age where the

Benedictines had fallen from their original position of cultural supremacy, and were taking on a more passive role as patrons. The fifteenth century saw the rise of a great body of polyphony conceived for votive observance, much of it focused around the votive antiphon, the Lady Mass and the Lady Office. It testifies to the emancipation of votive observance from its original context of appended devotion in community, to a far-reaching phenomenon of great importance, encompassing both communal and lay worship alike.

NOTES

1. Tolhurst, 162.
2. Tolhurst, 119.
3. Van Dijk, *The Origins of the Modern Roman Liturgy*, 268.
4. Tolhurst, 104.
5. *LU*, 273-276.
6. As, for example, Harrison, 'The Eton Choirbook, its background and contents'.
7. Discussed in Bowers, *Choral Institutions*, 4.5.4.
8. Van Dijk, *The Origins of the Modern Roman Liturgy*, and *Sources of the Modern Roman Liturgy*.
9. Tolhurst, 3.
10. Ker, *Medieval Manuscripts*, iii, 667.
11. Brady, Chester, 266.
12. Tolhurst, 6.
13. See Doe, 'Latin polyphony under Henry VIII' and Le Huray, *Music and the Reformation*.
14. Harrison, *Music in Medieval Britain*, 82.
15. Bailey, *The Processions of Sarum*, 27, 120.
16. Bailey, *ibid.*, 46.
17. Bailey, *ibid.*, 72.
18. Bailey, *ibid.*, 51.
19. Bailey, *ibid.*, 46, n.1.
20. Especially De Valois, *Salve regina*; Maier, *Studien zur Geschichte der Marienantiphon Salve regina*; Ingram, *The polyphonic Salve regina*; Leclercq 'Salve regina', *DACL*, 714-724.
21. Bernard, *PL*, clxxxv, 544.
22. See Bernard, *Tractatus*; Marosseki, 'Les origines du chant

Cistercien'.

23. For example Baumer, 'Hermann Contract est sans nul doute l'auteur de *Salve regina*', *Histoire du Brévaire*, i, 375.

24. Cited in Leclercq, *op. cit.*, 715.

25. Gushee, 'Hermannus Contractus', *The New Grove*; De Valois, *Salve regina*, 42.

26. Cited in Leclercq, *op. cit.*, 717.

27. Leclercq, *ibid.*, 715.

28. Cited in Leclercq, *ibid.*, 716-7.

29. Carter, *An Edition of William of Malmesbury's Treatise*, No.19.

30. Harrison, *Music in Medieval Britain*, 84-5.

31. McColl, *Large-scale settings of Marian antiphons*, 226-7.

32. Morel, Nos. 208-219.

33. Hartker, 19*.

34. Knowles, *The Monastic Order*, 553-4.

TABLES

Table 1.1 181

Table 1:1   THE STRUCTURE OF THE OFFICE
IN THE RULE OF ST BENEDICT

References to Timothy Fry (ed.), *RB 1980: The Rule of St Benedict in Latin and English with Notes*, Collegeville, 1981.

A: MATINS ON SUNDAYS AND FEASTS (SUMMER AND WINTER)

[Introduction:]		
Versicle, three times	*in primis versu tertio dicendum: Domine, labia mea aperies, et os meum adnuntiabit laudem tuam*	9:1
Psalm 3 with *Gloria Patri*	*tertius psalmus et gloria*	9:2
Psalm 94 with antiphon ('or at least chanted')	*psalmum nonagesimum quartum cum antiphona, aut certe decantandum*	9:3
Hymn	*Inde sequatur ambrosianum*	9:4
[First Nocturn:]		
6 psalms with antiphons	*deinde sex psalmi cum antiphonas*	9:4
Versicle	*versu*	9:5 11:2
Abbot's blessing	*benedicat abbas*	9:5
4 readings, each followed by a responsory, the final responsory with *Gloria Patri*	*quattuor lectiones cum responsoriis suis. Ubi tantum in quarto responsorio dicatur a cantante gloria*	11:2-3

[Second Nocturn (Pattern repeated):]		
6 psalms with antiphons	*alii sex psalmi cum antiphonas sicut anteriores*	11:4
Versicle	*et versu*	11:4
4 readings with 4 responsories	*aliae quattuor lectiones cum responsoriis suis*	11:5
[Third Nocturn:]		
3 canticles from the Prophets with *Alleluia*	*tria cantica de prophetarum . . . cum alleluia psallantur*	11:6
Versicle and Abbot's blessing	*versu et benedicente abbate*	11:7
4 New Testament lessons with 4 responsories	*aliae quattuor lectiones de novo testamento, ordine quo supra*	11:7
[Conclusion:]		
Te Deum	*hymnum Te Deum Laudamus*	11:8
Gospel reading	*lectionem de Evangelia*	11:9
Hymn, *Te decet laus*	*hymnum Te decet laus*	11:10
Blessing, then Lauds	*data benedictione incipiant matutinos*	11:10

B: MATINS ON WEEKDAYS IN WINTER (NOVEMBER 1 TO EASTER)

[First Nocturn] As Sunday Matins up to and including the first 6 psalms, then:		
3 readings with 3 responsories, the third with *Gloria Patri*	*tres lectiones, inter quas et tria responsoria cantentur . . . post tertiam vero lectionem, qui cantat dicat gloriam*	9:5-6

Table 1.1 183

[Second Nocturn:]		
6 psalms with Alleluia	*sequantur reliqui sex psalmi, cum alleluia canendi*	9:9
Epistle Reading (by heart)	*lectio apostoli sequatur, ex corde recitanda*	9:10
Versicle	*et versus*	9:10
Kyrie eleison	*supplicatio litaniae, id est Kyrie eleison*	9:10

C: MATINS ON WEEKDAYS IN SUMMER (EASTER TO 31 OCTOBER)

[First Nocturn] As Sunday Matins up to and including the first 6 psalms, then:		
Old Testament reading by heart, with short responsory	*una de veteri testamento memoriter dicatur, quam brevis responsorius subsequatur*	10:2
[Second Nocturn] As for Matins on weekdays in winter		

D: LAUDS (SUNDAYS AND WEEKDAYS)

[Fixed preliminary psalms:]		
Psalm 66 without antiphon	*in primis dicatur sexagesimus sextus psalmus, sine antiphona, in directum*	12:1 13:2
Psalm 50 with Alleluia	*Post quem dicatur quinquagesimus cum alleluia*	12:2 13:2

[Variable psalms:]		
Sunday: 117, 62	*centesimus septimus decimus et sexagesimus secundus*	12:3
Monday: 5, 35	*secunda feria, quintum et tricesimum quintum*	13:4
Tuesday: 42, 56	*tertia feria, quadragesimum secundum et quinquagesimum sextum*	13:5
Wednesday: 63, 64	*quarta feria, sexagesimum tertium et sexagesimum quartum*	13:6
Thursday: 87, 89	*quinta feria, octogesimum septimum et octogesimum nonum*	13:7
Friday: 75, 91	*sexta feria, septuagesimum quintum et nonagesimum primum*	13:8
Saturday: 142	*sabbatorum autem, centesimum quadragesimum secundum*	13:9
[Variable canticle:]		
Sunday: *Benedicite*	*Inde benedictiones*	12:4 13:9
Weekdays: Canticle from the Prophets, in accordance with Roman practice	*canticum unumquemque die suo ex prophetis sicut psallit ecclesia Romana dicantur*	13:10
Saturday: Canticle from Deuteronomy in 2 sections, with *Gloria Patri* after each section	*canticum Deuteronomium qui dividatur in duas glorias*	13:9
Psalms 148-150	*Post haec sequantur laudes*	13:11 12:4

Table 1.1 185

Reading:		
Sunday: from the Apocalypse, by heart	*lectionem de Apocalypsis una ex corde*	12:4
Weekdays: from an Epistle, by heart	*lectio una apostoli memoriter recitanda*	13:11
Responsory	*et responsorium*	12:4 13:11
Hymn	*ambrosianum*	12:4 13:11
Versicle	*versu*	12:4 13:11
New Testament Canticle	*canticum de Evangelia*	12:4 13:11
Litany	*litania*	12:4 13:11
Lord's Prayer	*oratio dominica*	13:12
Conclusion	*et completum est*	12:4 13:11

E: PRIME, TERCE, SEXT, NONE

Versicle	*versum, Deus in adiutorium*	17:3 17:5
Hymn	*hymnos earundem horarum*	17:5
3 psalms (4 at Sunday Prime), each with *Gloria Patri* and optional antiphons	*psalmi tres sigillatim et non sub una gloria . . . Si major congregatio fuerit, cum antiphonas, si vero minor, in directum psallantur.*	17:2 [18:2] 17:6
Reading	*lectionem*	17:5 17:4
Versicle	*et versu*	17:5 17:4
Kyrie eleison	*Kyrie eleison*	17:5 17:4
Dismissal	*et missas*	17:5 17:4

F: VESPERS

[No details of Introduction]		
4 psalms with antiphons	*quattuor psalmis cum antiphonis*	17:7 18:12
Reading	*lectio recitanda est*	17:8
Responsory	*responsorium*	17:8
Hymn	*ambrosianum*	17:8
Versicle	*versu*	17:8
New Testament Canticle	*canticum de Evangelia*	17:8
Litany	*litania*	17:8
Lord's Prayer and dismissal	*oratione dominica fiant missae*	17:8

G: COMPLINE

[No details of Introduction]		
Psalms 4, 90 and 133 (invariable) without antiphon	*trium psalmorum . . . directanei sine antiphona dicendi sunt. Ad completorios vero cotidie idem psalmi repetantur, id est quartum, nonagesimum et centesimum tricesimum tertium.*	17:9 18:19
Hymn	*hymnum eiusdem horae*	17:10
Reading	*lectionem unam*	17:10
Versicle	*versu*	17:10
Kyrie eleison	*Kyrie eleison*	17:10
Blessing and dismissal	*et benedictione missae fiant*	17:10

TABLE 1:2 THE PSALMODIC *CURSUS* FOR THE MONASTIC AND SECULAR USES

MONASTIC MATINS

Sunday	Monday	Tuesday	Wednesday	Thursday	Friday	Saturday
3, 94	3, 94	3, 94	3, 94	3, 94	3, 94	3, 94
20-31	32-34, 36 x 2, 37-41, 43,44	45-49, 51, 52-55, 57, 58	59-61, 65, 67 x 2, 68 x 2, 69-72	73, 74, 76, 77 x 2, 78-84	85, 86, 88 x 2, 92, 93, 95-100	101, 102, 103 x 2, 104 x 2, 105 x 2, 106 x 2, 107, 108

SECULAR MATINS

Sunday	Monday	Tuesday	Wednesday	Thursday	Friday	Saturday
94	94	94	94	94	94	94
1-3, 5-20	26-37	38-41, 43-49, 51	52, 54-61, 63, 65, 67	68-79	80-88, 93, 95, 96	97-108

MONASTIC LAUDS

Sunday	Monday	Tuesday	Wednesday	Thursday	Friday	Saturday
66, 50	66, 50	66, 50	66, 50	66, 50	66, 50	66, 50
117, 62	5, 35	42, 56	63, 64	87, 89	75, 91	142
Canticle	Canticle	Canticle	Canticle	Canticle	Canticle	Canticle
148-50	148-50	148-50	148-50	148-50	148-50	148-50

SECULAR LAUDS

Sunday	Monday	Tuesday	Wednesday	Thursday	Friday	Saturday
92	50	50	50	50	50	50
99	5	42	64	89	142	91
62, 66	62, 66	62, 66	62, 66	62, 66	62, 66	62, 66
Canticle	Canticle	Canticle	Canticle	Canticle	Canticle	Canticle
148-50	148-50	148-50	148-50	148-50	148-50	148-50

MONASTIC PRIME

Sunday	Monday	Tuesday	Wednesday	Thursday	Friday	Saturday
118 (vv.1-32)	1, 2, 6	$7\text{-}9^1$	$9^2\text{-}11$	12-14	$15\text{-}17^1$	$17^2\text{-}19$

SECULAR PRIME

Sunday	Monday	Tuesday	Wednesday	Thursday	Friday	Saturday
21-25 [certain Sundays only]						
53	53	53	53	53	53	53
117						
118 (vv. 1-32)	118 (vv. 1-32)	118 (vv. 1-32)	118 (vv. 1-32)	118 (vv. 1-32)	118 (vv. 1-32)	118 (vv. 1-32)

Sunday	Monday	Tuesday	Wednesday	Thursday	Friday	Saturday

MONASTIC TERCE

118 (vv. 105-128)	119-121	119-121	119-121	119-121	119-121

MONASTIC SEXT

118 (vv. 129-152)	122-124	122-124	122-124	122-124	122-124

118 (vv. 57-90)

MONASTIC NONE

118 (vv. 153-176)	125-127	125-127	125-127	125-127	125-127

118 (vv. 81-104)

SECULAR TERCE: 118 (vv. 33-80) on all days
SECULAR SEXT: 118 (vv. 81-128) on all days
SECULAR NONE: 118 (vv. 129-176) on all days

MONASTIC VESPERS

109-112	113-114, 115/116, 128	129-132	134-137	138 x 2, 139, 140	141, 143 x 2, 144^1	144^2, 145-147

SECULAR VESPERS

109-113	114-116, 119, 120	121-125	126-130	131, 132, 134-136	137-141	143-147

MONASTIC COMPLINE

4, 90, 133	4, 90, 133	4, 90, 133	4, 90, 133	4, 90, 133

SECULAR COMPLINE

$4, 30^1, 90, 133$	$4, 30^1, 90, 133$	$4, 30^1, 90, 133$	$4, 30^1, 90, 133$	$4, 30^1, 90, 133$

KEY

36 x 2 indicates a single psalm said in two parts
115/116 indicates two psalms said under a single *Gloria Patri*
$Psalm^1$ indicates the first part of a single psalm
$Psalm^2$ indicates the second part of a single psalm

Table 1:3 CONCLUSION OF THE HOURS IN
THE RULE OF ST BENEDICT

References to Fry, *RB 1980.*

Matins (summer)	Lauds follows after a very short interval (*sic temperetur hora ut vigiliarum agenda parvissimo intervallo, . . . mox matutini, qui incipiente luce agendi sunt, subsequantur*)	8:4
Matins (winter)	Versicle and Litany (*versus et supplicatio litaniae, id est Kyrie eleison. Et sic finiantur vigiliae nocturnae*)	9:10
Matins (festal)	Hymn and blessing (*et subsequatur mox abbas hymnum Te decet laus, et data benedictione incipiant matutinos*)	11:10
Lauds	Canticle, litany and conclusion. (*canticum de Evangelia, litania et completum est*)	12:4 13:11
Lauds and Vespers	Lord's Prayer read in full (*Plane agenda matutina vel vespertina non transeat aliquando, nisi in ultimo per ordinem oratio dominica*)	13:12
Other hours	Lord's Prayer from *Sed libera nos* (*Ceteris vero agendis, ultima pars eius orationis dicatur*)	13:14
Prime, Terce, Sext, None	Versicle, *Kyrie eleison*, dismissal (*versu et Kyrie eleison et missas*)	17:4-5
Vespers	Litany, Lord's Prayer, dismissal (*litania, et oratione dominica fiant missae*)	17:8
Compline	*Kyrie eleison*, blessing, dismissal (*Kyrie eleison, et benedictione missae fiant*)	17:10
At all hours	Commemoration of absent brethren during closing prayer (*et semper ad orationem ultimam operis Dei commemoratio omnium absentum fiat*)	67:2

Table 1:4   EXTANT ENGLISH SOURCES OF
THE RULE OF ST BENEDICT

Ob 48 [*O*]	s.viii[1]	At Worcester in the later Middle Ages
Ctc 0.2.30	s.x med.	Probably from St Augustine's, Canterbury
Cu Ee.2.4	s.x med.	Smaragdus of St Mihiel, *Expositio in Regulam S. Benedicti* (incomplete); from Glastonbury?
Occ 197	s.x[2]	*RB* with OE translation; at Bury St Edmunds by s.xi med., but not written there
Lbl 5431	*c*.1000	From St Augustine's, Canterbury
Ccc 57	s.x/xi	From Abingdon
Ccc 368	s.x/xi	Incomplete
Ccc 178	s.xi[1]	*RB* with OE translation; from Worcester
Lbl A.III, 118-163v	s.xi med.	From Christ Church, Canterbury. *RB* with interlinear OE gloss.
Lbl A.III, 103-105	s.xi med.	Ch.4 of *RB* with OE version
Lbl A.IV	s.xi med.	From Winchester [?] With OE translation
W s.n.	s.xi med.	Fragmentary; with OE translation
Cu Ll.1.14	s.xi[2]	*RB*; provenance unknown
DRc B.IV.24	s.xi[2]	At Durham since 1100; from Christ Church, Canterbury? RB with OE gloss
GL 35	s.xi[2]	Fragment of Ch.4 of OE version of *RB*
Lbl A.X	s.xii[1]	OE version of *RB*
Lbl D.III	s.xiii[1]	From Wintney, Hampshire; with early Middle English adaptation

Compiled from Mechthild Gretsch, 'Aethelwold's translation of the *Regula Sancti Benedicti*'.

Table 1:5 INTERPOLATIONS IN THE MEDIEVAL RECENSION OF
THE RULE OF ST BENEDICT

1. Elaboration on the eighth degree of humility	Chapter 7 (31:21-30)
2. Addition of *Deus in adiutorium* (with *Gloria Patri*) before *Domine, labia mea* at Vespers	Chapter 9 (33:11-12)
3. Addition of *Gloria Patri* to *Deus in adiutorium* at the beginning of Prime	Chapter 17 (37:8)
4. a) Addition of *preces* and other items after *Kyrie eleison*, to conclude Prime (*cum precibus et missae fiunt*)	Chapter 17 (37:10)
b) Likewise for Terce, Sext and None	Chapter 17 (37:13)
c) Likewise for Vespers, after the Lord's Prayer	Chapter 17 (37:19)
5. Athanasian Creed (*quae sequatur hymnus De fide catholica*) added to the four sections of Ps.118 said at Prime	Chapter 18 (38:3)
6. Specific texts (a series of versicles with responses and a collect) given for the blessings prescribed on Sunday after Lauds for outgoing and incoming kitchen servers	Chapter 35 (46:22-32; 47:4-11)
7. Three versicles and a collect to be said by the prior before the incoming mealtime reader begins his week of reading	Chapter 38 (48:15-24)
8. a) A series of versicles and a collect to be said by the superior or brother appointed to sit with guests lately arrived at the monastery	Chapter 53 (57:23-31)
b) A prayer to follow the versicle prescribed in earlier versions of *RB*, to be said after the abbot and the entire community have washed the feet of a guest	Chapter 53 (58:8-13)
9. a) A series of versicles and responses given for the commemoration of absent brethren to be observed at the closing prayer of each hour	Chapter 67 (69:21-31)
b) Versicles and a prayer to be said by the entire community when a brother returns from a journey	Chapter 67 (70:4-13)

[Compiled from *Ccc* 57 (s.x/xi) copied at Abingdon and edited by John Chamberlain as *The Rule of St Benedict: The Abingdon Copy*. Bracketed references to page and line numbers of this edition]

TABLE 2:1   UNIQUE ENGLISH FEATURES OF
REGULARIS CONCORDIA

1. Daily prayers for King, Queen and Benefactors

> *. . . ne ea, quae usu patrum pro rege ac benefactoribus, quorum*
> *beneficiis Christo larigente pascimur, intercessionis oramine*
> *consuete canimus . . .*   RC 74,2-4

2. Celebration of Morrow Mass for the King

> *Eadem uero matutinalis missa pro rege uel quamcumque inminente*
> *necessitate celebretur.*   RC 86,13-14

3. High Mass of the Holy Cross and BVM on Friday and Saturday

> *Hoc semper adtendendum ut sexta feria de cruce, sabbato de sancta*
> *Maria, nisi festiua aliqua dies euenerit, missa celebretur*
> *principalis.*   RC 90,1-3

4. Prescription of daily reception of the Eucharist

> *Post pacem fratres cotidie, nisi qui crimine se aliquo uel carnis*
> *fragilitate reos cognouerint, regulari studio prorsus intenti*
> *eucharistiam accipere non rennuant . . .*   RC 89,1-3

5. Recitation of the entire psalter on the *Triduum*

> *His tribus diebus Prima peracta psallant psalterium ex integro*
> *unianimiter in choro.*   RC 111,1-2

6. Prescription of a room with a fire during the winter

> *In huius quoque hiemis tempore propter nimiam imbrium*
> *asperitatem locus aptus fratribus designetur, cuius caumene refugio*
> *hibernalis algoris et intemperiei aduersitas leuigetur.* RC 95,11-96,1

7. Use of the chasuble by deacon and subdeacon in Lent

> *Tunc induti casulis sacerdos, diaconus ac subdiaconus peragant*
> *ministeria sua. Hic autem mos casularum tantummodo tempore*
> *quadragesimali et Quatuor Temporibus usu praecedentium patrum*
> *obseruetur.*   RC 104,8-11

8. Observance on the death of a monk from a neighbouring house

> *Quod si ex alio monasterio noto ac familiari frater quis nuntiatus*
> *fuerit defunctus, . . . septem penitentiae prostrati in oratorio*
> *modulentur psalmos hac subsequente oratione: Satisfaciat tibi*
> *domine deus . . .*   RC 145,2-5

9. Pealing of the bells during Christmas Week

> *Quia Gloria in excelsis Deo ob tantae festiuitatis honorificentiam*
> *ad missam celebratur, ad Nocturnam et ad Uesperam uti ad*
> *missam, sicut in usum huius patriae indigenae tenent, omnia signa*
> *pulsentur. Nam honestos huius patriae mores ad deum pertinentes,*
> *quos ueterum usu didicimus, nullo modo abicere sed undique, uti*
> *diximus, corroborare decreuimus.*   RC 100,5-11

10. Ban on lay dominion over monasteries

> *Secularium uero prioratum, ne ad magni ruinam detrimenti uti olim*
> *acciderat misserabiliter deueniret, magna animaduersione atque*
> *anathemate suscipi cenobiis sacris sapienter prohibentes . . .*
>   RC 75,15-76,1

11. Role of the King in abbatial elections

> *Praefato equidem sinodali conciliabulo hoc adtendendum*
> *magnopere cuncti decreuerunt, ut abbatum ac abbatissarum electio*
> *cum regis sensu et consilio sancte regulae ageretur documento.*
>   RC 74,17-75,1

12. Practice of Monastic Bishops [probably Winchester and Worcester only]

> *Episcoporum quoque electio uti abbatum, ubicumque in sede*
> *episcopali monachi regulares conuersantur, si domini largente*
> *gratia tanti profectus inibi monachus reperiri potuerit, eodem modo*
> *agatur . . .*   RC 75,1-4

TABLE 2:2 VOTIVE OBSERVANCES MODELLED ON PSALMS IN *REGULARIS CONCORDIA*

A. Self-contained Groups of Psalms

Content	Context	References	Votive Function	Non-votive Function	References to non-votive Functions
FIFTEEN GRADUAL PSALMS *(quindecim psalmi graduum)*					
Pss.119-133	Daily in the stalls, after the *Trina oratio*, as the bell rang for Matins. Said in three groups of five. Also recited singly; during Lent	82,9-17 105,1-14	Non-specific	None specified	None
SEVEN PENITENTIAL PSALMS *(paenitentiae psalmi; speciales psalmi)*					
Pss. 6, 31, 37, 50, 101, 129, 143 [sometimes with 85]	Daily during winter, after Prime and two further appended psalms (see below) preceding the Litany. The psalms also formed part of the *Trina oratio* and were recited singly, prostrate, during Lent	84,19 - 85,6 96,16 81,9 - 82,6 105,1-14	Non-specific	Visitation of a sick brother On receiving news of sickness After the death of a member of the community After death of a member of the confraternity Good Friday, as part of the Veneration of the Cross (modelled on the *Trina oratio* before Matins	141,14-16 146,1-5 142,10-15 145, 1-5 116,20-22
FIVE PSALMS FOR THE DEAD *(quinque psalmi pro defunctis)*					
Pss. 5, 6, 114, 115, 129	Daily; after Chapter	87,24-25 90,9-11	for departed brethren (*pro defunctis fratribus*)	None specified	None

Content	Context	References	Votive Function	Non-votive Function	Refs.
TWO PROSTRATE PSALMS (*psalmi prostrati*)					
One penitential and one gradual psalm, as a pair (6,119; 31,120; 37,121; 50,122; 101,123; 129,124; 142,125)	Daily, during Lent, 'prostrate on the floor of the oratory', after all hours except Matins	35,12-20	To effect 'some increase in divine worship', so that 'being freed from the bonds of sin we may rise to heavenly things by the steps of the virtues'	None specified	None
THE *MISERERE*					
Ps. 50	Daily, after Lauds, Vespers and Compline, in each case preceding the psalms for king, queen and benefactors	19,5-6; 25,39-49; 27,8-9	Non-specific	None specified	None
THE ENTIRE PSALTER (*psalterium ex integro*)					
Pss. 1-150	On the *Triduum*, after Prime, in choir.	40,1-3	Presumably as an act of particular devotion (*devotissime*)	Deacons chanted the entire psalter after the death of a member of the community; subdeacons recited fifty psalms	67, 11-16

B. Groups of Psalms with Additional Items

PSALMS FOR THE ROYAL HOUSEHOLD (*psalmi pro rege et regina ac familiaribus*)					
Pss. 6,19; 31,85; 12,56; 19,22; 66,101; 79,129; 84,142; 69,120; each pair with the same three specially appointed collects	Daily, one pair after each of the hours except Prime, and after High Mass.	18,1-19; 19,1-8; 20,19-22; 24,7-12; 25,20-22; 25,29-31; 25,39-42; 27,8-11	Said for king, queen and benefactors; later Benedictine sources often refer to identically-placed psalms as *psalmi familiares*, but *RC* seems to be unique in offering them for the royal family.	None	
	Omitted from the Octave of Easter to the Octave of Pentecost	56,18-23			
TWO PSALMS AFTER PRIME					
Pss. 37 and 50, both followed by *preces* and a collect	Daily, after Prime, replacing the psalms for the royal household said after the other offices	19,18-23	Ps.37 against fleshly temptation; Ps.50 for departed brethren	None	
PRECES					
Single verses or groups of verses from the psalms, sometimes with special collects	Incorporated into Prime	53,1-6	Not specified	Ash Wednesday, during the ashing ceremony	34,16
	Recited with the two psalms after Prime	19,18-21		Incorporated into secular Compline during Easter Week	53,17-21
	Recited after High Mass with psalms for benefactors	24,8-11			
	Incorporated into *Trina oratio* after Compline	27,30			

THE TRINA ORATIO (*Trina oratio; tres orationes; tres orationes*)

Tripartite structure. After Matins, Pt.I comprised Pss.6,31,37; Pt.II Pss.50, 101; Pt.III Pss.129, 143; each part with *Pater noster* and collects.	Three times daily: before the 15 Gradual Psalms preceding Matins; after Compline, and before Terce in winter and after Lauds in summer	16,1-20; 17,1-12; 20,16-19; 54,16-12	Essentially Trinitarian, but each part had its own emphasis after Matins: Pt.I: personal intentions, Pt.II: king, queen and benefactors; Pt.III: the faithful departed	Structurally-related observance on Good Friday	116,20-117,23
After Compline: Pt.I, Pss.12,42; Pt.II, Pss.66,126; Pt.III, Ps.129, each part with *Kyrie*, *Pater noster*, *preces* and collect.		27,11-38			

Table 2:2

201

C: Non-psalmodic votive observances in *Regularis Concordia*

		INDEPENDENT ANTIPHONS (*antiphonae*)			
Three antiphons, each probably followed by a versicle and collect	Daily, after the psalms for the royal household at both Lauds and Vespers. Omitted during Advent	19,5-11; 25,42-43; 29,23-27	Holy Cross, BVM, and patron saint respectively.	None	None
MORROW MASS (*Missa matutinalis*)					
Complete mass	Second mass of the day, attended by the community. On ferial days in winter it followed Terce and in summer it was delayed until after Prime and Chapter. The choice of formula seems to have been flexible, but the Morrow Mass was by no means invariably votive.	20,27-28; 23,4-5	On Sunday for the Trinity, unless a feast took precedence. On weekdays, for the king or any other pressing need	To mark the lesser of two feasts falling on the same day; or a Sunday if a feast fell on this day. When a member of the community died	67,5-6
MASS OF THE DAY (*missa principalis*)					
Complete mass	First and main mass of the day, attended by all. It was offered as a votive mass only on Friday and Saturday, unless a feast took precedence	24,5-7	On Friday for the Holy Cross, on Saturday for the Virgin	On most days related to the calendar cycle	None

TABLE 2:3   PSALMS FOR THE ROYAL HOUSEHOLD IN *REGULARIS CONCORDIA*
(*Psalmi pro regi et regina ac familiaribus*)

A) After Matins: Psalm 6 for the king; psalm 19 for king, queen and *familiares*

> *Peractis Nocturnis dicant duos psalmos Domine ne in furore tuo I et
> Exaudiat te dominus, unum uidelicet pro rege specialiter, alterum uero
> pro rege et regina ac familiaribus cum his collectis: Pro rege, Quesumus
> omnipotens deus . . . Pro regina, Rege quaesumus domine . . . Pro rege
> et regina ac familiaribus Deus qui caritatis dona . . . Et sic finitis
> omnibus regularibus horis semper agatur.*   83,1-15

B) After Lauds: Psalms 31, 85 [preceded by 50]

> *Post hoc sequantur diei Laudes. Post Miserere mei deus addant duos
> psalmos pro rege reginaque et familiaribus Beati quorum et Inclina
> domine aurem tuam.*   84,5-7

C) After Terce: Psalms 12, 56

> *. . . horam Tertiam. Post cuius terminum dicant pro rege atque regina
> et benefactoribus suis psalmos Vsquequo domine et Miserere mei deus,
> miserere mei, subsequentibus praescriptis collectis.*   86,7-9

D) After Mass of the Day: Psalms 19, 122 [with *preces*]

> *Omnibus namque diebus festiuis siue cotidieanis missa finita dicatur pro
> rege psalmos Aexaudiat te dominus et pro regina Ad te leuaui
> consequentibus precibus et oratione congrua, uidelicet—ut post missam
> eorum agatur memoria uti in missa et in omnibus aliis agitur horis.*
>   90,3-6

E) After Sext: Psalms 66, 101

> *Finita Sexta canant psalmum Deus misereatur nostri et Domine exaudi
> I, pro rege reginaque et familiaribus cum prescriptis collectis. Sequitur
> letania.*   91,11-13

F) After None: Psalms 79, 129

> *Peracta Nona dicant pro rege reginaque et familiaribus psalmos Qui
> regis et De profundis cum praenotatis collectis. Dehinc pergant ad
> mensam.*   91,17-19

G) After Vespers: Psalms 84, 142 [preceded by 50]

> *Vesperam uero canentes duos post Miserere mei deus pro rege reginaque
> et familiaribus addant psalmos, id est, Benedixisti domine et Domine
> exaudi II.*   91,25 - 92,2

H) After Compline: Psalms 69, 120 [preceded by 50]

> *Finito Completorio, et ad ultimum more solito Miserere mei deus decantato addantur duo psalmi Deus in adiutorium meum et Leuaui pro rege ac regina et benefactoribus.*   93,7-9

TABLE 2:4   THE *TRINA ORATIO* IN *REGULARIS CONCORDIA*
[*Trina oratio, tres orationes, tres oramines*]

A) Before the 15 Gradual psalms which preceded Matins

> *Finitis uero tribus orationibus a pueris sonetur secundum signum . . . canentibus quindecim psalmos graduum . . . atque finitis cum eisdem psalmis, incipiant Nocturnam.*   82,12-17

i. 'First prayer'	*In prima itaque oratione . . .*
for personal intentions	*pro seipso primum intercedendo.*
[consisting of:]	81,9-11
a) The first three Penitential Psalms	*decantet tres primos*
[6, 31, 37]	*penitentiae psalmos* 81,9-10
b) *Pater noster* [repeated as	*cum oratione dominica*
the second element in the two	*uti in sequentibus* 81,10
following prayers]	
c) Collect [complete text given	*Post hos orationem istam:*
in source]	*Gratias tibi ago . . .*
	in hac nocte 81,11-14
ii. 'Second prayer'	*Inde ueniat ad secundam orationem*
	. . . 81,14-15
for king, queen and *familiares*	*pro rege et regina atque familiaribus*
	81,15-82,1
a) Two [Penitential] Psalms [50, 101]	*duos dicat psalmos* 81,15
b) *Pater noster*	
c) Collect [complete]	*cum oratione Deus qui caritatis*
	. . . 82,1-4

iii. 'Third prayer'   *Inde ad tertiam orationem ueniens . .*

   for the faithful departed   *pro fidelibus defunctis* 82,5-6

   a) Two [Penitential] Psalms [129, 143]   *duos posteriores psalmos* 82,5

   b) *Pater noster*

   c) Collect [complete]   *cum oratione Inueniant*
                                    quaesumus domine 82,6-8

B) i. Before Terce (in winter)

     Peractis tribus a pueris oraminibus, uti prius a senioribus gestum fuerat,
     dispositi singuli in locis suis campana pulsata incipiant horam Tertiam.
                             86,5-7

  ii. After Lauds (in summer)

     Quod si luce diei ut oportet Matutinae fuerint finite, egredientes
     aecclesiam fratres calcient se, lauent, peractisque in ecclesia tribus
     oraminibus, sedentes in claustro uacent lectioni usque dum signum
     Primae auditum fuerit.   130,9-12

[No details of structure or texts are given for either of these hours]

C) After Compline

     Finito Completorio, ut in ultima hora canonica uti in exordio sanctae
     trinitatis ac indiuiduae unitatis reuerentia legitime a seruulis exibeatur
     catholicis, agant primum pueri tres orationes, post pueros agant fratres.
     93,9-12

Structure of *Trina oratio* after Compline

i. 'First Prayer'   *In prima oratione* 93,12
   [no intentions given]

   a) Psalms 12 and 42   *canant psalmos: Vsquequo domine et*
                                   Iudica me deus et discerne. 93,12-13

b) *Kyrie eleison*	*Kyrrie eleison* 93,13
c) *Pater noster*	*Pater noster.* 93,13
d) *preces* [Psalm 50, vv. 11-14]	*Preces Auerte faciem tuam. Cor mundum. Ne proicias me. Redde michi letitiam.* 93,14-15
e) Collect [complete]	*Oratio Gratias tibi ago . . . in hac die* 93,15-18
ii. 'Second Prayer'	*In secunda oratione* 93,18
a) Psalms 66 and 126	*Deus misereatur nostri. Nisi dominus* 93,19
b) *Kyrie eleison*	*Kyrrie eleison* 93,19
c) *Pater noster*	*Pater noster.* 93,19
d) *preces* as above	*Easdem preces quas supra.* 93,19-20
e) Collect [complete]	*Collectam Deus cui omne cor patet* 93,20-23
iii. 'Third Prayer'	*In tertia oratione:* 93,23
a) Psalm 129	*De profundis.* 93,23
b) *Kyrie eleison*	*Kyrie eleison.* 93,23
c) *Pater noster*	*Pater noster.* 93,23
d) *preces* as above	*Easdem praeces* 93,24
e) Collect [complete]	*Collecta. Omnipotens . . qui sitienti populo* 93,24 - 94,1
[two alternatives, both complete]	*Alia. Omnipotens . . . respice propitius* 94,1-3

[The community was then aspersed before retiring]

TABLE 2:5   DERIVATION OF COLLECTS IN
ACCRUED OBSERVANCES IN *REGULARIS CONCORDIA*

Collect	Concordant Sources	Context in Concordant Sources
Trina oratio before Matins		
1.*Gratias tibi . . in hac nocte*	MQ, 231	Personal devotion before Matins, said prostrate
2.*Deus qui caritatis dona*	Greg.Suppl., 1304 Jumièges, 263 Leofric C, 14, 191	Collect for *Missa pro familiaribus*
3.*Inueniant quaesumus Domine*	Gelas.Sac., 1670 Greg.Suppl., 1436 Leofric A, 197	Postcommunion of *Missa in agenda plurimorum mortuorum*
Trina oratio after Compline		
1.*Gratias tibi . . in hac die*	MQ, 260	Personal devotion after Compline
2.*Deus cui omne cor*	Alcuin, 446 Greg.Sac., 2325 Leofric A, 177	Collect of *Missa de gratia Sancti Spiritus postulanda*
3a.*Omnipotens mitissime Deus, qui sitienti*	Alcuin, 448 Jumièges, 259 Leofric A, 186	Collect of *Missa pro petitione lacrymarum*
3b.*Omnipotens mitissime Deus, respice propitius*	Alcuin, 450 Jumièges, 257 Leofric A, 188	Collect of *Missa pro tentatione cogitationum*

Psalms and Collects for the Royal Household

1.[For King] *Quaesumus omnipotens* *Deus, ut famulus tuus*	Greg.Suppl., 1270 Leofric A, 179 Fulda, 1270	Collect of *Missa cotidiana* *pro rege*
2.[For Queen] *Rege quaesumus Domine*	Gelas.Sac., 77 Greg.Sac., 2463 Leofric A, 72 Leofric C, 20	*Oratio super populum,* Sexagesima Postcommunion, *Missa pro regina*
3.[King, Queen and *Familiares*] *Deus qui caritatis*	As above	

Psalms and Collects after Prime

1.[Fleshly Temptation] *Ure igne*	Alcuin, 453 Jumièges, 258 Leofric A, 182	Collect of *Missa contra* *tentationem carnis*
2.[Departed Brethren] *Inueniant quaesumus* *Domine*	As above	

TABLE 2:6 WEEKLY CYCLES OF VOTIVE MASSES

	Alcuin	Leofric A	Jumièges	F: LH 330 (Winchester)	DRu V.V.6 (Durham)
Sunday	1. *De sancta Trinitate* 2. *De gratia Sancti Spiritus postulanda*	*De sancta Trinitate*	1. *De Sancta Trinitate* 2. *[In memoriam salvatoris Domini nostri]*	1. *De sancta Trinitate* 2. *In memoriam salvatoris Domini nostri*	
Monday	1. *Pro peccatis* 2. *Pro petitione lachrymarum*	*De sancta sapientia, que Christus est*	*Pro peccatis*	*Pro peccatis*	*De angelis*
Tuesday	1. *Ad postulanda angelica suffragia* 2. *Pro tentationibus cogitationum*	*De sancta caritate*	*Ad suffragia angelorum*	*Ad suffragia angelorum*	*De sapientia*
Wednesday	1. *De sancta sapientia* 2. *Ad postulandam humilitatem*	*De cordis emundatione per spiritum sanctum postulanda*	*De sapientia*	*De sapientia*	*Ob Sancti Spiritus gratiam*
Thursday	1. *De charitate* 2. *Contra tentationes carnis*	*Ad angelorum suffragia postulanda*	*De sancta karitate*	*De caritate*	1. *Ob caritatis donum* 2. *[Aut hoc]*
Friday	1. *De sancta cruce* 2. *Pro petitione lachrymarum*	*In honore sanctae crucis*	*De sancta cruce*	*De sancta cruce*	*[De sancta cruce]*
Saturday	1. *De sancta Maria* 2. *In commemoratione sanctae Mariae*	*In honorem sanctae Mariae*	*De sancta Maria*	[Manuscript incomplete]	*De sancta Maria*

TABLE 3:1   CHRONOLOGICAL LIST OF EXTANT DAILY
MONASTIC VOTIVE OFFICES

Source	Category	Date	Provenance	Intention	Content
[Ordericus Vitalis]	Life of Ethelwold	[963-84]	[Winchester]	1. BVM 2. Peter and Paul 3. All Saints	
Lbl D.XXVI-II	Private prayerbook	c.1023-35	Newminster, Winchester	1. Holy Trinity 2. Holy Cross 3. BVM	[V] [V] [V]
Ob 296	Psalter	1015-36	Crowland	Holy Trinity	V-S
Lbl A.III	Miscellaneous	c.1050	Christ Church, Canterbury	BVM	M-C
Lbl 2.B.V	Psalter with additions	c.1066-87	Winchester/ Canterbury	BVM	M-C
Cjc C.18	Psalter	c.1150-70	Wherwell [St Albans]	BVM	M-C
Lbl 21927	Psalter	c.1175	Muchelney	BVM	M-C
Lbl 1005	Ordinal	c.1234	Bury St Edmunds	BVM	[All hours]
WO F.160	Antiphoner	s.xiii[1]	Worcester	BVM	M-C
Ob 435	Customary	s.xiii	Eynsham	BVM	[C]
Lbl 157	Hours	s.xiii [?]	?	BVM	M-C
Llp 368	Psalter	s.xiii	Norwich	Holy Spirit	M-N [incomplete]
CA 6	Breviary	s.xiv[2]	Christ Church, Canterbury	BVM	M
Lbl 155	Psalter [later additions]	s.xiii	Christ Church, Canterbury	Holy Spirit	M-C
Ccc 441	Instruction for Novices	s.xiii ex	Christ Church, Canterbury	BVM	V
Ob e.1*	Breviary	c.1300	Hyde Abbey	BVM	M-C
D-Bds 194	Customary	c.1330-40	St Werburgh, Chester	BVM	V-N
Lbl C.XII	Customary	1330-40	St Augustine, Canterbury	BVM	All hours
Cjc D.27	Customary	c.1400	St Mary, York	BVM	C-N

Source	Category	Date	Provenance	Intention	Content
Ouc 169	Ordinal	1404	Barking	BVM	V-N
Llp 558	Hours	c.1400-25	Christ Church, Canterbury	BVM	M-C
Lbl 1804	Offices	s.xv[l]	Durham	BVM	M-C
DO 26543	Hours	s.xv med	Winchester	BVM	M-L [incomplete]
Mch 6717	Psalter	s.xv med	Godstow	BVM	M-C
Ob f.1	Hours	1425-75	Gloucester	BVM	M-C
Ob g.12	Hours	1521	Pilton [Malmesbury]	BVM	M-C
SECULAR FORMS					
	Ordinal	c.1270?	Sarum	BVM	V-N
	[Grandisson]	1337	Exeter	BVM	V-N

TABLE 3:2   EARLY APPEARANCES OF THE OFFICE OF THE DEAD

A 750-800   Ordo Romanus XVI   *Ad agendas uero mortuorum ad Uigilias*
                    '*Instruccio*   *tam psalmi quam et leccionibus cum*
                    Aecclesiastici Ordinis'   *responsuriis suis uel antephonis in*
                                                    Mattutinis Laudibus sine Alleluia de
                    CCM i, 21, 22-24.   *ipsis est canendum . . .*

B 778-97   Letter of Theodomarus,   *Si quis autem nocte obierit, supra id*
                    abbot of Casinen, to   *quod diximus, etiam nocturnum officium*
                    Theodoricus the Glorious   *cum novem psalmis tribusque lectionibus*
                                                    sive responsoriis sive Matutinum pro eis
                    CCM i, 135, 22-25.   *domino canitur.*

C s.viii/ix   Ordo Romanus XVII   *Agenda uero mortuorum ad Uigilias*
                    '*Breviarium Ecclesiastici*   *psalmi quoque et lectionis cum*
                    Ordinis'   *responsoriis uel antefonis in*
                                                    Matutinis Laudibus sine Alleluia de ipsis
                    CCM i, 44, 10-12.   *est canendum . . .*

D *c.*800-11	*Institutio* of Angilbert, abbot, *De Diuersitate Officiorum* *CCM* i, 301,30 -302,21	*. . . statuere curauimus, qualiter fratres . . . ob memoriam cunctorum fidelium defunctorum per singulos dies ac noctes Uespertinos, Nocturnos atque Matutinos deuotissime eo ordine, ut in sequentibus declaratur celebrare studerent . . . Omnibus horis uespertinis more solito celebratis . . . accedant [fratres] simul ad Sanctum Mauricium, ubi per singulos cotidianos dies ac noctes, sicut superius est insertum, Uesperos, Nocturnos et Matutinos ob memoriam omnium fidelium defunctorum persoluant.*
E 812, 817	*Supplex Libellus Monachorum Fuldensium Carolo Imperatori porrectus* *CCM* i, 321,20 -322,4	*. . . pro defunctis ergo fratribus nostris commemorationem illam, quam quotidie bis habuimus, id est post matutinam celebrationem et vespertinam, quae est antiphona videlicet Requiem aeternam et prima pars psalmi Te decet hymnus deus, versus et collecta; in kalendis vero omnium mensium unam Vigiliam et quinquaginta psalmos; pro Sturmi quoque abbate et fundatoribus monasterii istius in anniversaria obitus die unam Vigiliam et unum psalterium per singulos annos.*
F 816	Authentic Decrees of First Synod of Aachen, Cap. XI *CCM* i, 460, 3-5	*Ut si necessitas poposcerit ob operis laborem post refectionem uespertinam etiam et in Quadragesima pari modo et quando officio mortuorum celebratur priusquam lectio Completorii legatur bibant.*
G 817-21	*Capitula in Auuam Directa*, Cap. XI: [Attributed to Tatto and Grimalt] *CCM* i, 336, 12-16	*. . . ut defunctorum Uigilia hoc modo ab eis celebratur: Vespera solito finita statim Uesperam cum antiphonis celebrant pro defunctis. Et post Completorium Uigiliam cum antiphonis uel responsoriis plenissime atque suauissime canunt. Et post Nocturnas interuallo Matutinos pro mortuis faciunt.*
H 818-9	*Collectio Capitularis* *CCM* i, 536, 9-12	*Post octauam Paschae incipiant cantare Uigilias post Nonam et post cenam Deus auribus et post kalendas novembris dum pulsantur Uesperae Placebo domino, post Uesperas Dirige, post Matutinos Deus auribus.*

TABLE 3:3   THE OFFICE OF THE DEAD
IN THE WORCESTER   ANTIPHONER (*WO* F.160)

PM 1, xii, pp.435-8.   All items are given complete with music.

Common alternatives found in other sources are given in square brackets.

VESPERS

Antiphon	*Placebo domino*	Psalm	*Dilexi q[uonia]m*	114
	Heu me quia		*Ad d[omi]n[u]m*	119
	Dominus custodit		*Leuaui*	120
	Si iniquitates		*De p[ro]fundis*	129
	Opera manuu[m]		*Confitebor*	137

Versicle   *Req[u]iem aet[er]nam*   *[A porta inferi]*

Mag.Ant.   *Audiui uocem de celo*   *[Tuam deus deposcimus]*

Canticle   *Magnificat*

[Kyrie eleison]

Pater noster.

Psalms   *Lauda anima.* (145)
            Voce mea. (141)

Preces.

Versicles   *Requiem et[er]nam.*   *Et lux p[er]p[etua].*
            A porta inferi.   *Erue d[omi]ne sp[irit]u tuo.*
            Dominus uobiscum.   *Et cum sp[irit]u tuo.*

Collects   *D[eu]s indulgentiaru[m] d[omi]ne*
            Inclina d[omi]ne
            D[eu]s qui int[er] ap[osto]licos
            D[eu]s uenie largitor
            Miserere q[uesumu]s d[omi]ne
            Fidelium d[eu]s om[n]ium conditor.

[Dominus vobiscum. Requiescant in pace.]

VIGILS

[Invitatory   *Regem cui omnia vivunt*   (*Ccc* 391 only)]

[First Nocturn:]

Antiphon	*Dirige domine deus*	Psalm	*V[er]ba mea*	5
	Convertere d[omi]ne		*D[omi]ne ne* (i)	6
	Nequando rapiat		*D[omi]ne d[eu]s m[eu]s*	7

Versicle   *Requie[m] et[ernam]*   *[A porta inferi]*   *[Adiuva vos]*   *[Audivi vocem]*

Lessons   *Parce m[ih]i d[omi]ne*
           Tedet a[n]i[m]am mea[m]
           Manus tue fec[er]unt me

Responds	*Qui lazarum resuscitasti*	*[Credo quod redemptor]*
	Credo quod redemptor meus	*[Qui lazarum resuscitasti]*
	Heu michi domine	*[Domine quando veneris]*

[Second Nocturn:]

Antiphon	*In loco paschue*	Psalm	*D[omi]n[u]s reg[it]*	22
	Delicta iuve[n]tutis		*Ad te d[omi]ne*	24
	Credo uidere *[Videam domine]*		*D[ominu]s [illuminacio]*	26

Versicle   *A[n]i[m]a m[e]a t[u]rbata*   *[In memoria eterna]*

Lessons   *Quantas habeo iniquitates*
           Homo natus de muliere
           Quis michi tribuat

Responds	*Ne recorderis*	*[Subvenite sancti dei]*	*[Heu michi]*
	Domine quando	*[Heu michi domine]*	*[Ne recorderis]*
	Peccantem me	*[Libera me domine]*	*[Domine secundum]* *[Ne recorderis]*

[Third Nocturn:]

Antiphon	*Complaceat t[ibi]*	Psalm	*Expectans*	39
	Sana d[omi]ne. *[Tu autem domine]*		*Beatus q[ui] intelligit]*	40
	Sitiuit a[n]i[m]a mea		*Q[u]emad[modum]*	41

Versicle   *Audivi voce[m]*   *[Requiem eternam]*   *[A porta inferi]*

Lessons   *Sp[iritu]s m[eu]s attenuabitur*
           Pelli mee consumptis
           Quare de uulua *[Vir fortissimus]* *[Ecce misterium]*

Responds   *Domine secundum [Peccantem me cotidie]*
            Tibi soli peccaui   [Domine secundum actum]   [Requiem eternam]   [Quomodo
            Libera me domine   confitebor]
            [Pater noster]

[Psalms   *Ad dominum cum tribularer* (119)
            Voce mea (141)]

Versicle   *Audiui uocem de celo*

[Collects]

LAUDS

Antiphon   *Exultabunt domino*   Psalm   *Misere[re]*   50
            Exaudi domine   *Te decet*   64
            Me suscepit   *D[eu]s d[eu]s m[eu]s*   62
            Eruisti do[m]i[n]e [A porta inferi] *Ego dixi*
            Omnis sp[iritu]s   *Laud[ate]*   148

Versicle   *Requie[m] et[e]rna[m]*

Ben. Ant.   *Omne q[uo]d dat michi [Ego sum] [Verum auctor] [Tuam deus]*

Canticle   *Benedictus*

[Kyrie eleison]

Pater noster.

[Psalms   *Ad dominum*   (119)
            De p[ro]f[undis] (129)
            Voce m[e]a   (141)]

[Versicles and collects]

TABLE 3:4   MOBILITY OF THE OFFICES OF THE DEAD AND OF ALL SAINTS IN *RC*

1. Winter (1 Nov. to Lent)	2. Summer[1] (When two meals were taken)	Summer[2] (When a single meal was taken, *ad nonam*)	4. Summer[3] (When a single meal was taken, *ad vesperam*)
Matins of the Day	Matins of the Day	Night Office arrangement as for the summer pattern with two meals	
Vigils of the Dead Matins of All Saints[4] Lauds of the Day	Lauds of the Day Matins of All Saints[4] Matins of the Dead[5]		
[Single meal, *ad nonam*]	First meal, *ad nonam*		
Vespers of the Day	Vespers of the Day	Vespers of the Day	Vespers of the Day
Vespers of All Saints	Vespers of All Saints	Vespers of All Saints	Vespers of All Saints
Vespers of the Dead	Vespers of the Dead	Vespers of the Dead Vigils of the Dead	Vespers of the Dead
	Second meal, *Cena*		Sole meal, *Cena*
			Vigils of the Dead

1. Two meals were taken from the Octave of Pentecost to 14 September
2. A single meal *ad nonam* was taken on Rogation Days, Wednesdays and Fridays from the Octave of Pentecost to 14 September, and on all weekdays from 14 September to 1 November
3. *Cena* only was taken in Lent and on Quarter Tense Days
4. The Office of All Saints was omitted from Maundy Thursday to the Octave of Easter
5. The Office of the Dead was omitted from Maundy Thursday to the Octave of Pentecost

(Based on Symons, 'Monastic Observance', 146-7.)

TABLE 3:5   THE OFFICE OF ALL SAINTS
IN THE EINSIEDELN CUSTOMARY

Incipivnt Vespertine Lavdes de Omnibus Sanctis.
(Einsiedeln, 248,8-249,3)

Antiphona	*In consilio.*	*Psalmus*	*Confitebor tibi.* [110]
Antiphona	*Preciosa.*	*Psalmus*	*Credidi.* [115]
Antiphona	*Euntes ibant.*	*[Psalmus]*	*In conuertendo.* [125]
Antiphona	*Iusti confitebuntur.*	*Psalmus*	*Eripe me domine.* [139]
Lectio	*Scimus quoniam diligentibus deum.*		
Versus	*Mirabilis deus.*		
Ymnus	*Christe redemptor omnium.*		
Versus	*Letamini.*		
Antiphona	*Sancti dei omnes.*	*Psalmus*	*Magnificat.*
Pater noster.			
Preces	*Post partum virgo.*		

In conspectu angelorum.
Solue iubente deo.
Sancte Paule apostole.
In omnem terram.
Ora pro nobis beatae Emmeramme.
Sacerdos dei Martine.
Sanctissime confessor domini monachorum pater et dux.
Benedicte intercede pro nostra omnium salute.
Exultent iusti.
Collecta uel oratio.

In Matutinis Laudibus (Einsiedeln, 249,4-8)

prima antiphona	*Post partum uirgo.*	*Psalmus*	*Dominus regnauit.* [92]
Antiphona	*Angeli eorum.*	*Psalmus*	*Iubilate.* [99]
Antiphona	*Vos amici mei.*	*Psalmus*	*Deus deus.* [62]
Antiphona	*Sancti spiritus.*	*Psalmus*	*Benedicite.*
Antiphona	*Omnium sanctorum chori.*	*Psalmus*	*Laudate.* [148]
Lectio ut supra.			
Ymnus	*Ihesu saluator saeculi.*		

TABLE 3:6   VOTIVE OFFICES IN
THE PRAYER BOOK OF AELFWINE (*LBL* D.XXVII)

Asterisks mark antiphon incipits (incipit alone precedes psalms in each case.)

[IN HONORE SANCTE TRINITATE] ff.76-77

	D[eu]s in adiutoriu[m] meum intende. *D[omi]ne. [G]l[ori]a p[at]ri. Sicut erat.*
Antiphon	*O beata* et benedicta et gloriosa trinitas pater et filius et sp[iritu]s s[an]c[tu]s.*
Psalms	*D[eu]s in nomine tuo* (53) *Confitemini d[omi]no* (117) *Beati immaculati usq[ue]: i[n] fin[em]* (118) *Quicumq[ue] uult*
Chapter	*Tres sunt qui testimoniu[m] dant in celo. pater. et filius.* *et sp[iritu]s s[an]c[tu]s et hi tres unum sunt.*
Respond	*Benedicat nos d[ominu]s d[eu]s noster benedicat nos d[eu]s et* *metuant eum omnes fines terrae.* *V. Deus misereatur nostri et benedicat uos d[eu]s.* *[R.] et metuant*
Hymn	*Veni creator sp[iritu]s*
Versicle	*Sit nomen d[omi]ni benedictum.*
Magnificat *Antiphon*	*Te d[eu]m* patrem ingenitum te filium unigenitum te sp[iritu]m* *s[an]c[tu]m paraclitum s[an]c[t]am et indiuiduam trinitatem toto* *corde et ore confitemur laudamus at[que] benedicimus tibi* *gloria in secula.*
Canticle	*Magnificat.*
	Kyrriel[eison]. Christel[eison]. Kyrriel[eison]. *Pater noster. Credo in d[eu]m. Carnis r[esurrectionem].*
[Preces]	*Benedicamus patrem et filiu[m].* *Bendictus es d[omi]ne.* *Benedicat et custodiat nos summa et indiuidua trinitas.* *patris filii[que] ac sp[iritu]s s[an]c[t]i. omne[s]q[ue] facim[us] a nobis* *procul expellat.* *S[an]c[t]a et individua trinitas terge tuoru[m] petimus sub nixe* *flagitia seruorum. Uosq[ue] in tuo s[an]c[t]o conserva servitio.* *Benedicat et custodiat nos om[ni]p[oten]s d[eu]s. qui fecit celu[m]* *et terram mare et omnia quae meis sunt.* *Benedicta sit s[an]c[t]a trinitas atq[ue] indiuisa unitas* *confitebimur ei quia fecit nobiscum misericordiam suam.*

Collects   *O beata et benedicta et gloriosa trinitas . . .*
                      Te summa deitas unaq[ue] . . .

Appended prayers to the Trinity follow on ff.77-80.

IN HONORE S[AN]C[T]E CRUCIS ff.80-1v

                      D[eu]s in adiutorium meum intende. D[omi]ne. Gloria patri.
                      Sicut erat.

Antiphon   *Salua nos christe* saluator per uirtutem crucis qui salvasti*
                      petru[m] in mari miserere nobis.

Psalms   *D[eu]s in nomine tuo.* (53)
                      Confitemini d[omi]no. (117)
                      Beati immmaculati. usq[ue] in finem. (118)
                      Quicumq[ue] uult.

Chapter   *Christus peccata n[ost]ra p[ro]tulit in corpore suo sup[er] lignum.*
                      ut peccatis mortui iustitie uiuamus cuius uiuere sanati
                      sumus.

Respond   *O crux benedicta que sola fuisti digna portare regem celorum*
                      et dominu[m].
                      V. O crux admirabilis euacuatio uulneris restitutio sanitatis.
                      [R.] que sola.

Hymn   *Vexilla regis.*

Versicle   *Omnis terra ador[ent] te d[ominu]s.*

Magnificat   *Sup[er] omnia* ligna cedrorum tu sola excelsior. in qua uita*
Antiphon   *mundi pependit in qua christus triumphavit et mors mortem*
                      superauit. All[eluia].

Canticle   *Magnificat.*

                      Kyrriel[eison]. Christel[eison]. Kyrriel[eison].
                      Pater n[oste]r. Et ne nos inducas. Credo in d[eu]m. Carnis
                      resurr[ectionem].

                      Adoramus te christe. Hoc signum s[an]c[t]e crucis erit in celo
                      cum d[omi]n[u]s adiudicandu[m] uenerit. Dicite in nationibus.
                      Tuam cruce[m] adoram[us] d[ominus]. D[omi]ne exaudi.

                      Oration[es] de s[an]c[t]a cruce ac salubri.

                      D[eu]s cui cuncte obediunt creature et omnia in verbo . . .

Prayers to the Holy Cross follow on ff.80-81v.

IN HONORE S[AN]C[TA]E MARIAE *ff.81v-82*

D[eu]s in adiutorium meu[m] intende. D[omi]ne. Gloria [patri]. Sicut erat.

Antiphon	*Aue Maria* gratia plena dominus tecum benedicta tu in mulieribus alleluia.*
Psalms	*D[eus] in nomine tuo.* (53) *Confitemini d[omi]no.* (117) *Beati immaculati us[que] in fin[em].* (118) *Quicum[que] uult*
Chapter	*Ab initio et ante secula creata su[m] et usq[ue] ad futurum s[e]c[u]l[u]m non desinam. et in habitatione s[an]c[t]a coram ipso ministraui.*
Respond	*Beata es maria que omnium portasti creatore[m] d[eu]m genuisti qui te fecit et in eternu[m] p[er]manes uirgo.* *V. Aue maria gratia plena dominus tecum.* *[R.] genuisti.*
Hymn	*Ave mari[s] stella.*
Versicle	*Post partum uirgo.*
Magnificat Antiphon	*Succurre s[an]c[t]a* genitrix christi miseris ad te confugientibus adiuua et refoue omnes qui in te confidunt. ora p[ro] totius mundi piaculis. interueni pro clero intercede pro monachoru[m] choro exora pro sexu femineo.*
Canticle	*Magnificat.* *Kyrriel[eison]. Christel[eison]. Kyrriel[eison].* *Pat[er] n[oste]r. Et ne nos inducas. Credo in d[eu]m. Carnis resurr[ectionem].*
[Preces]	*Beata mater. Post partum uirgo. Aue maria. Specie tua. D[omi]ne exaudi.*
Collect	*Auerte, q[uesumu]s, d[omi]ne ira[m] tuam.*
Alia	*Famulorum tuorum, q[uesumu]s d[omi]ne delictis ignosce.*
Item	*Supplicationes seruorum tuorum.*

Miscellaneous prayers to the Virgin follow on ff.82-85v

TABLE 3:7   COMPARISON OF THE MARIAN OFFICES IN *LBL* A.III AND *LBL* 2.B.V

[All items are complete in the original, unless marked 'inc']

	Lbl A.III ff.107v-112v	*Lbl* 2.B.V ff.1v-6
	[AD MATUTINAS]	*[AD MATUTINAS]*
	Deus in adiutorium	
	Domine labia mea aperies x iii	*Domine . . ./ Deus . . .*
Psalm	3 (inc)	
Invitatory	*Aue maria gratia plena*	*Aue maria gr[ati]a plena*
Hymn	*Qvem terra pontvs etthera*	*Maria mater d[omi]ni*
Antiphon	*Sp[iritu]s s[an]c[tu]s in te*	*Exaltata es s[an]c[t]a d[e]i*
Psalm	8 (inc)	8 (inc)
Antiphon	*Virgo uerbo concepit*	*Dignare me laudare te*
Psalm	14 (inc)	14 (inc)
Antiphon	*Ecce Maria genuit*	*Sicut letantiu[m] om[n]iu[m]*
Psalm	86 (inc)	86 (inc)
Versicle	*Benedicta tu.*	*Specie tua*
	Pater n[oste]r	*Pater n[oste]r*
Preces	*Precibus et meritis*	*Precibus et meritis*
Blessing	*Pater de celis*	*Intus et exteri[us] purget*
Lesson	*Quas igitur tibi*	*Ecce tu pulchra es*
Respond	*S[anct]a et immaculata*	*S[an]c[t]a et immaculata*
	V. Benedicta tu	*V. Benedicta tu*
Blessing	*Beata interueniente*	*Om[n]i benedictione*
Lesson	*Recordare n[ost]ri*	*Que est ista*
Respond	*Beata es maria*	*Sup[er] salutem et om[n]em*
	V. Aue maria	*V. Ualde ea[m]*
Blessing	*Intercessio s[an]c[t]e marie*	*Gr[ati]a s[an]c[t]i sp[iritu]s*
Lesson	*O maria omni laude*	*Pulchra es amica mea*
Respond	*Te laudant angeli*	*Beata es uirgo maria*
	V. Ipsa [creatorem nostru]m	*V. Aue maria*
Canticle	*Te d[eu]m* (inc)	*Te d[eu]m* (inc added by later hand)
[John I, vv.1-14]	*In principio*	*In principio*
Hymn	*Te decet laus*	*Te decet laus*
Collect	*Famolor[um] tuor[um] q[uesumu]s*	*D[eu]s qui beate marie*

Table 3:7 221

	Lbl A.III	*Lbl* 2.B.V
	AD LA[V]DIBVS	*IN LAUDIB[US]*
	Deus in adiutorium	*Deus in adiutorium*
Psalm	66 (inc)	
Antiphon	*Post partum uirgo*	*Nigra sum*
Psalm	92 (inc)	92 (inc)
Antiphon	*Odor tuus s[an]cta d[e]i*	*Tota pulchra es*
Psalm	99 (inc)	99 (inc)
Antiphon	*In odorem unguentoru[m]*	*Ortus conclusus est*
Psalm	62 (inc)	62 (inc)
Antiphon	*Benedicta filia tua*	*Benedicta filia tua*
Psalm	*Benedicite* (inc)	*Benedicite* (inc)
Antiphon	*Cum iocunditate*	*Felix namque es*
Psalm	148[-50] (inc)	148[-50] (inc)
Chapter	*Ego quasi uitis* [Eccl.XXIV, 23-4]	*In om[ni]bus requie[m]* [Eccl.XXIV, 11-12]
Respond	*S[an]c[t]a maria mater* V. *Et impetrat[am] nob[is]*	*Adiuuabit eam d[eu]s* V. *D[eu]s in medio ei[us]*
Hymn	*Ave maris stella*	*O quam glorifica*
Versicle	*Speciosa facta es*	*Diffusa est gr[ati]a*
Ben. Ant.	*O gloriosa genitrix uirgo*	*Quomodo fiet istud*
Canticle	*Benedictus* (inc)	*Benedictus* (inc)
	Kyrie	*Kyrie* *Pater noster*
	[Preces]	*[Preces]*
Collect	*Concede q[uesumu]s*	*Concede nob[is] famulis tuis*

[Six memorials follow in *Lbl* A.III only]

	Lbl A.III	*Lbl* 2.B.V
	AD PRIMAM	*AD PRIMAM*
	Deus in adiutorium	*D[eu]s in adiutorium*
Hymn	*Maria mater do[mi]ni*	*A solis ortu[s]*
Antiphon	*Regali ex p[ro]genige* [sic]	*Missus est gabriel ang[e]ll[u]s*
Psalms	53	53 (inc)
		117 (inc)
	118 vv.1-16 (inc)	118 vv.1-8 (inc)
		118 vv.9-16 [inc]
	118 vv.17- (inc)	118 vv.17- (inc)
	Quicu[m]q[ue] uult (inc)	*Quicumq[ue] uult* (inc)
Chapter	*In omnibus requie[m]*	*In sion firmata sum*
Respond	[Absent]	*Adiuuabit eam d[eu]s*
		V. D[eu]s in medio eius
Versicle	*Beata mater et innupta*	*Diffusa e[st] gr[ati]a*
	Kyrie	*Kyrie*
	Pater	*Pater*
	Credo	
	Preces	*[Preces]*
	Confiteor/Misereatur	
Collect	*Beate et gloriose*	*Om[ni]p[oten]s sempiterne d[eu]s*

	Lbl A.III	*Lbl* 2.B.V
	AD TERTIAM	*AD TERTIA[M]*
	Deus in adiutorium	*D[eu]s in adiutoriu[m]*
Hymn	*Gabrihel dei archangelus*	*Domus pudici*
Antiphon	*Gaude dei genitrix*	*Aue maria gr[ati]a plena*
Psalms	118 vv.33-48 (inc) 118 vv.49-64 (inc) 118 vv.65-80 (inc)	118 vv.33 [-80] (inc)
Chapter	*In sion firmata sum*	*Eradicaui in populo*
Respond	[Absent]	*Diffusa e[st] gr[ati]a* *V. P[ro]pterea benedixit*
Versicle	*Specie tua*	*Dilexisti iustitia[m]*
	Kyrie	*Kyrie* *Pater*
	Preces	*Preces*
Collect	*D[eu]s qui salutis*	*Famulorum tuorum*
	AD VI	*AD SEXTAM*
	Deus in adiutorium	*D[eu]s in adiutoriu[m]*
Hymn	*Maria celi regina*	*Quem terra pontus*
Antiphon	*Succurre s[an]c[t]a genitrix*	*Ne timeas maria*
Psalms	118 vv.81-96 (inc) 118 vv.97-112 (inc) 118 vv.113-28 (inc)	118 vv.81 [-128] (inc)
Chapter	*Eradicaui in populo*	*Sicut cedrus*
Respond	[Absent]	*Specie tua V.Intende p[ro]spere*
Versicle	*Adiuuabit eam*	*Adiuuabit ea[m]*
	Kyrie *Pater noster* *[Preces]*	*Kyrie* *Pater noster* *P[re]ces ut supra*
Collect	*Concede q[uesumu]s*	*D[eu]s qui nos in tantis*

	Lbl A.III	*Lbl* 2.B.V
	AD NONAM	*AD VIIII*
		D[eu]s in adiutoriu[m]
Hymn	*Maria virgo virginum*	*Beata celi nuntio*
Antiphon	*Rogamus te uirgo*	*Sp[iritu]s s[an]c[tu]s in te*
Psalms	118 vv.129-44 (inc) 118 vv.145-60 (inc) 118 vv.161-76 (inc)	118 vv.129 [-176] (inc)
Chapter	*Sicut cinnamomu[m]*	*Sicut cinnamomu[m]*
Respond		*Adiuuabit ea[m] d[eu]s* *V.D[eu]s in medio ei[u]s*
Versicle	*Dif[f]usa est gr[ati]a*	*Diffusa est gr[ati]a*
	Kyrie *Pater noster* *[Preces]*	*Kyrie* *Pater noster* *P[re]ces ut supra*
Collect	*Porrige nob[is]*	*Porrige nobis*

	Lbl A.III	*Lbl* 2.B.V
	AD VESPERVM	*AD VESPERAM*
	Deus in adiutorium	
Antiphon	*Aue maria gratia plena*	*Benedicta tu in mulieribus*
Psalm	109 (inc)	109 (inc)
Antiphon	*S[an]c[t]a d[e]i genitrix*	*In odore[m] unguentoru[m]*
Psalm	121 (inc)	121 (inc)
Antiphon	*Gaude maria uirgo*	*Gaude maria uirgo*
Psalm	126 (inc)	126 (inc)
Antiphon	*Beata mater et innupta*	*Dignare me laudare te*
Psalm	131 (inc)	131 (inc)
Chapter	*Ab initio ante s[e]c[ul]a*	*Ego quasi uitis*
Respond	*Sancta Maria succurre miseris*	*Veni electa mea*
	V.Adsiste parata	*V.Specie tua*
Hymn	*O qvam glorifica*	*Aue maris stella*
Versicle	*Post partum uirgo*	*Post part[um] uirgo*
Mag.Ant.	*Virgo d[e]i genitrix*	*Succurre s[an]c[t]a genitrix*
Canticle	*Magnificat* (inc)	*Magnificat* (inc)
	Kyrie	*Kyrie*
	Pater noster	
	[Preces]	*Preces ut supra*
Collect	*Concede nos famulos*	*D[eu]s qui salutis*
	Two memorials	
	Little Office of Dead	
		Benedicamus d[omi]no

	Lbl A.III	*Lbl* 2.B.V
	[AD COMPLETORIUM]	*A[D] COMPLETORIVM*
	Conferte nos	*Converte nos*
	Deus in adiutorium	*D[eu]s in adiutorium*
Psalms	4 (inc)	4 (inc)
		30 (inc)
	90 (inc)	90 (inc)
	133 (inc)	133 (inc)
[Hymn verse]		*Memento n[ost]ri*
Hymn	*Christe s[an]c[t]or[um]*	*O qua[m] glorifica*
Chapter	*Ecce tu pulchra es*	*Tu autem in nobis*
Versicle	*S[anct]a d[e]i genitrix*	*Custodi nos*
Antiphon		*Ecce completa s[un]t*
Canticle		*Nunc dimittis seruum*
	Kyrie	*Kyrie*
	Pater	*Pater*
		In pace in idipsum
	Credo	*Credo in d[eu]m*
	Preces	*Preces*
Collects	*Protege q[uesumu]s d[omi]ne*	*Visita d[omi]ne habitation[em]*
	Benedicat nos d[eu]s pater	*Purifica q[uesumu]s*
		Da nob[is] d[omi]ne

[Litany follows]

TABLE 3:8 PSALMS FOR THE DAILY APPENDED VOTIVE OFFICE

MATINS

The Little Office of the Virgin

Lbl A.III	*c*.1050	Christ Church, Canterbury	3	8	14	86
Lbl 2.B.V	c.1066-87	Winchester/ Canterbury		8	14	86
Cjc C.18	*c*.1150-70	Wherwell [St Albans]		8	23	86
Lbl 21927	*c*.1175	Muchelney		8	23	86
WO F.160	s.xiii¹	Worcester	Cycle I	8	18	23
			II	44	45	47
			III	84	86	95
			IV	96	97	98
Lbl 157	s.xiii[?]	?		8	18	23
Ob e.1*	*c*.1300	Hyde Abbey		8	18	23
CA 6	s.xiv²	Christ Church, Canterbury		8	23	86
Cjc D.27	*c*.1400	St Mary, York		8	18	23
Llp 558	*c*.1400-25	Christ Church, Canterbury		8	23	86
Lbl 1804	s.xv¹	Durham		8	18	23
DO 26543	s.xv med	Winchester		8	18	21
Mch 6717	s.xv med	Godstow		8	18	23
Ob f.1	1424-75	Gloucester		8	18	23
Ob g.12	1521	Pilton [Malmesbury]		8	23	86
Sarum and Exeter			Cycle I Su,M,Th	8	18	23
			II Tu,F	44	45	86
			III W,Sa	95	96	97

The Office of the Holy Spirit

Llp 368	s.xiii	Norwich	1		
Lbl 155	s.xiii	Christ Church, Canterbury	1		
Mch 6717	s.xv med	Godstow	1		

The Office of the Holy Trinity

Ob 296	1015-36	Crowland	8	18	23

LAUDS

The Little Office of the Virgin

Lbl A.III	*c*.1050	Christ Church, Canterbury	66	92 99 62		*Benedicite*	148-150
Lbl 2.B.V 148-150	*c*.1066-87	Winchester/ Canterbury		92 99 62			
Cjc C.18	*c*.1150-70	Wherwell [St Albans]		92 99 62 66		*Benedicite*	148-150
Lbl 21927	*c*.1175	Muchelney		92 99 62 66		*Benedicite*	148-150
WO F.160	s.xiii[1]	Worcester		92 99 62 66		*Benedicite*	148-150
Lbl 157	s.xiii[?]	?	66 92	62		*Benedicite*	148-150
Ob e.1*	*c*.1300	Hyde Abbey		92 [99 62 66		*Benedicite*	148-150]
Cjc D.27	*c*.1400	St Mary, York		92 99 62 66		*Benedicite*	148-150
Llp 558	*c*.1400-25	Christ Church, Canterbury		92 99 62 66		*Benedicite*	148-150
Lbl 1804	s.xv[1]	Durham		92 99 62 [66]		*Benedicite*	148-150
DO 26543	s.xv med	Winchester		92 99 62 66		*Benedicite*	148-150
Mch 6717	s.xv med	Godstow		92 99 62 66		*Benedicite*	148-150
Ob f.1	1424-75	Gloucester		92 99 62 66		*Benedicite*	148-150
Ob g.12	1521	Pilton [Malmesbury]		92 99 62 66		*Benedicite*	148-150
		Sarum and Exeter		92 [99 62 66		*Benedicite*	148-150]

The Office of the Holy Spirit

Llp 368	s.xiii	Norwich	92
Mch 6717	s.xv med	Godstow	14

PRIME

The Little Office of the Virgin

Lbl A.III	*c.*1050	Christ Church, Canterbury	53		118 x 2 (vv.1[-16]; 17[-32])		*Quicumque*
Lbl 2.B.V	*c.*1066-87	Winchester/ Canterbury	53	117	118 x 3		*Quicumque*
Cjc C.18	*c.*1150-70	Wherwell [St Albans]	53		118 x 2 (vv.1[-16]; 17[-32])		
Lbl 21927	*c.*1175	Muchelney	53 (vv.1[-16]; 17[-32])		118 x 2		*Quicumque*
WO F.160	s.xiii¹	Worcester	53 (vv.1-32)		118 x 2	116	
Lbl 157	s.xiii[?]	?	53 (vv.1-16; 17-24; 25-32)		118 x 3		
Ob e.1*	*c.*1300	Hyde Abbey	Not specified				
Cjc D.27	*c.*1400	St Mary, York	Sun 53 1 2 6 116 Wk 53 116				
Llp 558	*c.*1400-25	Christ Church, Canterbury	2 6 116				
Lbl 1804	s.xv¹	Durham	Sun 53 1 2 5 116 Wk 53 118 x 2 (vv.1-16; 17[-32])				
Mch 6717	s.xv med	Godstow	53 116 [117]				
Ob f.1	1424-75	Gloucester	53 (vv.1-16; [17-32])		118 x 2	116	
Ob g.12	1521	Pilton [Malmesbury]	Sun 53 117 118 x 4 116 (vv.1-32) Wk 53 118 x 4 116				
	Sarum and Exeter		53 116 117				

The Office of the Holy Spirit

Llp 368	s.xiii	Norwich	53
Mch 6717	s.xv med	Godstow	53

TERCE

The Little Office of the Virgin

Lbl A.III	*c*.1050	Christ Church, Canterbury	118 x 3 (vv.33-48; 49-64; 65-80)
Lbl 2.B.V	*c*.1066-87	Winchester/ Canterbury	118 x 3 (vv.33[-80])
Cjc C.18	*c*.1150-70	Wherwell [St Albans]	118 x 3 (vv.33-48; 49-64; 65-80)
Lbl 21927	*c*.1175	Muchelney	118 x 3 (vv.33-48; 49-64; 65-80)
WO F.160	s.xiii[1]	Worcester	119 120 121
Lbl 157	s.xiii[?]	?	119 120 121
Ob e.1*	*c*.1300	Hyde Abbey	Not specified
Cjc D.27	*c*.1400	St Mary, York	119 120 121
Llp 558	*c*.1400-25	Christ Church, Canterbury	Sun 118 x 3 (vv.105-112; 113-120; 121-128) Wk 118 x 3 (vv.33-40; 41-48; 49-56)
Lbl 1804	s.xv[1]	Durham	118 x 3 (vv.33-48; 49-64; 65-80)
Mch 6717	s.xv med	Godstow	119 120 121
Ob f.1	1424-75	Gloucester	118 x 3 (vv.33-48; 49-64; 65-80)
Ob g.12	1521	Pilton [Malmesbury]	Sun/M 119 120 121 T/W/Th/F/Sa 118x6 (vv.33-80)
		Sarum and Exeter	119 120 121

The Office of the Holy Spirit

Llp 368	s.xiii	Norwich	69
Mch 6717	s.xv med	Godstow	*Confundatur*

The Office of the Holy Trinity

Ob 296	1015-36	Crowland	118 (vv.33[-80])

SEXT

The Little Office of the Virgin

Lbl A.III	*c*.1050	Christ Church, Canterbury	118 x 3 (vv.81-96; 97-112; 113-28)
Lbl 2.B.V	*c*.1066-87	Winchester/ Canterbury	118 x 3 (vv.81[-128])
Cjc C.18	*c*.1150-70	Wherwell [St Albans]	118 x 3 (vv.81-96; 97-112; 113-28)
Lbl 21927	*c*.1175	Muchelney	118 x 3 (vv.81-96; 97-112; 113-28)
WO F.160	s.xiii[1]	Worcester	122 123 124
Lbl 157	s.xiii[?]	?	122 123 123
Ob e.1*	*c*.1300	Hyde Abbey	Not specified
Cjc D.27	*c*.1400	St Mary, York	Su/M 122 123 124
Llp 558	*c*.1400-25	Christ Church, Canterbury	Su 118 x 6 (vv.81-128)
Lbl 1804	s.xv[1]	Durham	118 x 3 (vv.81-96; 97-112; 113-28)
Mch 6717	s.xv med	Godstow	122 123 124
Ob f.1	1424-75	Gloucester	118 x 3 (vv.81-96; 97-112; 113-28)
Ob g.12	1521	Pilton [Malmesbury]	Sun/M 122 123 124 T/W/Th/F/Sa 118 x 5 (vv.81-120)
		Sarum and Exeter	121 123 124

The Office of the Holy Spirit

Llp 368	s.xiii	Norwich	86
Mch 6717	s.xv med	Godstow	86

NONE

The Little Office of the Virgin

Lbl A.III	*c*.1050	Christ Church, Canterbury	118 x 3 (vv.129-144; 145-160; 161-176)
Lbl 2.B.V	*c*.1066-87	Winchester/ Canterbury	118 x 3 (vv.129[-176])
Cjc C.18	*c*.1150-70	Wherwell [St Albans]	118 x 3 (vv.129-144; 145-160; 161-176)
Lbl 21927	*c*.1175	Muchelney	118 x 3 (vv.129-144; 145-160; 161-176)
WO F.160	s.xiii[1]	Worcester	125 126 127
Lbl 157	s.xiii[?]	?	125 126 127
Ob e.1*	*c*.1300	Hyde Abbey	Not specified
Cjc D.27	*c*.1400	St Mary, York	Su/M 125 126 127
Llp 558	*c*.1400-25	Christ Church, Canterbury	Su 118 x 6 (vv.129-176)
Lbl 1804	s.xv[1]	Durham	118 x 3 (vv.129-144; 145-160; 161-176)
Mch 6717	s.xv med	Godstow	125 126 127
Ob f.1	1424-75	Gloucester	Su/M 125 126 127 T/W/Th/F/Sa 118 x 6 (vv.129-176)
Ob g.12	1521	Pilton [Malmesbury]	Sun/M 125 126 127 T/W/Th/F/Sa 118 x 6 (vv.129-176)
		Sarum and Exeter	125 126 127

The Office of the Holy Spirit

Llp 368	s.xiii	Norwich	127
Mch 6717	s.xv med	Godstow	92

VESPERS

The Little Office of the Virgin

Lbl A.III	*c.*1050	Christ Church Canterbury	109	121	126	131	
Lbl 2.B.V	*c.*1066-87	Winchester/ Canterbury	109	121	126	131	
Cjc C.18	*c.*1150-70	Wherwell [St Albans]	109	112	121	126	
Lbl 21927	*c.*1175	Muchelney	109	121	126	131	
WO F.160	s.xiii[1]	Worcester	[Vespers section missing]				
Lbl 157	s.xiii[?]	?	109	112	121	147	
Ob e.1*	*c.*1300	Hyde Abbey	121	122	123	124	125
Cjc D.27	*c.*1400	St Mary, York	[Vespers section missing]				
Llp 558	*c.*1400-25	Christ Church, Canterbury	121	122	123	124	125
Lbl 1804	s.xv[1]	Durham	121	122	123	124	
Mch 6717	s.xv med	Godstow	121	122	123	124	125
Ob f.1	1424-75	Gloucester	121	122	123	124	125
Ob g.12	1521	Pilton [Malmesbury]	121	122	123	124	125
		Sarum (not Tu) and Exeter	121	122	123	124	125
		Sarum [Tu]	109	110	111	129	131

The Office of the Holy Spirit

Mch 6717	s.xv med	Godstow	127

The Office of the Holy Trinity

Ob 296	1015-36	Crowland	143	144	145	146	147

COMPLINE

The Little Office of the Virgin

Lbl A.III	*c.*1050	Christ Church Canterbury	4		90	133		
Lbl 2.B.V	*c.*1066-87	Winchester/ Canterbury	4	30	90	133	*Nunc dimittis*	
Cjc C.18	*c.*1150-70	Wherwell [St Albans]	12	42	128	130	*Nunc dimittis*	
Lbl 21927	*c.*1175	Muchelney	4	30	90	133	*Nunc dimittis*	
WO F.160	s.xiii[1]	Worcester	[Compline section missing]					
Lbl 157	s.xiii[?]	?	4	30	90	133	*Nunc dimittis*	
Llp 368	s.xiii	Norwich	[Compline section missing]					
Ob e.1*	*c.*1300	Hyde Abbey		30	86	116	*Nunc dimittis*	
Cjc D.27	*c.*1400	St Mary, York		30	86	116	*Nunc dimittis*	
Llp 558	*c.*1400-25	Christ Church, Canterbury	4	30		133	*Nunc dimittis*	
Lbl 1804	s.xv[1]	Durham	12	42	128	130	*Nunc dimittis*	
Mch 6717	s.xv med	Godstow	12	42	128	[130]	*Nunc dimittis*	
Ob f.1	1424-75	Gloucester	4	30		133	*Nunc dimittis*	
Ob g.12	1521	Pilton [Malmesbury]		30	86	116	*Nunc dimittis*	
		Sarum and Exeter	12	42	128	130	*Nunc dimittis*	

The Office of the Holy Spirit

Mch 6717	s.xv med	Godstow	128	

The Office of the Holy Trinity

Ob 296	1015-36	Crowland	4	30	90	133	*Nunc dimittis*

TABLE 3:8   KEY TO PSALMS

(a) Matins

1 *Beatus vir qui non abiit*	86 *Fundamenta eius*
3 *Domine quid multiplicati*	95 *Cantate domino* (i)
8 *Domine dominus noster*	96 *Dominus regnavit* (i)
14 *Domine, quis habitat*	97 *Cantate domino* (ii)
18 *Celi enarrant*	98 *Dominus regnavit* (ii)
23 *Domini est terra*	
44 *Eructavit cor meum*	
45 *Deus noster refugium*	
47 *Magnus dominus*	
84 *Benedixisti domine*	

(b) Lauds

62 *Deus, deus meus*
66 *Deus misereatur nostri*
92 *Dominus regnavit*
99 *Jubilate deo*
148 *Laudate dominum de celis*
149 *Cantate domino canticum novum*
150 *Laudate dominum in sanctis*

(c) Prime

1 *Beatus vir*	117 *Confitemini domino et invocate*
2 *Quare fremuerunt*	118 vv.1-8 *Beati immaculati*
5 *Verba mea*	118 vv.9-16 *In quo corriget*
6 *Domine ne in furore* i	118 vv.17-24 *Retribue servo tuo*
53 *Deus in nomine tuo*	118 vv.25-32 *Adhesit pavimento*
116 *Laudate dominum*	

(d) Terce

69 *Deus in adiutorium*	
118 vv.33-40 *Legem pone*	
118 vv.41-48 *Et veniat super me*	119 *Ad dominum cum tribulare*
118 vv.49-56 *Memor esto*	120 *Levavi oculos*
118 vv.57-64 *Portio mea*	121 *Letatus sum*
118 vv.65-72 *Bonitatem*	
118 vv.73-80 *Manus tuae*	

(e) Sext

86 *Fundamenta eius*
118 vv.81-88 *Defecit*
118 vv.89-96 *In eternum*
118 vv.97-104 *Quomodo dilexi*
118 vv.105-112 *Lucerna pedibus*
118 vv.113-120 *Iniquos odio*
118 vv.121-128 *Feci iudicium*

122 *Ad te levavi*
123 *Nisi quia*
124 *Qui confidunt*

(f) None

118 vv.129-136 *Mirabilia*
118 vv.137-144 *Iustus es*
118 vv.145-152 *Clamavi*
118 vv.153-160 *Vide humilitatem*
118 vv.161-168 *Principes*
118 vv.169-176 *Appropinquet*

125 *In convertendo*
126 *Nisi dominus edificaverit*
127 *Beati omnes*

(g) Vespers

109 *Dixit dominus*
110 *Confitebor*
111 *Beatus vir*
121 *Letatus sum*
122 *Ad te levavi*
123 *Nisi quia dominus*
124 *Qui confidunt in domino*
125 *In convertendo*
126 *Nisi dominus*
127 *Beati omnes*
129 *De profundis*
131 *Memento domine*

143 *Benedictus dominus*
144 *Exaltabo te*
145 *Lauda anima mea*
146 *Laudate dominum*
147 *Lauda ierusalem*

(h) Compline

4 *Cum invocarem*
12 *Usquequo domine*
30 *In te domine speravi*
42 *Iudica me*
90 *Qui habitat*
116 *Laudate dominum omnes gentes*
128 *Saepe expugnaverunt*
130 *Domine non est*
133 *Ecce nunc*

TABLE 3:9   THE TWO FORMS OF COMPLINE
AT ST MARY'S YORK

Compline of the Day	Compline of the Little Office
Sentence	
Pater noster	
[*Confiteor / Misereatur*]	
Converte nos / Et averte	*Converte nos / Et averte*
Deus in adiutorium	*Deus in adiutorium*
	Psalm antiphon [incipit sung]
Psalms 4, 90, 133	Psalms 30, 86, 116 [spoken]
	Chapter [sung]
	Short Respond [sung]
Hymn	Hymn [spoken]
Chapter	
Versicle and response	Versicle and response
Preces	
	Antiphon [sung]
	Nunc dimittis [spoken]
Collect	Collect [sung]
Benedicamus domino	*Benedicamus domino* [sung]
Blessing	
	Post-Compline Antiphon

TABLE 4:1   CHRONOLOGICAL LIST OF EXTANT
COMMEMORATIVE OFFICES

Source	Category	Date	Provenance	Intention	Day

A: Three-Nocturn Forms

Source	Category	Date	Provenance	Intention	Day
Lbl 2.A.X	Breviary	c.1140-50	St Albans	BVM	Saturday
F-VAL 116	Breviary	s.xii med.	Winchcombe	BVM	
Ob 435	Customary	after 1230	Eynsham	BVM	
Owc 213	Miscellany	s.xiii²	Reading	BVM	
D-Bds 194	Customary	c.1330-40	St Werburgh, Chester	BVM	Saturday
Ouc 169	Ordinal	1404	Barking	BVM	Saturday
Ctc 0.7.31	Breviary	s.xvi in.	Battle	BVM	
Ob g.12	Book of Hours	1521	Pilton (Malmesbury)	BVM	[Saturday]
Cec S1.4.6	Printed Breviary	1528	Abingdon	BVM	
Lbl C.110.a.27	Printed Breviary	c.1535	St Albans	BVM	Saturday

B: Two-Nocturn Forms

Source	Category	Date	Provenance	Intention	Day
WO F.160	Antiphoner	s.xiii¹ [later addition]	Worcester	BVM St Oswald and St Wulstan St Thomas of Canterbury	Saturday Thursday Tuesday?
Ob 41	Breviary	c.1250-75	Evesham	BVM Relics	Saturday Thursday
Ccc 465	Customary	c.1260	Norwich	BVM	Saturday
	Statutes of General Chapter	1278		BVM Patron or Relics	

continued . . .

Ob 10	Antiphoner (Diurnale)	s.xiii	Gloucester	BVM St Peter St Benedict	Saturday
CA 6	Breviary	s.xiv²	Christ Church, Canterbury	BVM St Thomas of Canterbury Relics	
Lbl 43405-43406	Breviary	s.xiii²	Muchelney	BVM St Peter	
Cu Ii.4.20	Breviary	s.xiii²	Ely	BVM St Etheldreda St Peter	
Ob e.1*	Breviary	c.1300	Hyde Abbey	BVM Relics	Saturday
Cmc F.4.10	Antiphoner	s.xiv in.	Peterborough	BVM St Peter	Saturday Thursday
Ob 22	Psalter	early s.xiv	Peterborough	St Benedict St Peter BVM	
Llp 198/198b	Customary	1371	Peterborough	BVM Relics St Peter St Benedict	Saturday Tuesday? Thursday Wednesday/ Friday?
Ob g.10	Miscellany	c.1400	St Peter, Westminster	BVM St Peter and St Paul St Edward St Benedict	
Ob 17	Diurnale	after 1415	Peterborough	Relics St Benedict St Peter BVM St Oswald	
Ctc O.7.31	Breviary	s.xvi in.	Battle	St John Evangelist St Martin St Benedict	
Ob g.12	Book of Hours	1521	Pilton	Holy Cross St Aldhelm St Benedict	[Friday] [Monday]
Cec S1.4.6	Printed Breviary	1528	Abingdon	St Vincent and St Edward Relics St Benedict	
Lbl C.110 a.27	Printed Breviary	c.1535	St Albans	St Alban St Benedict	Tuesday Wednesday

Source	Category	Date	Provenance	Intention	Day

C: Probable One-Nocturn Forms

Source	Category	Date	Provenance	Intention	Day
Ccc 391	Portiforium	*c.*1065	Worcester	Holy Cross BVM	Friday Saturday
CH-E 235	Customary	*c.*970	Einsiedeln	Holy Cross BVM	Friday Saturday

D: Form Unspecified

Source	Category	Date	Provenance	Intention	Day
Lbl 1005	Ordinal	c.1234	Bury St Edmunds	BVM St Edmund	
Ccc 441	Instruction for Novices	s.xiii ex.	Christ Church, Canterbury	BVM Relics	
Lbl C.XII	Customary	c.1330-40	St Augustine, Canterbury	BVM Patrons	Saturday Tuesday
Cjc D.27	Customary	c.1400	St Mary, York	BVM St Benedict	Saturday Thursday

TABLE 4:2　VOTIVE OFFICES IN THE
WORCESTER PORTIFORIUM (*Ccc* 391)

FERIA VI. DE SANCTA CRUCE (Worc.Port. ii, 59-60)

Category	Text	Concordances within source	Concordances in *WO* F.160
	AD VESPERAS		
[Ant]	*O crux benedicta*	Ben, L, Exaltation	308
[Ant]	*Super omnia ligna cedrorum*	of Holy Cross	371
	[AD MATUTINAS]		
Lectio I:	*Crux igitur dominica angelis et hominibus*		
[R.]	*Dulce lignum dulcem clauum V. Hoc signum crucis*		308
Lectio II:	*Ergo de triumpho*		
R.	*Hoc signum crucis V. Cum sederit*		308
Lectio III:	*Aptissime uero et dignissime*		
R.	*Tuam crucem V. Adoramus te Christe*		
	IN LAUDIBUS		
Ant.	*Nos autem gloriari*		371
In evang. Ant.	*Ecce crucem domini*	L, Invention of Holy Cross	369
	AD PRIMAM		
Ant.	*Salva nos Christe*		371
	AD TERTIAM		
Ant.	*Ecce crucem domini*		371
	AD SEXTAM		
Ant.	*O crux admirabilis*		370
	AD NONAM		
Ant.	*Per signum crucis*	Mag, V, Exaltation of Holy Cross	371

SABBATO. SANCTA MARIA (Worc.Port. ii, 60-62)

[AD VESPERAS]

Ant.	*Ortus conclusus es dei genitrix*	A3, V, Nativity BVM	361

[AD MATUTINAS]

Lect. I:	*Sacrosancta et uenerabilis deus genitricis*	
R.	*Veni electa mea V. Specie tua*	355

Lect. II:	*Opere pretium quippe est*	
R.	*Ista est speciosa*	356
	V. Specie tua et pulchritudine tua	[Verse differs]

Lect. III:	*Haec tanta tamque sancta regia virgo*	
R.	*Super salutem V. Valde eam*	357

IN LAUDIBUS

[Ant.]	*Post partum virgo*	P, All Saints (2 Nov)
In evang. Ant.	*Ave Maria [gratia plena]*	Ben, L, Advent III

AD PRIMAM

Ant.	*Beata mater*	302

AD TERTIAM

Ant.	*Gaude Maria virgo*	268

AD SEXTAM

Ant.	*Speciosa facta es*	268

AD NONAM

Ant.	*Post partum virgo*	P, All Saints
		L, this office

TABLE 4:3 THE MARIAN COMMEMORATIVE OFFICE
IN THE ST ALBANS BREVIARY (*LBL* 2.A.X)

IN COM[M]EMORAT[IO] S[AN]C[T]E MARIE (*Lbl* 2.A.X, ff.135-140v)

[All items appear as complete texts in the manuscript unless marked here as incipits (inc)]

[Concordances in source]

[AD UESPERAS]

Antiphon	*Hec est regina uirginu[m]*	No concordance
Chapter	*Ab initio et ante s[e]c[u]la*	No concordance
Respond	*Speciosa facta.* (inc)	No concordance
Hymn	*Ave maris stell[a].* (inc)	V 1 & 2, T, Nativity BVM, V 1, Annunciation
Versicle	*Benedicta tu in mulieribus*	No concordance
Magnificat Ant.	*Aue regina cel[orum].* (inc)	Given complete on f.62r, headed *In veneratione sancte* *Marie ad vesperas*
Collect	*Concede nos famulos*	No concordance

[AD MATUTINAS] (Three Nocturns)

Invitatory	*In honore[m] beatissime Marie*	No concordance
Hymn	*Que[m] t[er]ra.* (inc)	M, Purification & Assumption

[First Nocturn]

Antiphons 1-6 (with psalm incipits)	1 *Ecce tu pulchra* Ps.8 2 *Sicut liliu[m]* 18 3 *Fauus distillans* 23 4 *Emissiones tue* 44 5 *Fons ortoru[m]* 45 6 *Ueniat dilectus* 47	No concordance " " " " "	
Versicle	*Benedicta tu in mulieribus.*	V, this office	
Lessons i-iv	i *O alma uirgo Maria* ii *Surge [er]go beata uirgo* iii *O sacratissima uirgo* iv *Adiuua nos beata dei*	No concordance " " "	

Responds I-IV	I	*S[an]c[t]a et immac[u]lata V. Benedicta tu*		No concordance
	II	*Sicut cedrus V. Et sicut cynamomu[m]*		"
	III	*Beata[m] me dicent V. Et mis[eri]c[or]dia*		"
	IV	*Felix nanq[ue] V. Ora pro pop[u]lo*		R II, M, All Saints

[Second Nocturn]

Antiphons 7-12	7	*Ueni in ortu[m]*	Ps.84	No concordance
(with psalm	8	*Comedi fauu[m]*	86	"
incipits)	9	*Descendi in ortu[m]*	95	"
	10	*Adiuro uos filie*	96	"
	11	*Qualis e[st] dilectus*	97	"
	12	*Dilectus m[eu]s*	98	"

Versicle	*Sicut myrra el[ecta]*		M & N, Asm, Pur, & Nat BVM

Lessons v-viii	v	*Exaudi nos gl[ori]osa*	No concordance
	vi	*O regina mundi*	"
	vii	*O felix Maria*	"
	viii	*O felix puerp[eri]um*	"

Responds V-VIII	V	*Ornata[m] monilib[us] V. Astitit regina*	No concordance
	VI	*Benedicta et uenerabilis V. Benedicta tu*	"
	VII	*Beata es uirgo Maria V. Aue Maria*	"
	VIII	*Ad nutu[m] d[omi]ni V.Ut uiciu[m] uirtus*	"

[Third Nocturn]

Canticle Antiphon	13	*Talis e[st] dilectus*	No concordance

First of three canticles	*Audite me diuini fruc[tum]*	"

Versicle	*Speciosa facta es*	"

Gospel reading	*Exurgens Maria abiit* (Luke I, vv.39-40)	

Lessons ix-xii	[ix]	*Quia p[er] te meritate[m]*	No concordance
	x	*Prior [er]go nobis*	"
	xi	*Gestans beata Maria in utero*	"
	xii	*Ut aute[m] audiuit salutatione[m]*	"

Responds IX-XII	IX	*Sup[er] salute[m] V. Ualde eam*	R IX, M, Asm
	X	*Ista est speciosa V. Ista est*	R X, M, Asm
	XI	*Beata es Maria V. Aue Maria*	R XI, M, Asm
	XII	*Styrps iesse V.Virgo d[e]i*	R XI, M, Anc & V2, Pur &Asm

Gospel reading	*Exurgens Maria* [Luke I, vv.39-47]	
Collect	*Concede nos fam[ulos].* (inc)	V, this office

[Alternative readings for Third Nocturn]

Gospel	*Loquente ih[es]u ad turbas*	

Lessons ix-xii	[ix]	*Magne deuotionis*	No concordance
	x	*Nos ig[itur] contra euticen*	"
	xi	*Uere eni[m] beata parens*	"
	xii	*At ille dixit. Quinimmo* (Luke 11, 28)	"

Gospel	*Factu[m] est eu[m]* (Luke 11, vv.27-8)	
Collect	*Concede nos famul[os].* (inc)	V and M, this office

IN LAUDES

Antiphons 1-5	1	*Beatam me dicent*	A1, L & P, Annunciation
(psalms not listed)	2	*Beata mater et innupta*	No concordance
	3	*Post partu[m] uirgo*	A4, L, Annunciation
	4	*Sicut myrra electa*	A3, L & S, Annunciation
	5	*Gaude Maria uirgo*	A5, L & N, Annunciation; A13, M, Nativity BVM

Chapter	*Ab initio et ante s[e]c[u]la.* (inc)	V1, this office
Respond	*S[an]c[t]a dei genet[ri]x.* (inc)	L, Nativity BVM
Hymn	*O gl[ori]osa femina.* (inc)	L, common to BVM
Versicle	*Post partu[m] uirgo.*	L, Nativity BVM
Benedictus ant.	*Succurre nob[is]*	No concordance

IN DIE AD VESPERAS

Antiphons 1-4	1	*Ecce tu pulchra.* (inc) 144 (i)	A1, M, this office
(with psalm	2	*Sicut liliu[m].* (inc) 145	A2, M, this office
incipits)	3	*Fauus distillans.* (inc) 146	A3, M, this office
	4	*Emissiones.* (inc) 147	A4, M, this office

Alternative psalms for days other than Saturday:	109
(incipits only)	121
	126
	131

TABLE 4:4 THE MARIAN COMMEMORATIVE OFFICE IN
THE WINCHCOMBE BREVIARY (*F-VAL* 116)

IN COMMEMOR[ATIONE] S[ANCTE] MARIE (F-VAL 116, f.257)

[All items given as incipits unless indicated otherwise]   Concordances in Source

[AD MATUTINAS] (Three Nocturns)

Invitatory:		*Ave Maria*	M, Annunciation
Hymn:		*Que[m] t[er]ra [pontus]*	Common to M of Marian feasts

[First Nocturn]

Antiphons 1-6	1	*Ecce tu pulc[hra]*	A1, M, Assumption
(psalms not listed)	2	*Sic[ut] liliu[m]*	A2 "
	3	*Fauus distillans*	A3 "
	4	*Emissiones*	A4 "
	5	*Fons ortorum*	A5 "
	6	*Venit dilectus m[eu]s*	A6 "
Versicle:		*B[e]n[e]dicta tu i[n] mulieribus*	M, Annunciation
Lessons i-iv:	i	*O alma uirgo Maria*	No concordance
(all complete)	ii	*Surge [er]go beata uirgo*	"
	iii	*O sanctissima uirgo*	"
	iv	*Sacrosanctam uenerabilis*	"
Responds I-IV:	I	*S[an]c[ta] et im[m]ac[u]lata*	?
	II	*Beata es Mar[ia]*	R III, M, Purification
	III	*Sicut cedrus*	R VII, M, Assumption
	IV	*Felix namque es*	R VIII, M, Assumption

[Second Nocturn]

Antiphons 7-12	7	*Veni i[n] ortu[m] meu[m]*	Ps. 84	A7, M, Assumption
with psalm	8	*Comedi fauu[m]*	86	A8, M, Assumption
incipits	9	*Ost[e]nde m[ih]i facie[m]*	95	No concordance
	10	*Sonet uox tua*	96	No concordance
(Antiphons 9-12	11	*Ort[us] conclus[us] amica mea*	97	A8, M, Nativity BVM
given complete)	12	*Que [est] ista q[u]e ascendit*	98	No concordance
Versicle:		*Speciosa [facta es]*		?

Lessons v-viii: (complete)	v vi vii viii	*Ope[re] p[re]ciu[m] q[ui]ppe* *Hec tanta ta[m]q[ue]* *O u[ir]go caput u[ir]ginu[m]* *O glo[ri]osa u[ir]go Maria*	No concordance " " "
Responds V-VIII: [VIII given complete]	V VI VII VIII	*Veni electa mea* *Que [est] ista* *Ista [est] speciosa* *Ornata[m] monilibus* *V. Astitit regina*	R VI, M, Assumption R IV, M, Assumption R II, M, Assumption R III, M, Assumption

[Third Nocturn]

Canticle antiphon (complete)	13 *Rogam[us] te uirgo u[ir]ginu[m]*	No concordance
First of three canticles	*Audite me diuini fruct[us]*	Nativity BVM, Octave of Assumption

[Lessons ix-xii omitted]

| Responds IX-XII:

[IX and XII
complete] | IX

X
XI
XII | *Beatam me dicent*
V. Magnificat anima
Sup[er] salute[m]
Beata es u[ir]go Maria
O s[an]c[ta] uirginitatis
V. Salve stella | No concordance

?
R X, M, Assumption
No concordance |

AD L[AUDES] f.258

Antiphons 1-5: (psalms not listed)	1 2 3 4 5	*Assumpta est Maria* *Maria u[ir]go assu[m]pta e[st]* *In odore ung[uentorum]* *Benedicta a filio tuo* *Pulc[hra] es et d[e]cora*	A1, L, Assumption A2 " A3 " A4 " A5 "
Respond:		*Aue Maria V. B[e]n[e]dicta*	L and V, Purification and Annunciation

TABLE 4:5   VARIED ANTIPHONS FOR
MATINS OF THE ASSUMPTION

1. *Lbl* C.110.a.27 (St Albans)

Antiphons		
	1	*Odor tuus sancta*
	2	*Te decus virgineum virgo*
	3	*Gaude dei genitrix*
	4	*O quam speciosa est maria*
	5	*O virgo maria que genuisti*
	6	*Gaude maria virgo*
	7	*Sancta et immaculata*
	8	*Succurre nobis genitrix*
	9	*Quam pulchra es*
	10	*Beata dei genitrix*
	11	*Beata es virgo maria*
	12	*Exaltata es sancta dei*
	13	*Beata virgo semper letare*

2. *Cu* Ii.4.20 (Ely) and *Lbl* 43405-6 (Muchelney)

Antiphons		
	1	*Adest dies preclara*
	2	*Hodie virgo maria*
	3	*Ad thronum maiestatis*
	4	*Hanc ergo salvator*
	5	*Ascendit hec virga iesse*
	6	*Ecce exaltata es*
	7	*Occurrit piissime*
	8	*Obviam procedunt cherubim*
	9	*Gloriam concinunt deo*
	10	*Sicut dies iusti*
	11	*Gaude virgo maria*
	12	*Exulta et lauda ierusalem*
	13	*Soror nostra paruula* (*Cu* Ii.4.20)
		Sancta maria genitrix (*Lbl* 43405-6)

TABLE 4:6 STRUCTURE OF THE TWO-NOCTURN MARIAN OFFICE

	Provenance	First Vespers from ps.ant.	First Vespers from Chapter	Common psalms at Matins [Series A]	Ferial psalms at Matins [Series B]	Five antiphons at Lauds	One antiphon at Lauds
WO F.160	Worcester Antiphoner		✓	All year			✓
Ob 41	Evesham Breviary	✓		Octave Easter to All Saints	All Saints to Ash Wednesday	✓	
Ccc 465	Norwich Customary		✓	Easter to All Saints	All Saints to Easter		✓
Ob 10	Gloucester Antiphoner				All year	Pur to Adv	Adv
Cu 4.20	Ely Breviary		✓	All year except 1 Nov to Chr and Pur to XL	1 Nov to Chr and Pur to XL		✓

continued. . . .

	Provenance	Vespers from ps. ant	Vespers from Chapter	Series A psalms	Series B psalms	Five antiphons at Lauds	One antiphon at Lauds
*Ob e.1**	Hyde Abbey Breviary		✓	?		Except Chr to Pur and Easter	Chr to Pur and Easter
Cmc F.4.10	Peterborough Antiphoner		✓	?			✓
Ob g.10	Westminster Offices		✓	All year		✓	
Ob 17	Peterborough Diurnale	✓			All year		
Ob g.12	Pilton Hours		✓		All year		✓

TABLE 4:7   SEASONAL VARIATION IN THE TWO-NOCTURN MARIAN OFFICE

	Advent	From Christmas	From Epiphany	From Oct Epiphany	From Purification	Lent	Easter-tide	From Oct Easter	From Trinity	Per Annum	Omitted
WO F.160	✓			a. to Pur b. to XL			✓		to Advent		
Ob 41	✓		to Advent								
Ccc 465	memorial only		to Pur		to XL (as *per annum*)	memorial only	to Trin [Mass texts]	to Asc	to AS [Vespers antiphons]		Adv, from XL, in Octs Ep, Asc, Trin
Ob 10	✓			to LXX			✓				
Cu 4.20	✓	to Pur					✓			✓	
Ob e.1*	✓	to Pur					✓			✓	
Cmc F.4.10		to Pur					to ?				
Ob g.10										✓	
Cjc D.27											Wk3 of Adv; Chr Eve to Oct Ep, Ash Wed to Oct Easter, in Octs Pent and CC
Ob 17		to Pur					✓			✓	
Ob g.12	✓	to ?					✓			✓	

TABLE 4:8 THE MARIAN COMMEMORATIVE OFFICE: THE PSALMODIC SERIES AT MATINS

SERIES A (Psalms for Marian feasts and Common of a Virgin Martyr)

Domine dominus noster	8	*Benedixisti Domine*	84
Celi enarrant	18	*Fundamenta ejus*	86
Domini est terra	23	*Cantate Domino* i	95
Eructavit cor meum	44	*Dominus regnavit* i	96
Deus noster	45	*Cantate Domino* ii	97
Magnus dominus	47	*Dominus regnavit* ii	98

Used at:

Three-nocturn forms

St Albans (both *Lbl* 2.A.X and *Lbl* C.110.a.27), Reading, Barking, Pilton BVM office, Abingdon, Battle

Two-nocturn forms

Worcester, Evesham (Octave of Easter to All Saints), Norwich (Easter to All Saints), Ely (Except 1 November to Christmas and Purification to Quadragesima), Westminster BVM office, [Sarum], [Exeter]

SERIES B (Saturday ferial psalms)

101	102	103i	103ii	104i	104ii
105i	105ii	106i	106ii	107	108

Used at:

Evesham (All Saints to Ash Wednesday)
Norwich (All Saints to Easter)
Ely (1 November to Christmas and Purification to Quadragesima)
Peterborough BVM office
[Fleury]

TABLE 4:9 THE COMMEMORATIVE OFFICE OF THE VIRGIN
IN THE WORCESTER ANTIPHONER (*WO* F.160)

Q[UA]NDO TAB[U]LA DE D[OMI]NA I[N] ADV[E]NTU (*PM* 1,xii p.238)

[Complete texts in both the commemorative office and concordant sources are marked with *]

Category	Text	Concordances within Source	*PM* Ref
AD V[ESPERA]S			
Respond	*Spec[i]osa*	1 V, CO in Pasch *	310
(by *ebdomadarii*)		2 S, DO in Adv *	8
		3 S, DO in Pasch *	310
		4 V, Vig. Asm *	352
		5 V during Oct Asm	359
Hymn	*Aue maris*	1 V1, Anc	301
		2 V1, Vig. Asm	352
		3 V1, Nat BVM	364
Versicle	*Post p[ar]tu[m]*	Several	
Magnificat antiphon	*Quomodo fiet* * [text and melody added complete by a later hand at the top of the leaf]	T, this office	238
[AD MATUTINAS]			
Invitatory	*Aue Maria* *	1 M, Anc * tmCon	301
		2 M, DO in Adv * tCon	7
Hymn	*Quem terra*	Common to M of BVM feasts	
In i n[octurn]o			
Antiphon	*Missus est*	1 M, DO, same season	7
		2 A1, M, Anc	301
either:	*Missus est Gabriel a deo*	3 Proc during Adv *	200
or:	*Missus est Gabriel angelus ad Mariam*	4 Ben, L, Wed after Adv III *	18

p[salm]i f[e]r[ia]les

Versicle	*Sicut mirra*	1 M & T, DO, same season	7
		2 T, this office	238
		3 M, Pur	268
		4 M, Nat BVM	364
		5 M, Vig. Asm and Asm	352,356
Responds I-III	I *Missus est Gabriel*	RI, M, Anc	301
	II *Aue Mar[ia]*	RIII, M, Anc	302
	III *Suscipe u[er]bu[m]*	1 RX, M, Anc	302
		2 R VI, M, Adv Sun *	4

In ii n[octurn]o

Antiphon	*Ne timeas*	1 S, this office	238
		2 S, DO, same season	8
		3 Mag, V2, Adv Sun *	8
		4 A6, M, Anc	301
Versicle	*Bened[i]c[t]a tu*	1 S, this office	238
		2 L, DO, same season	8

AD L[AUDES]

Antiphon	*P[ro]ph[et]e*	1 L, DO, same season	7
		2 A1, L, Wed. after Adv III *	18
Respond	*S[an]c[t]a dei genit[ri]x*	1 L, DO, Adv *	7
(by *ebdomadarii*)		2 C, DO, Easter *	310
Hymn	*O gl[ori]osa*	Common to L of BVM feasts	
Versicle	*Post p[ar]tu[m]*	V, this office	238
Benedictus antiphon	*Sp[iritus] s[an]c[tu]s*	1 Ben ii & T, DO in Adv	7,8
		2 L, Ben, Adv Sun *	7
		3 A5, M, Anc	301

AD .I.

Antiphon	*Ang[e]l[u]s*	1 Ben i & P, DO, same season	7,8
		2 Ben, L, Mon after Adv *	8
		3 A10, M, Anc	302

AD .III.

Antiphon	*Quom[od]o* [complete version at top of leaf]	V, this office [?]	238
Versicle	*Sic[ut] m[irra]*	1 M, this office	

AD .VI.

| Antiphon | *Ne tim[eas]* | 1 | A2, M, this office | |
| Versicle | *B[e]n[e]d[i]c[t]a tu* | 1 | M, this office | |

AD .IX.

Antiphon	*Ecce anc[illa]*	1	A8, M, Anc	301
		2	N, DO, Advent	8
Versicle	*Spec[i]osa*	1	N, DO, Advent	8
		2	N, Vig. Asm	353
		3	M, Nat BVM	367

Q[UA]N[DO] TAB[U]LA FU[ER]IT DE D[OM]INA
(OCTAVE EPIPHANY TO PURIFICATION PM 1,xii, p.59)

AD V[ESPERA]S

Respond	i	*Post p[ar]t[um]*	1	R2, V, CO in Pasch	310
			2	S, 1st of 3 R 358-9	
	uel			during Oct Asm	
	ii	*Glo[ri]osa*	1	V, 2nd of 3 R 359	
				during Oct Asm	
Magnificat	i	*Nesciens m[ate]r*	1	Mag i, V, DO, same season	59
antiphon			2	MA3 of Nat BVM after V2, 30 Dec	47
			3	N, Chr Day *	30
	u[el]				
	ii	*Virgo d[e]i*	1	Mag ii, V, DO, same season	59
			2	Ben, L, CO to Quad	360
	[either	*Virgo. . ex qua lux*	3	Ben, L, Anc	303
	or	*Virgo. . qui totus*	4	MA1 of BVM after V2, 30 Dec *	47]

[AD MATUTUINAS]

| Invitatory | *Laudamus d[eu]m uirginis** | M, CO, Eastertide * mCon only310 |

In i. n[octurn]o

| Antiphon with first psalm | *Virgo u[er]bo* | Ps. 8 | 1 M, DO, same season | 59 |
| | | | 2 MA2 after V2, Ho. In. * | 47 |

et c[etera] usque p[ur]ific[ationem]

Responds I-III	I	*Cong[ra]tulamini.*	R VI, M, Circ *	49
	II	*Contur[est]* [= *Continent?*]	R X, M, Circ *	50
	III	*Confirmatu[m]*	R VII, M, Circ *	49

In ii. n[octurn]o

| Antiphon | *Beat[us] uenter* | 1 L, Ben ii, DO same season | 59 |
| | | 2 MA 1 after V2, Ho. In. * | 47 |

AD L[AUDES]

Antiphon	*O admir[abile]*	1 L, DO same season	59
		2 A1, L, Circ *	50
Benedictus antiphon	*Ecce Mar[ia]*	1 N, DO, same season or	59
		2 A5, L, Circ *	50

AD HORAS

Ut s[upra] ad p[ri]uatas hor[as]   [See Table 4:10, pp.263-64 for texts and concordances]

Q[UA]N[DO] TABULA DE DOMINA [IN PASCHA TEMPORE] p.310

AD V[ES]P[ERA]S

Antiphon	*All[elui]a*		?

Respond	i	*Speciosa f[a]c[t]a es* *	1 S, DO, same season *	310
		V. In deliciis	2, S, DO in Adv *	8
			3 V, Vig Asm *	352
			4 V during Oct Asm *	359
	u[e]l			
	ii	*Post p[ar]tum*	1 R1, V, CO, Ep. to Pur.	59
		cu[m] All[elui]a	2 R1 of 3, V, during Oct Asm	358-9

c[eteras] ut s[upr]a

Magnificat	i	*P[ar]adisi*	1 V, Mag., DO, Easter	310
antiphon			2 S, Vig. Asm *	353
			3 MA of BVM after L, Th after Pasch *	135
	u[e]l			
	ii	*Int[ro]dux[it]*	V, Mag5 of 5, CO to Trinity *	360

[AD MATUTINAS]

Invitatory   *Laudem[us] d[eu]m virginis* *   M,CO, Ep to Pur * mCon only 59

In N[octurn]o

| Antiphon | i | *All[elui]a* | Ps. 8 | ? |
| | ii | *All[elui]a* | | ? |

[AD LAUDES]

| *Benedictus* | *P[ar]adisi* | V, Mag, this office | 310 |
| antiphon | | | |

c[eteras] ut su[pra] p[ost] p[ur]ificat[ionem]

AD HORAS

Antiphon   *All[elui]a ut sup[ra]*   ?

Hymn verse   *Quesumus auctor*   ?
(V[ersus] ad ymn[us])

Q[UA]N[DO] TAB[U]LA FU[ER]IT DE D[OMI]NA S[CILICET] AB OCT[AVIS]
EPIPH[ANIE] USQUE XL ET P[OST] T[RI]N[ITA TEM] USQUE ADV[ENTUM] pp.360-61

AD V[ESPERA]S

Magnificat	i	*Salue regina*	Mag, V1, Vig Asm *	352-3
antiphons	ii	*Aue regina celoru[m]* *	No concordance	
	iii	*Aue virgo* *	No concordance	
	iv	*Tota pulchra es* *	No concordance	
	v	*Introduxit me* *	Mag ii, V, CO in Pasch	310

AD L[AUDES]

Benedictus	*Virgo dei genitrix*	1 Mag ii, V, CO to Pur	59
antiphon		2 Mag ii, V, DO to Pur	59
[either	*Virgo. . ex qua lux*	3 Ben, L, Anc	303
or	*Virgo. . qui totus*	4 MA1 of BVM after V2, 30 Dec]	47

[AD PRIMAM]

Antiphon	*Ortus conclusus es* *	No concordance

AD III

Antiphon	*Beata dei genit[ri]x* *	No concordance

[In a later hand:]
AD VIa

Antiphon	*Beata mat[er]*	1 T, DO after Pur	272
		2 A11, M, Anc *	302

AD IX

Antiphon	*Sub tuam*	1 N, DO after Pur.	272
		2 N, Vig. Asm *	353
(Unrubricated antiphon)	*Anima mea liquefacta est* *	No concordance	

IN INTROITU POST P[RO]CESSION[EM]

Antiphon 1	*Ibo michi ad montem* *	No concordance
2	*Quam pulchra es* *	No concordance

TABLE 4:10 THE DAILY MARIAN OFFICE IN THE WORCESTER ANTIPHONER (*WO* F.160)

DE DOMINA IN ADVENTU [*PM*, 1,xii, pp.7-8]

Items appear as textual incipits in source, unless marked *, indicating complete text and music.

Category		Text	Concordances within source	*PM* Ref.
AD MAT[UTINAS] DE D[OMI]NA I[N] ADV[E]NTU				
Invitatory *		*Aue Maria gr[ati]a plena*	1 M, Anc * tCon only	301
			2 M, CO, Advent * tCon only	238
Hymn		*Q[ue]m t[er]ra.*	Common to M of BVM feasts	
Antiphon		*Missus [est].*	1 A1, M, CO, in Adv tCon	238
			2 A1, M, Anc	301
	either	*Missus est Gabriel a deo*	3 Proc during Adv *	200
	or	*Missus est Gabriel angelus ad Mariam*	4 Ben, L, Wed after Adv III *	18
Psalms	(a)	8, 18, 23	Common to M of BVM feasts	
seq[ue]ntibus noctibus:	(b)	44, 45, 47	"	
Ite[m]	(c)	84, 86, 95	"	
Ite[m]	(d)	96, 97, 98	"	
Et sic alt[er]natim.				
Versicle		*Sic[ut] mirra electa.*	1 M & T, CO, in Adv	238
			2 T, this office	7
			3 M, Pur *	268
			4 M, Nat BVM *	364
			5 M, Vig. Asm and M, Asm	352, 356
Lessons i-iii *	i	*S[an]c[t]a Mar[ia] u[ir]go u[ir]g[inu]m* No concordance		
*	ii	*S[an]c[t]a Mar[ia] piar[um] piissima*	"	
*	iii	*S[an]c[t]a d[e]i genit[ri]x*	"	
Responds I-III	I	*S[an]c[t]a et im[maculata].*	1 R VI, M, Chr Day *	29
			2 R I, M, Vig Asm	353
	II	*B[eat]a es M[aria].*	1 R IX, M, Pur *	270
			2 R IX, M, Asm	357
			3 R II, M, Vig Asm	353

	III *Felix n[amque].*	R VIII, M, Sun in Oct Asm *	357
[Hymn]	*Te D[eu]m*		
Q[ua]n[do] ad p[ri]ores laude[s]			
Versicle before Lauds	*B[eat]a mater et innupta u[ir]go*	No concordance	

IT[EM] AD LAUD[ES]

Antiphon	*P[ro]phe[te].*	1 L, CO in Advent	238
		2 A1, L, Wed after Adv III *	18
Psalms	92, 99, 62 with 66, *Benedicite* and 148	Common	
Respond *	*S[an]c[t]a dei genitrix* V. *Int[er]cede*	1 L, CO in Advent	238
		2 C, DO in Pasch * tCon only	310
Hymn	*O gl[ori]osa d[omina].*	Common to L of BVM feasts	
Versicle	*B[e]n[e]d[i]c[t]a tu i[n] mul[ieribus]*	M & S, CO in Advent	238
Benedictus Antiphons	i *Ang[e]l[u]s.*	1 P, this office	8
		2 P, CO in Adv	238
		3 A10, M, Anc	302
		4 Ben, L, Mon after Adv *	8
et seq[ue]ntibus noctibus alt[er]nat[im]	ii *Sp[iritus] s[an]c[tu]s.*	1 T, this office	8
		2 Ben, L, CO in Adv	238
		3 Ben, L, Adv Sun *	7
		4 A5, M, Anc	301
[A series of suffrages follows]			

AD I. DE D[OMI]NA IN ADV[E]NTU

Hymn	*V[ir]go sing[u]lar[is].*	Common to PTSN, this office	8
Antiphon	*Ang[e]l[u]s d[omini]*	As Ben i, L, this office	
Psalms	118 [2 sections], 116	Common	
Respond *	*Ih[es]u Christe fili dei* V. *Per intercessionem*	P, DO in Pasch * partial tCon	310
Versicle	*B[eat]a m[ate]r.*	No concordance	

AD. III. DE D[OMI]NA

Hymn	*Virgo s[ingularis].*	Common to PTSN, this office	7,8
Antiphon	*Sp[iritus] s[an]c[tu]s.*	As Ben ii, L, this office	7
Psalms	119, 120, 121	Common	
Respond *	*Exalta es s[an]c[t]a d[e]i genit[ri]x [V.] Sup[er] choros*	T, DO in Pasch * tCon only	310
Versicle	*Sicut mirra electa*	M, this office	

cet[era] u[t] s[upra]

AD. VI. DE D[OMI]NA IN ADV[E]NTU

Hymn	*Virgo sing[ularis].*	Common to PTSN, this office	7,8
Antiphon	*Ne timeas.*	1 A2, M, & S, CO in Adv	238
		2 Mag, V2, Adv Sun *	8
		3 A6, M, Anc	301
Psalms	122, 123, 124	Common	
Respond *	*Speciosa ff[a]c[t]a es V.In deliciis tuis*	1 S, DO in Pasch tCon only *	310
		2 V, CO in Adv	238
		3 V, CO in Pasch * tCon only	310
		4 V, Vig Asm * tCon only	352
		5 V, during Oct Asm	359
Versicle	*Bened[i]c[t]a tu in mulieribus.*	As L, this office	

c[etera] ut supra

AD IX. DE D[OMI]NA I[N] ADV[ENTU]

Hymn	*V[ir]go s[ingularis].*	Common to PTSN, this office	8
Antiphon	*Ecce anc[illa].*	1 N, CO in Adv	238
		2 A8, M, Anc	301
Psalms	125, 126, 127	Common	
Respond *	*Elegit eam V.Et in tab[er]naculo*	N, DO in Pasch * tCon only	310
Versicle	*Spec[i]osa ff[a]c[t]a es et suau[is].*	1 N, CO in Advent	238
		2 N, Vig. Asm	353
		3 M, Nat BVM	367

p.26 Christmas Eve rubric: *hore de d[omi]na i[n]t[er]mittant[ur] usque p[ost] oct[auem] epiph[anie]*

[FROM OCTAVE EPIPHANY TO THE PURIFICATION] p.59

AD MAT[UTINAS] DE D[OMI]NA

Antiphon	*Virgo u[e]rbo.*	1 A1, M, CO to Pur	59
		2 MA2 after V2, Ho. In. *	47

AD L[AUDES]

Antiphon	*O admir[abile].*	1 L, CO to Pur	59
		2 A1, L, Circ *	50
Benedictus antiphons	i *Maria aut[em].*	MA3 after V2, Ho. In. *	47
uel			
	ii *Beat[us] uent[er].*	1 A2, M, CO to Pur	59
		2 MA 1 after V2, Ho. In. *	47

AD I.

Antiphon	*Q[ua]n[do] nat[us].*	A2, L, Circ *	50

AD III

Antiphon	*Rubu[m].*	A3, L, Circ *	50

AD VI.

Antiphon	*Germinauit.*	A4, L, Circ *	50

AD IX.

Antiphon	*Ecce mar[ia].*	1 Ben, L, CO to Pur	59
		2 A5, L, Circ *	50

AD V[ESPERA]S

[Psalm antiphon erased]

Magnificat Antiphons	i *Nesciens m[ate]r.*	1 Mag i, V, CO to Pur	59
		2 N, Chr Day *	30
		3 MA3 of Nat BVM after V2, 30 Dec	47
uel			
	ii *Virgo d[e]i.*	1 Mag ii, V, CO to Pur	59
		2 Ben, L, CO to Quad	360

| [unclear: | either | *Virgo. . ex qua lux* | 3 Ben, L, Anc * | 303 |
| | or | *Virgo. . qui totus* | 4 MA1 of BVM after V2, 30 Dec * | 47] |

uel

	iii	*Virgo u[er]bo.*	1 As M, this office	
			2 A1, M, CO to Pur	59
			3 MA2 of BVM after V2, Ho. In. *	47

AD COMPL[ETORIUM]

| Antiphon | *Completi.* | A3, V1, Chr Day * | 27 |

| *Nunc* Antiphon | *Ecce completa* | A4, V1, Chr Day * | 27 |

C[etera] ut supra. Et sic fiat usque p[ur]if[f]icationem]

[Commemorative Office of BVM for the same season follows]

[FROM THE PURIFICATION TO EASTER] pp.272-73

AD MAT[UTINAS] DE D[OMI]NA

| Antiphon | *Gaude mar[ia].* | A5, M, Pur * | 268 |

AD L[AUDES]

| Antiphon | *Post p[ar]t[um].* | Mag, V2, Pur | 272 |

Benedictus	i	*In p[ro]le.*	A6, M, Pur *	268
Antiphons		*In iii. l[e]c[tiones]*		
	ii	*Dignu[m] nanque.* [sic]	A5, M, Nat BVM *	364
		In xii l[e]c[tionibus]		

c[etera] ut s[upra]

[AD I] DE D[OMI]NA

| Antiphon | *S[an]c[t]a dei* | A1, M, Vig. Asm * | 353 |
| | *gen[i]tr[i]x.* | | |

c[etera] ut s[upra]

[AD III] DE D[OMI]NA

Antiphon	*B[eat]a m[ate]r.*	1 S, CO to Quad	360
		2 T, CO after Pur	272
		3 A11, M, Anc *	302

c[etera] ut s[upra]

[AD VI] DE D[OMI]NA

Antiphon	*B[e]n[e]d[i]c[t]a.*	A6, M, Nat BVM *	360
		[several other possibilities]	

c[etera] ut s[upra]

[AD IX] DE D[OMI]NA

Antiphon	*S[u]b tuam*	1 N, CO to Quad	360
	p[ro]t[ectionem].	2 N, Vig. Asm *	353

c[etera] ut s[upra]

AD V[ESPERA]S DE D[OMI]NA

Antiphon	*Post p[ar]tum.*	As L, this office	
Magnificat	i *S[an]c[t]a Mar[ia]*	A2, V1, Asm *	354
Antiphons	*s[uccurre] m[iseris].*		
uel			
	ii *S[an]c[t]a d[e]i g[enitrix].*	As P, this office	
uel			
	iii *Aue o th[eotocos]*	A10, M, Nat BVM *	366

c[etera] ut s[upra]

AD CO[M]PL[ETORIUM] DE D[OMI]NA
ut s[upra] p[ost] oct[auem] epiph[anie]

DE D[OMI]NA I[N] PASCH[A] T[EM]P[OR]E   p.310

AD V[ESPER]AS

Antiphon	*Post p[ar]tu[m].*	L & V, DO after Pur	272
Respond *	*Gemma virginum*	No concordance traced	
	[V.]Memor esto tuor[um]		
Magnificat	*Paradisi.*	1 Ben, L, this office	
Antiphon		2 Mag i, V, CO in Pasch	310

| either | [Paradisi ianue] | 3 S, Vig. Asm * | 353 |
| or | [Paradisi porta] | 4 MA of BVM after L, Th after E * | 135 |

AD CO[M]PLETOR[IUM] DE DOMINA
et ad cet[er]as hor[as] a[ntiphona] ut s[upra] p[ost] p[ur]ific[ationem].

| Respond * | S[an]c[t]a dei genit[ri]x | L, DO in Advent * tCon only | 7 |
| | V. Intercede p[ro] nob[is] | | |

ut supra post purific[ationem]

AD L[AUDES]
Benedictus	Paradisi.	As Mag, V, this office
Antiphon		
c[eteris] ut s[upra]		

AD. I. DE D[OMI]NA
| Respond * | Ih[es]u Christe fili dei | P, DO in Advent * partial tCon | 7 |
| | V.Per int[er]cessionem | | |

AD. III.
| Respond * | Exalta es s[an]c[t]a dei | T, DO in Advent * tCon | 7 |
| | genit[ri]x V.Sup[er] choros | | |

AD VI.
| Respond * | Speciosa f[a]c[ta] es | 1 S, DO in Advent * tCon | 8 |
| | V.In deliciis tuis | 2 V, CO in Pasch * tCon | 310 |

Ad IX
| Respond * | Elegit eam d[eu]s | N, DO in Advent * tCon | 8 |
| | V.Et in tab[er]nac[u]lo suo | | |

[AFTER PENTECOST TO NATIVITY BVM] p.162

Et not[andum] q[uod] hec a[ntiphone] et cete[res] seq[uen]tes ca[n]te[n]t[ur] sing[u]lis diebus successiue ad u[espera]s de d[omi]na. In ew[angeliis] usque nat[iuitatem] ei[us].

[VESPERS]

Magnificat *	1	Osculetur me osculo	No concordances traced
Antiphons *	2	Pulchre sunt gene tue	"
		sicut turturis	
*	3	Ecce tu pulcher es	"
*	4	Si ignoras te	"
*	5	Veni dilecte mi	"
*	6	Sexaginta sunt regine	"
*	7	Aperi mihi in soror meas	"
*	8	Ferculum fecit sibi rex	"
*	9	Soror nostra parvula est	"

Table 4.11 267

TABLE 4:11 *MAGNIFICAT* ANTIPHONS FOR THE
DAILY VOTIVE OFFICE FROM PENTECOST TO THE NATIVITY
OF THE VIRGIN IN THE WORCESTER ANTIPHONER (*WO* F.160)

PM 1,xii, pp.162-63
[Words in brackets appear in the biblical verses (see under *Biblia Sacra* in bibliography) but not in the antiphons]

Text	Mode	Source
1. *Osculetur me osculo oris sui: quia meliora sunt ubera tua vino.*	1	*Song of Songs* I, 1
Fragrancia unguentis optimis.	"	I, 2a
Et odor unguentorum [tuorum] super omnia aromata.	"	IV, 10b
2. *Pulchre sunt gene tue sicut turturis collum tuum sicut monilia.*	2	"	I, 9
Murenulas aureas faciemus tibi vermiculatas argento.	"	I, 10
3. *Ecce tu pulcher es, dilecte mi, et decorus. Lectulus noster floridus.*	3	"	I, 15
Tigna domorum nostrarum cedrina laquearia nostra cypressina.	"	I, 16
4. *Si ignoras te, o pulchra [pulcherrima] inter mulieres, egredere, et abi post vestigia gregem [tuorum], et pasce hedos tuos juxta tabernacula pastorum.*	4	"	I, 7
5. *Veni dilecte mi, egrediamur in agrum, commoremur in vallibus [villis].*	5	"	VII, 11
Mane surgamus ad vineas, videamus si floruit vinea, si flores fructus partutiunt, si floruerunt mala punica: ibi dabo tibi ubera mea.	"	VII, 12

6. *Sexaginta sunt regine [et] octoginta*   6   "   VI, 7
   concubine, et adolescentularum
   non est numerus.
   Una est columba mea, perfecta mea,   "   VI, 8a
   una [est] matris sue, electa
   genetrici sue.

7. *Aperi mihi soror mea, amica mea,*   7   "   V, 2b
   columba mea, immaculata mea: quia
   caput meum plenum est rore, et
   cincinni mei guttis noctium.

8. *Ferculum fecit sibi rex Salomon*   7   "   III, 9
   de lignis Libani:
   Columnas ejus fecit argenteas,   "   III, 10
   reclinatorium aureum, ascensum
   purpureum: media charitate constravit
   propter filias Jerusalem.

9. *Soror nostra parva, et ubera*   8   "   VIII, 8
   non habet: quid faciemus sorori
   nostre in die quando alloquenda est?
   Si murus est, aedificemus super eum   "   VIII, 9
   propugnacula argentea: si ostium est,
   compingamus illud tabulis cedrinis.

TABLE 4:12 MODAL ORGANIZATION OF ANTIPHONS
IN *WO* F.160

Text	Mode	Source of text

Matins of the Assumption (PM 1-xii, p.354)

Antiphons, First Nocturn

Text	Mode	Source of text
1. *Ecce tu pulchra es*	1	*Song of Songs* I, 14
2. *Sicut lilium inter spinas*	2	" II, 2
3. *Favus distillans*	3	" IV, 2
4. *Emissiones tue paradisus*	4	" IV, 13
5. *Fons ortorum*	5	" IV, 15
6. *Veniat dilectus meus*	6	" V, 1

Antiphons, Second Nocturn

Text	Mode	Source of text
7. *Veni in ortum*	7	" V, 1
8. *Comedi favum cum melle*	8	" V, 1
9. *Ostende mihi faciem*	1	?
10. *Sonet vox tua*	2	?
11. *Ortus conclusus*	3	" IV, 12
12. *Que est ista*	4	" VI, 9

Antiphon, Third Nocturn

Text	Mode	Source of text
13. *Descendi in ortum*	7	" VI, 10

Matins of the Purification (PM 1-xii, p.268)

Antiphons, First Nocturn		Antiphons, Second Nocturn	
1. *Benedicta tu in mulieribus*	4	7. *Virgo concepit*	4
2. *Sicut mirra electa*	4	8. *Sicut letantium omnium*	7
3. *Speciosa facta es*	4	9. *Induere vestimentis*	7
4. *Dignare me laudare te*	4	10. *Dederunt hostiam*	1
5. *Gaude Maria virgo*	4	11. *Scriptum est enim in lege*	8
6. *In prole mater in partu*	4	12. *Optulerunt pro eo domino*	8
Antiphon, Third Nocturn		13. *Homo erat in ierusalem*	8

Matins of Nativity BVM (PM 1-xii, p.364)

Antiphons, First Nocturn		Antiphons, Second Nocturn	
1. *Hodie nata est beata virgo*	1	7. *Nativitas est hodie*	7
2. *Beatissime virginis Marie*	2	8. *Ista est speciosa*	8
3. *Quando nata est virgo*	3	9. *Felix namque es*	4
4. *Hodie nata est virgo*	4	10. *Ave O Theothocos virgo*	6
5. *Dignum namque est*	5	11. *Maria virgo semper*	7
6. *Benedicta et venerabilis*	6	12. *Celeste beneficium*	1
Antiphon, Third Nocturn		13. *Aula Maria dei*	6

Matins of Trinity Sunday (PM 1-xii, p.158)

Antiphons, First Nocturn		Antiphons, Second Nocturn	
1. *Adesto deus unus*	1	7. *Karitas pater est*	7
2. *Te unum in substantia*	2	8. *Verax est pater veritas*	8
3. *Te semper idem esse*	3	9. *Una igitur pater*	8
4. *Te invocamus te adoramus*	4	10. *In patre manet eternitas*	3
5. *Spes nostra salus*	5	11. *Ex quo omnia*	5
6. *Libera nos salva nos*	6	12. *Sanctus sanctus sanctus*	5
Antiphon, Third Nocturn		13. *Gloria et honor deo*	1

Lauds Antiphons		Vespers Antiphons	
1. *O beata et benedicta*	1	1. *Gloria tibi trinitas*	1
2. *O beata benedicta*	2	2. *Laus et perhennis gloria*	2
3. *O vera . . . trinitas*	3	3. *Gloria laudis resonet*	⸰ 3
4. *O vera . . . unitas*	4	4. *Laus deo patri*	4
5. *Te iure laudant te*	5		

Matins of St Wulfstan (PM 1-xii, p.248)

Antiphons, First Nocturn		Antiphons, Second Nocturn	
1. *Preclara festivitas*	1	7. *Quam salubre invocatum*	7
2. *In Wulstano cuius etas*	2	8. *Febres fugat tactus*	8
3. *Quem parentes*	3	9. *Reddit muto consonantis*	1
4. *Florem mundi*	4	10. *De sublimi preceps*	2
5. *Relinquens Wulstanus*	5	11. *Dum oraret sanctus*	3
6. *Vita verbo est Wulstanus*	6	12. *Perseverans ulcus*	4
Antiphon, Third Nocturn		13. *Decantemus domino*	6

Lauds Antiphons

1. *Benedictus sit dominus*   1
2. *Nomine eterno hereditavit* 2
3. *Ad te deus de luce*   3
4. *Sancte sacerdos deum*   4
5. *Rex virtutum assis*   5

Matins of the Deposition of St Oswald (PM 1-xii, 282)

Antiphons, First Nocturn		Antiphons, Second Nocturn	
1. *In lege domini Oswaldus*	1	7. *Oculi tui deus respexerunt*	7
2. *Seruiuit domino beatus*	2	8. *Habitat deus Oswaldus*	8
3. *Exaltasti domine caput*	3	9. *In uirtute tua*	1
4. *Signatus est beatus*	4	10. *Sacerdos domini Oswaldus*	2
5. *Intellexit deus clamorem*	5	11. *Elegisti domine deus*	3
6. *In universa terra nomen*	6	12. *Bonum est domine*	4
Antiphon, Third Nocturn		13. *O insignissime pater et dux*	5

Lauds Antiphons

1. *Electus a deo pontifex*   1
2. *In cordis leticia deo*   2
3. *De luce sanctus*   3
4. *Servi dei benedicite*   4
5. *Exultat in gloria*   5

Matins of St Cuthbert (PM 1-xii, p.292)

Antiphons, First Nocturn		Antiphons, Second Nocturn	
1. *Auctor donorum spiritus*	1	7. *Quandam vexatam demone*	7
2. *Qui Raphahelem*	2	8. *Multos hic sanavit*	8
3. *Dum iactantur puppes*	3	9. *Sanctus antistes*	1
4. *Edomans corpus*	4	10. *Sancte pater Cuthberte*	1
5. *Mirum dictu hinc*	5	11. *Sancte Cuthberte confessor*	4
6. *Adest frater*	6	12. *Iste est qui ante deum*	8
Antiphon, Third Nocturn		13. *Alme confessor*	1

Lauds Antiphons

1. *Christi fortis hic athleta* 2
2. *Qui de rupe promsit*   3
3. *In episcopatu suo*   4
4. *Hic tanguntur*   5
5. *Mox pater suos*   6

Matins of St Mary Magdalene (PM 1-xii, p.335)

Antiphons, First Nocturn	
1. *Adest preclara festivitas*	1
2. *Hec mulier sancta Christi*	2
3. *Alabastrum unguenti*	3
4. *Contemplative vite magna*	4
5. *Exemplum venie Maria*m	5
6. *Hanc ergo toto corde*	6

Antiphon, Third Nocturn

Antiphons, Second Nocturn	
7. *Lavit Maria lacrimis*	7
8. *Solempnitatem Magdalene*	8
9. *Magdalenam sua crimina*	1
10. *Condescende nobis pietatis*	3
11. *Tempore leticie*	6
12. *A Christo suscepta*	7
13. *Sit laus sit honor*	4

Lauds Antiphons	
1. *Intravit Maria in domum*	1
2. *Dixit dominus Symoni*	2
3. *Michi osculum non*	3
4. *Oleo caput meum*	4
5. *Ideoque dico tibi*	5

Magnificat antiphons for the Daily Votive Office
from Pentecost to Nativity BVM

Text	Mode	Source	
1. *Osculetur me osculo*	1	*Song of Songs*	I, 1,2a,10b
2. *Pulchre sunt gene tue*	2	"	I, 9-10
3. *Ecce tu pulcher es*	3	"	I, 15-16
4. *Si ignoras te*	4	"	I, 7
5. *Veni dilecte mi*	5	"	VII, 11-12
6. *Sexaginta sunt regine*	6	"	VI, 7-8a
7. *Aperi mihi soror mea*	7	"	V, 2b
8. *Ferculum fecit*	7	"	III, 9-10
9. *Soror nostra*	8	"	VIII, 8-9

TABLE 5:1 THE VOTIVE ANTIPHON
IN ENGLISH BENEDICTINE SOURCES

Date	Source	Text	Position
c.1259-83	*Lbl* C.XI Customary of St Peter's, Westminster	*Salve regina ex moderno et non ex veteri usu*	After Compline
s.xiii med.	*Ob* 358 St Albans Psalter	*Salve regina** with trope of three verses, Versicle *Ave Maria*, Collect *Omnipotens sempiterne Deus*	Not specified
c.1330	*D-Bds* 194 Customary of St Werburgh's, Chester	*Salve regina* with versicle *Post partum*	During Compline of BVM, between hymn and *Benedicamus Domino*
1343	Statute of Benedictine Chapter, issued at Northampton	Not specfied: *Salve* appears as a marginal note in one source	After Compline
1349-96 (Abbacy of Thomas de la Mare)	*Gestum Abbatum Monasterii S. Albani*, here referring to Redbourn Priory	*Antiphonam quoque de Sancta Maria*	After Compline
c.1400	*Cjc* D.27 Ordinal and Customary of St Mary's, York	*Salve regina** with trope of three verses, Versicle *Post partum*, Collect *Omnipotens sempiterne Deus*	Immediately after *Benedicamus* of Compline of BVM
c.1404	*Ouc* 169 Ordinal of the Nuns of Barking	*Salve regina*	After High Mass on Christmas Day and Feast of St Bridget
		Mater ora filium	After Compline on Feast of All Saints
1400-50	*Lbl* 1804 Office of BVM etc. from Durham Cathedral	*Salve regina** with Versicle *Ave Maria*, Collect *Omnipotens sempiterne Deus*	After Compline of BVM and memorial of the Passion
1400-50	*Llp* 558 Psalter with additions from Christ Church Canterbury	*Salve regina** with Versicle *Ave Maria*, Collect *Omnipotens* and Blessing *Per intercessionem*	After Lauds, None, Vespers and Compline of BVM, but preceding the suffrages and memorial of Passion where these occurred

Date	Source	Text	Position
1425-75	*Ob* f.1 Office of BVM etc. from St Peter's Gloucester	*Salve regina** with versicle *Post partum*, Collect *Omnipotens*	After Lauds, None, and Vespers of BVM, preceding memorial of Passion
		Sancta Maria non est*, Versicle *Post partum*, Collect *Protege Domine*	After Compline of BVM, the *Trina* *oratio* following Compline of BVM, and the Chapter meeting
1425	*US SM* 34.B.7 Processional of the Nuns of Chester	*Gaude dei genitrix, Ave* *regina celorum, Salve regina* with trope of five verses and *Alma redemptoris mater*	After miscellaneous prayers etc., following Compline
s.xv med.	*DO* 26543 Winchester Hours	*Salve regina** with Versicle *Ave Maria*, Collect *Omnipotens*	After ferial Compline, preceding memorial of the Passion
s.xv med.	*Mch* 6717 Godstow Psalter	*Salve regina** with trope of seven verses, Versicle *Ave* *Maria*, Collect *Omnipotens*	After Compline of BVM
		Gaude virgo mater*, Versicle *Exaltata*, Collect *Omnipotens*	After Compline of BVM
		Gaude flore virginali*, Versicle *O speciosa dei*, Collect *Domine ihesu christe*	After Compline of BVM
ante 1600	*Rites of Durham*	'the Salvi'	At 6 p.m. each day after prayer in the Chapter House

Antiphons marked with an asterisk appear as complete texts.

TABLE 5:2   FORMAL ADOPTION OF THE VOTIVE ANTIPHON

1218	Cistercian	*Omni die, finito Capitulo incipiat cantor Responsorium . . .*
		Finito Responsorio dicatur versus cum Gloria et repetitione
	[Cist.Stat. i, 484-5]	*Responsorii; et post incipiat cantor Salve Regina sub mediocri voce; quam cum inceperit, omnes veniam petant et sic maneant usque ad misericordiae, et tunc surgant fratres donec tota finiatur. Qua finita, dicat qui tenet conventum: Ora pro nobis sancta Dei Genitrix, conventu petente veniam et prono existente, donec ille collectas stando dixerit: Adsit nobis et Concede nos, quae non praemisso Dominus vobiscum dicentur et per Christum Dominum nostrum finientur.*

This requirement was modified to private daily recitation (*privatim*) in 1220:

| | [Cist.Stat. i,517] | *Antiphona videlicet Salve Regina de cetero non cantetur, sed privatim dicatur a singulis quotidie, cum collectis consuetis.* |

Restricted to recitation after Chapter on Fridays, 1228:

| | [Cist.Stat. ii,69] | *. . . omni sexta feria, dictis septem psalmis in ecclesia, mediocri voce cantetur responsorium Aspice Domine, antiphona Salve Regina, versus Ora pro nobis, et collecta* |

Daily recitation after Compline, 1251:

| | [Cist.Stat. ii,361] | *. . . ut singulis diebus finito ex toto Completorio et orationibus consuetis, cantor incipiat Salve regina . . . versus Ave Maria . . . collecta Concede nos. . .* |

| 1221 | Dominican | Adopted in Bologna, after Compline, as a processional observance (recorded in a letter of Jordan of Saxony): |

| | [Jordanus, 557] | *Huius praedicti fratris Bernadi tam fera vexatio fuit occasio, qua permoti antiphonam Salve regina post completorium decantandam instituimus apud Bononiam, qua de domo eadem per omnem postmodum Lombardiae coepit frequentari provinciam, et sic postmodum per universum Ordinem haec pia et salutaris invaluit consuetudo.* |

Widely observed throughout order by 1234

General Chapter at Limoges decreed formal adoption in 1334

1249	Franciscan	˙Four texts to be sung after Compline on a seasonal basis (recorded in a letter of John of Parma to Minorites of Tuscany):

	[Cited in Batiffol, 162]	*Beatae Virginis antiphonis, videlicet Regina caeli, Alma Redemptoris, Ave Regina Caelorum, et Salve Regina, quae post Completorium diversis cantantur temporibus . . .*

*c.*1140-45 Cluniac   Adopted as a processional observance on the Assumption and other occasions

Statute 76 of Peter the Venerable:

[Cluny, Pet.Ven., 105]   *Statutum est, ut antiphona de sancta maria domini facta, cuius principum est Salve regina misericordiae, in festo Assumptionis ipsius, dum processio fit a conventu cantetur, et insuper in processionibus quae a principali ecclesia apostolorum ad eiusdem matris virginis ecclesiam ex more fiunt . . .*

Adopted as a post-Compline observance throughout the order:

1301

Statute 37 of Bertrand I, Abbot of Cluny:

[Cluny, Statuta, i, 82]   *Item, quod in omnibus locis conventalibus Ordinis, in honore beate Marie Virginis, cantetur amodo post Completorium, alta voce et cum nota Salve regina, vel alia antiphona de eadem. Id idem, si bono modo possit fieri, in aliis locis non conventualibus fiat.*

1343	English Benedictines [Pantin, ii,33]	A Meeting of the General Chapter at Northampton specified recitation after Compline: *Hincque statuimus, ut singulis diebus statim post completorium, in honorem beate Virginis una in choro cantetur antiphona tractim pariter et devote, post quam subsequatur oracio de eadem.*

1350	Roman	Four texts, to be sung seasonally after Compline:

Rubric from 1478 Roman Breviary:

[*Rub. Nov.*, 390]   *Notandum est quod hec antiphona s. Alma Redemptoris Mater dicitur a sabbato primo de Adventu exclusive usque ad festum Purificationis; et hec ant. s. Salve Regina a festo Purificationis exclusive usque ad quartum feriam maioris hebdomade dicitur; et hec ant. s. Regina celi letare a festo resurrectionis Domini exclusive usque ad sabbatum individue Trinitatis dicitur; et hec ant. s. Ave regina celorum a sabbato vigilie sancte Trinitatis usque ad adventum Domini exclusive dicitur. Quas quidem anthiphonas Clemens VI ponifex max. ordinavit et in urbe statuit pontificatus sui anno VIII.*

TABLE 5:3   SEASONAL SCHEMES FOR THE VOTIVE ANTIPHON

	Roman Use (1350)	Franciscan Use (i) (1249)	Franciscan Use (ii) (s.xv)
Alma Redemptoris Mater	Advent Sunday to Purification	Advent Sunday to Quinquagesima	Advent Sunday to Quinquagesima
Ave Regina Celorum	Purification to Wednesday of Holy Week	Quinquagesima to Wednesday of Holy Week	Quinquagesima to Wednesday of Holy Week
Regina Celi	Easter Eve to Pentecost	Easter to Octave of Pentecost	Easter to Octave of Pentecost
Salve Regina	Octave of Pentecost to Advent	Octave of Pentecost to Advent	Octave of Pentecost to Nativity of BVM
Quam pulchra es			Nativity of BVM to Advent

TABLE 5:4 LITURGICAL PLACING OF FOUR
MARIAN ANTIPHONS IN ENGLISH BENEDICTINE SOURCES

	Alma Redemptoris	Ave Regina	Salve Regina	Regina Celi
Lbl 2.A.X St Albans c.1140-50		1. Mag, VI, CO BVM 2. Proc after V?		
WO F.160 Worcester s.xiii[1]	T, Anc	1. Mag, V1, Asm 2. Mag ii, CO of BVM, Oct Ep to Quad & Pent to Adv	1. Mag, Vig Asm 2. Mag i, CO of BVM, Oct Ep to Quad & Pent to Adv	
Ccc 465 Norwich c.1260	Mag i, CO of BVM Pur to Pent & AS to Adv	Mag ii, CO of BVM Pur to Pent & AS to Adv		
Ob e.1* Hyde Abbey c.1300	1. Mag, V2, Anc 2. Mag, V2, Oct Asm 3. Mag during Oct Asm 4. Mag ii, CO of BVM, pa 5. Proc, V2, Asm 6. Proc, V2, Nat BVM		1. Mag, during Oct Asm 2. Mag, CO BVM, Pasch	
D-Bds 194 Chester c.1330-40		BVM Proc, Sat	[VA during C.BVM]	
Cjc D.27 St Mary's, York c.1400	**Proc *ad introitum* Pur to Adv**	1. Proc *ad introitum* Pur to Adv 2. Proc, Tu Rog after Oct Easter	[VA after C.BVM]	MA of BVM after V2 during Easter week
Ouc 169 Barking 1404	1. Mag, Obl BVM 2. Proc during Pent	1. Proc during Pent 2. Proc for queen	[VA after HM, Chr Day & AS]	1. Mag, Anc 2. Mag, CO BVM, Easter to Trin

TABLE 5:5 LITURGICAL PLACING OF
MARIAN ANTIPHONS IN EUROPEAN MONASTIC SOURCES

	Alma Redemptoris	*Ave Regina*	*Salve Regina*	*Regina Celi*
I-Lc 601 Lucca s.xii in.				V. Easter Day to following Sat (Lucca, 215)
F-Pn 17296 St Denis s.xii	3rd of 6 proc A, marked *Ad Processionem* (Hesbert 2, 786)	2nd of 6 proc A, marked *Ad Processionem* (Hesbert 2, 786)		
I-BV V.21 Benevento s.xii ex				S, Pentecost (Hesbert 2, 439)
F-Pn 3719, f.99 ? c.1150			Mag/Ben, Office de Beata (Cited by Leclercq, 'Salve regina', *DACL*, 718)	
Lbl 18302 German? s.xii[1]			T, Asm	
CH-SGs 390 St Gall Addition of s.xii or s.xiii	Ben, L, Anc (Hartker, 10)		Mag [?], V2 Anc (Hartker, 10)	
F-O 129 Fleury s.xiii	1. Mag, day 2 of Oct Asm (Fleury 209,5) 2. Mag ii of iii, CO of BVM from Pur to Quad & Easter to Adv (Fleury 313,9)	Mag, day 3 of Oct Asm (Fleury, 209,21)	1. Mag, day 1 of Oct Asm (Fleury 208, 13) 2. Mag i of iii, CO of BVM from Pur to Quad & Easter to Adv (Fleury 313,9)	

TABLE 5:6 LITURGICAL PLACING OF MARIAN ANTIPHONS IN ENGLISH SECULAR SOURCES

	Alma Redemptoris	Ave Regina	Salve Regina	Regina Celi
Sar.Proc. [*Ob* d.4 and Pynson 1502]	V Proc, A3, *ad introitum*	V Proc, A2, *ad introitum*	A1 of non-specific series	A2 of non-specific series
Sar.Ant. 529 [*Cu* Mm.2.g] s.xiii[1]	V, MA3, Nat BVM	V, MA4, Nat BVM		
Exeter Ord. 1337	1. V Proc *ad introitum*, Mon to Sat during Easter wk 2. Proc *in redeundo* from cross, Sun after Trin	1. L Proc, A Th & Fri after Easter 2. V Proc to font, Th after Easter 3. Proc *in redeundo* from cross, Sun after Trin		1. V2 Proc *ad introitum*, Easter Day 2. VI Proc *ad introitum*, *Dom. in albis*
York.Brev. 1493	Mag, V, day 6 of Oct Asm	1. Mag, V, day 5 of Oct Asm 2. Mag, V, CO of BVM in Pasch 3. V Proc to font, Wed after Easter		
Hereford 1505	V Proc, A3, *Ad introitum* Sundays after Trin to Adv (Hereford iii,74)	1. V Proc, A1, *Ad introitum* Sundays after Trin to Advent (Hereford iii,74) 2. Ben, L, CO of BVM Pur to Quad & Oct CC to Adv (Hereford ii,35)		Ben, L, CO of BVM in Pasch (Hereford ii,239)

TABLE 5:7 TROPED VERSIONS OF *SALVE REGINA*

The Hymn *Virgo Mater*

1. *Virgo mater ecclesie*
Aeterna porta glorie
Esto nobis refugium
Apud patrem et filium.

2. *Gloriosa Dei mater*
Cujus natus est ac pater,
Ora pro nobis omnibus,
Qui memoriam agimus.

3. *Stella maris, lux refulgens,*
Stirps regalis, sancta parens,
Roga patrem et filium
Ut det nobis paraclitum.

4. *Virgo clemens, virgo pia,*
Virgo dulcis, O Maria,
Exaudi preces omnium
Ad te pie clamantium.

5. *Funde preces tuo nato,*
Crucifixo, vulnerato
Pro nobis et flagellato
Spinis puncto, felle potato.

6. *Alma mater summi regis,*
Lux et porta celsi celi,
Inclina te miserrimis
Gementibus cum lacrimis.
[From *AH*, xxiii, p. 57, no.82.]

Additional verses used with those of the hymn

Dele culpas miserorum
Terge sordes peccatorum
Dona nobis beatorum
Vitam tuis precibus.

Et nos solvat a peccatis
Pro amore sue matris
Et in regno claritatis
Ducat nos rex pietatis.

Supra celos exaltata (Mch 6717 only)
Et a nato coronata
In hac valle miserie
Sis reis vena venie

The trope in The Hartker Antiphoner (*CH-SGs* 390)

Virgo clemens, virgo pia,
Virgo dulcis, O Maria,
Exaudi preces omnium
Ad te pie clamantium.

Virgo mater ecclesie
Eterna porta glorie
Ora pro nobis omnibus
Qui tui memoriam agimus.

Gloriosa Dei mater
Cujus natus est et pater,
Esto nobis refugium
Apud patrem et filium.

Verses used by the Bridgettines of Syon

Salve celi digna
Mitis et benigna
Que es Christi flosculus
Amenitatis et rivulus
Salve mater pia
Et clemens O Maria.

Ave Christi cella
Nobis mundi mella
Semper da despicere
Et senum hostem vincere
Ave mater pia
Et mitis O Maria.

Vale pulchrum lilium
Nobis placa filium
Ut nos purget a crimine
Pro tuo pro peccamine
Vale mater pia
Et dulcis O Maria.

TABLE 5:8   SOURCES OF THE TROPED *SALVE REGINA*

Source	Date	Provenance	Content	Context	Verses (from hymn)
CH-SGs 390 'Hartker Antiphoner'	s.xi; s.xiii	St Gall (Benedictine)	Text with unheightened neumes, added s.xiii	*Magnificat* antiphon, Annunciation	4, 1', 2
Ob 358, f.145v Psalter	s.xiii med	St Albans (Benedictine)	Text only	Not specified	1, 4, 5
Ob d.4, ff.181-2v Processional	s.xiv²	Dublin (Sarum)	Text and music	Not specified	1, 4, 5, 2, *Dele culpas*
Cjc D.27, f.29v Ordinal	c.1400	St Mary's York (Benedictine)	Text and music	After Compline	1, 4, 5
US-SM 34.B.7 Processional	c.1425	Nuns of Chester (Benedictine)	Neither	After Compline	'with the fyve versus'
Ob D.4.7, f.60, Breviary; and Ob C.781, f.68v Breviary	c.1425-30	Bridgettines of Syon	Text only	Vigils and feasts of St John the Baptist, Sts Peter and Paul, Augustine, Michael; Vigils and feasts of BVM and St Bridget; Corpus Christi, Peter *ad vincula*, All Saints, St Anne	1, 4, 5; *Salve celi, Ave Christi, Vale pulchrum*

Source	Date	Provenance	Content	Context	Verses from hymn
Ob 6, f.100 Processional	s.xv med	Augustinians of Belton, Leics? (Sarum)	Text and music	Not specified	1, 4, 5, 2, *Dele culpas*, *Et nos solvat*
SB 152 Noted Breviary	s.xv²	? (Sarum)	Text only	?	1, 4, 5, 2, *Dele culpas*
Pynson Printed Processional	1502	Sarum	Text and music	Not specified	1, 4, 5, 2, *Dele Culpas*
Dunstable (*MB* viii, 46)	s.xv²	?	1 polyphonic setting	Not specified	1, 4, 5,
Power (*CMM* 1,10)	s.xv²	?	1 polyphonic setting	Not specified	1, 4, 5
Power (?) (*CMM* 1,22)	s.xv²	?	1 polyphonic setting	Not specified	1, 4, 5
WRec 178 Eton Choirbook	c.1480-90	Eton College	14 polyphonic settings — Browne (I & II), Cornysh, Davy, Fayrfax, Horwood, Huchyn, Hygons, Lambe, Sutton, Wylkynson (I)	After Compline	1, 4, 5
			Hacomplaynt, Wylkynson		1, 4, *Dele culpas*
			Hampton		1, 4, 5, *Dele culpas*

DESCRIPTIVE CATALOGUE

INDEX OF MANUSCRIPTS DESCRIBED

Ob e.1*	Hyde Abbey Breviary
Ob f.1	Gloucester Hours (with *Salve regina*)
Ob g.10	Westminster Commemorative Offices
Ob g.12	Pilton Hours
Ob 10	Gloucester Antiphoner
Ob 17	Peterborough Diurnale
Ob 22	Peterborough Psalter
Ob 41	Evesham Breviary
Ob 296	Crowland Psalter with Office of Trinity
Ob 358	St Albans Psalter (with *Salve regina*)
Ob 435	Customary of Eynsham
Ob 579	Leofric Missal
Ouc 169	Ordinal of the Nuns of Barking
Owc 213	Reading Commemorative Office
WO F.160	Worcester Antiphoner
D-Bds 194	Chester Customary
F-VAL 116	Winchcombe Breviary

INDEX TO PROVENANCE OF MANUSCRIPTS

DRu V.V.6	s. xi ex.	Gradual (from Canterbury)
Lbl 1804	s.xv	Hours (with *Salve regina*)

Ely
Cu Ii.4.20	s.xiii	Breviary and Missal

Evesham
Ob 41	*c*.1250-75	Portable Breviary (winter part)

Eynsham
Ccc 265	s.xi med.	*Aelfric's Letter to the Monks of Eynsham*
Ob 435	after 1230	Customary

Exeter
Lbl 2961	s.xi med.	*Leofric Collectar*

Glastonbury
Ob 579	s.x in.; s.xi	*Leofric Missal* (A, B, C)

Gloucester
Ob 10	s.xiii	Antiphoner (also used at Hereford)
Ob f.1	1425-75	Hours

Godstow
Mch 6717	s.xv med.	Psalter

Muchelney
Lbl 21927	s.xi	Psalter with additions
Lbl 43405-6	s.xiii	Breviary

Norwich
Ccc 465	1258-65	Customary

Peterborough
Cmc F.4.10	s.xiv in.	Antiphoner
Ob 22	early s.xiv	Psalter with additions
Llp 198-198b	1371	Ordinal
Ob 17	after 1415	Diurnale

Pilton (cell of Malmesbury)
Ob g.12	1521	Hours

Reading

Owc 213	s.xiii²	Miscellany

St Albans

Lbl 2.A.X	*c.*1140-50	Breviary
Ob 358	1246-60	Psalter with additions
Lbl C.110.a.27	*c.*1535	Breviary

Westminster

Ob g.10	*c.*1400	Miscellany
Lbl C.XI	1259-83	Customary

Wherwell (St Albans)

Cjc C.18	*c.*1150-70	Psalter with Office of BVM

Winchcombe

F-VAL 116	s.xii med.	Breviary

Winchester

Lbl B.III	s.x²	*Regularis Concordia*
Lbl 2.B.V	s.x; s.xi med.	Psalter with additions
Lbl D.XXVI-II	*c.*1023-35	*Prayerbook of Aelfwine*
Lbl A.III	s.xi²	*Regularis Concordia* with additions
DO 26543	s.xv	Hours

Winchester, Hyde Abbey

Ob e.1*	s.xiii	Breviary and Psalter
(with *Ob* 8)		

Worcester

Ccc 391	*c.*1065-56	Portiforium of St Wulfstan
WO F.160	*c.*1230; s.xiv	Antiphoner

York, St Mary's

Cjc D.27	*c.*1400	Customary

DESCRIPTIVE CATALOGUE OF MANUSCRIPTS

Manuscripts are indexed by classification mark in alphabetical order. Each entry contains the following information:

Classification mark (RISM siglum, followed by classification mark in full)
Title of manuscript, date and provenance
Brief description of manuscript (first paragraph)
Account of relevant votive material (second paragraph)
Edition (if any), together with short-title cross-reference
to bibliography (pp.353-363)
Bibliography of secondary sources

Ccc 265   (Cambridge, Corpus Christi College, MS 265, pp.237-268)

Aelfric's Letter to the   s.xi med.   Copied at Worcester for
monks of Eynsham   Eynsham

A customary written for the community of Eynsham (founded 1005), largely based on *Regularis Concordia*, with explanatory passages from Amalarius of Metz. It contains a few significant divergences from the practices of *RC*, such as the omission of any reference to the Easter sepulchre drama (in spite of the full treatment given to the first of *RC*'s Holy Week customs).

Most of the detail on votive observance duplicates that in *RC*; however, the direction that the Morrow Mass might be said for the king is omitted.

See **Aelfric**
Critical edition with analytical notes by Hadrianus Nocent, *CCM*, vii-3, (1984), 149-185.
See also Bateson, Hampshire Record Society, vii (1892), 171-98.

James, *Catalogue of Manuscripts at Corpus Christi*, ii, 14-21.
Ker, *Manuscripts containing Anglo-Saxon*, No.53.
Hall, 'Some Liturgical Notes'.

Ccc **391**   (Cambridge, Corpus Christi College, MS 391)

Portiforium of St Wulstan   1065-6   Worcester Cathedral Priory, from Winchester model

A 'portiforium' or travelling compendium, comprising calendar, psalter, litany, hymnal, collects, private prayers, *capitula*, antiphons, versicles and responds, with some neumatic notation. Concordances with *Ob* e.1* (the Hyde Abbey Breviary) suggest some affinity with Newminster, Winchester. There are several prayers for Winchester saints (Hedda, Grimbald, Brynston, Judoc, Swithun). Some antiphons concord with *WO* F.160, the Worcester Antiphoner, but others had clearly been abandoned by the time that the Antiphoner was copied (*c*.1230). The Worcester provenance is confirmed by an inscription on f.1: *Liber sce. Wygorniens[is]*. . . . Some of the later copying was possibly done by Heming of Worcester. The manuscript bears the title *Portiforium Oswaldi*, but a direct connection with the reformer Oswald, bishop of Worcester and archbishop of York, who died as early as 992 is difficult to substantiate. The Easter Table covers the years between 1064 and 1093, and it may well be that the source was made for Wulfstan, bishop of Worcester 1062-95.

Ccc 391 contains the earliest extant English instances of weekly commemorative offices, addressed to the Holy Cross (Friday) and the BVM (Saturday). The first part of the Office of the Holy Cross has neumatic notation. Several of the texts seem to be newly composed, rather than borrowed from the sanctorale. The Office of the Dead follows the two weekly offices.

See **Worc.Port.**
Edition of text with introduction by Anselm Hughes, *HBS*, lxxxix (1958), xc (1960).

James, *Catalogue of Manuscripts at Corpus Christi*, ii, 241-48.
Ker, *Manuscripts containing Anglo-Saxon*, No.67.
Kaufmann No.3.
McLachlan, 'St Wulfstan's Prayer Book'.

Ccc **441**   (Cambridge, Corpus Christi College, MS 441)

Instructio Noviciorum   s.xiii ex. [?]   Christ Church, Canterbury

A code of instructions for the novices of Christ Church, Canterbury. Knowles suggests that they were based upon a directory derived from Lanfranc's *Constitutions*.

Reference to commemorative offices of the Virgin and Relics (f.378; 379), suffrages and memorials, the Office of All Saints and extraneous psalmody.

See **Cant.Ch.Nov.**
Edition and parallel translation by David Knowles, *The Monastic Constitutions of Lanfranc*, 133-149.

James, *Catalogue of Manuscripts at Corpus Christi*, ii, 349-355.

Ccc **465**   (Cambridge, Corpus Christi College, MS 465)

Norwich Customary   1258-65   Norwich Cathedral

Although termed a customary (f.9: *Incipit Consuetud[inarum] ecclesie Norwyc[ensis]*), the book is less concerned with the affairs of the house than the day-to-day running of the liturgy, and thus in some ways is nearer to an ordinal. The manuscript may well bear traces of the Use of Fécamp, since Herbert Losinga, responsible for the establishment and endowment of the Norwich community (*c*.1100), had previously been prior of Fécamp. Tolhurst considered that the main body of *Ccc* 465 was written between 1258 and 1265, but that the calendar was slightly later (1279-88). He also identified substantial additions in at least five hands, some dealing with the minor reforms stipulated by the General Chapters of 1277 and 1279.

The main body of the book gives directions for a weekly commemorative office of the Virgin with several seasonal alternatives, the Office of the Dead, suffrages, the Morrow Mass and private masses, and various groups of psalms recited as accretions to the office. The source also reflects the influence of two reforming Benedictine Chapters, in later alterations made to the manuscript.

See **Norwich**
Edited with an introduction by Tolhurst, *HBS*, lxxxii (1948).

James, *Catalogue of Manuscripts at Corpus Christi*, ii, 396-7.

Cec **S1.4.6**   (Cambridge, Emmanuel College, MS S1.4.6)

Printed Breviary   1528   St Mary's, Abingdon
(*Pars Aestivalis*)

A breviary or portiforium printed for the community at Abingdon in 1528, as specified in the colophon: *Istud portiferium fuit impressum per Joannem Scholarem in monasterio beate marie uirginis Abendonensi. Anno incarnationis dominice millesimo quingencesimo uicesimo octauo. Et Thome Rowlande abbatis septimo decimo.* This volume consists only of the second part of the complete book (*secunda pars portiferii ad usum nigrorum monacorum Abendonie,* f.5); the *Pars Hiemalis* is missing. One further partial copy survives at Exeter College, Oxford (*Oec* 9M) comprising only the psalter and hymnal sections. All material in *Oec* 9M is duplicated in *Cec* S1.4.6. with the exception of the months May to August in the Calendar. Both temporale (f.5) and sanctorale (f.220) begin after Easter. The Common of Saints occupies ff.174-207. The Abingdon book is one of two printed breviaries issued shortly before the Reformation: the other is *Lbl* C.110.a.27, produced for St Albans in *c.*1535.

Four commemorative offices on ff.207-217v, in honour of the Virgin, Sts Vincent and Edward, Relics, and St Benedict. No weekdays are prescribed. All offices begin with first Vespers; Matins of the Virgin follows the three-nocturn structure with thirteen antiphons in total, the others each have a more condensed two-nocturn framework. The Office of the Dead appears on f.147v. Both Lauds and Vespers are followed by memorials in the usual way, but there is no mention of a post-Compline antiphon.

STC 15792; mentioned in Tolhurst, p.242.

Cjc **68** (Cambridge, St John's College, MS 68 C.18)

St Albans Psalter *c.*1150-70 St Albans and St Bertin, Wherwell

An illuminated psalter with canticles, creeds, the litany, and offices of BVM and the Dead, written in a very large, clear hand. Rodney Thomson identified a St Albans model for the calendar (with some Flemish influence) and decoration by the St Albans 'Simon Master', but he concludes that it was not intended for use there and was not even definitely made at St Albans. The selection of obits suggests that it was copied for a particular person rather than an institution. Shortly after its manufacture, it became the personal property of Matilda de Bailleul, abbess of Wherwell.

Daily Little Office of the Virgin from Matins to Compline on f.236, with integral memorials after Lauds and Vespers to the Trinity, the Holy Cross, St Bertin and All Saints. Three prayers with the rubric *ad S. Mariam* are given on f.226v. The Office of the Dead, copied in a thirteenth-century hand, appears on f.246.

James, *Catalogue of Manuscripts at St John's*, ii, 14-21.
Thomson, *Manuscripts from St Albans Abbey*, i, 56-61.

Cjc **D.27** (Cambridge, St John's College, MS 102. D.27)

Ordinal and Customary of *c.*1400 St Mary's, York
St Mary's York

Detailed customs of St Mary's Abbey, dealing with the manner of observance of the Divine Office, masses, processions and other miscellaneous information on the duties of members of the community. The prologue states that it was drawn up at the instance of the Archbishop of York in order to obtain uniformity of use. The ordinal proper, consisting mainly of incipits, really begins on f.125v, since the First Sunday in Advent deals with the general customs of the house in some detail. The ordinal consists of temporale only, ending with a list of obits and details on the care of a brother at the point of death. The observance of the community at St Mary's shows considerable divergence from other contemporary manuscripts. There is some borrowing from Sarum and a slight resemblance to the use of Muchelney (*Lbl* 43405-6), but many of the customs described in the source appear to be unique. There is some musical notation.

Extensive information on the daily Little Office of the BVM, the singing of a troped *Salve Regina* (complete with music in the source) after Compline, and the celebration of various masses of a votive nature, including a *Missa Familiaris*. There is also mention of the *Trina oratio*, the Office of the Dead and weekly commemorative offices of the BVM and St Benedict, memorials, suffrages, and certain groups of appended psalms.

See **York.SM.Ord.**
Edited with a short commentary and index by Laurentia McLachlan and J.B.L. Tolhurst as *HBS*, lxxiii (1936), lxxv (1937) and lxxxiv (1951).

James, *Catalogue of Manuscripts at St John's*, 135-7.
Frere, No.922.

Cmc **F.4.10**   (Cambridge, Magdalene College, MS F.4.10)

Antiphoner   early s.xiv;   Peterborough
                            late s.xv

One of two complete surviving English Benedictine antiphoners from this period: the other is *WO* F.160. The Peterborough provenance is confirmed by a note on f.8v: *Iste liber est s.petri de Burgo*. Laurentia McLachlan saw this source as representative of a later and more corrupt tradition than the Worcester manuscript, but more recent investigation by Josiah Brady suggests that the Peterborough source may in fact be a witness to an older use, primarily based on Corbie. The book consists of temporale, sanctorale, common, a hymnal and various appendages, including a series of later offices (Corpus Christi, the Visitation, Transfiguration, Name of Jesus, Erminilda and Anne) in a fifteenth-century hand on f.151. The book is one of four Peterborough manuscripts of roughly comparable date, the others being *Ob* 22, *Llp* 198-198b and *Ob* 17.

Two commemorative offices, both with music, to the Virgin and to St Peter with three sets of seasonal texts, consisting of Vespers to None.

James, *Catalogue of Manuscripts at Magdalene*, No.10.
Frere, No.934
Brady, *The Derivation of the English Monastic Uses*
PM, 1, xii, p.x

Ctc **O.7.31**   (Cambridge, Trinity College, MS O.7.31)

Breviary   s.xvi in.   Battle Abbey

A small breviary reputedly copied for Battle in a small, rather indifferent hand. There is no explicit reference to provenance, but there is some emphasis on St Martin and St John the Evangelist in the sanctorale and in the sets of memorials (f.117v) and blessings (f.118v) provided. The source contains very few rubrics.

Four commemorative offices to the Virgin, St John the Evangelist, St Martin and St Benedict on ff.196v-202. The BVM office is constructed with three nocturns, but with only a single antiphon for each group of psalms. Alternative texts are given for Advent. The other offices follow the usual two-nocturn pattern. A miscellanous series of antiphons emphasizing the same saints follows on f.202; these were presumably intended to function as memorials, although this is not stated precisely.

James, *Catalogue of Manuscripts at Trinity*, No.1359.
Frere, No.953.

Cu **Ii.4.20**   (Cambridge, University Library, MS Ii.4.20)

Breviary and Missal   s.xiii   Ely

A large manuscript, with material for both mass and office, partially incomplete, with some missing initials. A small amount of square black notation on red four-line staves accompanies the prefaces of the mass. The hand is at times unclear. The exorcism of salt, proper material for masses from the sanctorale, temporale and common and a series of votive masses occupy ff.172-198. Office material flanks this middle section.

Three commemorative offices to St Peter, St Etheldreda and the Virgin on ff.167-171v. All three offices are of identical two-nocturn construction. The BVM office has seasonal texts for Advent, Christmas to the Purification, Eastertide and *per annum*; St Peter for Eastertide and *per annum* only, and St Etheldreda only a single set of texts. Both of the latter offices were omitted from Advent to the Octave of the Epiphany. The Office of the Dead appears on f.165. Four of the votive masses are for general weekly use (Trinity, Holy Spirit, Holy Cross and BVM), one against the temptations of the flesh, and the rest of the series for the dead.

Frere, No.774

CA 6   (Canterbury Cathedral, Chapter MS Add. 6)

'Burnt Breviary'   s.xiv² [Ker]   Christ Church, Canterbury

The remains of a once extensive manuscript, now in two separate parts, both damaged in a fire at Canterbury in 1674. *CA* 6 (i), the sanctorale, is more severely impaired: only the lower part of the book survives, still attached to the original oak boards. *CA* 6 (ii), the temporale, consists of fewer leaves, but these are rather more complete than those of 6 (i), despite their charred state. A partially conjectural transcript by Dr C.S. Phillips of both manuscripts is boxed with the original material. Phillips also pointed out the close connection between *CA* 6 and *Lbl* 4664, the Coldingham Breviary: presumably Coldingham (via Durham) drew on Canterbury as a liturgical model. *DRu* V.V.6 also testifies to the connection between Canterbury and Durham. *CA* 6 has abundant detailed rubrics; Phillips suggested that it may even have incorporated much of the Canterbury ordinal. The source clearly bears some relation to *CA* 3, a collection of sixteenth-century fragments of a breviary of Canterbury Use, although the latter contains no votive material.

Three commemorative offices to the Virgin, St Thomas of Canterbury and Relics. No weekdays are specified, but all three offices were to be omitted on twelve-lesson feasts and during octaves. Matins of the BVM office (f.81) followed the two-nocturn pattern. Partial texts for a daily Little Office of the Virgin also survive, headed *Qualiter dicende sunt mat[utine] et hore de sancta maria sing[ulis die]bus priuatim per totum annum* (f.81v). These end incomplete in the middle of Matins. Further votive material comprises Offices of the Dead and of All Saints and a series of memorials (here termed *commemorationes*) to the Cross, BVM, St Thomas of Canterbury, St Aelfege and St Dunstan.

Ker, *Medieval Manuscripts*, ii, 303-5.
Phillips, *Canterbury Cathedral in the Middle Ages*, 18-26.
Brady, *The Derivation of the English Monastic Uses*.

DO **26543**   (Downside, Abbey Library, MS 26543)

Horae   s.xv med.   Winchester Cathedral Priory

A damaged fragment of a Book of Hours for monastic use. All leaves have been cut across the middle, and eighteen survive as half leaves only. The Winchester provenance is suggested by the local saints included in the suffrages on f.11v.

Matins and Lauds of the Little Office of the Virgin occur on ff.1-6v, incomplete; thereafter there are several leaves missing. A series of suffrages to the Trinity, the Cross, the Virgin, Apostles, Thomas of Canterbury (erased), Sts Birinus, Swithun and Ethelwold, St Benedict, St Katherine, Relics, Peace and All Saints is given on ff.9v-12v. An untroped form of *Salve regina* with versicle and collect appears on f.16, followed by a memorial of the Passion.

Ker, *Medieval Manuscripts*, ii, 445-47.
Tolhurst, 241.

DRc **A.IV.19**   (Durham, Cathedral Library, MS A.IV.9)

The Durham Collectar s.x (early):   Southern England
[Durham Ritual]
                    additions of later   St Cuthbert,
                    s.x and s.xi   Chester-le-Street

A manuscript compiled for a secular community, probably for a priest. The book is a collectar (900-25) with texts for the office copied from a continental exemplar. The additions include a gloss in Old English, collects to St Cuthbert, and a colophon dated 970. At least six hands are identifiable in the manuscript, in addition to that of the original scribe from southern England. Towards the end of the tenth century, additions were made by Aldred, the glossator of the Lindisfarne Gospels. He appended Anglo-Saxon glosses and signed the Latin collects for St Cuthbert (f.84) with his name, the place and the date: 10 August, 970. There are further additions of the eleventh century.

Sets of devotions comprising antiphons, versicles and collects, which seem to be early examples of memorials. These appear on ff.68v-71 and were probably added *c.*970. A set of Gallican *capitella* is given on ff.78-79, Celtic *capitella* on ff.80v-82.

See **Durham.Coll.**
Introduction and facsimile in T.J. Brown, *The Durham Ritual.*
Text also edited by U. Lindelöf, *SS,* 140 (1927).

Ker, *Manuscripts containing Anglo-Saxon,* No.106.
Temple No. 3.

DRc **B.IV.24**   (Durham, Cathedral Library, MS B.IV.24)

Lanfranc's	s.xi[2]	Canterbury, Christ Church
Constitutions		
etc.	additions of s.xi/xii	Durham

A miscellaneous collection of material, probably compiled shortly after the Conquest, from French models. In addition to the Rule of St Benedict, the manuscript contains the earliest extant copy of Lanfranc's *Constitutions,* which reflect the new liturgical code drawn up for the Benedictine community at Canterbury by Lanfranc shortly after the Norman Conquest. *DRc* B.IV.24 is one of a number of Canterbury manuscripts sent to Durham in the latter part of the eleventh century.

In spite of the apparent evidence of liturgical remodelling by the Normans, the *Constitutions* retain many of the observances of *Regularis Concordia:* the Offices of the Dead and of All Saints, the Morrow Mass, Masses for the Dead, the *Trina oratio* and appended psalms, and memorials. There is no reference to either the commemorative office or the Little Office of the BVM.

See **Lanfranc**
Knowles, *Decreta Lanfranci, CCM,* iii (1967), 1-149.
Knowles (with parallel translation), *The Monastic Constitutions of Lanfranc.*

Ker, *Manuscripts containing Anglo-Saxon,* No.109.

DRu **V.V.6**   (Durham, University Library, Cosin MS V.V.6)

Cosin Gradual   1066-1100   Christ Church Canterbury
              additions of   and Durham
              late s.xi and s.xii

A small precentor's book, comprising gradual, kyriale, tonary and processional with diastematic Anglo-Norman notation, partially erased. It was written at Christ Church, Canterbury in the last third of the eleventh century, but sent to the new cathedral-monastery of Durham with a number of other Canterbury books, probably in the early 1080s. Additions (mostly related to local feasts) were made to the manuscript at Durham in the late eleventh or twelfth century. The repertory as a whole has strong affinities with a group of sources associated with Winchester, Corbie and St Denis, suggesting common roots possibly derived from tenth-century foreign contacts in the time of Ethelwold. Liturgical ordering of the gradual may be the result of Norman influence from Bec.

Alcuin's series of votive masses, one for each day of the week, is given on f.83v. A set of *ordines* for various votive masses is added on f.125v.

Hartzell, 'An unknown English Benedictine Gradual'.

Lbl **A.III**   (London, British Library, Cotton MS Tiberius A.III)

Regularis Concordia   s.xi med.   Canterbury, Christ
with additions   [Ker]   Church [?]

Non-liturgical composite manuscript, including miscellaneous devotional material, the Rule of St Benedict (ff.118-63) and *Regularis Concordia* (ff.3-27v), both with interlinear Anglo-Saxon glosses, and both preceded by full-page miniatures. This is the later of only two surviving copies of *Regularis Concordia*, [see also *Lbl* B.III], with modifications, possibly for use at Canterbury. Temple considers that the provenance of the manuscript is identifiable by its table of contents (f.117) added in the twelfth century, which corresponds to an item listed in the fourteenth-century catalogue of the Christ Church Library. Inclusion of Winchester saints in parts of the source suggests a Winchester exemplar.

As *Lbl* B.III, but this later version of *RC* rearranges parts of the Prologue and adds a list of chapters and an Epilogue. A full Marian office similar to that in *Lbl* 2.B.V is appended, with a series of memorials after Lauds and Vespers. The Office of All Saints (Lauds and Vespers only) appears on f.57: Vespers is followed by a series of 'suffrages' which is not mentioned in the Winchester version of *RC*.

See *RC* and **Dewick**
RC edited by Symons, *CCM*, vii-3 (1984), 69-147; the Office of the Virgin on f.57 by E.S. Dewick, *HBS*, xxi (1901).

Ker, *Manuscripts containing Anglo-Saxon*, No.186
Backhouse No. 28
Temple No. 100.

Lbl **B.III**   (London, British Library, Cotton MS Faustina B.III)

Regularis Concordia   s.x^2 Canterbury, Christ Church
with OE translation

The earlier of two extant copies of *Regularis Concordia*, without a title and with some sections of the Prologue displaced. The main sequence of the manuscript breaks off during the course of Chapter 12; one of the missing folios can seemingly be supplied by f.177 of the later copy of *RC* (*Lbl* A.III), written in the same hand. This leaf has the antiphon *Hodie in pace*, complete with neumatic notation, appended in the margin. A variant form of the letter to be sent round to all monasteries on the death of a monk on f.198 of *Lbl* B.III is appended in another tenth-century hand: details recorded here confirm the connection with Christ Church, Canterbury.

Reference to the *Trina oratio*, psalms for the royal household after the office, miscellanous appended psalms, the Morrow Mass and private masses, antiphons after Lauds and Vespers, and the Offices of All Saints and the Dead.

Symons, *CCM*, vii-3

Ker, *Manuscripts containing Anglo-Saxon*, No.155.

Lbl **C.XI**   (London, British Library, Cotton MS Otho C.XI)

Westminster Customary   1259-83   St Peter's, Westminster

The extant material forms the fourth part of the Customary of St Peter's Abbey, Westminster, compiled (as the colophon indicates) under the authority of Richard de Ware, abbot 1259-83. The manuscript was badly damaged by fire in 1731.

Extensive information on the duties of the *custos* of the Lady Chapel, including a passage on the daily celebration of the Lady Mass. There is also reference to the singing of the Marian antiphon *Salve regina* after Compline, *ex moderno et non ex veteri usu*. The book is clearly related to *Lbl* C.XII (the Customary of St Augustine's, Canterbury), which E.M. Thompson considered to be modelled on it.

See **West.Cust.**
Thompson, *HBS*, xxviii (1904).

Lbl **C.XII**   (London, British Library, Cotton MS Faustina C.XII)

Customary of   c. 1330-40   St Augustine's, Canterbury
St Augustine's, Canterbury

A slightly later version of *Lbl* C.XI (the Westminster Customary). Deals with the general running of the house: excommunication, the refectory, the cloister, the chapter, admissions to confraternity etc.

Two weekly commemorative offices, one to the BVM (Saturday), the other to local saints (Tuesday) are mentioned.

See **Cant.SA.Cust.**
Thompson, *HBS*, xxiii (1902).

Lbl C.110.a.27 (London, British Library, Printed Book C.110.a.27)

Printed Breviary *c.*1535 St Albans

One of only two extant printed monastic breviaries, produced for St Albans by J. Herford. No title-page or colophon survives, and the pages are not numbered. The book comprises temporale, calendar, psalter, litany, blessings, suffrages and sanctorale, with several miscellanous additions.

Commemorative offices to the Virgin (Saturday), St Alban (Tuesday) and St Benedict (Wednesday) occur in a section headed *Capitulum de solitis commemorationibus beate Marie et beatorum Albani et Benedicti per hebdomadam faciendis*. The Marian office exhibits close textual correspondence with the commemorative office in the twelfth-century St Albans source, *Lbl* 2.A.X. A lengthy rubric indicates that all three offices were to be transferred on certain specified occasions, and omitted entirely from Advent to Epiphany, Ash Wednesday to Low Sunday, within octaves and on Rogation days. Offices to St Amphibalus (mostly borrowed from the Common) and the Trinity follow immediately in the manuscript, but without indication of context. It is possible that both were treated as commemorative offices without prescribed weekdays. The independent Office for Trinity Sunday itself (in the sanctorale) has very little proper material: the rubric simply indicates *cetera ut in commemoratione*.

STC 15793.5

Lbl D.XXVI-II (London, British Library, Cotton MS Titus D.XXVI-II)

'Prayerbook of Aelfwine' *c.*1023-35 Winchester, Newminster

Miscellaneous collection of private devotional material in Latin and Anglo-Saxon: prayers, devotions, offices, computistical texts, etc. Originally one manuscript; now bound in two separate parts. Two full-page 'Winchester' drawings (D.XXVII f.65v and f.75v) precede principal liturgical texts. Written for Aelfwine before his appointment to the abbacy of Newminster (1032-35), as shown in D.XXVII which records his ownership: *Aelwino monacho aeque decano . . . me possidit* (f.13v). Obits of Aelfwine's mother (1029) and of Abbot Byrthmear (1030) are given in a different hand, suggesting that the manuscript was complete by then.

Lbl D.XXVII contains three single office hours, presumably for use as private devotions, each of identical structure. These are addressed to the Trinity (f.76), Holy Cross (f.80) and BVM (ff.81v-85). Each hour is modelled on Vespers, but uses the normal arrangement of psalms for secular Prime. Antiphons appear to be mostly borrowed from the regular office (some concordances with *Ccc* 391, the Portiforium of St Wulstan). There are additional prayers to various saints appended to each private office.

Temple, *Anglo-Saxon Manuscripts 900-1066*, No. 77
Backhouse, No. 61
Ker, *Manuscripts containing Anglo-Saxon*, No.202
Tolhurst, 129-30.

Lbl **2.A.X** (London, British Library, Royal MS 2.A.X)

Breviary   s.xii med.   St Albans

Breviary with hymns, psalter, canticles, litany, small sanctorale (with propers for Purification, Assumption, Nativity BVM and Annunciation given separately on ff.111v-122v). K.D. Hartzell sees the manuscript as a 'portiforium' rather than a true breviary, on account of its small format; Rodney Thomson's analysis is similar: the sort of book 'which each monk would have had a copy when in choir'. Thomson considers that the presence of two distinctive hands and several liturgical details confirm the St Albans origin. There is also an inscription on f.2: *Hic est liber Sancti Albani quem qui abstulerit aut titulum deleuerit anathema sunt. amen.*

The source places some emphasis on Marian devotion. In addition to the four Marian feasts (see above), there is a Saturday commemorative office of the BVM (f.135), headed *In commemoratio Sancte Marie*, consisting of First Vespers, Matins (with twelve lessons), Lauds and Second Vespers. Most items are given as incipits only. Several texts appear to be borrowed from the Assumption, but some have no concordance elsewhere in the manuscript. The Marian antiphon *Ave regina celorum* with rubric *In ueneratione sanctae Marie. ad uesperas* is given separately on f.62, with no specific function prescribed. There is a three-lesson Office of the BVM (consisting of the three readings at Matins only) on f.201; twelve lessons *de sancto Albano* follow (ff.201-6v).

Thomson, I, 94, no.25.
Hartzell, *The Musical Repertoire at St Albans Abbey.*

***Lbl* 2.B.V**   (London, British Library, Royal MS 2.B.V)

Psalter etc   s.x med. with added   Winchester and Canterbury
                     leaves (*c.*1066-87)

Psalter with Anglo-Saxon gloss and Latin *scholia*, suggesting that it was copied for non-liturgical use (perhaps for teaching or reference purposes.) A prayer prefixed to the appended office at the beginning of the manuscript (see below) contains an appeal for the restoration of land originally donated to the house of supplicants, which was dedicated to Mary: Dewick suggests that this may have been the Nunnaminster (St Mary's), Winchester. Ker also notes the references to the Winchester saints Machutus and Eadburga in this preliminary prayer, which he considers to have been copied in the early eleventh century, but the Old English notes and the presence of a letter-mark show that the manuscript was at Christ Church, Canterbury in the eleventh century and later.

One of the earliest complete Little Offices of the Virgin, revealing both monastic and secular features, is given on the prefatory leaves of the manuscript. (Dewick suggests that these were appended during the second half of the eleventh century.) The overall structure of the office is mostly monastic, but the choice of psalmody suggests the influence of the secular *cursus*. Antiphons, hymns, responds and collects are largely borrowed from the Marian feasts, while all readings are from *The Song of Songs*. The office bears strong similarities to another complete Marian office in *Lbl* A.III. The prefatory supplication to Mary is of strongly conventual character and may be an indication that the office was intended for conventual rather than private use.

See **Dewick**
Text of office edited with an introduction and partial facsimile in Dewick, *HBS*, xxi (1902);

Ker, *Manuscripts containing Anglo-Saxon*, No.249.

Lbl **1005**   (London, British Library, MS Harley 1005)

Customary   *c.*1234   Bury St Edmunds

Gransden suggests a date of *c.*1234 for this manuscript, since the author of the customary had twice been one of the custodians of the pyx, although no more than this is known about him. The book relates to rights and duties of the abbot and his obedientiaries, monastic offices and miscellaneous customs. It represents a period at which new customs were proliferating, but life does not seem to have been particularly strict: certain customs forbidden by the General Chapter were accepted at Bury.

Two commemorative offices, one to the Virgin, the other to St Edmund, with the regulations pertaining to each. Also references to the Offices of All Saints and the Dead.

See **Bury**
Gransden, *HBS*, xcix (1973).

Lbl **1804**   (London, British Library, MS Harley 1804)

Miscellaneous Offices   s.xv[1]   Durham Cathedral

Little Office of BVM, suffrages, penitential psalms, litany, calendar, obits and other miscellanous psalms and devotions. Apparently for private use. Provenance confirmed on f.13: *Obituarum Ecclesiae Dunelmensis.*

Lttle Office of BVM with *Salve regina* after Compline and the memorial of the Passion which followed. Suffrages (f.65v) consisting of antiphon, versicle with response and collect, of Holy Spirit, Angels, John the Baptist, John the Evangelist, Peter and Paul, Andrew, Aidan and Oswald, Laurence, Thomas, bishop, Blasius, Holy Martyrs, Nicholas, Martin, Edmund, Benedict, Leonard, All Saints, Mary Magdalene, Katherine, Ebbe, Holy Virgins, Cuthbert, Relics, Peace.

***Lbl* 2961**   (London, British Library, MS Additional 2961)

Leofric Collectar   1046-72   Exeter [Probably one of
                             [Watson]   Leofric's gifts to Exeter]

A collectar containing the chapters and collects for the year with some
hymns appended, but no lessons. Antiphons and hymn incipits have
adiastematic notation appended. The manuscript was compiled for the use
of Leofric, bishop of Crediton (and later Exeter) 1046-72. There are four
hands in the manuscript, some of which appear to concord with parts of the
Exeter collection of books. Two marginal notes on the first page of the
manuscript refer to Leofric: the book may well have been the *collectaneum*
mentioned as one of Leofric's gifts to Exeter in *Ob* MS D.ii.16 and Exeter
MS 3501. Seemingly a manuscript for use at the secular cathedral of Exeter,
but related to *Ccc* 391 (Portiforium of St Wulfstan). Both appear to have
been influenced by the Low Countries.

Two sets of 'suffrages' for recitation after Vespers, each added at a later
date than the rest of the source, on a blank page. The second set bears
similarities to those in the Portiforium of St Wulfstan (*Ccc* 391). They are
addressed to the Virgin, the Holy Cross, and All Saints, consisting of
antiphon, versicle and collect. One or more of these elements changed in
certain specified seasons.

See **Leofric Coll.**
Frere, *HBS,* xlv (1914) and lvi (1921).

Drage, *Bishop Leofric and the Exeter Cathedral Chapter.*

***Lbl* 4664**   (London, British Library, MS Harley 4664)

Breviary   s.xiii   Coldingham (Durham)

Breviary with lavish illumination (as f.12v), but few rubrics and no musical
notation. The calendar emphasizes St Cuthbert, and there is an explicit
reference to Coldingham (cell to Durham) on 29 April: *Dedicacio altar[is]
S.Michael[is] in Coldingha[m].* The presence of the Translation of St
Margaret of Scotland on 19 July suggests that the book was compiled after
1259. C.H. Phillips pointed out the close correspondence between this book
and *CA* 6, the thirteenth-century 'Burnt Breviary' from Christ Church,
Canterbury. Further research by J.D. Brady has confirmed this connection,

and established the apparent independence of the Canterbury-Durham liturgy from other mainstream English practices.

Surprisingly, *Lbl* 4664 contains scarcely any reference to votive material with the exception of the usual memorials after Lauds and Vespers. There are no commemorative offices.

Phillips, unpublished introduction to transcript of *CA* 6
Brady, *The English Monastic Uses.*

Lbl 21927   (London, British Library, MS Additional 21927)

Psalter with additions   *c.*1175   Muchelney [?]

Psalter, calendar, creeds, litany, collects and Hours of BVM. Both Tolhurst and *Latin Service Books* suggest a Muchelney provenance.

The complete Little Office of the Virgin is given, from Matins to Compline (ff.101v-105v)

Lbl Catalogue, *Latin Service Books*, No.76
Tolhurst, 122, 239.

Lbl **43405-6**   (London, British Library, MSS Add. 43405-6)

Breviary   s.xiii[2]   Muchelney

A large breviary bound as two separate volumes. *Lbl* 43405 consists exclusively of the temporale, with moderately detailed rubrics. *Lbl* 43406 contains the calendar, psalter, litany, Office of the Dead, and the sanctorale (f.98). Rubrics are often faded and there is no musical notation. Both volumes have prefatory leaves covered in close cursive script, some of the material directly related to Muchelney.

A three-lesson commemorative office of the Virgin follows the Common on f.326, with alternative seasonal sets of lessons. Lessons for what appears to be a commemorative office of St Peter follow. There are also references to processions after Vespers and Lauds, some to the Lady altar, and memorials of the Cross, BVM and All Saints after these hours.

Llp 198-198b   (London, Lambeth Palace, MSS 198-198b)

Consuetudinary   1371 [Tolhurst]   Peterborough

This large consuetudinary is in three parts, copied in a similar script, but by different scribes. *Llp* 198 contains the first two parts, consisting of computational tables, a calendar, the temporale from Easter to Advent (f.9) and the sanctorale for the same period (f.161). 198b contains the third part, with calendar (f.10), and the summer *historiae* (f.18). There is a reference to Ricardum Asshton, abbot of Peterborough 1438-1476, on f.1 of 198b.

Four commemorative offices to the Virgin, Relics, St Peter and St Benedict.

James, *Catalogue of Manuscripts in the Library of Lambeth Palace*, ii, 309-312.

Llp 558   (London, Lambeth Palace, MS 558)

Psalter with   late s.xiii;   Christ Church, Canterbury
additions   additions of early s.xv

A small, illuminated psalter (ff.34v-155) with monastic canticles, miscellaneous hymns, the Office of the Dead and a list of masses for benefactors. Rubric on f.14 *Psalterium do[m]pni Ioh[ann]is Holyngbourne monachi eccl. christi. cant* confirms the Canterbury provenance, also that on f.250: *Hec sunt officia et beneficia fraternitatis ad que facienda quilibet monachus eccl. Chr. Cant. tenetur et obligatur, ut patet in illorum martilogio et multis aliis scripturis de officiis et beneficiis compositis et sigillo confirmatis*. Some musical notation.

Little Office of BVM on f.252 (*Inc[ipiunt] matut[ine] de domina sec[undum] usu[m] ecclesie Christi Cantuarie. hoc modo*). Three-lesson Matins; *Salve regina* with versicle *Ave Maria*, collect *Omnipotens* and blessing *Per intercessionem* to follow after Lauds, None, Vespers and Compline of Our Lady, but preceding the suffrages and memorial of the Passion where these occurred. A list of suffrages given from f.259v: Peter and Paul; St Andrew, apostle; St John, apostle and evangelist; Apostles; St Thomas of Canterbury (erased); St Elphege, Stephen, Laurence and other martyrs; Martyrs; St Dunstan; St Benedict; Relics; Confessors; St Mary Magdalene; Virgins; Peace; All Saints.

James, *Manuscripts in the Library of Lambeth Palace*, v, 761-765.
Frere, No.4.

Mch 6717   (Manchester, Chetham's Library MS 6717 (Mun A.6.74))

Psalter with Hours   s.xv med.   Godstow nunnery, near Oxford

A small psalter with miscellaneous additions: the Little Office of the Virgin
following the Use of Sarum (ff.116-126v), litanies, the Hours of the Trinity
and the Holy Spirit, and the Office of the Dead. The anathema on f.148v
confirms that it was written for the Benedictine nuns of Godstow: *Istud
psalterium dedit Iohannes Gyste armiger ad vsum monialium monasterii
Sancti Iohannis baptiste de Godestow et si quis illud alienauerit a dicto
monasterio anathema sit amen.*

A complete Little Office of the Virgin from Matins to Compline,
corresponding closely to the texts and forms of the Sarum Hours. There are
extensive suffrages after Lauds, including St Julian, St Gregory, and Sts
Katherine, Margaret and Mary Magdalene. Compline is followed by *Salve
regina* with a seven-verse trope. The Hours of the Holy Spirit on ff.22v-27
survive in only two other English Benedictine sources, *Llp* 368 and *Lbl* 155.

Ker, *Medieval Manuscripts*, iii, 352-3.
Frere, No. 633.

Ob e.1*   (Oxford, Bodleian, Rawlinson liturg. e.1*)

Breviary etc.   *c.*1300   Hyde Abbey, Winchester

One of two manuscripts copied for use at Hyde Abbey, Winchester,
probably during the abbacy of Symon de Kanings (1292-1304), since Robert
de Poman, his predecessor (d.1292) appears in the Calendar. The
manuscript comprises temporale, sanctorale from 9 January to 21
December, Common of Saints, and votive material. Tolhurst considered that
it may well have been intended for use in conjunction with *Ob* 8, on the
basis that this latter source supplied 'missing material'. Both books have
similiar bindings and layout, and although the scribe is likely to have been
different, Tolhurst considered that the illuminations in each source were
likely to be the product of one man.

Little Office and Saturday Office of BVM, Votive masses of Holy Trinity,
Holy Spirit, Holy Cross, BVM, Angels, relics, All Saints etc; Chapter
Office.

See **Hyde Abbey**
Edited with *Ob* 8 by Tolhurst as the Hyde Abbey Breviary: *HBS,* lxix
(1932), lxx (1933), lxxi (1934), lxxvi (1938), lxxviii (1939), lxxx (1942).

Van Dijk i,187;

***Ob* f.1**   (Oxford, Bodleian, MS Rawlinson liturg. f.1)

Hours   *c.*1425-75   St Peter's, Gloucester

A small book of hours, with French illuminations in the margins. The
liturgical material suggests that the manuscript was intended for private use:
there are no commemorative offices and the groups of psalms (gradual and
penitential) are familiar elements in books of hours. There are three
references to the monastery of St Peter's, Gloucester in the manuscript
(f.10v, f.53 and f.116).

The Little Office of the BVM with the Hours of the Cross and the Holy
Spirit worked in as an integral part; *Salve regina* after Lauds, None and
Vespers of BVM, preceding the memorial of the Passion, *Sancta Maria non
est* after Compline of BVM; *Trina oratio* after Compline and after Chapter;
the Office of the Dead (with Vespers added in a later hand); Gradual psalms
(f.116); Penitential psalms (f.125); Chapter office of Prime; Psalms for use
after Compline.

Van Dijk, iv,4.

***Ob* g.10**   (Oxford, Bodleian, MS Rawlinson liturg. g.10)

Commemorative Offices etc.   ?s.xiv ex.-s.xv.in.   St Peter's,
                                    ? Late s.xv [Van Dijk]   Westminster [?]

A small manuscript, possibly of Westminster provenance (Van Dijk's
observation on the basis of script). It contains four commemorative offices,
eight memorials, the propers for the Feast of All Saints, *preces* and graces,
and the Office of the Dead (f.13) with some musical notation.

Commemorative offices of BVM (f.31v), Peter and Paul (f.32), Edward, king and confessor (f.36v) and St Benedict (f.42v), all with two-nocturn Matins. Suffrages of Holy Trinity, Holy Cross, BVM, Peter, Edward, Dunstan, Benedict and Holy relics (from f.46). Additions concerning memorials f.71v, f.73.

See **West.Miss.**
Legg, *HBS,* xii, 1303-1384.

Van Dijk, No.347

Ob **g.12**   (Oxford, Bodleian, MS Rawlinson liturg. g.12)

Hours   1521   St Mary's Pilton, Devon
                                         [cell to Malmesbury Abbey]

A miscellaneous manuscript, but apparently for private rather than communal usage. A colophon on f.295 gives the date: *Anno domini mccccc. xxi. Laus et honor. Filius soli Deo. Nomen scriptoris Thomas Olston plenus amoris.* Olston was elected prior of Pilton in 1472.

Office of Our Lady with three-lesson Matins (f.1); Suffrages (*suffragia*) of Trinity, Cross, BVM, Peter and Paul, St Aldhelm, St Benedict, relics and All Saints to follow Vespers and Matins (f.79v); Office of Dead with three-lesson Matins (f.201) followed by *Verba mea, Domine in furore tuo* and *Domine Deus meus*; Commemorative offices of the Cross, BVM (with twelve-lesson Matins), St Aldhelm and St Benedict (f.228v). Prayers and devotions, some to local saints, on f.131.

Van Dijk iv,8.

***Ob* 10**   (Oxford, Bodleian, MS Jesus College 10)

Antiphoner	late s.xii	St Peter's Gloucester;
	with additions	St Guthlac's Hereford
	of s.xiii-s.xiv	

A rubricated portable Antiphoner consisting mostly of the Day Office, but with the antiphons for Lauds and hymns for Matins. Temporale and sanctorale are combined. There are some processions and a few masses. The manuscript has some musical notation. The Dedication of St Peter's (18 September) and the feast of the Cell of St Guthlac (17 October) are added in the Calendar in another hand.

Commemorative offices of BVM, St Peter and St Benedict. Memorial antiphons after Lauds and Vespers, those for Advent mostly borrowed from the commemorative office of the same season. There are also rubrics dealing with the Morrow Mass.

Van Dijk ii,136
Frere, No.537
Tolhurst, 289.

***Ob* 17**   (Oxford, Bodleian, MS Gough Liturg 17)

Diurnale   after 1415   St Peter's, Peterborough

A very small manuscript, without material for the Night Office. The Peterborough provenance is recognisable from an entry in the calendar for 28 September: *Dedicacio ecclesie burgi*, and an inscription on f.iv: *Liber ffratris Humfridi Matures monachi de burgo sancti Petri cuius anime Deus propicietur. Amen.* The book consists of temporale (ff.1-93), commemorative offices, calendar, psalter, litany, Office of the Dead, sanctorale and Common of Saints.

Five commemorative offices to the Virgin (Saturday), Relics, St Benedict, St Peter and St Oswald, all beginning with first Vespers, and all with two-nocturn Matins. A few seasonal alternatives, particularly for the BVM office.

Van Dijk, ii, 322b.

Ob **22**   (Oxford, Bodleian, MS Barlow 22)

Psalter   s.xiv¹   St Peter's, Peterborough

A lavishly-illuminated choir-psalter, with miniatures and borders, made by a Fenland workshop in the earlier fourteenth century and presented to Peterborough Abbey by Brother Walter de Rouceby (d.1341): *Psalterium fratris Walteri de Rouceby* (f.1). It includes additional weekly and daily canticles, the litany and the Office of the Dead.

Additions on f.2v of three lessons for votive offices of St Benedict, St Peter and BVM. These are clearly related to offices in three other Peterborough manuscripts (*Llp* 198-198b, *Ob* 17 and *Cmc* F.4.10). There is a prayer in honour of the Virgin, *O regina mundi*, on f.4v, and the Office of the Dead occurs on f.196.

Van Dijk ii, 18
Frere, No.177
Tolhurst, 240.

Ob **41**   (Oxford, Bodleian, MS Barlow 41)

Breviary (Winter part) *c.*1250-75   St Mary's, Evesham

Consisting of temporale, psalter, canticles and sanctorale from St Andrew to St Aplhege.

Two commemorative offices, to the Virgin (Saturday) and Relics (Thursday). Office of the Dead on f.242.

Van Dijk ii, 264
Frere, 99.

Ob 296   (Oxford, Bodleian, MS Douce 296)

Psalter with additions   s.xi med.   St Guthlac, Crowland

Choir-psalter with weekly and daily canticles, litany, private prayers etc. The provenance is suggested by the presence of St Felix, St Guthlac and St Pega in the Calendar. Two full-page illuminations.

One of the earliest extant daily votive offices, unusually addressed to the Trinity (*Cursus de Sancta Trinitate*) appears on ff.127v-130v. Vespers to Sext are given; None is missing. Matins has one nocturn. Prayers for use before and after the recitation of psalms for various intentions on f.120v.

Van Dijk ii, 7.

Ob 358   (Oxford, Bodleian, MS New College 358)

Psalter   s.xiii med.   St Albans

Portable psalter with canticles, litany etc. One full-page illuminated initial. Feasts in the calendar suggest a St Albans provenance. Edmund Rich, canonized in 1246 appears in the main hand at 16 November, the obits of the father, mother and uncle of Abbot John VI (Whethamstede) at 5 March.

Troped *Salve regina* with versicle and collect on f.145v, which Ker considers to have been added at the end of the thirteenth century; Office of Dead on f.140.

Ker, *Medieval Manuscripts*, iii, 667
Van Dijk ii, 16.

Ob 435   (Oxford, Bodleian, MS Bodley 435, ff.3-131)

Eynsham Customary   after 1230   Eynsham

Gransden considers that the customary was compiled after January 1228/9, since a Chapter ordinance of this year is mentioned at paragraph 120. The customary contains relatively little liturgical information, but concentrates on domestic matters and the duties of the obedientiaries. Liturgical matters were treated more extensively in a companion book (referred to several times as *alio consutudinario* in *Ob* 435), now lost. There are many citations from other sources, including Lanfranc, the twelfth-century *Liber Ordines* of the Austin Canons of St Victor's, Paris, the Customary of Westminster and that of St Mary's, York. The manuscript also has close connections with *Lbl* B.VI, the Abingdon Customary compiled in 1189.

Reference to a twelve-lesson Saturday commemorative office of the BVM and daily *Completorium dei genitricis*, which may have formed part of a complete Little Office of the BVM. There was also a *Collatio dei genitricis* after Compline.

See **Eynsham**
Edited with an introduction and index by Gransden, *CCM*, ii (1963).

Ob **579**   (Oxford, Bodleian, MS Bodley 579)

Leofric Missal	A	s.x in	Original section from Arras or Cambrai area
	B	969-78	Additions from S.W. England (Glastonbury)
	C	s.xi med; s.xii	Additions made at Exeter

The oldest extant Sacramentary, probably of English origin. The hand in parts of the manuscript suggests a continental scribe, but certain texts (such as the Coronation Service) point to execution in England. The source falls into three major parts: the original section, *Leofric A* (*c*.900), probably copied in the region of Arras or Cambrai; *Leofric B* (ff.38-58), *c*.970-80, consisting of a Calendar and other computistical matter from Glastonbury Abbey, and possibly executed before 978 since St Edward, King and Martyr is not included; *Leofric C* (additions of the eleventh and twelfth century made at Exeter). The manuscript was probably put together in its present form by Leofric, bishop of Exeter 1042-72 and presented by him to Exeter Cathedral, as recorded in the dedicatory matter at the beginning of the manuscript. There is some musical notation.

Votive masses (ff.212-40); masses for the dead (ff.240-45v).The source as a whole witnesses to the introduction of foreign liturgical models into England.

See **Leofric.Miss.**
Warren, *The Leofric Missal*, 1883

Van Dijk, i, 10
Temple, No. 17
Drage, *Bishop Leofric.*

Ouc **169**   (Oxford, University College, MS 169)

Ordinal of the Nuns   *c.*1400   St Mary and St Ethelburga,
of Barking   Barking

Written at the request of Sibille Fenton, Abbess of Barking 1394-1419, and presented by her to the convent in 1404 for her own use and that of her successors. The directions are almost exclusively concerned with the choir. The opening words of the hymns are given with square notation.

Office of the BVM with twelve-lesson Matins on Saturday; the Psalter and fifteen psalms of BVM, weekly recitation of *Dirige* with nine lessons, retention of the Office of All Saints, suffrages of the saints, directions for the Chapter Mass and recitation of *Salve regina* after High Mass.

See **Barking**
Tolhurst, *HBS*, lxv (1927), lxvi (1928).

Van Dijk iii, 217

Owc **213**   (Oxford, Worcester College, MS 213)

Miscellany   s.xiii²   Reading

A collection of annals, tracts, meditations and miscellaneous devotions given to Reading Abbey by the prior, Alan: *Hunc librum dedit Alanus prior deo et beate marie de Rading'* . . . (p.2). Ker points out that there is some emphasis on St James, who was held in special honour at Reading. Two leaves of polyphonic music were bound into the manuscript as flyleaves (now bound separately).

A commemorative office of the Virgin with seasonal texts appears on p.340 (*incipit seruitium de beata uirgine maria*), ending incomplete in the middle of the tenth Matins reading for the Advent period. There is also a series of readings for Matins of the Little Office of the Virgin, one set for each day of the week: *incipiunt lecciones de domina nostra* (pp.329-32).

Ker, *Medieval Manuscripts*, iii, 726-732.

WO **F.160**   (Worcester, Cathedral Library, MS F.160)

Worcester Antiphoner   *c.*1230   Worcester Cathedral
                           with s.xiv additions

Antiphoner, processional, calendar, psalter, hymnal, collectar, tonary, Kyriale, gradual and fragmentary proser, with some quadratic notation, copied at Worcester. Portions of the antiphoner section are incorrectly bound (correctly reconstructed in *PM*).

A Saturday commemorative office of the Virgin with seasonal alternatives, mostly borrowed from the sanctorale, but with a few *unica* particularly in the antiphon repertory. There is a further weekly office to Sts Oswald and Wulstan and mention of one to Thomas of Canterbury in some of the later rubrics, partly erased. There is also an appended daily Little Office of the Virgin, again with seasonal texts, and a series of nine proper *Magnificat* antiphons, all *unica*, for use during the summer. The Offices of the Dead and All Saints also appear, with a series of suffrages and references to *psalmi familiares* and the *Trina oratio*.

See **Worc.Ant.**
Facsimile edition edited as *PM*, 1, xii (1922)

Extensive introduction by McLachlan, *PM*, 1, xii (1922)
Brady, *The Derivation of the English Monastic Office*.

D-Bds 194   (Berlin, Deutsche Staatsbibliothek, cod. 194, ff.141-48v)

Customary   *c.*1330-40   St Werburgh, Chester

A miscellaneous source including various treatises, with the *Consuetudinarium . . . in monasterio Cestrensi* on f.141. Brady considers that internal evidence points to the Chester community of monks not nuns (reference to *novicii* and a *prelatus* as superior). The text of the customary is concerned exclusively with liturgical matters: it makes no reference to constitutional or aesthetic concerns. Even so, its treatment of liturgy is far less extensive than, for example, *Cjc* D.27 (the St Mary's York Ordinal). Brady analyses its fundamental concern as 'the coordination and resolution of coincidences of various elements of the regular and supernumary office'. There are signs of influence from Bec, but also many individual practices. Exact dating is not possible: the *Ars kalendarii* is dated 1330, so the source probably post-dates this.

Memorials (termed *commemorationes*) of the BVM and All Saints after Vespers; twelve-lesson Saturday observance of BVM (*Synaxis / Commemoratio de S. Maria*); *Salve regina* as an integral part of Compline of BVM; processions to the Lady altar; Hours of the Cross; Saturday Mass of BVM; daily Little Office of BVM; penitential psalms but no *psalmi familiares*.

See **Chester.Cust.**
Brady, *CCM*, vi (1975), 259-308.
Albers, IV.

Ker, *Medieval Libraries of Great Britain*, 49.

F-VAL 116   (Valenciennes, Bibliothèque Municipale, MS 116)

Winchcombe Breviary   s.xii med.   Winchcombe

The ealiest extant English breviary, roughly contemporary with *Lbl* 2.A.X, but considerably more extensive. Particular emphasis on the Apostle Peter and St Kenelm. The book is small, and written with a legible hand similar to that in *Lbl* 2.A.X. Rubrics are somewhat sparse. Almost all of the texts are given in full, except for repeated sections and psalms. The book comprises calendar, psalter, litany, votive masses, temporale, sanctorale, common etc.

A twelve-lesson commemorative office of the Virgin, consisting of Matins and Lauds only (f.257). Some correpsondence with that in *Lbl* 2.A.X. Votive masses and a Mass of Relics (f.268v), the Office of the Dead (f.258).

Leroquais, *Brévaires Manuscrits*, iv, No.853.

APPENDICES

OSCULETUR ME OSCULO

Mode 1

Os - cu - le - tur me os - cu - lo o - ris su - i

qui - a me - li - o - ra sunt u - be - ra tu - a vi - no,

fra - gran - ci - a un - guen - tis op - ti - mis,

et o - dor un - guen - to - rum tu - o - rum

su - per om - ni - a a - ro - ma - ta.

Magnificat

PULCRE SUNT GENE TUE

Mode 2

Pul - cre   sunt   ge - ne tu - e si - cut tur - tu - ris,

col - lum tu - um si - cut   mo - ni - li - a,

mu - re - nu - las au - re - as fa - ci - e - mus ti - bi,

ver - mi - cu - la - - tas ar - gen - to.

Magnificat

ECCE TU PULCHER ES

SI IGNORAS TE

Mode 4

Si   ig – no – ras te o pul – cra in – ter mu – li – e – res

e – gre – de – re et a – bi post ue – sti – gi – a gre – gum

tu – o – rum et pas – ce e – dos tu – os iu – xta

ta – ber – na – cu – la pa – sto – rum.

Magnificat

VENI DILECTE MI

Mode 5

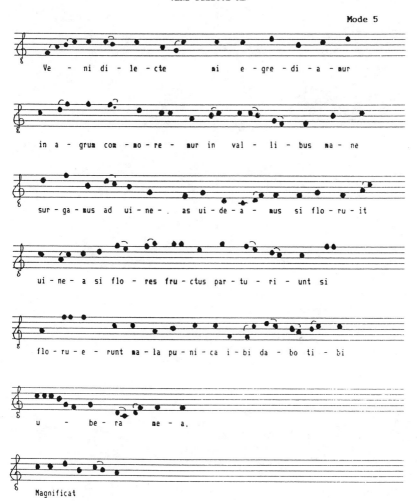

Ve – ni di – le –cte   mi   e – gre – di – a –mur

in a – grum com – mo – re – mur in   val – li – bus ma – ne

sur – ga – mus ad ui – ne – . as ui – de – a – mus si flo – ru – it

ui – ne – a si flo – res fru – ctus par – tu – ri – unt si

flo – ru – e – runt ma – la pu – ni – ca i – bi da – bo ti – bi

u – be – ra me – a.

Magnificat

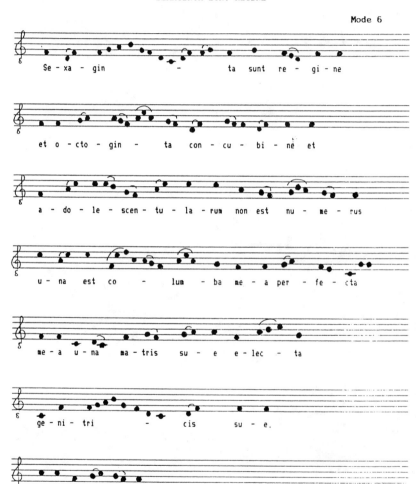

SEXAGINTA SUNT REGINE

Mode 6

Se - xa - gin - ta sunt re - gi - ne

et o - cto - gin - ta con - cu - bi - ne et

a - do - le - scen - tu - la - rum non est nu - me - rus

u - na est co - lum - ba me - a per - fe - cta

me - a u - na ma - tris su - e e - lec - ta

ge - ni - tri - cis su - e.

Magnificat

APERI MIHI SOROR MEA

Mode 7

A - pe - ri mi - hi so - ror me - a a - mi - ca me - a

co - lum - ba me - a im - ma - cu - la - ta me - a

qui - a ca - put me - um ple - num est ro - re

et cin - cin - ni ca - pi - tis me - i gut - tis no - cti - um.

Magnificat

FERCULUM FECIT SIBI

Mode 7

Fer - cu - lum fe - cit si - bi   rex   Sa - lo - mon

de li - gnis   li - ba - ni co - lum   -   pnas e - ius

fe - cit   ar - gen - te - as re - cli - na - to - ri - um

au - re - um a - scen - sum pur - pu - re - um

me - di - a ca - ri - ta - te con - stra - vit pro - pter

fi - li - as ie - ru - sa - lem.

Magnificat

SOROR NOSTRA PARUULA EST

Mode 8

So - ror no - stra par – uu - la est et u - be - ra

non ha - bet quid fa - ci - e - mus so - ro - ri no - stre

in di - e quan - do al - lo - quen - da est si mu - rus est

e - di - fi - ce - mus su - per e - am pro - pu - gna - cu - la

ar - gen - te - a si ho - sti - um con - pin - ga - mus

il - lud ta - bu - lis ce - dri - nis.

Magnificat

MELODIC VARIANTS IN *SALVE REGINA*

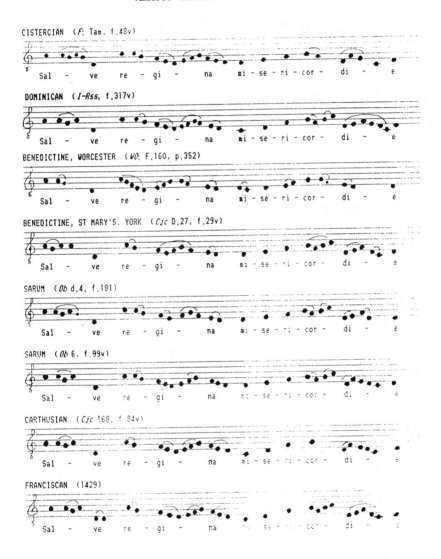

CISTERCIAN (*F*: Tam, f.48v)

Sal - ve re - gi - na mi - se - ri - cor - di - e

DOMINICAN (*I-Rss*, f.317v)

Sal - ve re - gi - na mi - se - ri - cor - di - e

BENEDICTINE, WORCESTER (*WO*: F.160, p.352)

Sal - ve re - gi - na mi - se - ri - cor - di - e

BENEDICTINE, ST MARY'S, YORK (*Cjc* D.27, f.29v)

Sal - ve re - gi - na mi - se - ri - cor - di - e

SARUM (*Ob* d.4, f.181)

Sal - ve re - gi - na mi - se - ri - cor - di - e

SARUM (*Ob* 6, f.99v)

Sal - ve re - gi - na mi - se - ri - cor - di - e

CARTHUSIAN (*Cjc* 168, f.84v)

Sal - ve re - gi - na mi - se - ri - cor - di - e

FRANCISCAN (1429)

Sal - ve re - gi - na mi - se - ri - cor - di - e

CISTERCIAN (*F-Tam*, f.48v)

Vi - ta dul - ce - do et spes no - stra sal - ve

DOMINICAN (*I-Rss*, f.317v)

Vi - ta dul - ce - do et spes no - stra sal - ve

BENEDICTINE, WORCESTER (*WO*; F.160, p.352)

Vi - ta dul - ce - do et spes no - stra sal - ve

BENEDICTINE, ST MARY'S, YORK (*Cjc* D.27, f.29v)

Vi - ta dul - ce - do et spes no - stra sal - ve

SARUM (*Ob* d.4, f.181)

Vi - ta dul - ce - do et spes no - stra sal - ve

SARUM (*Ob* 6, f.99v)

Vi - ta dul - ce - do et spes no - stra sal - ve

CARTHUSIAN (*Cjc* 168, f.84v)

Vi - ta dul - ce - do et spes no - stra sal - ve

FRANCISCAN (*Ob* e.14, f.52v)

Vi - ta dul - ce - do et spes no - stra sal - ve

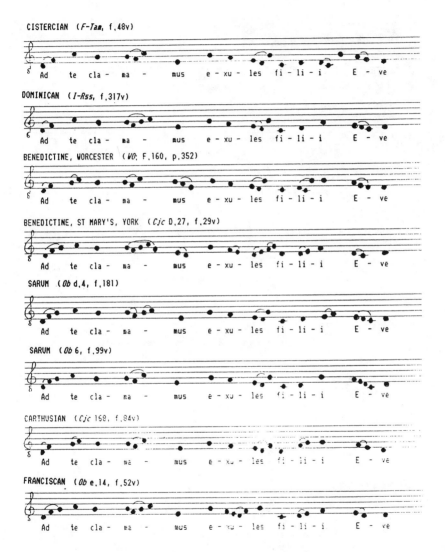

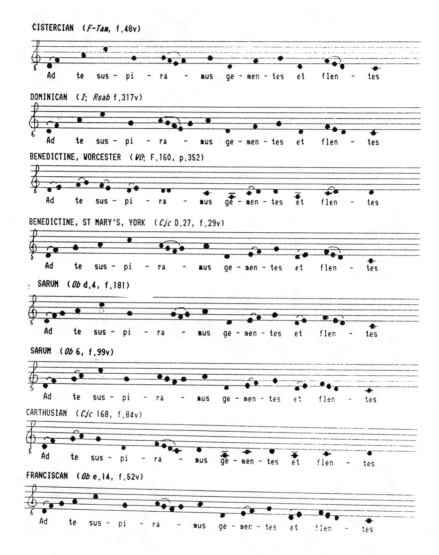

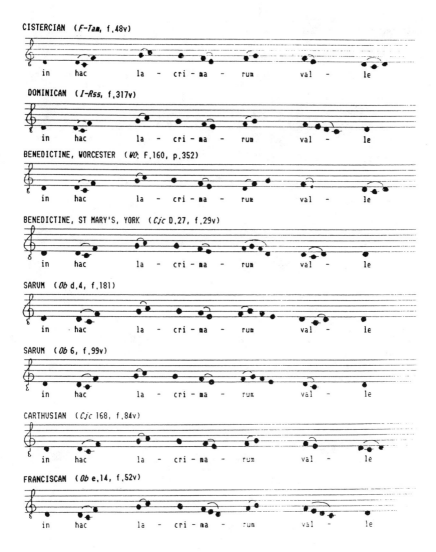

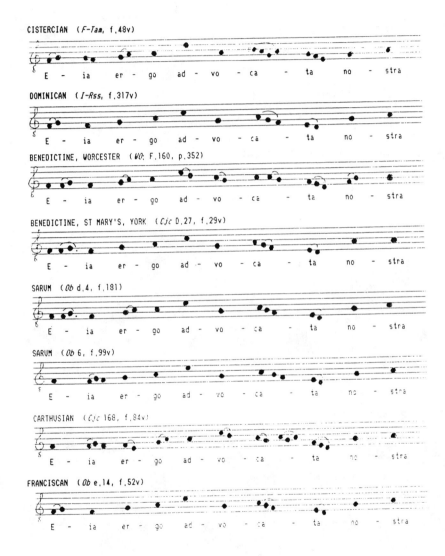

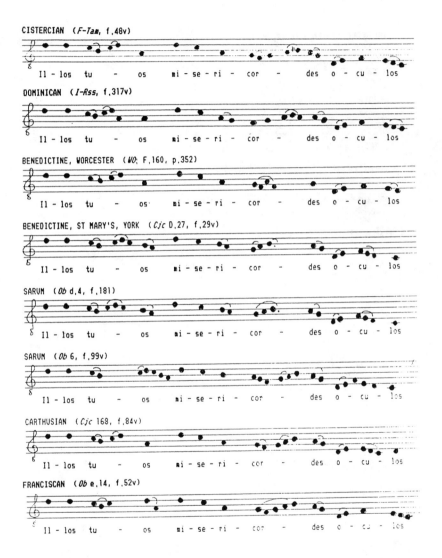

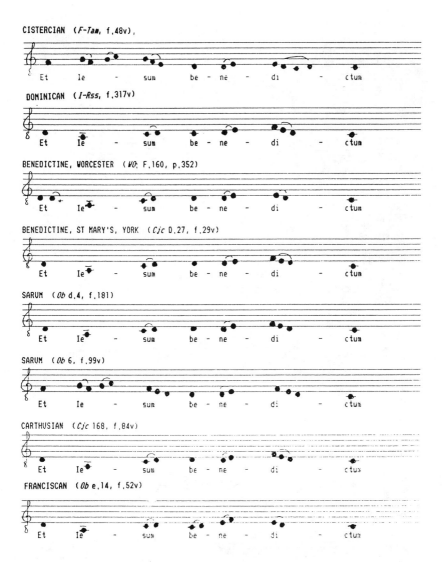

CISTERCIAN (*F-Tam*, f.48v),

Et Ie - sum be - ne - di - ctum

DOMINICAN (*I-Rss*, f.317v)

Et Ie - sum be - ne - di - ctum

BENEDICTINE, WORCESTER (*WO*; F.160, p.352)

Et Ie - sum be - ne - di - ctum

BENEDICTINE, ST MARY'S, YORK (*Cjc* D.27, f.29v)

Et Ie - sum be - ne - di - ctum

SARUM (*Ob* d.4, f.181)

Et Ie - sum be - ne - di - ctum

SARUM (*Ob* 6, f.99v)

Et Ie - sum be - ne - di - ctum

CARTHUSIAN (*Cjc* 168, f.84v)

Et Ie - sum be - ne - di - ctum

FRANCISCAN (*Ob* e.14, f.52v)

Et Ie - sum be - ne - di - ctum

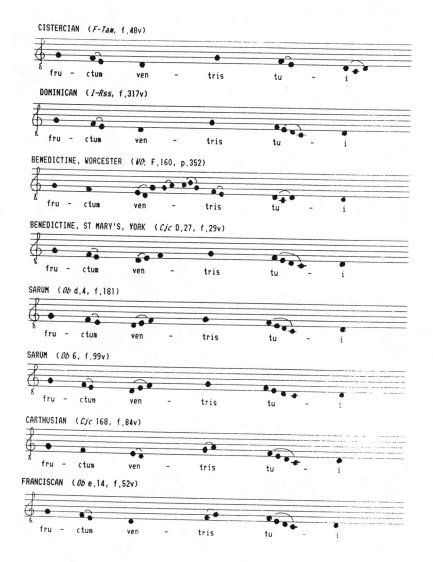

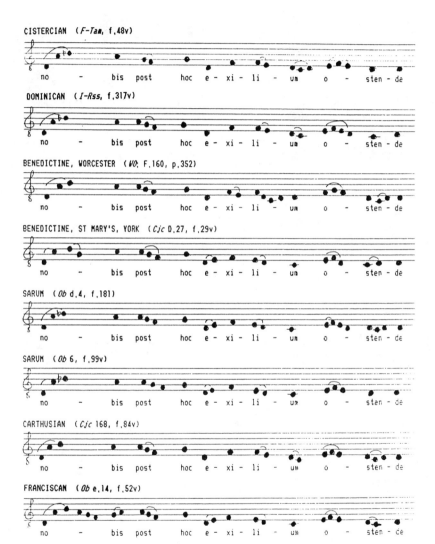

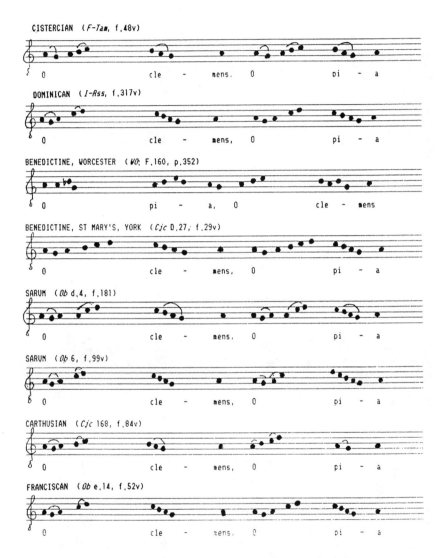

Ob e.14 presents the last seven notes a third too high

BIBLIOGRAPHY

BIBLIOGRAPHY

Primary Sources: Printed Editions

All sources are cited in the main text in the abbreviated form given in the left margin. Items followed by manuscript sigla are also given in the descriptive catalogue on p.285.

Abingdon   *Chronicon Monasterii de Abingdon* (8 vols.), ed. J. Stevenson, *RS*, ii, 1858.

Aelfric   *Aelfrici Abbatis Epistula ad Monachos Egneshamnenses*
(Ccc 265)   directa (post 1004), rev. edn. by Hadrianus Nocent, *CCM*, vii-3 (1984), 149-185.

'Aelfric's Abridgement of St Aethelwold's *Concordia Regularis*', ed. Mary Bateson, in *Compotus Rolls of the Obedientaries of St Swithun's Priory, Winchester*, ed. G.W. Kitchin, Hampshire Record Society, vii (1892), 173-198.

AH   *Analecta Hymnica Medii Aevi* (55 vols.), ed. G.M. Dreves, C. Blume, H.M. Bannister, 1-55, Leipzig, 1886-1922; repr. Frankfurt, 1961.

Alberic   *Chronica Albrici Monachi Trium Fontium*, *MGH*, xxiii (1874).

Albers   Albers, B., *Consuetudines monasticae*, i, Stuttgart, 1900; ii, Monte Casino, 1905; iii (1907); iv (1911), v (1912).

Alcuin   Alcuin, *Liber Sacramentorum*, *PL*, ci, 445-66.

Amalarius,   Amalarius, *De Ecclesiasticis Officiis libri quatuor*, *PL*, cv,
Eccl.Off.   985-1242.

Amalarius,   Amalarius, *Liber Officialis*, ed. I.M. Hanssens, *Amalarii*
Lib.Off.   *episcopi opera liturgica omnia* ii, *Studi e Testi*, cxxxix (1948); repr. 1967.

353

Amalarius, Amalarius, *Liber de Ordine Antiphonarii,* ed. I.M.
Lib.Ord. Hanssens, *Amalarii episcopi opera liturgica omnia* iii, *Studi e Testi,* cxl (1950), 13-109; repr. 1967.

Aachen 816 *Synodi primae Aquisgranensis decreta authentica (816),* ed. J. Semmler. *CCM,* i (1963), 451-468.

Aachen 817 *Synodi secundae Aquisgranensis decreta authentica (817),* ed. J. Semmler, *CCM,* i (1963), 469-481.

Aachen *Legislationis monasticae Aquisgranensis collectio sancti*
St Martial *Martialis Lemovicensis (ante 850),* ed. J. Semmler, *CCM,* i (1963), 555-561.

Aniane *Regula sancti Benedicti abbatis Anianensis, sive*
Coll.Cap. *Collectio Capitularis (818 / 819?),* ed. J. Semmler, *CCM,* i (1963), 501-536.

Aniane *Ordo diurnus Anianensis (post 821),* ed. C. Molas,
Ord.diurn. M. Wegener, *CCM,* i (1963), 305-317.

Aniane, *Vita S. Benedicti Anianensis, PL,* ciii, 355-84.
Vita

Apoc. *The Apocryphal New Testament—Being the Apocryphal Gospels, Acts, Epistles and Apocalypses,* ed. M.R. James, Oxford, 1926.

Barking *The Ordinale and Customary of the Benedictine Nuns of*
(Ouc 169) *the Nuns of Barking Abbry,* (2 vols.) ed. J.B. Tolhurst, *HBS,* lxv (1927); lxvi (1928).

Bateson, M., see Aelfric

Bec *Consuetudines Beccenses,* ed. Marie Pascal Dickson, *CCM,* iv (1967), 150-419.

Bede.EH Bede, *Ecclesiastical History of the English People,* ed. Bertram Colgrave and R.A.B. Mynors, (Oxford Medieval Texts), Oxford, 1969.

Bede.Lives *Lives of the Abbots of Wearmouth and Jarrow*, ed. J.F. Webb and D.H. Farmer (Penguin Classics), Harmondsworth, 1965; repr. 1983.

Bernard *Opera Omnia S. Bernardi* (4 vols.), *PL*, clxxxii-clxxxv.

Bernard Tractatus Bernard, *Prefatio seu Tractatus de Cantu seu Correctione Antiphonarii*, *PL*, clxxxii, 1121-1132.

Biblia Sacra *Biblia Sacra iuxta Vulgatam Clementinam*, ed. A. Colunga and L. Turrado, Madrid, 1977.

Bosworth Psalter The Bosworth Psalter, ed. F.A. Gasquet and E. Bishop, London, 1908.

Bury (*Lbl* 1005) *The Customary of Bury St Edmunds*, ed. Antonia Gransden, *HBS*, xcix (1973).

Cassian Cassian, *De Coenobiorum institutis libri duodecim*, *PL*, xlix, 53-477.

Caesarius Caesarius, *Regula ad monachos*, *PL*, lxvii, 1097-1104.

Cant.SA., Cust. (*Lbl* C.XII) *The Customary of St Augustine, Canterbury*, ed. Edward Maunde Thompson, *HBS*, xxiii (1902).

Cant.Ch.Nov. (*Ccc* 441) *Instructio Noviciorum secundum Consuetudinem Ecclesie Cantuarensis* (*The Instruction of Novices according to the Custom of the Church of Canterbury*), ed. David Knowles (Nelson's Medieval Classics), London, 1951, 133-149.

Chamberlain, J., see *RB*.Abingdon

Chester (*D-Bds* 194) *Consuetudines Cestrenses*, ed. Josiah D. Brady, *CCM*, vi (1975), 259-308.

Chester Proc. *The Processional of the Nuns of Chester*, ed. J. Wickham Legg, *HBS*, xviii (1899).

Cist.Stat.	*Statuta Capitulorum Generalium Ordinis Cisterciensis ab anno 1176 ad annum 1786*, (8 vols.), ed. J.M. Canivez, Louvain, 1933-39.
Cluny Ant.	*Consuetudines Cluniacensium Antiquiores cum Redactionibus Derivatis*, ed. Kassius Hallinger, *CCM*, vii-2 (1983).
Cluny Pet.Ven.	*Statuta Petri Venerabilis, Abbatis Cluniacensis IX*, (1146-7), ed. Giles Constable, *CCM*, vi (1975), 19-106.
Cluny Statuta	*Statuts, Chapitres Généraux et Visites de l'Ordre de Cluny*, ed. G. Charvin, Paris, 1965.
Cluny Ulric	*Ulric's Cluny Consuetudinary*, ed. J.P. Migne, *PL*, cxlix, 635-778.
	Colgrave, B., see Eddius
	Colgrave, B. and R.A.B. Mynors, see Bede, *E.H.*
Columbanus	*Sancti Columbani Opera*, ed. with introduction, notes and translation by G.S.M. Walker, *Scriptores Latini Hiberniae* ii, Dublin, 1957.
	Consuetudines Monasticae, see Albers
CCM	*Corpus Consuetudinum Monasticarum [CCM]*, (7 vols.), ed. Kassius Hallinger *et al*, Siegburg, 1963-.
	Davril, A., see Fleury
Dewick	*Facsimiles of Horae de Beata Maria Virgine, from English Manuscripts of the Eleventh Century*, ed. E.S. Dewick, *HBS*, xxi (1901).
	Dickson, M.P., see Bec
	Dreves, G.M., see *AH*.
Durham.Coll (DRc A.iv.9)	*The Durham Ritual, a Southern English Collectar of the Tenth Century, with Northumbrian Additions*, Early English Manuscripts in Facsimile, xvi, Copenhagen, 1969.

The Durham Collectar, ed. U. Lindelöf, *SS*, cxl (1927).

Durham Rites *The Rites of Durham*, ed. James Raine, *SS*, cvii (1902).

Eadmer   *Eadmer, The Life of St Anselm, Archbishop of Canterbury*, ed. with introduction, notes and translation by R.W. Southern, repr. with corrections (Oxford Medieval Texts), Oxford, 1972.

Eddius   *Eddius Stephanus, Life of Wilfrid*, ed. Bertram Colgrave, Cambridge, 1927.

Einsiedeln *Redactio Sancti Emmerammi dicta Einsidlensis (saec.x)*, ed. Maria Wegener, Candida Elvert, *CCM*, vii-3, 187-256.

Ethelwold *Vita S. Ethelwoldi auctore* . . . *Wolstano*, *PL*, cxxxvii, 81-114

Evesham *Officium Ecclesiasticum Abbatum Secundum Usum Eveshamensis Monasterii*, ed. H.A. Wilson, *HBS*, vi (1893).

Exeter.Ord. *Ordinale Exoniense* (3 vols.), ed. J. Dalton, *HBS*, xxxvii-xxxviii (1909); lxiii (1926).

Eynsham *The Customary of the Benedictine Abbey of Eynsham in*
(Ob 435) *Oxfordshire*, ed. Antonia Gransden, *CCM*, ii (1963), 1 *passim*.

Fleury   *Consuetudines Floriacenses Saeculi Tertii Decimi*, ed. Anselm Davril, *CCM*, ix (1976).

Fulda   *Sacramentarium Fuldense saec. x., Cod. theol. 231 der K. Universitätisbibliothek zu Göttingen*, ed. G. Richter, A. Schönfelder, Quellen und Abhandlungen zur Geschichte der Abtei und der Diözese Fulda, ix (1912); repr. *HBS*, ci (1972-1977).

Gelas.Sac. *Sacramentarium Gelasianum vetus*, ed. L.C. Mohlberg, L. Eizenhöfer, P. Siffrin, *Liber Sacramentorum Romanae Aecclesiae ordinis anni circuli. (Cod. Vat. Reg. lat. 316 / Paris, Bibl. Nat. 7193, 41 / 56. Rerum ecclesiasticarum documenta. Series maior. Fontes* iv (1960); 1968.

Gesta Abbatum S. Albani, see St Albans

Giraldus   *Giraldus Cambrenis, Opera Omnia*, ed. J.S. Brewer, J.F.
                  Dimock and G.F. Warner, *RS*, xxi, vols. 1-8, 1861-91.

                  Gransden, A., see Eynsham.

Greg.Sac.   *Sacramentarium Gregorianum*, ed. J. Deshusses, *Le
                  Sacramentaire Grégorien. Ses principales formes d'après
                  les plus anciens manuscrits Edition comparative. 1. Le
                  Sacramentaire, le Supplément d'Aniane. Spicilegium
                  Friburgense* xvi (1971); 2. *Textes compémentaires pour la
                  messe. Spicilegium Friburgenese*, xxiv (1979).

Greg.Suppl.   *Sacramentarii Gregoriani Supplementum*, ed. H.A. Wilson,
                  *The Gregorian Sacramentary under Charles the Great,
                  edited from three manuscripts of the ninth century*, *HBS*, xlix
                  (1915).

                  Hanssens, I.M., see Amalarius.

Hartker   *Antiphonaire de l'office monastique, transcrit par
                  Hartker: Manuscrits Saint-Gall 390-391 (980-1011)*,
                  ed. J. Froger, *PM* sér.2-i, Berne, 2nd ed., 1970).

Hereford   *The Hereford Breviary edited from the Rouen edition of
                  1505 with collation of manuscripts*, (3 vols), ed. W.H.
                  Frere, L.E.G. Brown, *HBS*, xxvi (1904), xl (1911), xlvi
                  (1915).

Hesbert.1   *Corpus Antiphonalium Officii*, ed. R.-J. Hesbert,
                  1. *Manuscripti cursus romanus, Rerum Ecclesiasticarum
                  Documenta, Séries Maior*, vii, Rome, 1963.

Hesbert.2   *Corpus Antiphonalium Officii*, ed. R.-J. Hesbert,
                  2. *Manuscripti cursus monasticus, Rerum Ecclesiasticarum
                  Documenta, Séries Maior*, viii, Rome, 1965.

Hyde Abbey   *The Monastic Breviary of Hyde Abbey, Winchester*, (6
(*Ob* e.1*)   vols.), ed. J.B. Tolhurst, *HBS*, lxix (1932); lxx (1933); lxxi
                  (1934); lxxvi (1938); lxxviii (1939); lxxx (1942).

Jordanus   *Jordanus, Vita S.Dominici Confessoris, Acta Sanctorum Bollandiana*, Augusti vol.1, Antwerp, 1733, 545-559.

Jumièges   *The Missal of Robert of Jumièges*, ed. H.A. Wilson, *HBS*, xi (1896).

Knowles, D., see Lanfranc, Cant.Ch.Nov.

Lanfranc   *Decreta Lanfranci Monachis Cantuariensibus transmissa*, revd. ed. with introduction by David Knowles, *CCM*, iii (1967), 1-149.

The Monastic Constitutions of Lanfranc, ed. David Knowles (Nelson's Medieval Classics), London, 1951.

Leof.Coll.   *The Leofric Collectar (Harl. 2961) with an appendix*
(Lbl 2961)   *containing a litany and prayers from Harl. MS 863*,
1. Text with 18 plates, *HBS*, xlv (1914); 2. *The Leofric Collectar compared with the Collectar of St Wulfstan together with kindred documents of Exeter and Worcester* (ed. W.H. Frere), *HBS*, lvi (1921).

Leof.Miss   *The Leofric Missal, as used in the Cathedral of Exeter*
(Ob 579)   *during the Episcopate of its first bishop AD 1050-1072, together with some account of the Red Book of Derby, the Missal of Robert of Jumièges, and a few other early Manuscript Service Books of the English Church*, ed. Frederick E. Warren, Oxford, 1883, repr. 1968.

Lib.Vit.   *Liber Vitae: Register and Martyrology of New Minster and Hyde Abbey, Winchester*, Hampshire Record Society, vii (1892).

LU   *Liber usualis with introduction and rubrics in English*, ed. Benedictines of Solesmes, Tournai, 1961.

Lucca   *Le Codex 601 de la bibliothèque capitulaire de Lucques, Antiphonaire Camaldule (xiie siècle)*, ed. A Mocquereau, *PM* sér.1-ix, Tournai, 1905-9.

Mabillon   *Annales Ordinis S. Benedicti*, (5 vols), ed. J. Mabillon, Paris 1703-13.

Mansi   *Sacrorum conciliorum nova et amplissima collectio*, (vols.
           1-54), ed. J.D. Mansi, Florence and Venice, 1759-98; 1769;
           repr. Leipzig, 1901-1927.

Martène   Martène, E. (ed.), *De antiquis ecclesiae ritibus*,
           (4 vols.), 2nd edn. Antwerp, 1736-38.

Maydeston *The Tracts of Clement Maydeston with the remains of
           Caxton's Ordinale*, ed. C. Wordsworth, *HBS*, vii (1894).

           McCann, J., see *RB*

MQ   *Memoriale Qualiter (saec. viii. fin. et saec. x.)*, ed. C.
           Morgand, *CCM*, i (1963), 177-282.

Muir   Muir, Bernard James (ed.), *A Pre-Conquest English
           Prayer-Book (BL Mss Cotton Galba A.xiv and Nero A.ii
           (ff.3-13))*, *HBS*, ciii (1988)

Norwich   *The Customary of the Cathedral Priory Church of
(Ccc 465) Norwich, (Ccc 465)* ed. J.B. Tolhurst, *HBS*, lxxxii (1948).

Ord.Rom.   *Ordines aevi regulae mixtae (post saec. viii med.)*, ed.
           Kassius Hallinger, *CCM*, i (1963), 3-91.

Osbert   *The Letters of Osbert of Clare*, ed. E.W. Williamson,
           London, 1929.

Pantin   *Documents illustrating the activities of the General and
           Provincial Chapters of the English Black Monks
           1215-1540* (3 vols.), ed. W.A. Pantin, *CS*, series 3, xlv
           (1931); xlvii (1933); liv (1937).

PL   *Patrologica cursus completus . . . series latina*, ed. J.P.
           Migne (221 vols), Paris, 1844-1900.

Petrib.   *Chronicon Angliae Petriburgense*, ed. J.A. Giles, Caxton
           Society, 1845.

Rabanus   Rabanus Maurus, *De clericorum orationibus*, *PL*, cvii, 293.

RB   *The Rule of St Benedict in Latin and English with Notes
           (RB 1980)*, ed. Timothy Fry, Collegeville, 1981.

The Rule of St Benedict in Latin and English, ed. Justin McCann, London, 1952.

The Rule of St Benedict (Oxford, Bodleian Library, Hatton 48), ed. D.H. Farmer, *Early English Manuscripts in Facsimile*, xv, Copenhagen, 1968.

RB.Abing. *The Rule of St Benedict: The Abingdon Copy*, ed John
(Ccc 57) Chamberlain, Toronto, 1982.

RC *Regularis Concordia Anglicae Nationis Monachorum*
(Lbl A.III) Sanctimonaliumque, rev.edn. with introduction by Thomas
(Lbl B.III) Symons, *CCM*, vii-3 (1984), 69-147.

The Monastic Agreement of the Monks and Nuns of the English Nation, ed. with introduction, notes and translation by Thomas Symons (Nelson's Medieval Texts), London and New York, 1953.

RM *La Règle du Maître*, ed. A. de Vogüé, *Sources Chrétiennes*, 105-107, Paris, 1964-65.

Rub.Nov. 'Appunti per la storia del Breviario Romano rei sec. xiv-xv, tratti dalle 'Rubricae novae', *Studi e Testi*, lxxvii (1937), 362-394.

Sacrorum conciliorum, see Mansi

St Albans *Chronica Monasterii S. Albani*, ed. H.T. Riley, *RS*, xxviii (12 vols., 1863-76).

Sar.Ant. *Antiphonale Sarisburiense*, ed. W.H. Frere, (6 vols.), London, *PMMS*, 1901-25, repr. Farnborough, 1966.

Sar.Brev. *Breviarum ad Usum Sarum*, (3 vols.), ed. Francis Procter and Christopher Wordsworth, London, 1879-86.

Sar.Grad. *Graduale Sarisburiense*, ed. W.H. Frere (2 vols.), London, *PMMS*, 1894, repr. in 1 vol., Farnborough, 1966.

Sar.Miss. *The Sarum Missal*, ed. J.Wickham Legg, Oxford, 1916.

Missale Sarum, ed. F.H. Dickinson, Burntisland, 1861-3.

The Sarum Missal in English (2 vols.), London, 1911.

Sar.Proc. *Processionale ad Usum Sarum*, ed. W.G. Henderson, Farnborough, 1969.

Sar.Proc.
Pynson
Richard Pynson: Processionale ad Usum Sarum 1502, ed. R. Rastall, Boethius Press (Musical Sources no.16), Clairabricken, 1980.

Sar.Use *The Use of Sarum*, (2 vols.) ed. W.H. Frere, Cambridge, 1898, 1901, repr. Farnborough, 1969.

Subiaco *Caeremoniae Regularis Observantiae Sanctissimi Patris Nostri Benedicti ex ipsius Regula sumptae, secundum quod in sacris locis, scilicet specu et monasterio Sublacensi practicantur*, ed. Joachim F. Angerer, *CCM*, xi-1 (1985).

Symons, T., see *Regularis Concordia*; Aelfric.

Syon *The Bridgettine Breviary of Syon Abbey from the Manuscript with English rubrics, F.4.11 at Magdalene College, Cambridge*, ed. A. Jeffries Collins, *HBS*, xcvi (1963).

Trier *Consuetudines et Observantiae Monasteriorum Sancti Mathiae et Sancti Maximi Treverensium ab Iohanne Rode Abbatae Conscriptae*, ed. Peter Becker, *CCM*, v (1968).

Warren, F.E., see Leof.Miss

West.Cust.
(*Lbl* C.XI)
The Customary of St Peter Westminster, ed. Edward Maunde Thompson, *HBS*, xxviii (1904).

West.Miss. *Missale ad Usum Ecclesiae Westmonstariensis nunc primum typis mandatum*, (3 vols.), ed. J. Wickham Legg, *HBS*, i (1891); v (1893); xii (1897).

Winc.Miss. *The Missal of the New Minster, Winchester*, ed. D.H. Turner, *HBS*, xciii (1962).

Winc.Tro. *The Winchester Troper*, ed. W.H. Frere, *HBS*, viii (1894).

Worc.Ant.   *Antiphonaire Monastique, xiiie siècle, Codex F.160*
(WO F.160)   *de la Bibliothèque de Worcester*, ed. André Mocquerau, *PM* sér.1-xii, Tournai, 1922.

Worc.John   *The Chronicle of John of Worcester, 1118-1140, being the continuation of the Chronicon ex Chronicis of Florence of Worcester, Anecdota Oxoniensia*, Medieval and Modern series, xiii, Oxford, 1908.

Worc.Port.   *The Portiforium of St Wulstan*, ed. Anselm Hughes (2
(Ccc 391)   vols), *HBS*, lxxxix (1956), xc (1957).

York.Brev.   *Breviarum ad Usum Insignis Ecclesiae Eboracensis*, (2 vols.), ed. Stephen W. Lawley, *SS*, lxxi, lxxv (1880-3).

York.Hours   *The Prymer or Hours of the BVM, according to the Use of the Illustrious Church of York*, ed. Christopher Wordsworth, *SS*, cxxxii (1920).

York.Lay   *The Lay Folks Mass Book and Offices in English according to the Use of York*, ed. Thomas F. Simmons, *EETS* (OS) lxxi, London, 1879.

York.Proc.   *Manuale et Processionale ad Usum Insignis Ecclesiae Eboracensis*, ed. W.G. Henderson, *SS*, lxiii (1875).

York.Miss   *Missale ad Usum Insignis Ecclesiae Eboraensis*, (2 vols), ed. W.G. Henderson, *SS*, lix-lx (1874).

YorkSM.   *Chronicle of St Mary's, York*, ed. H.H.E. Craster and
Chron.   M.E. Thornton, *SS*, cxlviii (1933).

YorkSM.   *The Ordinal and Customary of the Abbey of* St Mary's,
Ord.   York, (3 vols.), ed. J.B. Tolhurst and the Abbess
(Cjc D.27)   of Stanbrook, *HBS* lxxiii (1936); lxxv (1937); lxxiv (1951).

Catalogues

Alexander, J.J.G (ed.), *A Survey of Manuscripts illuminated in the British Isles*, i. *Anglo-Saxon Manuscripts from the Sixth to the Ninth Centuries* (ed. Elżbieta Temple), London, 1976; iii. *Romanesque Manuscripts 1066-1190*, (ed. C.M. Kauffmann), 1975.

Backhouse, Janet, D.H. Turner, Leslie Webster (eds.), *The Golden Age of Anglo-Saxon Art 966-1066*, (British Museum Publications), London, 1984.

[British Library], *Class Catalogue of Manuscripts*, lxxvi, *Service Books* (2 vols.), *1. Latin, 2. Latin and Modern Languages*, on deposit in the Students' Room, British Library.

Frere, Walter Howard, *Bibliotheca Musico-Liturgica. A descriptive handlist of the Musical and Latin-liturgical Manuscripts of the Middle Ages preserved in the Libraries of Great Britain and Ireland* (2 vols.), Plainsong and Medieval Music Society, London, 1901, 1932; repr. 1967.

Gneuss, Helmut, 'Manuscripts written or owned in England up to 1100', *ASE*, ix (1981), 1-60.

Hughes, Andrew, *Forty-seven Medieval Office Manuscripts in the British Museum: A Provisional Inventory of Antiphonals and Breviaries*, typescript (1976) on deposit in the Students' Room, British Library.

James, Montague Rhodes, *A Descriptive Catalogue of the Manuscripts in the Library of Corpus Christi College, Cambridge* (2 vols.), Cambridge, 1912.

——, *A Descriptive Catalogue of the Manuscripts in the Library of Magdalene College, Cambridge*, Cambridge, 1909.

——, *A Descriptive Catalogue of the Manuscripts in the Library of St John's College, Cambridge*, Cambridge, 1913.

——, *A Descriptive Catalogue of the Manuscripts in the Library of Trinity College, Cambridge* (4 vols.), Cambridge, 1900-1904.

—— and Claude Jenkins, *A Descriptive Catalogue of the Manuscripts in the Library of Lambeth Palace* (2 vols.), Cambridge, 1930-1932.

Kauffmann, C.M., see Alexander

Ker, Neil Ripley, *Catalogue of Manuscripts containing Anglo-Saxon*, Oxford, 1957.

————, *Medieval Libraries of Great Britain, A List of Surviving Books*, (Royal Historical Society Guides and Handbooks No.3), 2nd edn. London, 1964.

————, *Medieval Manuscripts in British Libraries*, i. *London*, Oxford, 1969; ii. *Abbotsford to Keele*, 1977; iii. *Lampeter to Oxford*, 1983.

————, 'A Supplement to Catalogue of Manuscripts containing Anglo-Saxon', *ASE*, v (1976), 121-131.

Leroquais, Victor, *Les Brévaires manuscrits des bibliothèques publiques de France* (6 vols.), Paris, 1934.

————, *Livres d'Heures manuscrits des bibliothèques publiques de France* (2 vols.), Paris, 1927-43.

————, *Les Psautiers manuscrits latines des bibliothèques publiques de France* (3 vols.), Paris, 1940-41.

————, *Les Sacramentaires et les Missels manuscrits des bibliothèques publiques de France* (4 vols.), Paris, 1924.

Pollard, A.W. and G.R. Redgrave, *A Short-Title Catalogue of Books printed in England, Scotland and Ireland and of English Books printed abroad 1475-1640 [STC]* (2 vols.), 2nd rev. edn. W.A. Jackson, F.S. Ferguson and Katharine F. Pantzer, London, 1976-1986.

Temple, E., see Alexander

Thomson, Rodney M., *Manuscripts from St Albans Abbey 1066-1235* (2 vols.), Woodbridge, 1982.

Van Dijk, Stephen J.P., *Handlist of the Latin Liturgical Manuscripts in the Bodleian Library* (6 vols.), typescript (1951) on deposit in Duke Humfrey's Library.

Watson, Andrew G., *Catalogue of Dated and Datable Manuscripts c. 700-1600 in the British Library*, London, 1979.

Musical Sources

Facsimiles and editions of liturgical sources with music are indexed in the
first section of the bibliography, Primary Sources (pp.353-63).

Dunstable   *John Dunstable: Complete Works*, ed Manfred Bukofzer,
                     MB, viii (1953), rev. edn. by Margaret Bent, Ian Bent and
                     Brian Trowell, 1970.

EECM viii   *Fifteenth-century Liturgical Music: i. Antiphons for Holy
                     Week and Easter*, ed. Andrew Hughes, *EECM*, viii (1969).

Eton   *The Eton Choirbook*, ed. F. Ll. Harrison, 2nd edn.,
Choirbook   *MB* x-xii (1959-66).

Power   *Leonel Power: Complete Works*, ed. Charles Hamm,
                     CMM, 1 (1966-76).

PMFC xvi   *English Music for Mass and Office*, i, ed. F.Ll. Harrison,
                     E.H. Sanders and P.M. Lefferts, *PMFC*, xvi (1983).

Secondary Sources

Alexander, J.J.G., 'The Benedictional of St Aethelwold and Anglo-Saxon Illumination of the Reform Period, in Parsons (ed.), *Tenth-Century Studies*, 169-183.

————, *Insular Manuscripts from the sixth to the ninth century*, London, 1978.

Apel, Willi, *Gregorian Chant*, London, 1958.

Bailey, Terence, *The Processions of Sarum and the Western Church* (Pontifical Institute of Medieval Studies: Studies and Texts, xxi), Toronto, 1971.

Baltzer, Rebecca A., 'Another Look at a Composite Office and its History: The Feast of *Susceptio Reliquiarum* in Medieval Paris', *JRMA*, cxiii (1988), 1-27.

Bannister, H.M., 'Fragments of an Anglo-Saxon Sacramentary', *JTS*, xii (1911), 451-4.

Barlow, Frank, *The English Church 1000-1066*, 2nd edn., London and New York, 1979.

Barré, Henri, 'Antiennes et répons de la Vierge', *Marianum*, xxix (1967), 153-254.

————, *Prières Anciennes de l'Occident à la Mère du Sauveur des origines à S. Anselme*, Paris, 1967.

————, 'Un plaidoyer monastique pour le samedi marial', *RevB*, lxxvi (1967), 375-99.

————, and J. Deshusses, 'A la recherche du Missel d'Alcuin', *EL*, lxxxii (1968), 1-44.

Bateson, M. 'Rules for Monks and Secular Canons after the Revival under King Edgar', *EHR*, ix (1894), 693-99.

Battiscombe, C.F. (ed.), *The Relics of St Cuthbert*, Durham, 1956.

Baümer, Suitbert, *Geschichte des Breviers*, Freiburg-im-Breisgau, 1895; Fr.edn. *Histoire du Brévaire*, tr. R. Biron, Paris, 1905.

Benedictines of Stanbrook, *In a Great Tradition: Tribute to Dame Laurentia McLachlan, Abbess of Stanbrook*, London, 1956.

Bestul, T.M., 'St Anselm and the Continuity of Anglo-Saxon Devotional Traditions', *AnnMed*, xviii (1977), 20-41.

Biddle, Martin, '*Felix Urbs Winthonia*: Winchester in the Age of Monastic Reform', in Parsons (ed.), *Tenth-Century Studies*, 123-140.

Billet, B., 'Culte et devotion à la Vierge dans l'Ordre Monastique aux viii-ix siècles', *De Cultu Mariano Saeculis vi-xi: Acta Congressus Mariologici-Marian Internationals in Croatia anno 1971 celebrati*, Rome, 1972.

Bishop, Edmund, *Liturgica Historica: Papers on the Liturgy and Religious Life of the Western Church*, Oxford, 1918.

Bishop, T.A.M., 'Manuscripts connected with St Augustine's Abbey, Canterbury', *Transactions of the Cambridge Bibliographic Society*, ii (1957), 324.

Blair, Peter Hunter, *The World of Bede*, London, 1970.

Bonniwell, William R., *A History of the Dominican Liturgy*, New York, 1944.

Borg, Alan, and Andrew Martindale (eds.), *The Vanishing Past, Studies of Medieval Art, Liturgy and Metrology presented to Christopher Hohler*, (British Archaeological Reports Series iii), 1981.

Bowers, Roger D., *Choral Institutions within the English Church, 1340-1500*, unpubd. Ph.D thesis, University of East Anglia, 1975.

Brady. J.D., *The Derivation of the English Monastic Office Books as seen in the core of the Liber Responsalis*, unpubd. M.Litt. diss., University of Cambridge, 1963.

[British Library Publication], *The Benedictines in Britain,* London, 1980.

Brooke, Rosalind and Christopher, *Popular Religion in the Middle Ages*, London, 1984.

Bryden, J.R. and D.G. Hughes, *An Index of Gregorian Chant* (2 vols.), Cambridge (Massachusetts), 1970.

Bullough, D.A., 'The Continental Background of the Reform', in Parsons (ed.), *Tenth-Century Studies*, 20-36.

Burstyn, Shai, 'Early 15th-Century Polyphonic Settings of Song of Song Antiphons', *ActaM*, xlix (1977), 200-227.

Butler, C., *Benedictine Monachism*, London, 1924.

Butler, Lionel, and Chris Given-Wilson, *Medieval Monasteries of Great Britain*, London, 1979.

Cabaniss, A., *The Emperor's Monk: A Contemporary Life of Benedict of Aniane by Ardo*, Newton Abbot, 1979.

Cabrol, J. and H. Leclercq (eds.), *Dictionnaire d'Archéologie Chrétienne et de la Liturgie [DACL]*, (15 vols.), 1903-53.

Canal, J.M., 'En torno a la antîfona "Salve Regina". Punctualizando', *Recherches de Thélogie Ancienne et Médiévale*, xxxiii (1966), 342-355.

———, 'Salve regina misericordiae: Historia y leyendas en torno a esta antifona', *Temi e Testi*, ix (1963), 1, *passim*.

Carter, P.N., *An Edition of William of Malmesbury's Treatise on the Miracles of the Virgin Mary with an account of its place in his writings and in the development of Mary legends in the twelfth century*, unpubd. D.Phil. thesis, University of Oxford (Merton), 1959.

Cattin, Giulio, *Music of the Middle Ages*, i, Cambridge, 1984.

Chaney, William A., *The Cult of Kingship in Anglo-Saxon England: The transition from paganism to Christianity*, Manchester, 1970.

Clayton, Mary, *An examination of the cult of the Virgin Mary in Anglo-Saxon England, with special reference to the vernacular texts*, unpubd. D.Phil. thesis, University of Oxford (St Hilda's), 1983.

————, 'Feasts of the Virgin in the Liturgy of the Anglo-Saxon Church, *ASE*, xiii (1984), 209-233.

Constable, Giles (ed.), *Medieval Monasticism* (Toronto Medieval Bibliographies vi), Toronto, 1976.

Corbin, Solange, 'L'Office de la Conception de la Vierge', *Bulletin des études portugaises et de l'institut Français au Portugal*, xiii (1943), 105-66.

Coulton, G.G., *Five Centuries of Religion* (4 vols), Cambridge, 1923-50.

Cramp, Rosemary, 'Anglo-Saxon Sculpture of the Reform Period', in Parsons (ed.), *Tenth-Century Studies*, 184-199.

Cross, F.L. and E.A. Livingstone (eds.), *The Oxford Dictionary of the Christian Church* (2nd edn.), New York, 1974.

Dauphin, H., 'Le renouveau monastique en Angleterre au xe siècle et ses rapports avec la réforme du saint Gérard de Brogne', *RevB*, lxx (1960), 177-196.

Davis, H.F., 'The Origins of Devotion to Our Lady's Immaculate Conception', *DubR*, ccviii (1954), 375-92.

Davies, J.G., *A Dictionary of Liturgy and Worship*, London, 1986.

Deanesly, Margaret, 'The *familia* at Christchurch Canterbury, 597-832', *Essays in Medieval History presented to Thomas Frederick Tout*, ed. A.G. Little and F.M. Powicke, Manchester, 1925, 1-13.

————, *The Pre-Conquest Church in England*, London, 1961.

De Hamel, Christopher, *A History of Illuminated Manuscripts*, Oxford, 1986.

Delatte, Paul, *Commentary on the Rule of St Benedict*, London, 1921.

Deshman, Robert, 'The Leofric Missal and tenth-century English art', *ASE*, vi (1977), 145.

Deshusses, Jean, 'Les Messes d'Alcuin', *ALw*, xiv (1972), 7-41.

———, 'Le "Supplément" au Sacramentaire Grégorien: Alcuin ou Saint Benôit d'Aniane?', *ALw*, ix (1965), 48-71.

De Valois, J., *Le Salve Regina*, Paris, 1912.

De Valous, Guy, *Le Monachisme Clunisien des Origines au XVe Siècle* (2 vols.), Paris, 1970.
Diringer, David, *The Illuminated Book: its History and Production*, New York, 1967.

Doe, Paul, 'Latin Polyphony under Henry VIII', *PRMA*, xcv (1968-9), 81-96.

Drage, Elaine M., *Bishop Leofric and the Exeter Cathedral Chapter (1050-1072): a reassessment of the manuscript evidence*, unpubd. D.Phil. thesis, University of Oxford (Lady Margaret Hall), 1978.

Duby, Georges, *Le Temps des cathédrales: L'art et la société 980-1420*, 1976; Eng.edn. *The Age of the Cathedrals, Art and Society 980-1420*, tr. Eleanor Levieux and Barbara Thompson, London, 1981.

Ducange, C., *Glossarium Mediae et Infimae Latinitatis* (10 vols.), rev. L. Favre, Niort, 1883-87; repr. Graz, 1954.

Dugdale, W., *Monasticon Anglicanum* (6 vols.), London, 1817-1830; 1849.

Duschesne, L.M., *Origines du Culte Chrétien*, Paris, 1925.

Edwards, Kathleen, *The English Secular Cathedrals in the Middle Ages*, Manchester, 1949, rev.edn., 1967.

Ellard, G., *Master Alcuin, Liturgist. A Partner of our Piety*, Chicago, 1956.

Farmer, David H., 'The Progress of the Monastic Revival', in Parsons (ed.), *Tenth-Century Studies*, 10-19.

——, *The Oxford Dictionary of Saints* (4th edn.), Oxford, 1982.

Ferrari, Guy, *Early Roman Monasteries* (Studi di Antichità Cristiana xxiii), Vatican, 1957.

Finucane, Ronald C., *Miracles and Pilgrims: Popular Beliefs in Medieval England*, London, 1977.

Fry, Timothy (ed.), *RB 1980: The Rule of St Benedict in Latin and English with Notes*, Collegeville, 1981.

Genestout, A., 'La Règle du Maître et la Règle de Saint Benoît', *Revue d'Ascétique et de Mystique*, xxi (1940), 51-112.

Gibson, Margaret, *Lanfranc of Bec*, Oxford, 1978.

Gordon, Cosmo A., 'Manuscript Missals: The English Uses', *The Sandars Readership in Bibliography: Lectures delivered at Cambridge, 13 and 20 November, 1936, typescript and autograph of the lectures and supplementary lists of the Alleluia verses for the Sundays after Pentecost in British Library MS Add. 44920-1*, typescript on deposit in the Students' Room, British Library.

Gougaud, L. *Devotional and Aesthetic Practices in the Middle Ages*, London, 1927.

Graef, Hilda, *Mary: A History of Doctrine and Devotion* (2 vols.), London and New York, 1963.

Gransden, Antonia, 'Cultural Transition at Worcester in the Anglo-Norman Period', *Medieval Art and Architecture at Worcester Cathedral, British Archaeological Association I, Conference Transactions for the year 1975*.

Gray, Douglas, *Themes and Images in the Medieval English Religious Lyric*, London and Boston, 1972.

Gretsch, Mechthild, 'Aethelwold's translation of the *Regula Sancti Benedicti* and its Latin exemplar', *ASE*, iii (1974), 125-151.

Guiver, George, *Company of Voices: Daily Prayer and the People of God*, London, 1988.

Hall, J.R., 'Some Liturgical Notes on Aelfric's Letter to the Monks at Eynsham', *DownR*, xciii (1975), 297-303.

Harrison, Frank Ll., 'An English *Caput*', *ML*, xxxiii (1952), 203-214.

'The Eton Choirbook: Its background and contents', *AnnMus*, i (1953), 151-175.

———, *Music in Medieval Britain*, London, 1958, 2nd edn, 1963.

Hartzell, K.D., *The Musical Repertoire at St Albans Abbey, England, in the Twelfth Century*, unpubd. Ph.D. thesis, University of Rochester, New York, 1971.

———, 'An unknown English Benedictine Gradual of the Eleventh Century', *ASE*, iv (1975), 131-144.

Hergott, Marquat, *Vetus disciplina monastica*, Paris, 1726.

Hesbert, René-Jean, 'Les Antiphonaires Monastiques Insulaires', *RevB*, xcii (1982), 358-375.

Hiley, David, 'Recent research on the origins of Western chant', *EM*, vxi (1988), 203-211.

Hope, D.M., *The Leonine Sacramentary. A Reassessment of its Nature and Purpose*, Oxford, 1971.

———, 'The Medieval Western Rites', in Jones *et.al.* (ed.), *The Study of Liturgy*, 220-240.

Hughes, Andrew, 'Chants in the Rhymed Office of St Thomas of Canterbury', *EM*, xvi (1988), 185-201.

———, *Medieval manuscripts for Mass and Office: A guide to their organization and terminology*, Toronto and London, 1982.

———, 'Modal order and disorder in the rhymed office', *MD*, xxxvii (1983), 29-52.

Ingram, Sonja Stafford, *The Polyphonic Salve Regina 1425-1550*, unpublished Ph.D. thesis, University of North Carolina at Chapel Hill, 1973.

John, Eric, 'The King and the Monks in the Tenth-century Reformation', *Bulletin of the John Rylands Library*, xlii (1959), 61-87.

——, 'Some Latin Charters of the Tenth-century Reformation in England', *RevB*, lxx (1960), 333-359.

——, 'The Sources of the English Monastic Reformation: A Comment', *RevB*, lxx (1960), 197-203.

Jones, Cheslyn, Geoffrey Wainwright and Edward Yarnold (ed.), *The Study of Liturgy*, London, 1978.

Jungmann, Josph A., *Missarum Solemnia* (2 vols.), 1948; Eng. edn., *The Mass of the Roman Rite: Its Origins and Development*, tr. J.A. Brunner (2 vols.), Benziger, 1950.

Kantorowicz, Ernst Hartwig, *Laudes Regiae: A Study in Liturgical Acclamations and Medieval Ruler Worship* (University of California Publications in History, xxxiii), Berkeley, 1946.

Kauffmann, C.M., 'Manuscript Illumination at Worcester in the Eleventh and Twelfth Centuries', *Medieval Art and Architecture at Worcester Cathedral* (British Archaeological Association) Worcester, 1978.

King, Archdale A., *Liturgies of the Past*, London, 1959.

——, *Liturgies of the Religious Orders*, London, 1955.

Kishpaugh, M.J., *The Feast of the Presentation of the Virgin Mary in the Temple*, Washington, 1941.

Knowles, David, *Great Historical Enterprises; Problems in Monastic History*, London, 1963.

——, 'The Monastic Horarium 970-1120', *DownR*, xli (1933), 706-725.

——, *The Monastic Order in England: A History of its Development from the Times of St Dunstan to the Fourth Lateran Council, 940-1216*, Cambridge, 1940, 2nd edn., 1964.

——- and Dimitri Obolensky (ed.), *The Christian Centuries, ii, The Middle Ages*, London, 1969.

———, C.N.L. Brooke and V.C.M. London, *The Heads of Medieval Religious Houses: England and Wales, 940-1216*, Cambridge, 1972.

Lackner, Bede K., *The Eleventh-Century Background of Citeaux* (*CSS* viii), 1972, 1-39.

Lawrence, C.H., *Medieval Monasticism: Forms of Religious Life in the Middle Ages*, London, 1984.

Leclercq, Jean, *L'Amour des lettres et le désir de Dieu: Initiation aux auteurs monastiques du moyen âge*, 1957; Eng.edn. *The Love of Learning and the Desire for God*, tr. Catherine Mishrai, New York, 1961.

———, 'Formes Anciennes de l'Office Marial', *EL* lxxiv (1960), 89-102.

———, 'Fragmenta Mariana', *EL*, lxxii (1958), 292-305.

Le Huray, Peter, *Music and the Reformation in England 1548-1660*, Cambridge, 1967, repr. 1978.

Madan, F., 'Hours of the Virgin Mary (tests for localization)', *BQR* iii (1920), 41-44.

Maier, J., *Studien zur Geschichte der Marienantiphon Salve Regina*, Regensburg, 1939.

Marosseki, Solutor, 'Les origines du chant Cistercien', *Analecta Sacri Ordinis Cisterciensis*, viii (1952), 1-179.

Maskell, W., *The Ancient Liturgy of the Church of England*, Oxford, 1882.

Mayr-Harting, Henry, *The Coming of Christianity to Anglo-Saxon England*, London, 1972.

McColl, Sandra, *Large-scale Marian Antiphon Settings by English and Scottish Composers, 1460-1558*, unpubd. M.A. thesis, University of Melbourne, 1982.

McIntyre, Elizabeth A., *Early Twelfth-Century Worcester Cathedral Priory with special reference to the Manuscripts written there*, unpubd. D.Phil. thesis, University of Oxford (St Anne's), 1978.

McKinnon, James, 'The Late Medieval Psalter: Liturgical or Gift Book?', *MD*, xxxviii (1984), 133-157.

McLachlan, Laurentia, 'St Wulfstan's Prayer Book', *JTS*, l (1928-9), 174-7.

Moorman, John R.H., *A History of the Church in England*, London, 1953.

The New Catholic Encyclopaedia (20 vols.), Washington, 1967.

Niermeyer, J.F. (ed.), *Mediae Latinitatis Lexicon Minus*, 1976.

Norton, C. and D. Park (eds), *Cistercian Art and Architecture in the British Isles*, Cambridge, 1986.

Nussbaum, O., 'Kloster, Priestermönch und Privatmesse', *Theophaneia*, xiv (1961).

Oury, Guy, 'Les Matines solennelles aux grandes fêtes dans les anciennes églises françaises', *EG*, xii (1971), 155-62.

————, 'La Structure cérémonielle des vêpres solennelles dans quelques anciennes liturgies françaises', *EG*, xiii (1972), 225-36.

Parsons, David (ed.), *Tenth-Century Studies: Essays in Commemoration of the Millenium of the Council of Winchester and Regularis Concordia*, London and Chichester, 1975.

Pfaff, Richard W., *Medieval Latin Liturgy: A Select Bibliography* (Toronto Medieval Bibliographies ix), Toronto, 1982.

————, *New Liturgical Feasts in Later Medieval England*, Oxford, 1970.

Phillips, C.S., *Canterbury Cathedral in the Middle Ages* (S.P.C.K. pamphlet), London, 1949.

Pickering, F.P., 'The Calendar Pages of Medieval Service Books: An Introductory Note for Art Historians', *Reading Medieval Studies*, i, unpubd. monograph, British Library, 1980.

Platt, Colin, *The Abbeys and Priories of Medieval England*, London, 1984.

Rosenwein, B.H., 'Rules and the "Rule" at Tenth-Century Cluny', *Studia Monastica* xix (1977), 307-20.

Salmon, Pierre, 'L'Office Divin au Moyen Age', *Lex Orandi*, xliii, Paris, 1967.

Sandon, Nick, 'Mary, meditations, monks and music: poetry, prose, processions and plagues in a Durham Cathedral MS', *EM* x (1982), 43-55.

Schmitz, Philibert, *Histoire de l'Ordre de Saint-Benoît*, Maredsous, 1942.

Sicard, Damien, *La Liturgie de la mort dans l'eglise latine des origines à la réforme carolingienne* (Liturgiewissenschaftliche Quellen und Forschungen Bd.63), Münster Westf., 1978.

Southern, Richard W., 'The English Origins of the Miracles of the Virgin', *Medieval and Renaissance Studies* iv (1958), 176-216.

Stenton, Frank M., *Anglo-Saxon England*, 3rd edn., Oxford, 1971.

Symons, Thomas, 'Monastic Observance in the Tenth Century. The Offices of All Saints and of the Dead', *DownR*, l (1932), 449-464; li (1932), 137-152.

———, 'A Note on *Trina Oratio*', *DownR*, xiii (1924), 67-83.

———, 'The *Regularis Concordia*', *DownR*, xl (1922), 15-30.

———, '*Regularis Concordia*: History and Derivation', in Parsons (ed.), *Tenth-Century Studies*, 37-59.

———, 'The *Regularis Concordia* and the Council of Winchester', *DownR*, lxxx (1962), 140-156.

———, 'Some Notes on English Monastic Origins', *DownR*, lxxx (1962), 55-69.

Szövérffy, Joseph, *Die Annalen der Lateinischen Hymnendichtung. Ein Handbuch. 1. Die lateinischen Hymnen bis zum Ende des 11. Jahrhunderts, 2. Die lateinischen Hymnen vom Ende des 11. Jahrhunderts bis zum Ausgang des Mittelalters*, Berlin, 1964-5.

Thomson, Rodney M., 'The Library of Bury St Edmunds Abbey in the Eleventh and Twelfth Centuries', *Speculum*, lxvii (1972), 617-45.

Tolhurst, J.B.L., *Introduction to the English Monastic Breviaries (The Monastic Breviary of Hyde Abbey, Winchester*, vi), *HBS* lxxx (1942).

Traube, L., *Textgeschichte der Regula S. Benedicti*, 2nd edn., rev. H. Plenkers, Munich, 1910.

Turner, Derek H., 'The Crowland Gradual: An English Benedictine Manuscript', *EL*, lxxiv (1960), 168-74.

———, 'The Evesham Psalter', *Speculum*, xxxix (1964), 23

———, 'The Penworthan Breviary', *BMQ*, xxviii (1964), 85-8.

Van Dijk, Stephen J.P., 'The origin of the Latin feast of the Conception of the BVM', *DubR*, ccviii (1954) 251-67; 428-42.

———, *Sources of the Modern Roman Liturgy* (2 vols), Leiden, 1963.

——— and Joan Hazelden Walker, *The Origins of the Modern Roman Liturgy. The Liturgy of the Papal Court and the Franciscan Order in the Thirteenth Century*, London, 1960.

Vogüé, Adalbert de, 'Origine et Structure de l'Office Bénédictin', *Collectanea Cisterciensia*, xxix (1967), 195-199.

Wagner, Peter, *Introduction to the Gregorian Melodies: A Handbook of Plainsong* (2nd edn.), 1901.

———, 'Das Salve Regina', *Gregorianische Rundschau*, ii (1903).

Ward, Benedicta, *Miracles and the Medieval Mind. Theory, Record and Event 1000-1215*, Philadelphia, 1982.

Warner, Marina, *Alone of All her Sex: The Myth and Cult of the Virgin Mary*, London, 1976.

Warren, F.E., 'The Anglo-Saxon Missal at Worcester', *The Academy*, xxviii (1885), 394-5.

———-, *The Liturgy and Ritual of the Celtic Church*, 1881, 2nd edn. with introduction and bibliography by Jane Stevenson, Woodbridge, 1987.

Waterton, Edmund, *Pietas Mariana Britannica*, London, 1879.

Wieck, Roger S., *The Book of Hours in Medieval Art and Life*, London, 1988.

Willis, G.G., 'Early English Liturgy from Augustine to Alcuin', *Further Essays in Early Roman Liturgy* (Alcuin Club Collections l), London, 1968.

Wilmart, André, *Auteurs Spirituels et Textes Dévots du Moyen Age Latin*, Paris, 1931.

———, 'Prières Medievales pour l'adoration de la croix', *EL*, 46 (1932), 22.

Wilson, D.M., 'Tenth-Century Metalwork', in Parsons (ed.), *Tenth-Century Studies*, 200-207.

Winterbottom, M., 'Three Lives of St Ethelwold', *MAev*, 41 (1971), 191-201.

Woolf, Rosemary, *The English Religious Lyric in the Middle Ages*, Oxford, 1968.

Wormald, Francis, and C.E. Wright (ed.), *The English Library before 1700*, London, 1958.

INDEX